Content Area Literacy

Interactive Teaching for Active Learning

Third Edition

ANTHONY V. MANZO

ULA C. MANZO

THOMAS H. ESTES

JOHN WILEY & SONS, INC.
New York • Chichester • Weinheim • Brisbane • Singapore • Toronto

KH

EDITOR	Maureen E. Prado Roberts
MARKETING MANAGER	Alison Fichter
PRODUCTION SERVICES MANAGER	Jeanine Furino
PRODUCTION MANAGEMENT SERVICES	Ingrao Associates
SENIOR DESIGNER	Dawn Stanley
ILLUSTRATION EDITOR	Sandra Rigby
PHOTO EDITOR	Jill Tatara
COVER PHOTO	© Historical Picture Archive/Corbis

This book was set by PRD Group and printed and bound by Malloy Lithographing. The cover was printed by Phoenix Color Corp.

This book is printed on acid-free paper. ∞

Library of Congress Cataloging-in-Publication Data:
Manzo, Anthony V.
   Content area literacy : fusing curriculum, culture & community in the wired classroom / Anthony V. Manzo, Ulna C. Manzo, Thomas H. Estes — 3rd ed.
     p.   cm.
   Includes bibliographical references.
   ISBN 0-471-36561-0 (cloth : alk. paper)
   1. Content area reading—United States.   2. Language arts—Correlation with content subjects.   3. Interdisciplinary approach in education.   I. Manzo, Ula Casale.   II. Estes, Thomas H., 1940–   III. TItle.

LB1050.455.M36 2001
428.4'07—dc21   00-027524

Printed in the United States of America

10 9 8 7 6 5 4 3 2 1

Photo credits: Andy Sacks/Tony Stone Images, p. 4; Tom & Dee Ann McCarthy/The Stock Market, p. 24; Will & Deni McIntyre/Photo Researchers, p. 44; Chip Henderson/Tony Stone Images, p. 70; Jose L. Pelaez/The Stock Market, p. 106; Charles Gupton/The Stock Market, pp. 130, 282; Elizabeth Crews/Stock Boston, pp. 160, 264; Tom Stewart/The Stock Market, p. 192; Aaron Haupt/Photo Researchers, p. 240; Joseph Schuyler/Stock Boston, p. 320; Chuck Savage/The Stock Market, p. 346; Walter Hodges/Tony Stone Images, p. 376.

10/25/04

Preface

"Welcome, you've got mail," is already as ubiquitous as a telephone call. More incredible than getting e-mail is the fact that you can send it easily to almost anyone, almost any time you wish. We are rapidly merging teaching, reading, writing, business, and telecomputing. The commerce taking place in ideas, while not winning many headlines, is far more vast and far-reaching than any that is occurring in finance or products.

If communication is a major stimulus to brain development, what must be happening to our collective consciousness as these messages whirl about the globe? Surely we all are becoming better informed, but is the purpose of this book, which is to have us become wiser and more literate, being achieved? Are we becoming better processors of information, or just better mechanical "browsers" of it? How can education help to define the best possible future?

The merging of the internet, education, and commerce is amazing, exciting, and a wide-open frontier. So, don't just sit there and hear from us. Let us hear from you. Maybe we'll be overwhelmed by your e-mails, but more than likely we'll answer many and incorporate others into our web sites and book revisions. In any case, you have a chance to interact and influence that has never been feasible before. Let's continue the experiment and see where it takes us.

Anthony V. Manzo   manzoa@umkc.edu
Ula C. Manzo   umanzo@aol.com
Thomas E. Estes   the@virginia.edu

Contents

SECTION I

Foundations of Content Area Literacy

The first three chapters introduce some of the basic ideas, goals, and frameworks for improving reading, writing, and thinking in almost any content area. Several practical methods are described and illustrated to anchor these foundational principles. By the beginning of the next section, you will have much of the knowledge base needed to begin to select specific methods based on student needs and your own style of teaching/learning.

CHAPTER 1

Why and What Teachers Should Know About Content Literacy

No one can reveal to you aught but that which already lies half asleep in the dawning of your knowledge.

—Kalil Gibran

✦ Fore Words ✦

This introductory chapter encourages teachers in all fields to reflect on their potential roles as content area literacy facilitators. The chapter is constructed around the emergence of the *content area reading* movement: the questions that impelled it, and its evolution into its current, more accurate descriptor, *content area literacy*. The likely role of the coming wired classroom also is briefly set out in terms of its implications to multiple literacies, culture, communications, and contemporary life and learning. The fundamental theme of the chapter and the book, however, is that teaching students to learn on their own moves them toward becoming literate, more than simply not being illiterate. This is illustrated in one broadly applicable method called Listen-Read-Discuss.

THE FIRST DAY OF SCHOOL

New teachers often come away from their first classes feeling that they had wonderful lessons prepared, but the wrong students showed up. This mismatch in expectations happens largely because many teachers still feel that teaching is a process of transmitting information. This view is strengthened by the fact that some students can receive new information relatively effortlessly. They have sufficient background of information, appropriate independent learning strategies, and motivation to learn more about the subject. For many students in most subjects, however, merely presenting information is not enough. Most new learning is far from effortless. It requires some prior knowledge and, ideally, some concrete experience with the topic. Next, learners must somehow become engaged, or interested in and attentive to the new information and ideas at hand. Further, learners must explore the information by questioning, comparing, and testing it against those elements of prior knowledge and experiences. Finally, learners must categorize and connect the new information with what they already knew—which often means adding to and even revising previously held ideas. For these reasons, learning has been called a *constructive* process. To initiate this process—to grab students' interest, and then maintain and focus it—teachers must start from where students are—socially, emotionally, and intellectually. This means that teachers need to have a good sense of what interests students, what background of information and experience they are likely to have, and what obstacles and misconceptions might prevent them from actively participating in the learning process. Students have been shown to sense when teachers show such caring and to respond positively to their strategies for reading and learning (Moje, 1996).

FROM CONTENT AREA *READING* TO CONTENT AREA *LITERACY*

The field of content area reading evolved from an idea sparked in the 1920s into a movement that swept the nation by the 1960s. In recent years, the field has continued to evolve into the broader dimensions suggested by the label *content area literacy* (CAL). Before the 1920s, education tended to follow a survival-of-the-fittest model. Those who fell behind simply were permitted to drop from the system. A growing awareness of the need for an educated citizenry led to mandatory schooling legislation. It eventually became clear, however, that equal access to education meant more than requiring all students to stay in school until a certain age. If all students were to profit from staying in school, then schools would need to find ways to help them learn while they were there. In this context, educators began to believe that instead of simply presenting information, we could and should find ways to help students to *learn how to learn*—and especially how to learn through reading. This was a dramatic role change for schools and for teachers. It raised a host of questions. Just who was supposed to be responsible for figuring out why some students learn to learn and others do not? Who was supposed to help those who fell behind? And how could this be done? Some educators still question whether it really *can* be done, or even really *should* be done, given spiraling costs and competing priorities.

Nevertheless, this new concept of public education was an idea whose time had come. The need to equalize opportunities for all citizens was growing into a national priority that was fueled by the civil rights movement and the increasing skill demands of the job market. Today, most schools and teachers understand that they are not merely responsible for teaching a subject but for teaching all students to be flexible and independent learners. It is this shift in perspective that has driven the rapid development of the content area reading movement.

Early proponents of this movement laid the foundations for extending the definition and practices of reading instruction from an elementary grade focus on merely learning how to read to a new and broader focus on learning from reading. To meet this expectation, schools and teachers needed answers to immediate and pressing questions about how students learn and about how to help students to become better learners. They welcomed the answers that the field of study known as content area reading was beginning to offer. In many cases, however, these answers conflicted with teachers' attitudes and expectations. Changing teachers' views of their roles and responsibilities, like most change, has not been easy. It has been an ongoing process that continues to unfold within one teacher at a time, among both practicing and beginning teachers.

THE COMING WIRED CLASSROOM AND HOW IT IS AFFECTING SCHOOLING AND LITERACY

You do not have to be the Delphic Oracle to realize that telecomputing is changing the face and the functions of education at every level. Since this is one of those things that is in progress, rather than historically analyzed and evident, our aim here is to set out some of the influences it seems to be exerting and the implications that are becoming evident. To date, it appears that telecomputing is having unparalleled effects on daily life and learning.

+ It is generating more reading and writing than ever before.
+ It is, through *chat rooms* and specialized web sites, the ultimate niche-maker and server to individual reading interests and tastes.
+ It is, through the *surfing* option, the greatest means ever of promoting multiple literacies and broadened interests and tastes.
+ It is more current and interactive than any prior media.
+ It is a form of connection that ends much of the isolation that has characterized schools and classrooms to date.
+ It is creating new communities of learners that are blind to a person's color, ethnicity, age, and background.
+ It is blurring lines between services, business, entertainment, information, and education.
+ It is democratizing the power of individuals to speak across political boundaries and be heard by a potentially wide audience.
+ It is, through *homepaging*, producing some of the greatest wealth-making opportunities since free land homesteading.

The authors are heavily involved in the evolutionary process that telecomputing has set in motion. You will read about how we began in the early seventies to create a reading-writing-teaching method (called REAP) that now serves as the vehicle for electronic sharing by readers and how we are now advocating for and extending it through what is being called *WebQuesting,* and social and economic entrepreneurism. However, we will proceed for much of the next two sections by preparing you with the knowledge base that content area literacy has provided to us for making the most of the connections and possibilities that telecomputing seems to be offering to education and contemporary life. See if you find the stories of CAL and the World Wide Web (WWW) to be, as we do, a tale of two merging technologies.

THE SECONDARY SCHOOL READING PROGRAM

Whose Job Is It?

In its early years, the slogan of the fledgling field of content area reading was "Every teacher a teacher of reading." This slogan probably did the field more harm than good, since most junior high and high school teachers saw themselves as teachers of their subject areas, and thought of reading as a basic skill that should have been mastered in the elementary grades. The following line of questioning represents the major points in the reasoning process that many experienced secondary teachers have worked through.

1. *Haven't students learned to read by the time they finish grade school?* The answer to this question must begin with a basic definition of *reading.* Many people think of learning to read as learning to *decode,* or translate the little squiggles we call letters into the sounds we call words. Reading, however, means much more than this simple translation process. It means constructively comprehending, or making meaning from, print. Reading comprehension generally is defined as follows:

✦ *Understanding* the author's intended message (reading the lines)
✦ *Interpreting* the message's meaning and implications (reading between the lines)
✦ *Applying* the message in meaningful ways (reading beyond the lines)

Most children do master the decoding aspects of reading by about the fourth grade. At each higher grade level, however, the reading materials become more difficult. To express increasingly complex ideas and information, authors must use more technical vocabulary and more complex language forms. Thus, learning to read is a process that continues as long as one continues to learn.

Even children who master beginning reading in elementary school must continue to develop effective strategies for learning from more difficult materials and about increasingly specialized subjects. Some students acquire these strategies rather effortlessly, but many others do not. Even in elementary school, some children begin to fall behind their peers in comprehending what they read. As middle and high school teachers' expectations increase, these children begin to have more frequent unsuccessful experiences in attempting to learn from reading. And, of course, a few children fail to master even basic decoding.

For these reasons, content area teachers can expect to have several categories of students in their classes. A few students will still have basic decoding problems. Some will have fairly serious comprehension problems. Many will simply need assistance in acquiring the comprehension strategies appropriate to each higher grade and subject area. Finally, some students will continue to read and develop the needed comprehension strategies on their own. In the past, teachers could concern themselves primarily with presenting information and materials to the latter category of students. Learning to read content materials was treated as a sink-or-swim challenge: you figured out how to do it, or you failed to learn the subject.

Today, most teachers are willing to accept more responsibility for helping *all* children to learn to read and think. As they do so, they are accepting the challenge to teach in ways that don't simply *require* but that help students *acquire* the thinking strategies they need to actively construct meaning from print.

2. *If some students acquire reading–thinking strategies naturally, simply by reading increasingly difficult materials, why do others fail to do so?* The fundamental premise of this book, and a large sector of the content area literacy movement, is that *if all students did spend time reading and working at understanding in every subject through the grades, they all might continue to develop the reading–thinking strategies they need.* However, for a variety of reasons, this does not always happen.

One simple reason why some students do not spend sufficient time reading and working at understanding every subject is that at each higher grade level students' personal interests begin to influence how much reading they do in different subjects. They read more in subjects they prefer and often avoid reading in subjects they do not like. Thus, they may continue to acquire the specialized vocabulary, language, and thinking strategies needed in some subjects but not in others.

Another reason why some students do not do enough reading to make so-called natural progress is related to their personal experiences with being taught to read. Reading instruction, even in the elementary grades, often is structured and conducted in ways that cause some children to see themselves as poor readers. For example, when children are grouped for reading, children placed in the low group know that they are seen as poor readers by their teacher and their peers and learn to see themselves as poor readers. The strength of this learning is evidenced in the fact that they seldom advance to a higher group. When children begin to view themselves as poor readers, for whatever reason, they read less, and progress at a slower rate. By the time these struggling readers reach secondary school, they have had years of negative experiences with reading.

Thus, at each higher grade, in any given subject, there are students who have fallen behind in acquiring the necessary natural reading–thinking strategies: some simply because of stronger interest in other areas, and some because prior failures have caused them to stop trying. Secondary teachers, faced with increasing numbers of students who cannot or will not learn from reading, sometimes make the well-meaning but ironic attempt to present information in other ways that involve little or no reading. The irony in this approach is that it removes any possibility of students' acquiring greater ease and self-confidence in reading. Even those students who might have developed grade-level reading strategies through continued reading may fail to do so if no reading is required. The better alternative, and one of the most influential things a secondary teacher can do, is to use teaching methods that structure reading-based lessons in ways that enable more students to have more successful experiences with reading. It is only through repeated successful reading experiences that appropriate thinking strategies are acquired, and the effects of years of negative experiences can be counteracted.

3.   *Aren't there some students who just can't be taught to read better?* Since reading comprehension is almost synonymous with thinking, many educators once believed that there was a simple, one-to-one relationship between general intelligence and reading comprehension. It was assumed that intelligent students would acquire the ability to read and comprehend well and that unintelligent ones would not and could not be taught to do so. Today, few educators hold this simplistic view. We now know, for example, that intelligence is much more multifaceted than is measured by most conventional tests of intelligence. Several aspects of critical and creative thinking, in fact, appear to be only minimally related to conventional IQ test scores. In fact, some educators have proposed that poor reading comprehension may be a causal factor in low IQ scores, rather than the reverse. In recent years, educational researchers have provided convincing evidence that thinking can be improved and that the methods for doing so are not terribly complex. Content area literacy is based on the premise that all students can be taught to read, learn, and think better, and that all teachers can share the challenges and rewards of helping them to do so.

4.   *Why can't reading be taught in a separate pull-out class?* For those few students who have not acquired basic decoding strategies, reading *should* be taught in a separate class by a reading specialist. Reading disabilities this severe usually have multiple causes and may be accompanied by emotional and behavioral disorders.

Students who can decode adequately but simply do not seem to understand what they read are a different matter. At the beginning of the content area reading movement, and sometimes still today, separate reading classes were designed for these students. The problem with the separate-class approach is that, even though it seems to be the most logical solution, it simply doesn't work very well. Why it doesn't work seems to be related to at least three conditions. First, whenever students are grouped by ability, a multitude of negative factors tend to outweigh the logical advantage that might be gained by offering them instruction that is geared to their achievement level. Second, as discussed previously, most secondary students are stronger readers in some subjects than in others. Identifying which students are lagging in which subjects and trying to provide this level of individualized assistance is practically impossible. Finally, the pull-out approach assumes that students will be taught general reading–thinking strategies that they will then modify and apply when reading their various subject area assignments. This kind of transfer of training is a higher-order thinking process that is, almost by definition, what poor readers have difficulty doing.

Gradually, after years of trying various approaches, two things have become clear: (1) Pull-out programs are necessary for those students who have not mastered basic decoding. (2) However, all students, including those receiving separate remediation, need specific coaching in the particular grade-appropriate reading–thinking strategies of each subject. And, who is more experienced in reading, thinking, talking, and questioning in the respective subject fields than the content teachers themselves?

5. *How can content teachers be expected to find* time *to teach reading and thinking?* The fact that content teachers are being held responsible for the learning of *all* students is the strongest argument for all teachers to be prepared to coach students in the particular reading strategies relevant to their subject areas. Coaching reading and thinking need not be done *in addition to* teaching content. In fact, it is best done *while* teaching content. When such coaching accompanies the teaching of content, students (including mainstreamed students with learning disabilities) become more able to learn independently. Thus, in the big picture, teachers who help students to read on their own are able to teach more content rather than less.

Teaching methods that result in effective coaching of subject area reading and thinking have two important characteristics that make them appropriate for subject area teachers. These methods tend to be concurrent and interactive. *Concurrent* methods permit the teacher to teach toward several objectives at the same time. *Interactive* methods are designed to encourage what is called the *constructivist* side of education—that is, increasing student involvement in instructional exchanges and supporting the use of thinking strategies for making, or constructing, meaning. Many good teachers teach some reading without labeling, or even realizing, it as such. Teachers are teaching reading, for example, when they introduce a reading selection in a way that engages students' interest, or when they invite meaningful discussion following reading, or even when they just ask some questions to check comprehension following reading. Teachers who do these things naturally will want to know more; those who do not do so naturally need to know more.

6.   *Why should all subject areas be included in the schoolwide reading program?* Some content areas, such as English, science, and social studies, have an obvious connection with reading. Others, such as physical education, art, music, and mathematics, traditionally involve far less reading. Yet most states require that all teacher certification programs include at least one course in the teaching of reading. This consensus is in part due to two concepts that are central to effective schools. First, schools are more effective when *all teachers accept responsibility for the overall goals of the school,* not simply for those of their own discipline and classes. Accordingly, every teacher is expected to contribute to the schoolwide literacy program. In some subject areas, this contribution may be as simple as including just a few reading-based lessons that are carefully designed to permit even poor readers to have more successful experiences as readers in that subject. Second, effective schools are organized not merely to teach a given body of information but also to develop interests and abilities that will allow students to continue to be reasonably well versed in their subjects in the future. In this information age, it is not enough to merely acquire information; students must know how to acquire it and, more importantly, to interpret and use it. This new challenge is stirring many to grapple with questions like: What counts as literacy? and, how must the term *literacy* be re-invented in "new times"? (Luke & Elkins, 1998; Moje, Young, Readence & Moore, 2000; Vacca, 1998).

7.   *What level of reading achievement can content teachers expect students to have, and how can they evaluate their students' reading?* Naturally, the higher the grade, the higher the overall average reading level of the class. However, this fact tends to mask another more important one: the higher the grade, the wider the *range* of students' reading abilities from lowest to highest. This is because children who encounter difficulty in beginning reading often make far less than a year's progress for each year in school. Others, however, make more than a year's progress in a school year. Thus, a typical seventh-grade class may be expected to have reading levels ranging from the third- to the tenth-grade level, while a tenth-grade class is likely to range from the fourth-grade to the college level.

Some basic information about students' reading levels usually can be gathered from standardized test scores that are on file. Students with particularly low scores can be noted and observed during the first weeks of school to verify this test-based information. As discussed previously, however, students' reading abilities are likely to vary from subject to subject according to their personal interests, experiences, and prior knowledge. Subject area teachers can use a variety of techniques to cross-verify standardized test score information. These include observation, informal assessment procedures, and systems for portfolio collection, all of which are detailed in Chapter 9.

8. *How can students of varying reading achievement levels learn from a single textbook or supplementary material that is written more or less on grade level?* Over the years, the field of content area reading has proposed and explored many solutions to this logistical question. Most of the early solutions were logical but not very practical. One popular suggestion, for example, was to collect a variety of reading materials on the same topic but at different difficulty levels, and to match these with student reading levels. Individual students, or groups of students, could then explore the topic of study by reading at their own levels. Another suggestion was to prepare reading guides at different difficulty levels and to assign these based on student reading level. For example, lower-achieving readers were guided through acquiring the basic information, and more advanced students were asked questions that required more complex analysis of the information. These early attempts, while reasonable and still viable in some situations, tend to require an extraordinary amount of preparation and continuous monitoring. They also raise troublesome questions about how to evaluate students' work on these differentiated assignments and about whether lower-achieving students would be penalized rather than assisted by a steady diet of literal-level questions and easy material.

Content area literacy has moved to simpler, more manageable, and more equitable solutions. The core approach is based on *interactive methods* for teaching reading–thinking *concurrently* with subject area knowledge and applications. Regular use of such methods from grade to grade and across subject areas supports student development of independent reading–learning strategies and empowers even relatively poor readers to read and learn from materials that they otherwise would find difficult.

Content Area Literacy

The research-supported answers and perspectives that have evolved in response to the preceding questions represent a fairly complete picture of the traditional field of content area reading. A substantial body of research now supports the propositions that teachers *can* teach reading–thinking strategies, that they *can* meet the needs of a fairly wide range of student reading levels in a single classroom, and that the most effective schoolwide reading programs are those that enlist the participation of *every* educator in the school. With that groundwork established, the field has begun to broaden its focus, viewing reading within the broader context of literacy. Whereas the term *reading* connotes acquisition of strategies needed to successfully complete schooling, the term *literacy* speaks more to the breadth of education needed to function in modern life, where ordinary citizens are given the executive power of the vote but also must live in a milieu of rapid technological change and job displacement.

In today's world, the acquisition of large amounts of information is less important than the acquisition of effective strategies for accessing and evaluating information, problem solving, and communicating and inter- acting with interested parties. We once assumed that learners must first acquire information before they could be challenged to critically analyze and apply it. Many frustrating hours have been spent in trying to teach/ learn isolated history facts, math facts, grammar rules, and the like. These required so many hours that teachers often despaired of students ever acquiring sufficient information to enable them to operate at higher levels of evaluation and application. Research in the field of learning theory is refocusing our attention on what many effective teachers have long intu- ited: if students are initially engaged in an authentic, relevant problem, situation, or challenge, the relevant information is acquired almost effort- lessly and in a fraction of the time.

Similarly, reading and subject area specialists are redirecting their atten- tion toward creating educational environments in which students are chal- lenged to analyze, reflect, communicate, and create. In such environments, effective strategies for reading, writing, speaking, listening, and thinking are more likely to develop more naturally and easily than when these are addressed as isolated elements. Thus, there is a growing trend to refer to this emerging field as *content area literacy.* This reorientation shifts the emphasis from reading as a somewhat isolated function toward its role in overall communication and higher-order thinking. Ironically, the need to write and to read highly technical information has been greatly intensified by telecomputing and related technologies that once were expected to reduce the demand for every citizen to be highly literate.

On a Professional and Personal Career Level

So who, in conclusion, should have knowledge about content area literacy? In our judgment, everyone who teaches, and certainly anyone who will teach in a conventional school setting, should know about content area literacy. The interactive teaching methods of content area literacy permit students with a wide range of reading levels to learn from the same reading materials and in the same classroom. These methods offer practical ways to satisfy today's expectation that students of quite varied learning apti- tudes and even those with special learning needs and from diverse cultural backgrounds should have the opportunity to learn in the traditional class setting. And, given the additions of new electronic communication and computing systems, traditional class settings are now anything but tradi- tional. Nonetheless, all teachers, including those who might think they have the least need for content literacy methodology, have the obligation to be informed about what constitutes enlightened instruction so that they can participate in the school's primary mission.

On a more personal career level, an understanding of content area literacy precepts and practices prepares all who work in a school setting to be ready to step in for their colleagues and to have sufficient flexibility and preparation in their education to be able to take on other related jobs, as often as is required over a typical lifelong career. It is not unusual today for those who originally prepared to teach in a conventional classroom to find themselves teaching in other settings: in adult basic and high school equivalency programs; in one of the burgeoning educational programs within business and industry; or extending their certification to work as school-based consultants or central office administrators. (See Appendix A for a sample portfolio system to help teachers better record and prepare for such varied career options.)

The Listen-Read-Discuss (L-R-D) method was created as a "starter" method for bridging from traditional instruction to a more interactive approach. Traditional reading-based instruction typically begins by having students read the assignment, listen to a brief lecture or overview by the teacher, and then discuss their responses to questions. The L-R-D simply inverts the first two steps.

LISTEN-READ-DISCUSS: A SELF-INITIALIZING METHOD

Effective learning, including learning how to be an effective teacher, needs something to get it started, something to keep it going, and something to keep it from becoming random or misguided (Bruner, 1971). The L-R-D method (Manzo & Casale, 1985) tends to meet these requirements for both teachers and students. It is a simple lesson design that can be tried almost immediately and that offers several variations that can be phased in as a personal program of professional development. The L-R-D is a heuristic, or hands-on, activity designed to induce self-discovery about effective teaching by teachers and about effective learning by students.

Steps in the L-R-D

Step 1	Review the reading selection, and prepare a brief, organized overview that points out the basic structure of the material, relevant background information, and important information to look for, and generates interest in the topic.
Step 2	Present the summary orally to students. (See Figure 1.1.)
Step 3	Have students read the textbook version of the same material. Students will then be empowered to read material with which they have some familiarity.

Figure 1.1
Example of an L-R-D prereading script.

This sample prereading script is based on the article "Dance and Sport: The Elusive Connection," which follows in this figure.

Did you know that football coaches sometimes have their players take ballet lessons? Can you see Frank over there in a tutu? (Frank is one of the school's star football players.) Well, this article tells about where this idea came from, and why it seems to work. Look for seven things dancers learn, and think about why these would be useful for football players. Write these down when you come to them—there're listed in one of the first paragraphs. Then the author tells how some sports are more like dance than others. In dance, it is the mastery over one's movement that is important. In sport, it is the result of mastery over one's movement that is important. Look for the difference between "open skill" sports and "closed skill" sports, and how one type is more like dance than the other. The title of the article is "Dance and Sport: The Elusive Connection." Elusive means something that seems to keep slipping away. Read to see why the connection between dance and sport might keep slipping away.

Students then read the article below, from the *Journal of Physical Education, Recreation, and Dance.*

DANCE AND SPORT—THE ELUSIVE CONNECTION

Techniques and principles effectively used in teaching dance can be applied to teaching sport

Sandra Minton
Bradford Beckwith

(1) What are the functional connections between dance and sport and the benefits that are derived from participation in both pursuits? This article presents ideas which are applied to both dance and sport in order to enhance performance and reduce injury.

(2) Many well-known people have recognized a connection between dance and sport skills. It may have been this kinship that convinced Knute Rockne, famed football coach at Notre Dame, to require his players to enroll in dance classes. Maybe it was the similarity between dance and sport that caused Woody Hayes, former Ohio state head coach, to expect his players to take dance as part of their practice procedures (Lance, 1981). Lynn Swan, three-time Pro Bowl wide receiver while playing with the four-time World Champion Pittsburgh Steelers, studied dance for 14 years and attributed his graceful athletic abilities to dance.

(3) It is possible that each of these individuals witnessed movement competencies shared by dance and sports. Some of these shared abilities include centering, balance, focus, breathing, transfer of weight, relaxation and the ability to use space, time, and energy with mastery. Such abilities are taught specifically in dance classes, while in athletics they are only alluded to as a part of skill instruction.

(4) The basic difference between dance and sport is that sport takes place within the conditions of a game, while dance is performed in other contexts. A game is a contest in which opposing interests are given specific information and are then allowed a choice of moves with the object of maximizing wins and minimizing losses. A game entails dominance over an opponent and the acquisition of some mutually coveted symbol. The athlete, by improving his or her movement abilities, will then improve sport skills.

(5) Dancers, on the other hand, are process-oriented rather than product-oriented. The goal in dance is the improvement of movement quality.

(6) Similarities between dance and sport outweigh their differences. Participants in both areas train to go faster and farther, while moving with increased control. The dancer and the sport participant both work to expand their movement vocabulary so they can use a particular action when the situation demands. Biomechanical analysis has been used for many years by physical educators to help their students learn. In recent years, dancers have also begun to use biomechanics to analyze movement with the goals of sharpening perception of movement, decreasing learning time, and enhancing performance (Laws, 1984). Dance and sport are similar in another respect. While some would say a dance was choreographed but a sport contest was not planned, further examination indicates that all the X's and O's used in game strategy simply represent another form of choreography.

(7) Some sport activities are more similar to dance training than others. The concept of open and closed skills helps explain this point. In a closed skill, one strives to master an effective and efficient motor program with the goal of being able to duplicate this program with each repetition. Environmental conditions remain relatively constant, and the performer attempts to be consistent in the execution of the skill. Sports such as the shot put, diving, and gymnastics are closed skills. Open skills exist in a changing environment, and the selection of appropriate movement responses is as variable as the environment itself. Baseball, football, soccer, and basketball are open skill activities (Sage, 1977). Both open and closed skill athletes can benefit from dance training. The abilities which are taught in dance classes used by both kinds of athletes are different, but are not less applicable to their sports' requirements.

Figure 1.1, *continued*

(8) The principle of relaxation can be used as an example. Dancers frequently talk about using the right amount of tension in one part of the body while allowing other body areas to remain relaxed. The main idea is to use energy efficiently and only where needed to perform a movement. Efficient movement is characterized by using the appropriate muscle groups in proper sequence. The use of the wrong muscle group at the wrong time can be deleterious to the skill and possibly to the performer. Another common word heard in dance class is "centering." Centering is finding the body's center of weight and manipulating it effectively in relation to gravity. It also brings the mind and body together to produce better concentration. Achieving a heightened perception of and facility with space, time, and energy is another principle used in teaching dance. Dancers are asked to look at the direction or level of a movement, its speed in relation to an underlying pulse, or the quality of energy used to propel actions through space. Such movement descriptions are provided in dance classes to help students see movement more clearly and to enhance understanding of the expressive aspects of each action (Minton, 1984).

(9) The point is that these principles are used in teaching dance, but generally not in teaching sport. In dance, these ideas are singled out in the classroom and used as learning tools. The examples given here are several of the techniques used in teaching dance that could be applied profitably to the teaching of sport.

REFERENCES
Lance, J. (1981). Practicing for touchdowns. *Journal of Physical Education, Recreation, and Dance,* 5, 38.
Laws, K. (1984). *The Physics of Dance.* New York: Macmillan, Inc.
Minton, S.C. (1984). *Modern Dance: Body and Mind.* Englewood, CO: Morton.
Sage, G.H. (1977). *Introduction to Motor Behavior: A Neuropsychological Approach* (2nd. ed.). Reading, MA: Addison-Wesley.

This article is reprinted with permission of the *Journal of Physical Education, Recreation and Dance,* May/June 1986, pp. 26 and 54. JOPERD is a publication of the American Alliance for Health, Physical Education, Recreation and Dance, 1900 Association Drive, Reston, VA 20191.

Sandra Minton is coordinator of the Dance Program at the University of Northern Colorado, Greeley, CO 80639. Bradford E. Beckwith is a doctoral candidate, psychological kinesiology, at the same school.

Step 4   Discuss the material students have heard and read. Begin
            the discussion with the information and ideas students
            were directed to look for.

Other Values and Benefits of Listen-Read-Discuss

Use of the L-R-D tends to benefit teachers, students, and the school program
in ways that are not always immediately apparent. One such value emerges
almost immediately in the lesson-planning stage. When teachers select
textual material for use in an L-R-D lesson, they find themselves looking
at the textbook more carefully and from more points of view than they
might otherwise. They begin, quite naturally, to sense where students'
comprehension is likely to falter and to better align the phrasing, facts, and
organization of the lecture material they are preparing with the textbook
material that students will read. With better alignment and organization,
teachers automatically begin to heed a basic dictum of effective reading
instruction: to stimulate active reading by preteaching key terms, pivotal
questions, and new concepts before reading. Better organization and alignment also are likely to raise teachers' levels of tolerance for reasonable
digressions in the form of comments about how the new information relates
to real-life events and experiences. In so doing, teachers help students to
better recall and develop relevant background information and appropriate
anticipation, both of which have been shown to be natural to proficient
readers and of great value in effective comprehension (Crafton, 1983;
Harste, 1978; Stevens, 1982).

Careful preparation of L-R-D lessons actually raises students' ability to
read a particular piece beyond their typical reading and thinking levels.
This can be a positive and enabling experience for students and teachers.
It tends to become a new benchmark for students to strive for in learning
from text and for teachers to strive for in helping students to learn from
text.

Following the lecture and empowered reading, the lesson design calls
for discussion, providing a third repetition and elaboration of the material.
This built-in redundancy factor is a most basic—and often overlooked—
practice of effective teachers and principle of effective learning.

Finally, a teacher who follows the L-R-D guidelines will have begun to
restructure class time and expectations from the typical 90% lecture format
to one containing greatly increased proportions of purposeful reading and
informed discussion. This achieves yet another important practice of effective teachers and precept of effective learning: increased time on task.
Some have argued that the simple lack of attention to reading in typical
content classes accounts for a great part of the current higher-literacy
crisis in the schools. This conclusion seems justified by the fact that several
observational studies of subject teaching at the postelementary levels reveal that virtually no purposeful reading goes on during class time (Feath-

ers & Smith, 1987; Greenewald & Wolf, 1980; Mikulecky, 1982; Ratekin, Simpson, Alvermann, & Dishner, 1985).

Overall, the greatest value of the L-R-D seems to be its ability to provide a simple, hands-on way to introduce and initiate oneself to the principles and practices of content area literacy. The reapportioning of class time offers teachers with defensive teaching styles—who overuse either lecture or seatwork—an opportunity to experiment with reasonable alternatives. This in turn, often leads to a greater willingness to try more sophisticated teaching methods and potentially benefit more fully from in-service workshops, consultations, and graduate coursework (Watkins, McKenna, Manzo, & Manzo, 1995).

Figure 1.2
Ladder of variations and elaborations on Listen-Read-Discuss.

1. Have students reread the information covered in the L-R-D format rapidly to increase their speed of reading and thought processing. Reading speed tends to rise as a result of increases in prior knowledge, although it can also be easily improved simply by systematic attention and practice.

2. Inform the class that you will lecture, intentionally omitting a few important details that they will need to read their texts to discover. This gives practice in recognizing what is not yet known and experience in careful reading and knowledge seeking.

3. Inform the class that your lecture will cover all the details of a lesson but that they will need to read to discover what questions these details answer. This is one way to teach students to actively seek an understanding of the concept base, or central question, around which an area of study is focused.

4. Inform the class that a quiz will follow the L-R-D sequence. Allow a short study period. This is recommended to activate a high level of focused attention, give practice in test taking, and set the stage for questions and discussion about how to study effectively.

5. Invert the core process occasionally by having the class R-L-D, or read (for about fifteen minutes), then listen, and finally discuss. This variation tends to focus and improve listening attention and the ability to learn from an effective lecture. This effect can be further heightened when joined with the other listening training and note-taking techniques covered ahead.

6. Watch a videotape, educational film, or multimedia presentation on a text topic *before* reading about it in the text. Such visual representations are compatible with the habits of contemporary youngsters and can help build new bridges to print. (See Figure 1.3.)

A Self-Instructional Ladder

To help teachers' self-discovery, that is, to ease their way into the actual use of more sophisticated, interactive teaching methods, and to provide rich alternatives for different learning styles, we have developed a self-instructional ladder for trying variations and elaborations on the basic L-R-D procedure (see Figures 1.2 and 1.3). You can use L-R-D variations and elaborations to develop your sophistication as an interactive teacher and to explore possible diverse student learning style needs. Try ascending this ladder as your own readiness and students' needs suggest. It's a good idea to keep notes of your thoughts and questions as you try different

7. Ask students which portions of the text struck them as inconsiderate, that is, poorly written, poorly organized, or presuming too much prior knowledge. This activity can help students learn when to ask for help with textual and class material. It also helps the teacher become more aware of student learning needs. Analysis of the writing in texts is also a good way to informally teach some of the basics of effective writing.

8. Provide the class with a definitive purpose for reading and discussing that will require critical and/or creative expression or application. State that purpose clearly on the chalkboard for easy reference, for example, "As you read this section on the steam engine, try to determine why it was bound to be replaced by the gasoline engine." This will serve as a reminder to read actively and with reference to real-life problem solving.

9. Hold postreading discussions on teaching and learning strategies. Make the discussion positive by asking students what they or you may have done that resulted in solid learning. Such discussion gives credit to student intuition, develops reciprocity, and furthers metacognitive processing, or thinking about thinking.

10. Create research teams, and provide time for students to delve into a topic in greater depth. One group could simply see what other textbooks say on the topic. Another could check with other authoritative references—persons, books, and the Internet. Another could write a best estimate of which real-life problems the information learned might help solve or answer. Still another group, where appropriate, could try to identify and discuss theme-related stories, poetry, music, or art. Activities such as these provide links between text topics and nonprint resources and among school learning, artistic expression, multicultural perspectives, and the rest of the real world.

Figure 1.3
Example of L-R-D elaboration 6: Viewing a videotape or film before reading in a world geography class.

Purposes for Viewing

Teacher: Today we are going to continue our study of Kenya by focusing on the Maisi tribe of Southern Kenya. First, we will watch a 20-minute National Geographic tape on this most unusual tribe of people. Listen carefully as you watch for two things, which you will then read about: the diet of the Maisi and the names of three other tribes of the north whom few people know of but who figure in Kenyan life in a big way.

Brief Review Following Viewing

Teacher: Okay, what were the two points we listened for?

Student: The Maisi basically live off their cattle, eating meat and drinking their blood and raw milk.

Teacher: And?

Student: Well, there were three other tribes mentioned, but I can't remember any of them.

Teacher: Okay, read pages 66 to 71 in your text now to learn more about the Maisi diet, and let's get the names of those tribes. If you happen to finish reading early, there are a few copies of a recent magazine report on cholesterol here on my desk that might help answer the question, "Why aren't the Maisi dying of clogged arteries and heart failure from their high-fat diet?"

Postreading Discussion

Teacher: What did you understand best from what you watched and read about?

Student: The names of the three other tribes.

Teacher: Say and spell them, and I'll write them on the board.

Student: Samburu, Turkana, and Hamitic.

Teacher: What did you understand least from what you watched and read about? [When students have understood what they have viewed and read, they will take this question to mean pretty much the same thing as the next one: What questions or thoughts did this lesson raise in your mind?]

Student: I pretty much understood what was said, but I don't understand why the Maisi don't raise things the way the other tribes do.

Teacher: The land they live on is not arable. There is poor topsoil and little water. But that really doesn't explain why they don't move to where there is arable land.

Student: I was wondering about their high-fat diet, so I read fast to get to the article you talked about. It seems that there are at least two reasons why they don't have high blood cholesterol. The raw milk has enzymes that break down fat in the blood. Also, they lead very active lives. They burn off the fat as fast as they put it on.

Teacher: If raw milk is so good for you, why do we homogenize and pasteurize ours, I wonder? Why don't you ask Mrs. Shell in science today if she can help us out with this?

variations. Your notes and thoughts will be useful in discussions with your instructor and coursemates and in processing your own teaching experiences.

✦   *After Words*   ✦

Chapter 1 described the evolution of the field of content area literacy, and offered practical and research-based arguments for urging all teachers to become content area literacy providers. It offered a simple method, Listen-Read-Discuss, as an example of this dynamic instructional technology. The next chapter focuses on the theoretical bases for making reflective and effective instructional decisions.

CHAPTER 2

Concepts and Terminology to Help You Get Started

Everyone who teaches has a theory of teaching, even if they don't realize that they do.

—Harry Singer

✦ Fore Words ✦

This chapter opens with a summary of what is known about the reading process, beginning with the three distinct levels of reading that can be identified for every person. Three theories, or models, of reading process are analyzed, and the *interactive* model is interpreted in terms of what effective readers do as they begin, continue, and conclude a typical content reading task. The chapter concludes with an example of a simple teaching method, the Oral Reading Strategy, and how it facilitates learning from print.

READING TO LEARN: A CLOSER LOOK

Reading can be defined, simply, as unlocking and constructing literal, interpretive, and applied meanings from a coded message. What is not so simple is why some things are easy to read and others are hard or why one student can accurately decode a page and comprehend 95% of the information while another student accurately decodes the same page but comprehends only 60%. To answer these questions, it is necessary to consider what happens when one reads. The cognitive processes involved in reading are quite complex, and, for the most part, are performed subconsciously. Therefore, what we know about reading is in the form of various theories and findings from research designed to test the accuracy of these theories.

One thing we know for sure about reading is that, for each of us, some things are easy to read, other things are more difficult, and still others are next to impossible. The next section introduces the terminology and specific criteria for categorizing and examining these levels of reading. To know these is to have the conceptual basis and the language for understanding and discussing much of what needs to be done instructionally in a content class to ensure that students will be able to learn from textual material.

Levels of Reading

The level at which materials are easy to read is technically referred to as the *independent level*. Reading feels effortless at this level, because we often know something about the topic and are familiar with the language, style, and vocabulary used. All we need to do is fit the new information into existing categories. At this level, we are able to read and comprehend without assistance. The independent level typically is defined as the highest level at which we can accurately decode 99% of the words and comprehend with 90% accuracy. For most people, independent-level reading—whether it is nonfiction, news, or novels—is enjoyable, relaxing, and entertaining. When a reading selection is at our independent level, we can begin at the beginning, and read straight through without stopping. We literally can "absorb" the information without much active effort at all.

Most of us occasionally have had the experience of reading and suddenly realizing that we have not understood the last few sentences, paragraphs, or even pages. What usually has happened is that we have been trying to read something that is somewhat difficult for us, using the same passive reading process that works for independent-level reading. When the topic, language, style, and/or the vocabulary are less familiar to us, we reach what is referred to as our *instructional level reading.* To comprehend material at this level, we often need to create new categories or stop to decipher the meanings of unfamiliar words and/or language patterns. This is the level at which we probably would be able to read and comprehend with the type of assistance a teacher might provide in a classroom setting, or by using a study-reading technique we have internalized. This level is defined as the highest level at which we can accurately decode 95% of the words and comprehend with 75% accuracy. Instructional level reading cannot be done by reading straight through, passively, from beginning to end. It requires an active stance and can be painstakingly slow.

Beyond this point, some reading materials are so difficult for us that they are next to impossible to understand without an extraordinary level of effort and assistance. This *frustration level* is defined as the point at which decoding falls below 90% or at which we comprehend with less than 50% accuracy. It is next to impossible to learn from materials at frustration level, even with the assistance a teacher could provide within a regular classroom.

Considering the reading process in this way, essentially as three *different* processes, helps to explain why many teachers fail to see the need for providing guidance in reading strategies. One reason is the frequent misinterpretation of the *grade-level* designation of textbooks. We tend to assume that this designation means that students at that grade should be able to use the book for independent study. In fact, it means that the book is intended to match the *instructional* level of the student's grade. It should be manageable for them, but only with a reasonable degree of guidance from the teacher. A second reason why teachers sometimes fail to provide reading strategy instruction is that they simply are uninformed about these levels and about the dramatic difference between passive, independent-level reading and active, instructional level reading. Textbooks that are written at students' instructional level require the use of active thinking strategies for constructing meaning. Since these same textbooks will be at the teacher's independent level, the teacher can read them quite easily and passively and may be puzzled as to why students are not understanding what seems perfectly clear. This misunderstanding is probably the reason for the fact that many middle and high school teachers still rely on "round robin" reading. In this familiar activity, students take turns reading aloud, a paragraph or two at a time. For this kind of "straight through" reading to be comprehensible, it must be at the readers' *independent* level. Since this is seldom the case, few students gain much that is profitable from this activity. Better readers are bored, most others are occupied with looking ahead to the section they will be reading, and struggling readers are dreading humiliation.

Teachers' ability to provide guidance in instructional-level reading strategies depends largely on their understanding of the nature of the reading process. What do teachers think *they* do when reading? Recent research related to the reading process suggests that many of our assumptions about the reading process may be inaccurate. This research is changing not only the way beginning reading is taught but how it is guided through the upper grades and even through professional school levels.

Comprehension as Guided Problem Solving

The scientific basis for the study of the comprehension process began around the time of World War I with a study designed to demonstrate that acquiring understanding from reading was far more than the simple act of reading words. Edward L. Thorndike (1917), one of the most eminent educational psychologists of the twentieth century, made the following observation:

> Understanding a paragraph is like solving a problem in mathematics. It consists in selecting the right elements of the situation and putting them together in the right relations, and also with the right amount of weight or influence or force for each. The mind is assailed as it were by every word in the paragraph. It must select, repress, soften, emphasize, correlate and organize, all under the influence of the right mental set or purpose or demand. (pp. 327–328)

In this single paragraph, Thorndike makes it clear that reading comprehension is a process of actively engaging text. It requires that the reader be attentive, analytical, purposeful, flexible, self-aware, world-aware, and emotionally sound.

Even as readers ourselves, it is difficult to identify the cognitive processes that yield such a complex product. Reading remains an unobservable act. We can see what goes in, and test what comes out, but what goes on in between can still be known only in the form of theory. Theories of reading comprehension typically are presented in the form of models that attempt to describe or illustrate, in flowchart form, the sequence in which various elements of the process are activated and the ways in which they interrelate.

MODELS OF THE READING PROCESS

Models of the reading process tend to be categorized as primarily bottom-up, top-down, or interactive. *Bottom-up models* assume that the reader builds upward from details and specifics toward a global concept. *Top-down models* assume that the reader begins with a sketchy grasp of the global concept and uses reading to build downward, filling in details and specifics. *Interactive models* concur with top-down model assumptions, but add a strong dimension of direct instruction. Each of these three categories of models has distinct implications for how reading should be taught.

Bottom-Up Models

Bottom-up models define reading as a text-driven process that begins with perception and recognition first of letters, then of phonetic elements, then of words, then of word groups, and ultimately of sentence meaning and passage meaning. The reader's role is to process these units accurately and rapidly, building meaning from the smaller to the larger units—that is, from the bottom up. It is assumed that if children master each successive reading subskill, they eventually will attain overall reading competency (Gough & Cosky, 1977). Bottom-up theories of reading are the product of behaviorist learning theory, in which the learner was viewed as a "blank slate" to be inscribed by experience. Therefore, for educators who hold bottom-up models of reading, the most important thing a teacher can do is to select and organize the information and skills to be taught, and present these in a logical sequence. If this is done, and each child is permitted sufficient time to master each step, then all children will learn (see Figure 2.1). For example, a bottom-up foreign language teacher would begin an introductory level class by requiring students to learn the alphabet and sound system of the new language, and several sets of high-utilitarian words such as days of the week, months of the year, numbers, colors, and so forth. Learning would be reinforced through a variety of drill and practice activities. Subsequent instruction would introduce the rules governing basic sentence structure, verb tense, and the like, while continuing to practice vocabulary and add practice with short phrases. Most of the class would be conducted in the students' first language.

Behaviorist learning theory held sway in psychology until the early 1970s, but the seeds of change were sown much earlier:

> In 1956, a group of psychologists, linguists, and computer scientists met at the Massachusetts Institute of Technology for a symposium on information science [Gardner, 1985]. This three-day meeting was the beginning of a cognitive revolution in psychology. . . . That scientific revolution became a movement, and eventually a discipline, called cognitive science. Cognitive scientists study how our minds work—how we think, remember, and learn. Their

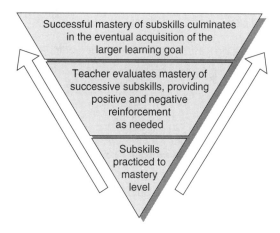

Figure 2.1
Bottom-up (behaviorist) models of the reading process. (Bruer, J. T., *Schools for Thought: A Science of Learning in the Classroom.* © 1993, The MIT Press, New York.

studies have profound implications for restructuring schools and improving learning environments. Cognitive science—the science of mind—can give us an applied science of learning and instruction. (Bruer, 1993, pp. 1–2)

Top-Down Models

Top-down models describe reading as a meaning-driven process. The learner is not seen as a blank slate, but as an individual whose needs and interests drive attention and learning. Reading begins with the reader's incomplete perception of the whole, and proceeds as an active process of recalling relevant prior knowledge and experience to reconstruct the author's meaning and construct related new meanings. Educators who hold top-down models see education not as something done to the learner, but as enriched environments structured for the learner (see Figure 2.2). For example, the founders of the popular whole language movement (Goodman, Bird, & Goodman, 1991) state that if children are immersed in a literate environment, they do not even need to be taught to read but will acquire print literacy in the same way they acquire spoken language. Another top-down theorist once proposed that comprehension cannot be taught, and that the only thing that accounts for reading gains is *time* spent reading (Carver, 1985). A top-down foreign language teacher would begin an introductory level class quite differently from the bottom-up teacher described above. This teacher would enter the classroom speaking the new language, call the roll in the new language, begin to make simple requests and communications supported by gestures and expressions and reference to concrete objects, and continue to conduct the class almost entirely without use of the students' first language.

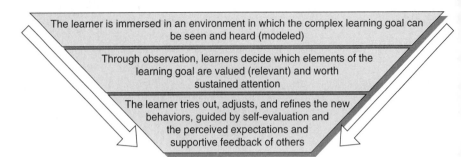

Figure 2.2
Top-down (cognitive) models of the reading process.

Interactive Models

While top-down models appear to align more closely with natural learning processes than bottom-up models, their limitation is that they tend to describe how learning occurs under ideal circumstances and without the physical and temporal constraints of classroom teaching and learning. Interactive models accept all the tenets of top-down models, but *add* direct attention to essential elements of the learning task: elements that might naturally be acquired over time, but that, given the realities of classroom instruction, need to be identified and directly taught. These essential elements often are similar to the subskills that might be identified in a bottom-up model approach. However, interactive models are *not* simply a combination of bottom-up and top-down theories. In the first place, learning *always* is initiated as a top-down process rather than as isolated skills practice. However, instead of relying solely on creating ideal learning environments (as would top-down theorists), interactive theorists begin with this and then move quickly to the identification of the essential bottom-up components of the learning task. While top-down teachers might argue that enthusiastic learners will, in most cases, deduce the underlying principles of an area of study, interactive teachers would place more importance on the fact that not *all* will do so in, say, a semester, largely because not all learners are enthusiastic. A second way in which interactive models are not simply a combination of the other two is that in many cases the bottom-up components identified from an interactive perspective are quite different from those identified from a more purely bottom-up perspective.

With respect to reading comprehension, as an example, bottom-up theorists identify subskills such as identifying the main idea, identifying cause and effect, recalling events in proper sequence, drawing supportable conclusions, and so on. Interactive theorists, on the other hand, identify aspects of the reader's active *self-talk* about what the words are saying and what they seem to mean. The goal of instruction, from this latter point of view, is to have students internalize their interactions with the teacher and peers so as to improve their silent interactions with self in analyzing text.

Interactive models, then, are not at all a combination of traditional bottom-up and avant-guard top-down theories. Rather, they are a real-world and research-based implementation of top-down models with the addition of a revisited and revised version of bottom-up components of learning. Interactive models differ from top-down models primarily in their emphasis on identifying specific bottom-up strategies for direct instructional intervention; they differ from bottom-up models in the *nature* of the strategies identified.

To return to the example of foreign-language instruction from the previous sections, the *interactive* teacher would enter and begin the class in exactly the same manner as the top-down teacher, and most of the class would be conducted in the new language. However, initial instruction would focus on students' mastery of the same high-utility vocabulary words from the bottom-up teacher's lists (days, months, numbers, colors, etc.), to facilitate initial communication, and fundamental rules of grammar and syntax would be directly taught in the students' first language.

The interactive teacher plans instruction by considering how the material would naturally be learned in a top-down manner, and providing as much of that environment as is reasonably possible. The teacher then analyzes the fundamental thinking strategies, principles, and concepts to be learned to determine which would best be taught directly (see Figure 2.3).

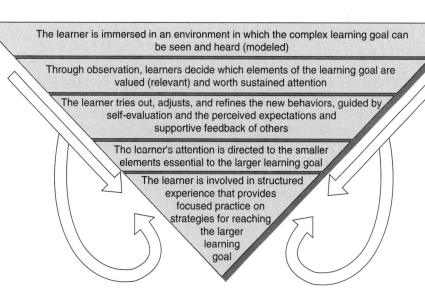

Figure 2.3
Interactive (intervention) models of the learning process.

The interactive model views reading as an active, strategic process of questioning, predicting, confirming, and self-correcting. The top portion of the triangle in Figure 2.3 is exactly the same as the top-down model in Figure 2.2, but a bottom portion has been added. Notice that the bottom portion is quite different in nature from the behaviorists' bottom-up model. Rather than emphasizing skills and facts, the intervention model calls attention to essential elements of the learning goal, and emphasizes direct teaching of strategies for internalizing these. Intervention models acknowledge that these strategies can be acquired naturally, over time, but focus on the assumption that they also can and should be taught.

If being in a conducive environment and doing as others around you do were all that was natural and necessary for learning, no one enthusiastic for a sport such as golf would ever have to take lessons in how to play. Nor would there be the need for master classes in playing the violin or the piano. Of course, many children learn to read without being taught, and continue to make developmental progress through the grades without much coaching. Most of us, however, with the exception of an occasional Tiger Woods type, need someone to lean over and say, "Tuck your elbow in when you swing," or, more to literacy and learning, "Turn that heading into a question and you'll get much more out of that selection."

For further information on models of reading, see Geyer (1972), Harker (1972–1973), Lovett (1981), Mitchell (1982), Ruddell and Ruddell (1995), Samuels (1977), Schell (1988), Singer (1976), Singer and Ruddell (1976), and Williams (1973).

HOW READERS ACTIVELY CONSTRUCT KNOWLEDGE FROM PRINT

Intervention models of reading describe what readers do in three basic stages of the process: as they begin to read, while they are reading, and after they have read. The thinking strategies readers use in each of these stages are more or less automatic in independent-level, or easy, reading. For instructional-level, or study-type, reading, however, the strategies must be used much more actively and consciously.

Prereading

Effective reading begins with readers quickly scanning some or all of the selection, consciously calling to mind what they know about the topic, and making some initial predictions about the content and the difficulty level of the selection. This process, in general, is called *schema activation*.

Schema is a term used in learning psychology to refer to an organization of information and experiences about a topic. *Schemata* (the plural form) are unique to each individual, both in content and in organization. A reader's schema for a topic can be thought of as a kind of net that screens incoming information and experience. The more information and experience that readers have related to a topic (the more finely woven the net), the better able they will be to learn, or catch, the new information (see Figure 2.4). This relatively passive process, which simply involves adding to and refining information and categories within the existing net, was described earlier in the chapter as independent-level reading. When readers have an undeveloped schema for a particular topic (very few strands in the net), it is more difficult to read and to learn. At this instructional level, reading requires active construction or reorganization of the net to recognize, evaluate, categorize, and retain new information.

Put simply, the more you know, the better able you are to learn more. However, there is another important aspect of the function of schemata in learning. No matter how much one knows about a topic, it must be consciously called to mind in order to function effectively as a *learning net*. *Schema activation*, is the most essential element of the prereading stage. Other related thinking strategies for prereading involve:

✦ Looking for organizing concepts

✦ Recalling related information, experiences, attitudes, and feelings

✦ Deciding how easy or difficult the reading selection is likely to be

✦ Setting a purpose for reading

✦ Trying to develop a personal interest

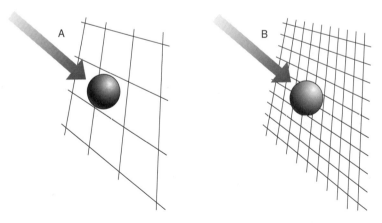

Figure 2.4
Schema theory.
Source: From *Teaching Children to Be Literate: A Reflective Approach,* by A. V. Manzo and U. C. Manzo, 1995, Fort Worth, TX, Harcourt Brace College Publishers. Copyright 1995 by Harcourt Brace College Publishers. Reprinted by permission.

Active Silent Reading

Once the reader has an appropriate mindset for reading a particular selection, the general characteristic of active silent reading is referred to as *metacognitive monitoring.* Metacognitive monitoring is the continuous awareness of when one is understanding and when one is beginning to lose the thread of meaning. It involves continuous and active questioning: Is the author saying that . . . ? Is this like when . . . ? Does this really mean that . . . ? or simply, What does this mean?

Metacognitive monitoring helps readers avoid lapsing into a passive, unproductive independent reading mode. When comprehension begins to falter, active readers use a variety of *fix-up strategies* to actively construct meaning even from difficult text (Baker & Brown, 1984). Depending on the situation, these may include simply pausing to reflect and refocus, rereading, reading aloud, identifying problematic terms and using context to predict or confirm possible meanings, paraphrasing difficult sections, forming mental images, or even asking for help. Thinking strategies for active silent reading involve:

- ✦ Translating ideas into own words
- ✦ Comparing ideas to personal experience
- ✦ Trying to identify main ideas—stop and question when this is unclear
- ✦ Noting important details
- ✦ Rereading whenever necessary for clarification
- ✦ Pausing to reflect whenever necessary to make relevant connections to prior knowledge and experience
- ✦ Consolidating ideas into meaningful groups
- ✦ Noticing unfamiliar vocabulary and predicting meanings based on context when possible
- ✦ Forming mental pictures
- ✦ Evaluating the author's purpose, motive, or authority when appropriate
- ✦ Inventing study strategies as needed
- ✦ Managing time to sustain concentration

Postreading

In the final stage of active instructional-level reading, readers check basic comprehension and appropriate interpretations, and decide on relevant applications of the new information. To do so, they may use any of a variety of strategies for *schema enhancement, schema building,* or *schema restructuring.* These terms correspond to the learning processes that developmental psychologist Jean Piaget called *assimilation* and *accommo-*

dation. The reader consciously compares the new information to existing schema categories and either adds it (assimilation) and constructs a new category or categorization system to incorporate it, or alters existing schema structures in order to fit the new information (accommodation). This process is best done through review and reflection and can best be taught through some form of writing in response to reading and/or questions and activities that require discussion and application of the new information. Strategies for postreading comprehension development involve:

✦ Checking basic comprehension by reciting ("What did I learn?")

✦ Organizing information into chunks of manageable size ("How can I remember it?")

✦ Deciding what is important ("How much should I understand this?")

✦ Trying to clarify ambiguous ideas ("Did I really understand this?")

✦ Evaluating new information in terms of previous knowledge and experience ("Does this make sense?")

✦ Developing study strategies according to class demands or personal purposes ("What should I do to remember this?")

✦ Reviewing material periodically ("How much do I remember now?")

✦ Relating what has been learned from reading back to real-life experiences and related learnings ("How does this answer some question, issue, or goal that I and/or others have been grappling with?")

Having provided an overview of the levels, theories, and stages of the reading process, we turn next to the more practical problems faced by teachers in translating this information into interactive classroom practice. This is followed by a simple interactive teaching method designed to help students acquire reading–thinking strategies by aligning instruction with what is known about the reading process. In doing so, it simultaneously causes teachers to discover many of the principles and guidelines for successful teaching.

ALIGNING INSTRUCTION WITH THEORY

Problems Facing Students

Schooling and education cannot always be the same, but educators must continue to try to align them. The reason is simple. Students tend to have the greatest difficulty internalizing appropriate strategies for independent learning when classroom practices are markedly incompatible with natural processes for learning. Accordingly, the goal of effective instruction is to try to parallel our best understanding of natural learning processes, since such practices are more likely to put the wind at the students' backs as they try to learn and at the teachers' backs as they attempt to teach. Of course, even meeting this objective is no panacea for all possible problems, since students have differing and unique styles of learning.

Nonetheless, the interactive teaching approach advocated here intentionally tries to parallel the interactive, and presumably natural, model of the reading process previously described. In this way, both teacher practices and student learning processes move in the same direction. Ideally, too, each of these processes periodically should guide the other since the necessarily more contrived aspects of operating institutions called *schools* occasionally conflict with the more natural ways that humans learn.

Problems Facing Teachers

At every career stage, there are developmental problems to face and resolve in working toward ideal goals. For most new teachers, it is much easier to teach in the traditional manner they experienced as students than it is to acquire a more interactive teaching style. Most of us have had far fewer personal experiences with interactive teaching than with traditional methods. Furthermore, for new teachers who have been successful students, it can be difficult to realize the problems that many of their peers experienced in those more familiar instructional settings. These impediments are intensified by the fact that they must learn to use these new methods while standing before a class of youngsters who have their own preoccupations, unique histories, and concerns. In a typical classroom setting, teachers must continually evaluate progress toward instructional goals and make many complex "in-flight" decisions based on their perceptions (Padak, 1986). The high potential for stress and job frustration that exists when youngsters with growing pains are brought together with young professionals who are also feeling their way along a new developmental path suggests the need to support teachers so that they can effectively support students.

Interactive Teaching (IT) Methods Benefit Students and Teachers

The IT methods of content area literacy parallel the needs of students and teachers during these difficult decision-making periods. They are fashioned around what research has revealed about what effective readers and teachers do. Interactive methods such as the Listen-Read-Discuss procedure, described in Chapter 1, are designed to produce a well-thought-out, but not confining, teaching–learning environment in which students can observe and try out a variety of thinking strategies. This is accomplished in several ways:

✦ Because IT methods are step-by-step guides, they help keep instruction and learning on course through most student disruptions as well as during teacher lapses resulting from inexperience. This structure helps to create a classroom environment that is conducive to the kind of cognitive and social risk taking that is essential to effective learning.

✦ Because IT methods are general enough in nature to be easily applied across grade levels, subject areas, and types of reading materials, they can reduce lesson-planning time. They can be drawn on to create a lively interaction in virtually any teaching–learning situation, freeing teachers to add as much subject-specific creativity as time and physical and mental resources permit.

✦ Because IT methods are designed to encourage greater student participation, teachers tend to be more responsive and empathetic. Teaching and learning become more interesting and engaging for both students and teachers.

In the next section, see how these characteristics are translated into a simple teaching method.

The Oral Reading Strategy: A Simple Interactive Method

The Oral Reading Strategy (Manzo, 1980) is a simple, direct way to model thinking strategies for prereading and active silent reading. The teacher reads a brief portion of the selection aloud to students while they follow along on their copies of the selection. While reading, the teacher makes a conscious attempt to think aloud; that is, to model the thinking strategies that proficient readers might use to focus attention, develop and maintain interest, and monitor comprehension. A similar method is called the *Think Aloud* (Davey, 1983). The Oral Reading Strategy calls for the teacher's oral reading to be *brief* so that students can maintain attention and have an immediate opportunity to emulate the model as they continue to read silently. (The literacy specialist or teacher with opportunity for individual tutoring may wish to have students attempt a think-aloud while reading to get a sense of what students may or may not be saying to themselves while reading.)

Steps in the Oral Reading Strategy

Step 1　　*Teacher preparation.* Preview the reading selection, trying to "see" it from your students' perspectives. On a photocopy of the first page or so (depending on print formatting), make notes of the thinking strategies that would be useful to model for students as you read the first few paragraphs aloud just before students' independent silent reading of the assignment. The prereading and active silent reading strategies listed above are a good place to start.

Step 2   *Teacher oral reading.* Tell students that you will read a little of the beginning of the reading assignment aloud to show them how to read actively when they are reading silently. Using the notes you have prepared, read and think aloud. Encourage students to answer your think-aloud questions.

Step 3   *Release responsibility to students.* At a reasonable stopping point (after no more than about three to five minutes), tell students to continue immediately to read silently, trying to use the same active thinking strategies you have just demonstrated. See the example in Figure 2.5 to get a sense of how the teacher can use this think-aloud process to demonstrate active reading strategies in a direct and interactive way.

Figure 2.5

Example of the Oral Reading Strategy with "Dance and Sport—The Elusive Connection."

The Oral Reading Strategy was used toward the end of class, to scaffold students' independent reading of a supplementary reading selection. In this example, the teacher has used the Oral Reading Strategy with this class several times before.

After distributing copies of the article, the teacher begins the interaction by stating, "Before you start to read this article, I will read the first part out loud to remind you of some of the ways we have to think actively when we're reading to learn something new."

The teacher then reads the first three paragraphs aloud (the boldface portions below), with the think-alouds inviting student responses as shown in parentheses.

DANCE AND SPORT—THE ELUSIVE CONNECTION

(*T:* Okay, when we read to learn something new, we start right off to do what?)
(*S:* Talk to ourselves.)
(*T:* Great, so, then, let's stop and think about the title, dance and sport—how *might* they be connected?)
(*S:* You have to learn to move in both.)
(*S:* You have to practice both.)
(*T:* Okay. Let's think some more about the title. If dance and sport are connected, how might the connection be *elusive?*)
(*S:* What does elusive mean?)

Figure 2.5, *continued*

(*T:* That's a good strategy question—what's the word culprit? Elusive means hard to hold on to or hard to pin down—in this case, it probably means hard to hold on to.)

(*T:* So, how might the connection be *elusive?*) (*after no immediate response, T:* Well, if we're not getting it, we could . . . ?)

(*S:* Read on a little bit.)

(*T:* Okay.)

Techniques and Principles Effectively Used in Teaching Dance Can Be Applied to Teaching Sport

(*T:* Let's stop and think about the rest of the title. Does this remind you of anything you've heard about?)

(*S:* I've seen how some football coaches make their players do ballet.)

(*T:* And how might that connection be elusive?)

(*S:* The guys probably feel kind of dumb doing it.)

(*T:* I think we've got a prediction about where the title is leading us; let's read on a little.)

1   **What are the functional connections between dance and sport and the benefits that are derived from participation in both pursuits? This article presents ideas which are applied to both dance and sport in order to enhance performance and reduce injury.**

(*T:* Let's stop for a second and boil that down.)

(*S:* By doing both dance and sport you can do your own thing better and not get hurt.)

(*T:* Any questions about this?)

(*S:* Do ballet dancers benefit from learning to play football?)

(*T:* Good question. Let's read on a little.)

2   **Many well-known people have recognized a connection between dance and sport skills. It may have been this kinship that convinced Knute Rockne, famed football coach at Notre Dame, to require his players to enroll in dance classes.**

(*T:* There's your football/ballet connection.)

Maybe it was the similarity between dance and sport that caused Woody Hayes, former Ohio state head coach, to expect his players to take dance as part of their practice procedures (Lance, 1981). Lynn Swan, three-time Pro Bowl wide receiver while playing with the four-time World Champion Pittsburgh Steelers, studied dance for 14 years and attributed his graceful athletic abilities to dance.

(*T:* What's the point of this paragraph?)

(*S:* Examples of people who have seen the connection between football and dance.)

(*T:* Let's read on a little bit.)

Figure 2.5, *continued*

3   It is possible that each of these individuals witnessed movement competencies shared by dance and sports. Some of these shared abilities include centering, balance, focus, breathing, transfer of weight, relaxation and the ability to use space, time, and energy with mastery. Such abilities are taught specifically in dance classes, while in athletics they are only alluded to as a part of skill instruction.

(*T:* What's important here?)
(*S:* Those look like the things that people need for both dance and sport.)
(*T: The "functional connections"?) (after nods, T:* Can we predict where this is going?)
(*S:* Maybe it's going to tell more about these things, like centering, and balance? Or tell about some other things that are the same in both?)
[Teacher writes on the chalkboard: "What are the functional connections between dance and sport?"]
(*T:* Any questions about this?)
(*S:* I still wonder whether any ballet dancers have tried to play football.)
[Teacher adds to the chalkboard; "Do the connections go both ways, or only from sport to dance?"]
(*T:* Do you have any other questions before you continue reading by yourselves?)
[No questions are raised.]
(*T:* Okay, continue reading to find answers to these questions. Remember to use the strategy phrases as you go.)

4   The basic difference between dance and sport is that sport takes place within the conditions of a game, while dance is performed in other contexts. A game is a contest in which opposing interests are given specific information and are then allowed a choice of moves with the object of maximizing wins and minimizing losses. A game entails dominance over an opponent and the acquisition of some mutually coveted symbol. The athlete, by improving his or her movement abilities, will then improve sport skills.

5   Dancers, on the other hand, are process-oriented rather than product-oriented. The goal in dance is the improvement of movement quality.

6   Similarities between dance and sport outweigh their differences. Participants in both areas train to go faster and farther, while moving with increased control. The dancer and the sport participant both work to expand their movement vocabulary so they cular action when the situation demands. Biomechanical analysis

Figure 2.5, *continued*

has been used for many years by physical educators to help their students learn. In recent years, dancers have also begun to use biomechanics to analyze movement with the goals of sharpening perception of movement, decreasing learning time, and enhancing performance (Laws, 1984). Dance and sport are similar in another respect. While some would say a dance was choreographed but a sport contest was not planned, further examination indicates that all the X's and O's used in game strategy simply represent another form of choreography.

7 Some sport activities are more similar to dance training than others. The concept of open and closed skills helps explain this point. In a closed skill, one strives to master an effective and efficient motor program with the goal of being able to duplicate this program with each repetition. Environmental conditions remain relatively constant, and the performer attempts to be consistent in the execution of the skill. Sports such as the shot put, diving, and gymnastics are closed skills. Open skills exist in a changing environment, and the selection of appropriate movement responses is as variable as the environment itself. Baseball, football, soccer, and basketball are open skill activities (Sage, 1977). Both open and closed skill athletes can benefit from dance training. The abilities which are taught in dance classes used by both kinds of athletes are different, but are not less applicable to their sports' requirements.

8 The principle of relaxation can be used as an example. Dancers frequently talk about using the right amount of tension in one part of the body while allowing other body areas to remain relaxed. The main idea is to use energy efficiently and only where needed to perform a movement. Efficient movement is characterized by using the appropriate muscle groups in proper sequence. The use of the wrong muscle group at the wrong time can be deleterious to the skill and possibly to the performer. Another common word heard in dance class is "centering." Centering is finding the body's center of weight and manipulating it effectively in relation to gravity. It also brings the mind and body together to produce better concentration. Achieving a heightened perception of and facility with space, time, and energy is another principle used in teaching dance. Dancers are asked to look at the direction or level of a movement, its speed in relation to an underlying pulse, or the quality of energy used to propel actions through space. Such movement descriptions are provided in dance classes to help students see movement more clearly and to enhance understanding of the expressive aspects of each action (Minton, 1984).

Figure 2.5, *continued*

---

9   The point is that these principles are used in teaching dance, but generally not in teaching sport. In dance, these ideas are singled out in the classroom and used as learning tools. The examples given here are several of the techniques used in teaching dance that could be applied profitably to the teaching of sport.

References

Lance, J. (1981). Practicing for touchdowns. *Journal of Physical Education, Recreation, and Dance,* 5, 38.

Laws, K. (1984). *The Physics of Dance.* New York: Macmillan.

Minton, S. C. (1984). *Modern Dance: Body and Mind.* Englewood, CO: Morton.

Sage, G. H. (1977). *Introduction to Motor Behavior: A Neuropsychological Approach* (2nd ed.). Reading, MA: Addison-Wesley.

Sandra Minton is coordinator of the Dance Program at the University of Northern Colorado, Greeley, CO 80639. Bradford E. Beckwith is a doctoral candidate, psychological kinesiology, at the same school.

Source: Sandra Minton and Bradford Beck with *JOPERD,* May/June (1986).

✦   *After Words*   ✦

The concepts and theoretical background presented in this chapter, along with the Oral Reading Strategy for putting it all into practice, should have you ready, set, and able to continue your quest to be a competent content teacher and literacy provider. The next chapter outlines the elements of interactive instruction and frameworks for selecting dynamic teaching methods. These are some of the schemata that you will need to activate to be a reflective practitioner.

CHAPTER 3

Elements and Frameworks for Interactive Instruction in Content Area Reading and Writing

We have to change the way teachers interact with students in the classroom—and the changes must be grounded in an understanding of how children learn.

—John T. Bruer (1993, p. 7)

✦ *Fore Words* ✦

This chapter provides an overview of the instructional elements that distinguish interactive teaching/learning from more traditional approaches. These elements are then translated into an instructional framework for planning and teaching any reading-based lesson in any subject at any level. The simple three-part framework described is rooted in the stages of the reading process described in Chapter 2: prereading schema activation, metacognitive monitoring of silent reading, and active postreading schema building. An example is given of how the three-step framework can be implemented using a method referred to as the *Three-Phase Graphic Organizer*. The second half of the chapter addresses two forms of writing: informal writing to learn, and formal writing of papers.

THE MORE THINGS CHANGE . . .

Recently one of us (A. Manzo) had occasion to visit Wyandotte High School in Kansas City, Kansas. This truly beautiful inner-city building was as pristine as it must have appeared at its opening in 1937. The pleasant feeling of nostalgia in being at this venerable site was interrupted by the realization that instruction here, as in many other secondary schools, hasn't changed much since that time either. Students have changed, society has changed, and our understanding of the learning process has changed, yet life in many classrooms goes on much the same. The theory underlying robust, interactive instruction is not even very new. Its origins have been traced from a 1956, three-day symposium of psychologists, linguists, and computer scientists, to a full-blown movement by the mid-1970s. However, the movement has yet to make significant inroads into actual school practice:

> Cognitive science—the science of mind—can give us an applied science of learning and instruction. Teaching methods based on this research . . . are the educational equivalents of polio vaccine and penicillin. Yet few outside the educational *research* community [emphasis added] are aware of these breakthroughs or understand the research that makes them possible. (Bruer, 1993, p. 2)

We believe that this is partly due to the fact that, until very recently, all of the component parts needed for practical school implementation were not fully developed or readily available to real teachers in real schools. But times have changed dramatically with development of specific teaching methodologies and widespread access to the Internet. Many, if not all of the parts necessary for robust, interactive teaching and learning seem to be in place now. See if you agree, as you review the following brief descriptions of the elements of interactive instruction and learning.

ELEMENTS OF THE INTERACTIVE CLASSROOM

Three elements distinguish interactive teaching from more traditional approaches. These are: *preassessment, use of authentic/evocative tasks and materials,* and *strategy instruction.*

Preassessment Through Diagnostic Teaching

Preassessment refers to the knowledge about the particular group of students that a teacher draws upon in lesson planning. Planning an interactive lesson must begin not only with the content to be taught, but with knowledge and informed observations of students' information, abilities, and attitudes. Experienced teachers begin their planning with a rich background of informed assumptions about each new group of students. For beginning teachers and teachers new to a school, standardized test scores and prior grades in school can provide some basic information about students' general achievement and ability levels. Daily interactions during the first few days of school help teachers to begin to accumulate information about the nature and extent of students' prior knowledge and experiences, as well as their personal interests, talents, and possible areas of learning difficulty. As instruction progresses, each lesson provides preassessment information for the next. This process of planning and implementing instruction in ways that intentionally provide ongoing informal assessments is referred to as *diagnostic teaching.* More specific assessment information can be collected from structured observations of students and from a variety of informal assessment techniques. Several of these techniques and instruments are described in Chapter 9.

Accessing Multiple Literacies Through Supplementary Reading Materials

There is a growing recognition that traditional school-based definitions of *literacy* represent a narrow strand of the broader, real-world literacies needed to function in today's complex society. Therefore, young adolescents need to be encouraged to engage in "multiple literacies": reading, writing, and speaking in many arenas—fashion, sports, economics, interpersonal relationships, ethics—both in and out of school. This should not be so difficult to do since they encounter information and fictional events via television, movies, magazines, and the Internet. They communicate via telephone, through (forbidden) written notes, e-mail, and in chat rooms. The degree to which they make these literacy activities a public part of their public and private lives depends more on peer approval than upon school sanctions. In fact, school sanction often equals peer disapproval, and has the effect of driving many students' discovery of and interest in literacy activities "underground." In an article with the captivating title, "On every page someone gets killed! Book conversations you don't hear in school," Worthy (1998) describes her middle school son and his friend as "renegade readers." The study begins with a familiar scenario:

> Both Chase and Jared had followed a typical course of development in all academic and social areas and had been average to above-average students during their earlier school years. Each had grown up in homes in which literacy was valued and reading materials were abundant, and in which they had rich access to books, magazines, and comics of their choice. Both had enjoyed reading in their preschool and primary years, and both had begun to resist school reading in their upper elementary years and continued to do so. (Worthy, J., On every page someone gets killed! Book conversations you don't hear in school. International Reading Association © 1998.)

Chase and Jared were reluctant readers in school, but had animated conversations about their self-selected reading outside of school. Another literacy researcher undertook a study with his two adolescent daughters to document the girls' various real-life literacy activities. Not unexpectedly, the report co-authored by father and daughters revealed differing patterns related to the girls' different ages and interests, but very little overlap between in-school and out-of-school literacy involvement (Bean, Bean, & Bean, 1999).

Until recently, it was difficult to imagine an alternative to teacher-selected classroom reading materials: a single textbook or class sets of novels and supplementary books. Newspaper and magazine articles could not be easily reproduced until the cost of copying came down to practical levels. Simply locating materials related to an instructional unit was difficult. As schools and classrooms go on-line, these financial and logistical restrictions are dissolving. Search engines facilitate location of information on virtually any topic, by the teacher and/or students themselves. The use of high-interest, real-world supplementary readings on unit topics has a number of benefits:

- ✦ High-interest nontextbook-type short readings are an ideal way to provide top-down engagement for any subject at any level.
- ✦ For classes with traditional textbooks, supplementary readings can be selected to parallel, correspond to, or contrast with the textbook author's treatment of the topic to stimulate critical analysis.

✦ Supplementary readings can provide a simpler version, or a more detailed version, depending upon the students' interest and prior knowledge for the topic.

✦ Supplementary readings can add currency in rapidly changing subject areas.

✦ Supplementary readings can link abstract new concepts to familiar real-world events.

✦ In subjects where textbooks often are not available, occasional reading-based activities and supplementary readings can introduce students to sources for pursuing their interests outside of and beyond the classroom.

✦ At the next level, "WebQuest" sites make it easy for students to select from a wide range of potential sources of information on a given topic, and to access these at their own pace (see http://webquest.com).

Cognitive Modeling of Thinking Strategies

The third fundamental premise of interactive instruction is that *thinking* is not completely, or even primarily, a function of intelligence. Rather, it is a constellation of strategies and cognitive habits, or "habits of mind" that can be identified and taught through cognitive modeling.

Thinking strategies are *mental scripts used in active learning*. Thinking strategies for active study reading include, for example:

1. "Stop and think about the title."
2. "Where does this seem to be going?"
3. "How would I say this in my own words?"
4. "Maybe I'd better reread that part."

These phrases should, of course, be worded in language that is comfortable to the individual teacher, and appropriate to the age and level of the class.

Cognitive modeling is *thinking aloud to demonstrate a particular thinking strategy*. Although modeling has long been used to teach complex manual procedures, as in art and craft apprenticeships, it is only in relatively recent memory that it has been intentionally applied to teaching *thinking* processes which are otherwise hidden from view. The idea of cognitive modeling was sparked by a simple realization. This realization was that just as toddlers first learn to speak by interacting with skillful language users, each of us continues to acquire more sophisticated language and thinking processes in much the same way: by observing models of these behaviors, imitating those models, and self-evaluating our progress toward some personally desired level of competence. Another special value of cognitive modeling is based on the principle that "more is caught than can be explicitly taught." That is, when information is presented in ways that model relevant thinking strategies, students acquire not just the information in the day's lesson, but they begin to internalize the tools for acquiring similar information, as well as a host of other more holistic behaviors. These might include collateral factors such as body language, attitude, social poise, and even the civility with which something is spoken.

The essence of strategy instruction is intentional, frequent repetition of the strategy phrases, and intentional, frequent cuing of students to use the strategy phrases. The intent is to help students to internalize the phrases to the point where they automatically occur in the appropriate contexts. Modeling and direct instruction in thinking strategies have the effect of enabling at-risk students while building self-awareness and confidence in developmental and advanced students as well.

This planned, structured interpretation of cognitive modeling may be one of the great discoveries of modern pedagogy. It has several interlocking features that have emerged from various quarters over recent years: *engagement, scaffolding/fading, reciprocity,* and *structured peer interactions.*

Engagement

Engagement, simply speaking, is *focused attention to the learning task at hand.* It is, logically, the single most essential element in teaching/learning: if the learner is not paying active attention to the learning task or challenge, none of the subsequent elements can be achieved. While traditional instruction has tended to rely on external sources of motivation (such as grades) to encourage, or force, engagement, the interactive approach emphasizes building internal motivation through top-down engagement with the essential principles and concepts.

Points to Ponder

What! No star, and you are going out to sea?
Marching, and you have no music?
Traveling, and you have no book?
What! No love and you are going out to live?

—Translated from the French (author unknown)

The poem above represents the intent of top-down engagement. In traditional instruction, it is the teacher who presumably has the larger vision: the "star," the "music." The students' job is to be patient, cooperate, practice the parts as presented, and trust that at some point it will all come together. It is somewhat like trying to teach a child to speak without ever letting her or him hear spoken language or experience its value. One of the authors (U. Manzo) once observed a preschool classroom in which children, as they entered, were invited to come to the carpet, where they were given a black circle-shaped paper and shown how to punch holes of various shapes in the paper with special hole-punchers. Some children willingly began to punch holes, and try out different shapes and patterns. Four or five others, however, didn't show much interest in the activity, and wandered around the classroom looking for something else to do. After about ten minutes, all the children were asked to come to the carpet and sit in a circle. The lights were turned off, and an overhead projector was placed on the floor with the light projecting up to the ceiling. The teacher then began placing the children's hole-punched papers on the overhead screen to project the patterns of variously shaped "stars" onto the ceiling. There were audible rounds of awed "oohs" and "aahs," every teacher's dream response. Needless to say, the "wanderers" quickly found their unpunched papers and began to enthusiastically produce patterns of their own.

Many children will accept the teacher's authority and attempt seemingly aimless activities. But learning becomes more focused, animated, and rapid when they can see the "stars" before they begin. It is not always easy to work backwards to the driving questions and fundamental issues of a discipline, and then to translate these into classroom experiences. However, WebQuests on the Internet are offering a rapidly growing collection of interactive resources for providing this kind of top-down engagement. This is why several such sites are referenced throughout the text and on the accompanying web site. Teaching and learning have never been so richly supported, responsive, exciting, and accessible "24/7"—twenty-four hours a day, seven days a week.

Scaffolding/Fading

Scaffolding refers to elements of instruction that support the learner during the early stages of learning. Any truly new learning involves the "burning-in" of some new pathways. This takes much more time than all subsequent learning and is characterized by a high-risk trial-and-error period that, in the social context of a classroom, can threaten the learner's self-esteem. One of the best ways to build internal motivation and strengthen self-esteem is to design lessons with sufficient scaffolding to build students' sense of their own competence as learners. For interactive instruction to occur, learning situations must be structured in ways that reduce the social risks of active participation, and encourage the learner to experiment with new ways of thinking and communicating. One important function of cognitive modeling is to "externalize thinking" in ways that honestly portray the initial awkwardness and increasing competence in acquiring new knowledge and skill.

As students attain confidence and automaticity in using a set of strategies with a particular content, the teacher *gradually removes the scaffolding*, a process referred to as fading. This happens to some extent within each lesson, and more obviously over the course of a semester or year. It is during this fading process that learners internalize new learning strategies by adjusting them into forms and formats for personal use.

Reciprocity

Reciprocity is the opportunity for students to influence the teacher's thinking and one another's thinking, as well as to be influenced. While this often happens by chance in many classroom interactions, interactive teaching intentionally structures situations that encourage it. In reciprocal teaching situations, the teacher is still responsible for outlining and maintaining the general content and direction of instruction, but interactions are structured in ways that require the teacher to allow student response and encourage students to learn from one another. When teachers and students are connected reciprocally, they tend to create a communal learning spirit in which everyone, including the teacher, learns.

Structured Peer Interactions

In the traditional classroom, any active participation can be a risky proposition. Yet, genuine learning is virtually defined by active participation. By talking to others we discover what we think and feel; by listening to others we learn to consider other points of view. In recent years the early, complex versions of *cooperative learning* have evolved into more fluid, flexible *cooperative structures* for managing the complex social dynamics of the classroom. A cooperative structure is *an activity intended to produce active interactions among participants and create a sense of classroom community.* Kagan (1994) uses the acronym PIES to represent the elements of an effective cooperative structure:

✦ *Positive interdependence.* Interactions are structured in ways that students come to rely on their peers in positive ways.

✦ *Individual accountability.* Each student is, however, responsible for his or her own learning.

✦ *Equal participation.* All students are actively involved in the interactions for the same amount of time.

✦ *Simultaneous interaction.* A number of interactions occur at the same time.

A THREE-STEP FRAMEWORK FOR INTERACTIVE READING-BASED INSTRUCTION

Some subjects, such as social studies, science, and English, clearly are reading-based; others traditionally rely far less on students' acquiring information from print. In either case, the range of student reading ability within any one class has tended to reduce teachers' expectations that students will complete reading assignments independently. Bintz (1997) details the problems that teachers face with reading-based instruction:

✦ Students who experience daily difficulties learning from text materials

✦ Students who regularly refuse to do required reading out of class

✦ Students who do read but fail to comprehend the most important information

✦ Students who are bored or uninterested in much of what they read.

The fact is, in most middle and secondary school classes, most students need some guidance in reading, some need a great deal, and those who need little to no assistance benefit a great deal by becoming more aware of the strategies they are using. Following is a simple framework for structuring any reading-based lesson. See Figure 3.1 for an illustration of

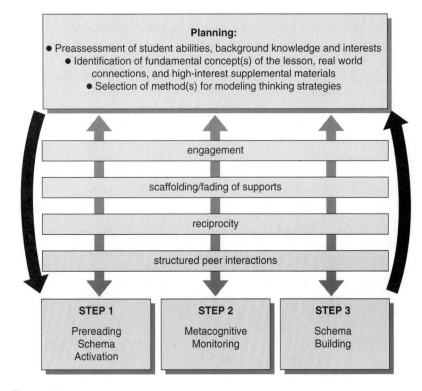

Figure 3.1
Planning elements and a three-step framework for interactive reading-based instruction.

how the elements of interactive instruction should be woven into the reading-based lesson.

Planning

Lesson planning is a matter of finding a match between content to be taught and student readiness to learn. In most instruction, the basic content is a given; therefore the task is in designing enabling learning situations that build on students' background information and experiences, and engage them in exploring new ideas. Planning for any reading-based instruction should begin with envisioning students actually doing the reading. Then, try to envision the essential concept(s) to be taught. Next address these questions: What is the range of abilities in the group? What do you know about student background knowledge, experience, and interests related to the topic? What real-world connections to the lesson topic can be drawn? In that context, what key terminology will students need in order to access the new ideas, and what basic questions will direct them toward the essential concept(s)? Considering where your students are, and where you want them to go, what real-world connections might serve to engage their interest and attention? What authentic, real-world, reading, writing, viewing, listening, speaking activities can be structured to provide these connections? If the core concepts are presented in a class textbook, how might these be brought to life through brief, high-interest supplemental reading materials, poignant video clips, and/or directed peer interactions? What on-line resources are available, and how can these be accessed and woven into the lesson planning?

The instructional framework described next provides a guide for designing reading-based lessons in which more students are likely to be more successful more of the time. This simple three-step framework parallels the interactive model view of the reading process. Remember, this framework is not a teaching method but a structure to guide and facilitate planning.

Step 1: Prereading Schema Activation

When the difficulty level of a reading selection is above the reader's independent level, good readers use a variety of active thinking strategies to consciously call to mind relevant schema structures for the general topic, including personal prior knowledge, experiences, and attitudes. This schema activation permits the reader to anticipate the structure, organization, and general content of the selection. Approaches to teaching prereading anticipation strategies may involve brainstorming, inquiry training, and/ or guided prediction. The intent is to engage students in observing and practicing effective anticipation strategies for initiating study reading. Some general guidelines for structuring anticipation include the following:

1. Consider visual and aural prompts to aid in schema activation.

2. Model anticipation strategies such as:

   "I need to stop and think about the title."
   "What do I know about this already?"
   "What are some categories that might be included in this topic?"
   "I'll look this over quickly to . . . [see how detailed it is] [see if I see any unfamiliar words]."
   "What's the main thing that I might be learn from this?"
   "After I read this, what should I be able to do with it or who might I talk to about it?"

3. Generate clear purpose questions to focus student reading.

4. Provide low-risk, scaffolded opportunities for students to practice these anticipation strategies.

5. Consider preteaching any vocabulary terms that may be unfamiliar to most students and central to the meaning of the selection.

Step 2: Metacognitive Monitoring

Having anticipated the basic structure and something of the general content of the piece, the reader begins to attempt to reconstruct the author's basic meaning, and to construct personal connections with and responses to it. In easy, or independent level reading, this can begin as an almost autonomic process of moving the eyes across the print and passively absorbing the author's meaning. In more difficult, instructional-level materials, the reader must monitor comprehension more consciously and more continuously. Silent reading can be guided by asking students to do various things as they read. One traditional approach is to provide students with a "reading guide"—a set of questions to consider and answer as they read. Silent reading strategies can also be taught through various think-aloud methods that are modeled by the teacher and practiced aloud by students. Guidelines or exercises for teachers to better understand and provide for the needs of students might include the following:

+ Try reading the selection yourself as if you had only your students' background of information, and their limited experience in reading material of this type. Anticipate possible misunderstandings and trouble spots, and alert students to these in whatever form of silent reading guidance is used.

+ Use the Oral Reading Strategy occasionally, to model silent reading strategies such as:

  "How would I say that in my own words?"
  "What's the main point here, and why is it important?"

"What would be an example of this?"
"How could I cluster the ideas I've read about so far?"
"Am I finding answers to the purpose question(s) yet?"
"Where is this going next?"
"Here's an unfamiliar word—what does it seem to mean in the way it's used here?"
"Can I picture in my mind what is going on here?"
"Does this make sense, according to my own experience?"
"Can I trust this author's accuracy/authority/objectivity?"

✦ When using the Oral Reading Strategy, remember to also model fix-up strategies for when students *realize* that they have lost the train of thought:

"Let me reread that last part, more slowly this time."
"Let me think about that for a minute."
"Is there a certain word here that is throwing off my understanding?"
"Let me read ahead a little, to see if getting the larger picture helps."

✦ Incorporate these fix-up strategies into other forms of silent reading guidance provided to students. Occasionally ask them to think aloud as they read. Ask better students to do this first so that there will be some peer models from which to learn.

Step 3: Postreading Schema Building

Postreading strategies for connecting what has just been read with existing schema begins with a simple comprehension check to add new information to existing schema, and include numerous strategies for analyzing and interpreting the author's message to add new schema structures or alter existing ones. Approaches to helping students acquire postreading strategies, as well as just correct answers, include peer discussion, writing, and traditional teacher-directed discussion. Peer discussion and writing activities help students to process and formulate their responses to reading in preparation for a larger group discussion. Guidelines for structuring the postreading stage of reading-based instruction include:

✦ Address all three levels of reading comprehension: basic or reconstructive comprehension (what did the author say?), interpretation (what did the author mean?), and application (how can this be used?). These do not always need to be addressed in sequence. Beginning with an interesting application question or activity can increase incentive to review and clarify basic facts and information.

✦ Model consolidation strategies, such as:

"Did we raise the best purpose question(s) for this selection?"
"What were the main points made?"

"Are there any parts/key terms that still are unclear? Do we need to reread any portions of this?"

"How can this information be organized or 'chunked' to remember it better?"

"Does this make sense when compared to my own experience and knowledge?"

"How could we use this information?"

"If what the author says is true, does it change what I thought before I read this?"

"How could this be confirmed or challenged?"

✦ Structure writing prompts and cooperative group activities to engage students in practicing asking and answering the strategic questions above.

This three-step framework is not terribly different, on the surface, from one of the first published content area reading frameworks: Russell Stauffer's (1969) Directed Reading–Thinking Activity (DR–TA). Intuition and good sense often outrun theory and research. Stauffer's DR–TA recommended five steps for a reading-based content area lesson: preparation for reading, reading the material silently, developing comprehension, rereading, and followup. We have translated this generic framework into the version described above primarily to place a stronger emphasis on the type of thinking strategy instruction that has evolved into a powerful instructional technology over the thirty years since Stauffer's groundbreaking publication. See Figure 3.1 for a graphic illustration of the relationships among the elements of interactive instruction and the three-step framework.

Using a Graphic Organizer to Plan and Teach a Reading-based Lesson

A graphic organizer is a two-dimensional picture of the logical organization of textual material. In one standard format, called a *structured overview*, the main topic is placed in the center, subtopics are arranged around it, and details related to each subtopic are noted alongside each. Other forms of graphic organizers include venn diagrams, flow charts, pyramid charts, and herringbone charts (see Figure 3.2 for examples).

Graphic organizers can be used in many ways to help students make concrete connections with abstract ideas and relationships. They can be used to structure brainstorming, to encourage active silent reading, or to prompt postreading reflective discussion or writing. In the following method, a graphic organizer is used to do all of the above.

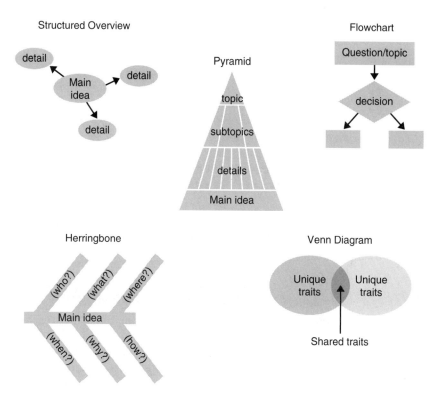

Figure 3.2
Graphic organizer formats.

Steps in the Three-Phase Graphic Organizer

Preparation

Analyze the reading selection to determine a graphic organizer format that illustrates its organization. Prepare a graphic organizer that includes all important information in the selection.

Step 1   *Prereading schema activation. Without showing the prepared graphic to the class,* announce the topic, and ask students what they think they will read about in the selection. As students make suggestions, begin a rough construction of the graphic organizer on the board or overhead, while students copy it on their papers. Typically, the first suggestions made will be details, rather than major subtopics. For example, in a selection about spiders, one of the students' first suggestions would likely be that "they have eight legs," rather than the subtopic, "body parts." For some selections, students will be able to generate the needed subtopics or anchor information; for other selections, the teacher will need to supply some if not most of these. During this interaction, the teacher should be open to modifying the planned structure of the graphic organizer if students make reasonable alternative suggestions. For maximum support, the teacher may show students where to draw blank lines for information to find in their reading. By the end of the prereading session, students will have an incomplete graphic organizer that they have helped to develop (see Figure 3.3).

Step 2   *Metacognitive monitoring.* Students read silently to complete the graphic organizer. While they read silently, students add information to their graphic organizers as they find it in the selection. The incomplete graphic organizer produced in step 1 provides a ready-made "reading guide," reminding students to read actively, question their understanding, and note important points, details, and relationships.

Step 3   *Schema building.* Once students have read, the teacher guides a discussion based on students' additions to the prereading graphic organizer, or students are directed to compare their work in cooperative groups. Optionally, the graphic organizer (GO) may be used as a writing prompt. For example, the GO may be divided into sections, with each section assigned to a small group of students. Each group then works together on their portion of the organizer to retranslate it from pictorial form into a connected paragraph (see Figure 3.3 for another variation on this idea) or to add some deeper level of understanding and research on the topic.

Notes on Graphic Organizers

Many content textbooks now include graphic organizers at the beginning or end of each chapter. Recent research indicates, however, that graphic organizers have little influence on reading comprehension if they are simply *given* to students before or after reading. Their effectiveness lies in students' participation in creating them. For this reason, in the prereading portion of the Three-Phase Graphic Organizer, the teacher uses the prepared graphic merely as a reference for guiding a brainstorming session on students' background knowledge about the topic.

Graphic organizers have been found to be especially useful in helping readers deal with what has been called *inconsiderate text*, that is, textual material that is too difficult because of poor writing and/or faulty assumptions about the reader's level of familiarity with the topic (Alvermann & Boothby, 1983). They do this by visually highlighting important ideas and

Figure 3.3
Example of a Three-Phase Graphic Organizer.

This example is based on a short article entitled, "How Do I Know if I Am, or Could Be, Creative?" as used by high school art teacher, Jeanette. Working from notes for a complete graphic organizer, Jeanette wrote the topic *"Are Some People More Creative Than Others?"* in the center of the chalkboard. She told the class, "I found an interesting article on the Internet about creativity. Before I have you read it, let's think together about some of the ideas you have about creativity—who is creative and who isn't." As I put your ideas on the chalkboard, each of you should copy them onto your own paper. This will make a kind of worksheet for you to use as you read the article. Now, what is something you would expect to find in an article on this topic?" [Note: Jeanette reworded the topic for the graphic organizer because she thought that the title of the article would lead the prereading brainstorming down the wrong paths.] The next interactions went something like this:

Student: Well, sure. look at Sheila. She always comes up with ideas for her projects that no one else would have thought of. [Sheila jokingly replies, "Maybe I'm just weird."]

Jeanette: So, one answer could be "yes." Creativity is something you're born with—something innate. [Jeanette adds the word "yes," followed by the phrase "Creativity is innate" to the GO, indicating that students should copy these terms and their placement on their papers.] Is that what you think?

Student: Yes. [Several students nod.]

Jeanette: Okay, then, think about creativity: what kind of mental process is it? How do you know it when you see it? [She adds "Define creativity" to the GO.]

Student: I don't know about that, but some people might be kind of creative but not, like, show it—because they don't want to be different or something.

Jeanette: Ah, so there may be people who are *potentially* creative? [adds the word "no", and the phrase "Some just have unrealized potential?" to the GO]. Anyone could be creative, but for some reason some people just don't use their potential. Maybe because they don't want to be different [adds the phrase "looking different" to the GO]—can you think of any other reasons why someone might not realize their creative potential?

Student: Well, like you said, what do you mean by "creative"? Some people might be creative in some things that they're interested in, but not in other things that don't interest them as much.

Figure 3.3, *continued*

> *Jeanette:*   Good, so, "motivation" would be a reason for not realizing
> creative potential [adds "motivation" to the GO], and we're
> back to trying to define "creativity." Let's stop here and go
> the the article. Add a few lines to your graphic organizers to
> show where there is information to look for [adds lines].
> While you're reading, look for how the author describes cre-
> ativity—be sure to put these into your own words—and two
> other reasons why some people may have unrealized cre-
> ative potential. Also look for what the author says about test-
> ing creativity.

By the end of these exchanges, Jeanette and the students had created
the following incomplete graphic organizer. Its structure and contents follow the one Jeanette had prepared, with one point ("looking different")
added from a student's contribution. Jeanette also added a few points to
direct students to key points in the article.

Prereading Incomplete Graphic Organizer:

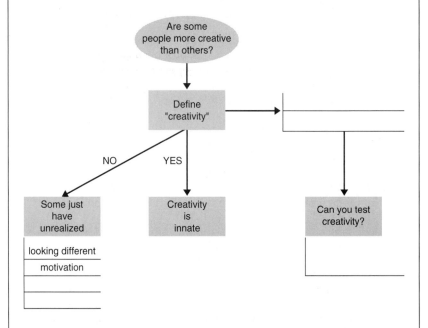

Students now read the article to complete their graphic organizers:

HOW DO I KNOW IF I AM, OR COULD BE, CREATIVE?

Every living, breathing human being has the potential to be creative.
Each of us is a unique individual capable of creating . . .

Figure 3.3, *continued*

it comes with the human territory. We are, simply, quite a creative species.

All people can be creative but those who are recognized as being creative have an awareness that others don't. Creative people seem to be able to tune in more to their thought patterns and glean great ideas. People who do not use their creative potential don't know how to do this or aren't even aware it is possible. Creative people can start thinking about something, then forget it.

Meanwhile, their brains are still thinking about it. Later on, the person will start thinking about whatever it was again and their brain will say, "Excuse me, I've been thinking about this while you were off doing other things and I have a few ideas. Care to hear them?" Noncreative people don't know that their brains are working for them offshift—they don't know what they don't know!

This is not to say that people tremendously fluctuate in their creativity day to day and hour to hour; the opposite is often believed—that some individuals are generally more creative most of the time than others. The reasons why some people are more creative, however, are many.

5. Without the abilities needed to do the creative act, it is highly unlikely the individual will do the act. Just because a person has the ability to do something, however, does not necessarily mean that the person will do it. This is why researchers examine people's motives.

6. Without the motivation to do so, it is unlikely that a person would complete an act, regardless of the person's abilities.

7. Lastly, opportunities in the environment can affect the creativeness of individuals and groups of individuals.

If you've ever generated a novel response to a problem or challenge then congratulate yourself as being creative. If you do this on a regular basis, say every day, then put the "creative person" badge on yourself. With practice, your ability to generate novel and useful responses to problems and challenges will greatly improve.

One aspect of a creative personality is the fluency with which he/she generates a number of new ideas. Not only does the creative person think of good ideas, but he/she can think of many ideas, explore them, and record them. If you feel a need to quantify your creative ability, go to a local psychologist and ask about taking a test to measure your creative ability. If you live near a college or university approach their psychology department with this request. But recognize that creative ability can be learned, improved upon, and increased over time.

Am I Creative? © 1999, Creativity Web <http://www.ozemail.com.au/ ~caveman/creative>charles©mpx.com.au.

Figure 3.3, *continued*

> After students have read the article and completed their graphic organiz-
> ers, students are directed to go to their home groups (four students
> each), compare what they have written, and make corrections or addi-
> tions as needed. They are then asked to number off within groups. Stu-
> dents 1 and 2 are directed to develop the strongest arguments they can
> for the position that some people are naturally more creative than others.
> Students 3 and 4 are directed to develop their strongest arguments for
> the alternate position. They are given about 5 minutes to complete this
> discussion, and then students 1 and 3 are asked to relate their argu-
> ments to the other pair in their group. As a final step, students are asked
> to write, on the back of their graphic organizer, one paragraph stating
> and defending the position of their own choice.

playing down irrelevant and potentially distracting points. In the example shown in Figure 3.3 the description of creativity is not clearly laid out in the article: part of the description is toward the beginning, and part at the end.

Notice that in the Three-Phase Graphic Organizer lesson example, students spend a good deal of time speaking, listening, and writing, as well as reading. Cooperative groups are used to encourage students to talk about what they have read, and to develop points for an argument. After they have predicted, read, taken notes, compared notes with peers, and discussed an arguable position, they are asked to write a summary of what they have discussed. This intermingling of listening and speaking, reading and writing, is a key characteristic of interactive teaching and learning.

The next section takes a closer look at two instructional uses of writing: writing to learn, and writing papers. Guidelines are given for increasing the use of writing to learn—possibly the most underused teaching/learning tool at secondary teachers' disposal. The *writing process* is offered as a framework for guiding students' writing of various types of papers, from research papers to creative writing activities. The writing process is widely acknowledged as a means of teaching students how to write rather than simply grading the products of their writing.

WRITING: ENCOURAGING THE PROCESS AND THE PRODUCTS

The process of simply writing something down—a note while reading, an item on a to-do list, a message to a friend, or an answer to a study guide question—adds a slight but significant element of commitment to that thought that it previously did not have. It becomes more real, more concrete, more likely to be remembered. Any form of writing prior to reading or listening tends to activate prior knowledge and experience and heighten the reader's anticipation of the author's focus and key points. This could be called *engaged* reading and listening. It is a more active, interactive, and memorable mode of operating than is the passive, or disassociated reading and listening that tends to occur in school. Additionally, each effort to write *after* reading also provides considerable benefits to learning. It requires active reconstruction of text and thereby increases sensitivity to the text's content, logic, and organization. Further, each effort to write in reaction to or evaluation of text constitutes that invigorating plunge into the unknown where language and thought trigger one another to discover and organize the "inchoate lump of meanings" (Henry, 1974) that we often are left with following typical passive reading.

Simply put, a routine requirement to write something—almost anything—before or after reading ignites more active thinking before, during, and following reading. In spite of these benefits, writing tends to be an underused tool in content classrooms. There are three primary reasons for this nonwriting orientation in school.

1. Most teachers have not themselves experienced a requirement for frequent writing as students, other than for an occasional book report or essay in English class and perhaps a research paper in social studies.
2. Relatedly, teachers are unaware of the many informal ways in which writing can be used as an aid to thinking.
3. Most teachers are reluctant to require frequent writing because of the time required to provide feedback.

Speaking to each of these three points now, let's see if we can become the generation of teachers that sets the example for others to follow. Our chances of accomplishing this goal are much improved over those who have preceded us. There is much that is new in the literature on writing, reading, and thinking to call upon, in addition to the enabling possibilities inherent in telecomputing in increasingly wired classrooms.

Righting Writing Across the Curriculum: Road Under Construction

The most important point to be made about writing as a thinking tool is that teachers should help students to distinguish between writing as a tool and writing as a product. When writing is used as a tool, *not everything students write has to be graded, or even read, by the teacher.* In the suggestions below, student writing may be followed by short cooperative group sharing of their writing, or added to a folder to be collected for "credit/no credit."

Before Reading

+ *Timed prewriting:* Tell students the topic of a reading assignment, and give a short time (3–5 minutes) to write on what they think it will be about.

+ *Prompted prewriting:* Give a specific prompt related to the content of a reading assignment, and have students write brief responses before reading.

While Reading

+ *Main idea notes:* Give the reading assignment with directions to write the author's main points (in students' own words), with supporting details noted.

+ *Factoids:* Direct students to look, while reading, for brief, interesting facts as might appear on CNN television, or set out in bold print to capture a reader's interest in a magazine or textbook.

+ *Rewrite for different audiences:* Direct students to look, while reading, for a section to rewrite for a different audience (e.g., a younger person; a grandparent; corporate/government leader).

+ *Write the author:* Direct students to think, while reading, about how the material might be presented more clearly or interestingly, and to write a note to the author informing him or her of their ideas.

+ *Add to it:* Direct students to write a paragraph or two that could/should be added to make the information clearer.

+ *Write an example:* Direct students to look for points that remind them of relevant examples or stories that help to make the author's point.

After Reading

+ *Press release:* A public relations press release on a worthy idea or finding.

+ *More information:* A letter of request to an author or other authority for more information.

+ *Connections:* Tell about a related television program, web site, book, article, idea, or related moral/ethical conflict.

Notice that most of these suggestions can be done quickly, and with little preparation. However, they add considerably to a student's anticipation and/or deeper processing of almost any fundamental set of information and ideas. It's a good bet that you can see yourself doing any of these. With another few moments of thought, you surely can come up with many similar and manageable writing–learning activities for almost any discipline, from the more obvious content areas such as English and social studies, to some that at first blush may seem less amenable to writing, like physical education, music, and art.

Next, we turn to the nuts and bolts of guiding effective writing and thinking. Traditional efforts to teach writing have focused on the final *product*. More recently, an instructional framework for guiding student mastery of the *process* of writing has evolved. This instructional framework was designed to parallel the process one would reasonably go through in writing. Therefore, it has come to be called simply the *writing process*. The writing process framework is analogous to the three-step framework for planning prereading, guided silent reading, and postreading instruction. It indicates what should be done at each stage in general terms but leaves considerable latitude in just how to do it.

THE WRITING PROCESS: A FRAMEWORK FOR GUIDING THE PROCESS OF PAPER-WRITING

Writing is not easy to learn or to teach. It is a habit of mind and often is hard work. The prolific writer and economist John Kenneth Galbraith has said it most sincerely, "There are days when the result is so bad that no fewer than five revisions are required. In contrast, when I'm greatly inspired, only four revisions are needed" (interview, CNBC, May 1996). For novice writers, the mere prospect of writing any type of paper is daunting. Traditionally, writing is a sink-or-swim proposition. A topic is assigned, and a due date is given. Sometimes a draft is critiqued by the teacher, but most of the real work of writing occurs before the initial draft is produced. The writing process framework is a way to provide guidance, from initial reflections through final editing stages.

Steps in the Writing Process

Step 1   *Prewriting: Getting It Together.* In the idea-building phase, the teacher prepares students for writing by:

1. Raising motivation and interest
2. Calling up relevant prior knowledge and experiences
3. Encouraging exploration of the topic, and suggesting resources
4. Reminding students to document sources of possible materials located in the library or on the Internet
5. Eliciting additional details, reasons, or examples
6. Providing basic expectations for the final product, usually in the form of a rubric

Step 2   *Drafting: Getting It Down.* In the drafting phase, students attempt to shape the unwieldy ideas, purposes, facts, personal feelings, and biases into the linearity of words and structure. This includes finding out what you really think and then how to say it best. During this phase, the teacher's role is:

1. Helping students express initial thoughts and ideas on paper.
2. Reminding students to refer to prewriting notes and experiences. Word processors are a tremendous aid at this stage. Notes can be copied and pasted quickly and easily.
3. Helping students to keep in mind the audience who will be reading their work, as a guide to the form and character of the composition.
4. Encouraging the free flow of ideas, by emphasizing content rather than mechanics or structure.

Step 3   *Revising: Getting It Organized.* Revising is an evaluative and reconstructive phase. It requires a good deal of introspection and willingness to critique oneself, to be critiqued, and, in several strategies described later, to think like an editor and to critique the work of others. In this phase, the teacher provides guidance by:

1. Arranging for students to receive feedback from peers and/or various audiences. Drafts copies can be e-mailed to a family member, an on-line tutor, or other willing helper.
2. Encouraging students to reorganize, rewrite, and revise as needed for fluency and coherence.
3. Guiding discussions that clarify and thereby point to specific areas of composition that require rewriting.
4. Encouraging redrafting as needed with an eye toward initial purpose and audience.
5. Helping students to consider how well others have understood and interpreted their writing.

Step 4   *Editing: Getting It Right.* In the final editing phase, the composition is reviewed for correct mechanics such as spelling, grammatical usage, and punctuation. The teacher assists by:

1. Encouraging students to fine-tune their work. Here again, word processors are quite useful in checking spelling and grammar.
2. Noting common mechanical problems and providing class instruction in these areas.

Step 5   *Publishing: Going Public.* In the publishing phase, the final copy is shared with an audience. This can be done in a variety of formal and informal ways. The point is that writing becomes more real and serious when it is to be read by someone other than the teacher. The teacher aids in this process by:

1. Employing methods that ensure that there will be readers for students' efforts. The Internet opens unlimited opportunities for creative ways of publishing student work.
2. Offering evaluative feedback based on a rubric for the assignment.
3. Offering opportunities for student papers to serve as a foundation for reading, discussion, or study.

✦ *After Words* ✦

Now you've had a chance to enrich your schema and understanding of the elements and frameworks for powerful content area literacy instruction. The concrete examples offered are extended in the next section into a rich menu of teaching methods from which to choose and plan daily instruction and units of study.

SECTION II

Reading and Learning from Text

The four chapters that you are about to engage contain the research-based and experiential core of content area literacy instruction. Knowledge of the content of these chapters will place you among the most technically competent of teachers. Skill in *delivering* a representative group of the methods in the chapters ahead will cause you to be among the most competent and influential of teachers. Read now about the best means available by which to guide reading and learning before, during, and following encounters with content-rich textual material.

CHAPTER 4

Methods for Prereading Schema Activation

To know how to question is to know how to become literate.

—Angelo V. Ciardiello

✦ *Fore Words* ✦

This chapter explains the importance of the objectives, goals, and practices of prereading instruction. It focuses first on the role of teacher questioning and its impact on student self-questioning and curiosity. It then discusses the process of *mental modeling*, which is the fundamental technique employed in several prereading methods. Finally, it describes a variety of other research-supported methods for providing this "frontloading" element of content area literacy instruction.

IMPORTANCE OF PREREADING

Effective comprehension depends largely on the reader's "readiness": entering the page with an appropriate mental set, or orientation. In a survey of teaching practices, professors specializing in content area literacy ranked prereading methods as the most important thing content teachers could do to help students learn from text (Gee & Rakow, 1987). Prereading instruction helps students to establish an appropriate orientation to the reading task. This orientation has three dimensions: *attitude, background,* and *reading strategies.*

Attitude Orientation: For Reader Engagement
1. Focus attention and reduce distractions.
2. Pique interest in the topic and the task.
3. Motivate for sustained effort.

Background Orientation: For Schema Activation
✦ Activate appropriate schema: relevant background knowledge and experiences.
✦ Preteach key concept terms and unfamiliar allusions.
✦ Correct possible misunderstandings.
✦ Provide necessary new ideas and information.
✦ Establish a sense of the organization and sequence of the reading selection.

Reading Strategies Orientation: For Active Meaning-Making
✦ Preview to establish a sense of the organization and sequence of the selection.

- ✦ Identify reading aids such as headings, graphics, pictures, and terms in italics.
- ✦ Predict possible outcomes based on prior knowledge and experience.
- ✦ Raise factual and evaluation-type questions that can serve as purposes for reading.

Of course, these components are not taken up in a tedious, step-by-step fashion. Rather, they should be addressed selectively, depending upon the particular needs of students and the challenges presented by the materials to be read. The methods in this chapter each address some combination of these elements, but in a focused, brisk, and interactive manner.

GOALS OF PREREADING INSTRUCTION: READER ENGAGEMENT, SCHEMA ACTIVATION, AND ACTIVE MEANING-MAKING

Reader Engagement

Successful reading begins with genuine attention to the task: the reader must be actively "engaged" in the process (Rosenshine, 1984). Thus, one goal of prereading instruction is to help students develop the attitudes and interests that build the habit of active engagement as an initial component of the study reading process.

Schema Activation

In a previous chapter, schema was defined as the sum of one's prior knowledge and experience about a given topic. Schema provides the "grid" for receiving and organizing information. However, simply *having* a broad background of information and experience about a topic may not ensure effective comprehension. To read with comprehension, the reader must consciously recall the schema structures that are relevant to the reading selection, so that she or he can actively form connections between this personalized organization of facts, perspectives, and experiences, and the new information from the text. Thus, how readers *use* what they know can be as important as how *much* they know.

Active Meaning-Making Through Questioning

The final goal of prereading instruction is to demonstrate and build strategies for constructing meaning from print. Most such strategies, beginning with formulating appropriate purposes for reading, are grounded in questioning.

Why Students *Don't* Ask More Questions

Interest and motivation are expressed through questions. New knowledge is built by means of questioning. Yet most students in most traditional content classrooms ask very few lesson-related questions. One of the primary reasons for "teacher burnout," in fact, is teachers' perception that students lack interest and motivation. For the most part, however, lack of interest and motivation is only a secondary symptom. Inquiry and learning are natural human inclinations. The primary cause of apathy, in most cases, is that students simply do not know how to ask questions in the classroom environment, which can be layered with subtle inhibitions to student questioning. One layer of inhibitions is composed of peer interactions. Asking a question in class amounts to a public admission of ignorance and an acknowledgment of the teacher's expertise and authority. Another layer of inhibitions is composed of the cognitive aspects of inquiry. Each subject area is, in a way, a foreign language, with unique terminology and thinking "grammars" that need to be employed in order to formulate useful questions. (Understanding a foreign language is always easier than speaking it.) Moreover, research and intuition suggest that rather than encouraging and supporting student questioning, teachers too often behave in ways that actually teach students *not* to question. Figure 4.1 elaborates on the most common of these. See if any sound familiar. As illustrated in the figure, the way in which teachers ask *and answer* questions can do much to overcome the inhibitions to active curiosity and questioning that seem to become instilled in the typical classroom.

Teaching students to ask as well as answer questions is what Aristotle was explaining when he said, "these, then are the . . . kinds of questions we ask and *it is in the answers to these questions that our knowledge consists*" (McKeon, 1947, p. 73, as quoted by Ciardiello, 1998). The simple goal of teaching students to engage in active questioning is to put them into an intelligent, ongoing "search mode," to use a telecomputing metaphor. In this way, the quest to learn is more likely to continue after a particular lesson is over, the book is closed, and the classroom lights dimmed.

Of further aid in teaching with questions is to know more about the types of questions that can be posed, and the cognitive demands that each involves.

Question Types

No discussion of questioning can be complete without reference to how questions can be classified by cognitive levels, or types. The rationale for this is fundamental: the types of questions that teachers ask influence the nature of the thinking and discourse that follows, as well as the thinking patterns that students will anticipate and internalize.

The most widely used system for characterizing questions is loosely based on a hierarchy of difficulty called the Taxonomy of Educational

Figure 4.1
Why students stop asking questions.

The Squelch.
Teachers sometimes respond to questions with sarcastic replies. Often, the questions that receive these replies are the kind of passive-aggressive questions that students raise when they are fearful or defensive. Before a test, for example, teachers often hear this flurry of questions: "Do we have to skip a line after every answer?"; "Do you want last names first?"; "Can we use notebook paper?"; "Can we use pencil?" Faced with these irrelevant, time-consuming questions, teachers sometimes get *too* skilled at squelching student questions with responses like, "Is today any different from yesterday?"; or "Are you new here?" Students, however, don't always see the distinction between relevant and irrelevant questions. If they come to expect sarcastic replies, they will be less likely to raise genuine, on-task questions. Overuse of the squelch is partly a matter of personal style, in which case it should still be used sparingly and in good humor. In general, we find that where a good rapport is established in a classroom, the passive-aggressive questions that deserve a squelch seldom occur.

The Sting.
As teachers, we occasionally *use* questions as a kind of "weapon" against student misbehavior. When we suspect that a student is unprepared, or is not paying attention, we may call on him or her to answer a question. Or when a student persists in talking while we are trying to explain a point to the class, we might use a punishing question like, "John, will you please explain this to the class?" When students feel and observe the sting of punishing questions, they often overgeneralize, and become fearful of asking and being asked *any* question. They fear that to ask a question is to challenge the teacher, and that to be asked a question is to be suspected of some misdeed. Even worse, more aggressive students begin to intentionally use questions to undermine the teacher's authority.

Figure 4.1, *continued*

The Void.

"Any questions?" is a popular teacher tool for encouraging students to raise clarifying inquiries. When students are asked this question in an inappropriate context, however, they quickly lose confidence in their ability to ask good questions. They often don't know what it is that they don't know; and/or, don't know how to articulate a vague thought into a clear question; and/or are unsure of how to frame the question so as not to annoy the teacher or alienate their classmates. Ironically, the more one knows about a topic, the easier it is to ask questions about it. With this in mind, it is important for the teacher to anticipate points of the lesson that may be unclear, and guide student questioning into those areas: "Can someone ask a good question to clarify when we need to change signs in an equation?"; then "What other questions could be asked about signs?"; and finally the more general question, "Any other questions about anything discussed today?"

The Volley.

Teachers too often fall into the habit of answering a question with a question, like the classic approach of indirect psychiatry. While there is a place and a time for this technique, if students expect that they will be put on the spot with a return question, they will grow reluctant to ask questions. Admittedly, this technique can be useful in "buying time" to think of an answer to a question that has come seemingly out of the blue. However, even in these instances, the more helpful teaching strategy is to think aloud through the processes needed to come up with an answer. This provides a perfect opportunity to demonstrate the teacher's role as a coach, rather than an encyclopedia.

Figure 4.2
Question types.

1. **Recognition questions.** Recognition questions require identifying the answers from available choices (e.g., multiple-choice questions).

2. **Recall questions.** Recall questions require remembering the answers with little prompting and no clues ("When was the Battle of Hastings?").

3. **Translation questions.** Translation questions entail transferring something from one symbolic form to another ("Can you describe this picture?"; "Can you tell in your own words what the author said in this paragraph?"; "Can you say what you just heard in your own words?").

4. **Inference questions.** Inference questions have the reader combine available textual information to reach an answer that is compellingly logical but not explicitly stated in the text ("What is the relationship between Jack and Joseph in this story?").

5. **Conjecture questions.** Conjecture questions involve an inferential leap, because all the information is not yet, or may never be, available ("As we read ahead, do you suppose that Jack's life will rise above his father's?").

6. **Explanation questions.** Explanation questions require verification of a previous point. They may involve reference to the text and/or to other sources ("Why do you think Jack's life will rise above his father's?").

7. **Application questions.** Application questions require critical and constructive thinking and problem solving ("In similar circumstances, how might a person like Jack avoid hurting his father?").

8. **Evaluation questions.** Evaluation questions are a specialized type of application question that requires critical thinking, aesthetic sense, and personal judgment ("How do you feel about the story? the characters? the style of writing? the moral to be drawn?").

Objectives: The Cognitive Domain (Bloom, 1956). There are eight basic question types that we have derived from this and several other authoritative sources (Aschner, Gallagher, Perry, Afsar, Jenne, & Farr, 1962; Barrett, 1967; Sanders, 1969). See Figure 4.2 for a description of each.

The most effective way to help students develop the complex cognitive and affective elements of effective questioning is *not* simply to teach them about the various types of questions; although, arguably there could be some benefit to this as well (Ciardiello, 1998). In general, questioning may be too complex, both cognitively and affectively, to be guided by a set of rules. It appears best to address it by providing opportunities for students to interact with models of effective questioning in real and simulated reading-thinking situations. Ideally, this should be done in a hands-on "apprenticeship" setting that is suitably matched to the complexity of this task, and to overcoming the social inhibitions noted.

MENTAL MODELING: A FORM OF APPRENTICESHIP TRAINING

Modeling is a form of teaching in which the instructor demonstrates a desired outcome and encourages the learner to imitate it. It is the traditional means of apprenticeship training in trades and crafts, where the objective is to teach complex motor skills. It is only fairly recently that learning psychologists and educators have begun to recognize and explore the power of this form of teaching when applied to cognitive, rather than motor, learning (see Figure 4.3).

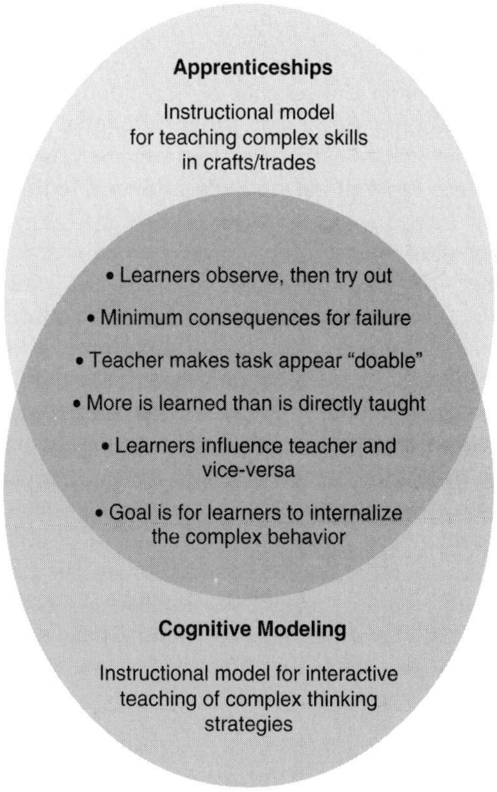

Apprenticeships

Instructional model
for teaching complex skills
in crafts/trades

- Learners observe, then try out
- Minimum consequences for failure
- Teacher makes task appear "doable"
- More is learned than is directly taught
- Learners influence teacher and vice-versa
- Goal is for learners to internalize the complex behavior

Cognitive Modeling

Instructional model for interactive
teaching of complex thinking
strategies

Figure 4.3
Cognitive modeling and apprenticeship training.

The human inclination to observe and imitate one another is the most familiar and frequently used mode of human learning outside of school. A prime example of its use is in natural language acquisition. Only a very small percentage of the words and language forms we know did we acquire as a result of direct instruction. A mother may teach her child to say some important words like "mommy," "hot," "chair," and so on, but the child picks up an enormous number of words on his or her own. A parent or teacher may remind the child to say "he ran" instead of "he runned," but the majority of what the child learns about word order and language structures is learned incidentally. In fact, when the child says, "he runned," she or he is demonstrating his subconscious mastery of English grammar.

The way we speak, the words we use, and the way we feel when using these words are the direct result of the speech patterns and concerns of the models to whom we were exposed and with whom we have interacted. From the models we select to emulate, we learn motives and attitudes as well as words and actions. Thus, *inquiring minds beget inquiring minds.*

In any situation, however, there are various models available from whom to choose. Selection of the model to be emulated is based on subjective assessments of the degree to which those around us appear to have mastery over a given environment or situation. In school settings, the student does not automatically choose the teacher or the good student as a model. There is an ongoing competition with other influential peers and adults in the home and community. Instructional strategies that employ modeling must include devices for winning students' attention to the desired models and behaviors.

Modeling of mental operations has its rational basis in "social and imitation learning" theory (Bandura & Walters, 1963; Miller & Dollard, 1941). Simply put, the idea is that we tend to copy and internalize a larger array of a model's character and behaviors than merely those traits that are essential to the task at hand. By taking advantage of this additional, "incidental" learning dimension, it becomes possible to teach very complex and subtle behaviors along with key target behaviors, and in a much shorter period of time. Further, the mental image of the model serves as a mental "template," or set of guidelines, that the novice can use to monitor and evaluate subsequent attempts to apply and refine the new thinking strategy in different situations. In short, internalization of the target strategy is most likely to occur only after youngsters have used a cognitive operation in situations where adults and other peer experts have modeled and given them some form of feedback on their performance (Camperell, 1982; Manzo, 1969a, 1969b; Vygotsky, 1978).

Conditions for Effective Mental Modeling

Modeling is a very *efficient* means of teaching complex tasks; however, its *effectiveness* is likely to vary depending on the management of certain conditions. The six conditions listed below are particularly relevant to translating this natural teaching-learning process into techniques and methods for classroom instruction.

1. When the student's attention is drawn to a desired model

2. When the impression can be made that the model is doing something masterful and desirable

3. When there is a reduced social risk entailed in imitating a desired behavior

4. When the new behavior appears "doable," as when a student observes someone from his or her peer group engaged in the behavior

5. When students are permitted to interact with the model in an affective (feeling) manner as well as in purely cognitive, or "school-like" ways

6. When *reciprocity* is used to help students develop a sense of "agency" or the feeling that they have some reasonable level of influence ove the instructional environment

The last element, reciprocity, serves other critical purposes in effective teaching and learning. It raises student competence while inviting the student's individuality to emerge. In this way, students come to learn generalized strategies for effective learning that are *personalized*, and owned by them, rather than continuing merely to *copy* the behavior and objectives of the model alone.

As you study the teaching methods ahead that feature social and mental modeling, remember to look for the specific action(s) of the teacher that might attract students' attention and desire to emulate available models of question asking, reflecting, and answering. Initially, this is likely to be the teacher, but eventually it will include peers and, finally, a personal quest to ask and puzzle about things—some of which may never be known. It is at this point that a student can be said to be fully engaged, or in an active "search mode." Ideally, this mode becomes internalized as a life strategy as much as a school learning strategy.

PRE-READING METHODS FOR READER ENGAGEMENT, SCHEMA ACTIVATION, AND ACTIVE MEANING-MAKING

The short article in Figure 4.4 is used for examples of the prereading methods in this section. Skim through the article before beginning to read about the ReQuest procedure.

Figure 4.4
Sample Reading Selection
"Vaulting Vampires" (*Discover*, March 1998, 19:3).

(1) On most nights a vampire bat tries to drink about half its body weight in blood. After feasting, the blood-bloated bat launches itself into the air. But unlike other bats, which simply drop from their perches to initiate flight, vampire bats jump from the ground into the air. How do they manage their takeoffs?

(2) "They can't run to get up a head of steam like a swan or a goose does," says William Schutt, a zoologist at Bloomfield College in New Jersey. Schutt recently managed to give biologists their first detailed look at the dynamics of a vampire bat takeoff.

(3) Of the world's 900 or so bat species, only the common vampire bat, Desmodus rotundus, is able to maneuver as well on the ground as it does in the air. "They can hop, move backward, side to side—like little spiders," says Schutt.

(4) To study how the bats launch themselves, Schutt put them on a force-measuring platform and recorded their movements with a high-speed camera. The animal begins with all four limbs on the ground. Then it extends its hind knees and tips itself forward, so the center of mass is over the forelimbs. For the actual jump, it extends the forelimbs and pushes itself off the ground with the tremendously large pectoral muscles," he says. Schutt found that the pectorals are the major flight muscles in bats, just as in birds. The triceps muscle and the bat's very long thumb also generate some force. The thumb is the last part of the body to leave the ground and helps steer the bat's takeoff.

(5) The entire jump lasts a mere 30 milliseconds, but during that time the bat catapults itself three to four feet off the ground. The transition from jump to flight is almost seamless, says Schutt. At the end of the jump "all the limbs are pointed toward the ground, which is the equivalent of a downstroke. So now it just has to bring the forelimbs into an upstroke position and it can begin to power itself in flight."

(6) Since vampire bats do most of their feeding on level surfaces, their deftness is a definite advantage. "If they are feeding on a cow's foot, and the cow takes a step back, they need to be quick to get out of the way," Schutt says, "and they also need to be fast on the ground to get away from predators."

Source: Kathy A. Svitil © 1998. Reprinted with permission of *Discover Magazine.*

ReQuest Procedure

The Reciprocal Questioning or ReQuest procedure (Manzo, 1969b) is a well-proven and robust method that introduced the idea of "mental modeling" to educational intervention. It is a constructivist method designed to permit the teacher to model good questioning and question answering (Ciardiello, 1998). It encourages students to *focus on the teacher and competent peers* as effective models of question asking and answering. However, while the teacher is the initial focus, ReQuest emphasizes strategy more than skill learning by teaching students how to set their own purposes for reading. As importantly, the *reciprocal* step gives students a good deal of control, and makes a learner of the teacher as he or she grows in understanding of students' different constructions of what they have read.

ReQuest can be used to introduce an in-class reading activity, or at the end of a class period for a home reading assignment. It has been used from the primary grades to graduate school levels.

Steps in the ReQuest Procedure

Preparation: Teacher and students should have copies of the reading selection. ReQuest can be used by directing students to look only at one sentence at a time, without reading ahead. When possible, it is useful to have the first portion of the selection on an overhead transparency, so that it can be shown one sentence at a time (title and first sentence together first, then the second sentence, the third, etc., to about the fifth sentence). The teacher should prepare at least four questions *each*, over: the title and first sentence, and each of the next sentences, through about the fourth sentence. These should be questions that students would probably *not* ask, since students will have the chance to ask questions first.

Step 1   The first time the method is used the teacher should explain the purpose; for example, "Before you read this selection, we will look at the first few sentences together and ask each other some questions. The purpose of this activity is to improve your ability to set a good purpose for reading."

Step 2   The teacher guides the students through as many sentences of the selection as necessary to formulate a logical purpose to guide silent reading. This is done in the following way:

   a. Students and teacher read the title and first sentence. Students are told that they may ask the teacher as many questions as they wish about the title and first sentence only (see Figure 4.5). Students are told that they should try to ask the kinds of questions a teacher might ask, in the way a teacher might ask them.

   b. The teacher answers each question fully, but without excessive elaboration, and without asking questions back. How much to "tell" in answering a question will be a judgment call in any lesson. The objectives at this stage of the lesson are: to encourage and reinforce questions that activate relevant schema; to fill in needed background information (but only in answer to questions); to stay

Figure 4.5
Example of the ReQuest procedure with "Vaulting Vampires."

The teacher prepared the following questions for the lesson.

Title & Sentence 1: *Vaulting Vampires: On most nights a vampire bat tries to drink about half its body weight in blood.*
- What are two other words for "vaulting"?
- How big is a vampire bat?
- What type of creatures feed at night?
- Who has ever seen one?
- Does anyone know where their natural habitats are?

Sentence 2: *After feasting, the blood-bloated bat launches itself into the air.*
- Why is "feast" a good word to use here?
- Where do you think the vampire bat launches from?
- Does this sound like any other animal you know?

Sentence 3: *But unlike other bats, which simply drop from their perches to initiate flight, vampire bats jump from the ground into the air.*
- Why might it be important for vampire bats to be able to jump into flight from the ground?
- What would it take to be able to do this?
- How many kinds of bats do you think there are?

Sentence 4: *How do they manage their takeoffs?*
- How do you think they manage?
- How might a scientist study this question?

Possible purpose questions:
   How do vampire bats launch into flight from the ground?
   How have scientists studied this ability?
   Why is it important for vampire bats to have this ability?

The short selection was distributed to students familiar with the ReQuest procedure. Students were asked to keep their papers face down, while they used ReQuest to set a relevant purpose for reading. The title and first sentence were shown on the overhead:

Title & Sentence 1: *Vaulting Vampires: On most nights a vampire bat tries to drink about half its body weight in blood.*

Figure 4.5, *continued*

Teacher:	Who has a question about just the title and first selection of this article?
Student 1:	What does "vaulting" mean?
Teacher:	Good vocabulary question. It means leaping. Springing or jumping high.
Student 2:	How much do vampire bats weigh?
Teacher:	Hum, I'm just guessing here, maybe 3 pounds.
Student 3:	Whose blood do they drink?
Teacher:	Large animals, like cows. That's a good question, because it gets at why it's important for them to be able to vault.
Student 3:	Why is that?
Teacher:	To get out of the way if their prey tries to shoo them off.
Teacher:	No other questions? Okay, my turn.
	Has anyone ever seen a live vampire bat?
[Several students raise their hands]	
	Jake, you have? Where was it?
Student 4:	At the zoo, they make a big show out of the vampire bats' "feeding time."
Teacher:	Has anyone seen them in the wild?
[No hands]	
	Why does it say "on most *nights*"?
Student 4:	Bats sleep during the day, and feed at night.
Teacher:	Yes, and what's another name for creatures that do this?
Student 2:	Nocturnal animals.
Teacher:	Good. Let's go on to the next sentence. After you've read it, you can ask me questions.
Sentence 2:	*After feasting, the blood-bloated bat launches itself into the air.*
Student 5:	Do they jump off the cows' backs?
Teacher:	Not usually.
Student 5:	What do they jump off?
Teacher:	The ground.
Student 2:	Can they fly?
Teacher:	Yes.
Student 6:	Can they walk on the ground.
Teacher:	Yes, they can move very easily and quickly on the ground. No more questions? Okay, my turn.
	Why is "feasting" an especially good word to use here?
Student 1:	Because they eat, or drink I guess (yuck) so much.
Teacher:	If you picture yourself as a bat, what muscles do you think you would use to launch yourself into flight?
Student 7:	My leg muscles.
Teacher:	Maybe. Do you think other kinds of bats launch into the air in this way?

Figure 4.5, *continued*

Student 5:   Maybe other ones just drop off the branches they're hanging from.

Teacher: Okay, let's look at the next sentence.

Sentence 3: *But unlike other bats, which simply drop from their perches to initiate flight, vampire bats jump from the ground into the air.*

Teacher: So that was a good prediction, John. What questions could we ask now? Remember, we're trying to predict what the rest of this article is about, and write a purpose question.

Student 8:   How many kinds of bats are there?

Teacher: Actually, this article says that there are over 900.

Student 1:   So they have to jump into the air to get out of the cows', or whatever's, way. Is this going to explain how they do that?

Teacher: That's a good prediction. Let's put it up here.

[Writes "How vampire bats vault" on the board]

Student 7:   Is it about what muscles they use?

Teacher: Another good prediction.

[Writes "What muscles?' on the board]
          Any others?

[No hands]

Teacher: Okay, well, how do you think a scientist might try to find out how the vampire bat launches itself from the ground?

Student 9:   Take a video?

Teacher: Good idea. What if it's too fast to really see on the tape?

Student 9:   Put it in slow motion.

Teacher: Good prediction. [At the risk of creating a digression, the teacher may occasionally wish to add other sidebar information, such as "By the way, when something is filmed for slow-motion the film/tape often needs to move much faster, except if it is 'time-lapse' photography."] In any case, how can you tell how hard it has to push off?

Student 6:   What if you put a scale, like you weigh yourself on, under it. Would that show how hard it was pushing down to jump?

Teacher: Good idea. Let's see what we have.

[Writes "Use videotape & scales to study?" on board]
          Can we put these predictions into one or two purpose questions?

Student 2:   What muscles do vampire bats use to vault, and how did scientists find out?

Teacher: Terrific.

[Writes prediction question on board:
"What muscles do vampire bats use to vault, and how did scientists find out?"]

Teacher: Okay, turn your papers over, and let's go ahead and read to see if we find answers to this question.

Figure 4.5, *continued*

[Students read article]
Teacher: Was this a good purpose question for the article?
Student 2:   Yes, it told what muscles, and how scientists found out.
Student 3:   But it seemed like the point of the article was the part at the end, about why it was important for this kind of bat to be able to do this.
Teacher: To get out of the way if the cow started kicking! That came up in our discussion before we read. So, just from the title, we might have added another purpose question:
[Writes, "Why is it important for them to vault?"]

Discussion continues with what students learned about how one scientist studied these bats, and what he learned.

---

focused on setting a good purpose for reading; and to model good question-answering behaviors.

c. Once students have asked all their questions about the title and first sentence, the teacher follows up with a few additional questions. Some question types to consider include: *basic information, translation, inference, personal experience,* and *evaluation.* The purpose in this followup questioning is to model the kinds of prereading questions that activate schema and help to set good purposes for reading.

d. The pattern used to review the first sentence—silent reading, followed by student questions, followed by teacher questions—is continued through the second, third, and fourth sentence, and/or continuing until enough information has been generated to form a good purpose for reading.

Step 3   After *about* the fourth sentence, the teacher should conclude his or her questions on the sentence by asking students what they think the rest of the selection will mostly be about. Briefly note student responses on the chalkboard, and then ask students to form one or more of these ideas into a question. Write the purpose question(s) on the board. If students are to read the remainder of the selection outside class, have them copy the purpose question(s).

Step 4   Following silent reading, the teacher's *first* question should be "Did we set a good purpose for reading this selection?" If so, discussion can begin with what was learned in answer to this question; if not, a better purpose question should be stated, and then answered (Manzo, 1985).

Notes on ReQuest: Tips on Implementation

✦ The first time you use ReQuest with a group, it is quite likely that when you direct them to ask questions over the title and first sentence, they will respond with blank stares. Be calm. Count to ten. Take confidence from the fact that you know *why* you are making this seemingly strange request, and you know *where* the lesson is going. You know that the purpose of spending time at the beginning of a difficult reading selection is like initializing a computer disk: it helps the brain to recognize and process the information that is coming. You also know that while there are only a handful of fact questions that can be asked about a single sentence, there are many more inference and beyond-the-lines questions that would be helpful in recalling prior knowledge and experience in order to set a good purpose for reading. Most importantly, you know that pupils have been conditioned *not* to ask questions in the classroom, and that you are willing to try to counter this conditioning. Much of this counterconditioning is accomplished simply by setting up the game-like ReQuest situation, in which students are directed to ask as many questions as they can over a single sentence at a time. So, don't despair in waiting for that first question. If wait time isn't enough, you can say something like, "This is a different kind of lesson, I know. Any question you can come up with is fine. It will help to try to think of the type of questions teachers might ask. You've heard a few questions asked, I take it." When the first question or two come, answer them respectfully: another important element in counterconditioning students' reluctance to ask questions is the way the teacher *responds* to them—discussed next.

✦ When students take you up on your offer to answer any questions on a sentence in ReQuest, you can expect a few "unexpected" questions: ones for which you do not know or cannot quickly formulate answers. Be ready for this. It's your chance to show students that you *aren't* threatened or frightened by questions you can't answer, and that you won't respond with sarcasm or by asking a question back. Instead, you will give the question a thoughtful, measured response. If it is a relevant, schema-activating question, you will say so, and give an honest explanation as to why you can't answer it, if only to say you just can't remember: "That's exactly the kind of question we're trying to bring up here. It is information the author assumes the reader knows. And, do you know, I can't remember that fact myself." At this point, another student may know the answer. Since it's not your turn to ask questions, turn to the person who asked the question, and tell him or her that another student is willing to help you out. If the question that "stumped" you is clearly off the subject, the teacher might say something like, "Because of the way the title was worded, I didn't think the author was going in that direction, so I haven't tried to remember what I might know about that. It's an interesting point, but I don't think I'll get myself off the subject with it right now."

✦ When calling on students to *ask* you questions, keep an eye on students who typically do not participate in discussion. With the ReQuest structure, you've given at-risk students a much more possible situation for involvement. They don't have to answer a question—they only have to ask one. Call on them, and be supportive in your answers.

✦ When it is your turn to ask questions, you will need to have several questions prepared for each sentence that students probably won't ask. Prepare four or five such questions for each sentence, even though you may not use them all. How many questions you ask on each sentence will depend on how many and what kind of questions the students ask. In general, you should ask at least two questions when it is your turn, trying to ask questions of different *types* than the students have asked. Basic facts will probably be covered by student questions. In fact, the reason ReQuest uses single sentences for questioning is that this places a limit on the number of fact questions that can be asked. Once these are covered, both teacher and students are challenged to ask schema-connecting beyond-the-lines questions.

✦ While it is somewhat gamelike in the back-and-forth questioning, ReQuest should *not* take on a "stump-the-teacher"/"stump-the class" tone, which tends to get off the track of a clear focus on setting a good purpose for reading a specific selection. This can happen if the teacher asks questions that the class clearly cannot answer—students will begin to ask the same types of questions back. Be careful to ask questions that *can* be answered by prediction, inference, judgment, evaluation, and experience.

✦ ReQuest should move along briskly, taking no more than about fifteen minutes. If it is extended too long, it can become tedious and lose focus. This can be difficult to keep in mind. While student questions can be intimidating at times, it also can feel satisfying to finally have students asking the questions to which we are obliged to teach them the answers. Careful, though; it is easy to go into too much detail in answering.

✦ The questions generated from the first three or four sentences usually yield enough context for students to form a good purpose question or two. When preparing your own questions, you usually can predict a good stopping point. You should have a possible purpose question in mind, in order to help guide students' suggestions.

See Figure 4.5 for an example of the ReQuest procedure with "Vaulting Vampires," from *Discover* magazine.

Further Background on ReQuest

ReQuest was first developed for one-on-one teaching. However, it proved equally effective in content classrooms with heterogeneous groups (Manzo, 1973), in programs to promote personal-social adjustment in juvenile delinquents (Kay, Young, & Mottley, 1986), in mainstreaming learning-disabled students (Alley & Deshler, 1980; Hori, 1977), with second-language students (McKenzie, Ericson, & Hunter, 1988), and as a significant part of an instructional program to improve social studies education (Ciardiello, 1998; Ciardiello & Cicchelli, 1994). It also has become the basis for a larger movement in education called Reciprocal Teaching (Palincsar & Brown, 1984). A recent survey of over 450 teachers revealed that based on descriptions of ten leading comprehension improvement methods, teachers would most like further information and training in ReQuest (Spor & Scneider, 1999).

Cooperative ReQuest

Even with ideal participation in a ReQuest lesson as described above, if four different students asked a question about each of the first four sentences of a selection, only sixteen students, half a traditional classroom, would have actively participated. Once students have become familiar with the method, try this Kagan-like, cooperative structure variation. Our sense is that it increases active involvement of more students. Several of these suggestions also add more of the elements of what Ciardiello (1998) calls TeachQuest, or explicit teaching about and cueing of question types to students.

Preparation

+ Prepare an overhead transparency with the title and first four sentences or so of the selection, or write these on the chalkboard, with strips of paper taped over each sentence to be removed to uncover one sentence at a time; for even more cueing of the type recommended by Ciardiello (1998), prepare a worksheet for each group, with space after each sentence for questions to be written.

+ The teacher should prepare questions over the title and first four sentences, as described for ReQuest, above (personal experience, translation, inference, background information, evaluation, and prediction questions).

✦ Form groups of four. A good way to form heterogeneous groups for the topic of a given reading selection is to have students form a Kagan-type "lineup" from "no knowledge or experience with the topic of xxx" at one end, to "lots of knowledge and/or experience with the topic of xxx" at the opposite end. Then count off by the number of groups needed to form groups of four. Have students, in groups, number off or self-select roles such as: recorder, speaker, discussion starter, and encourager. Roles can be rotated for each sentence.

✦ Have copies of the reading selection available for each student.

Step 1   Assuming that students are familiar with ReQuest, show the title and first sentence, and tell students that they have two minutes in their groups to come up with as many questions as they can over that portion of the reading. Tell students that they may not need to use each of the questions in the discussion that will follow, but that you will collect all of their questions at the end of the lesson.

Step 2   Proceed as with ReQuest, calling on the speaker in one of the groups to begin. Not every group needs to be called on for each sentence.

Step 3   At a reasonable point, have groups write possible purpose questions for the selection. Have the writer from each group write their group's purpose question(s) on a designated spot on the chalkboard. Review these together with the class and select from or combine these to form the best collaborative purpose question(s).

Step 4   Have students read silently to answer the purpose question(s).

Step 5   Ask whether a good purpose was set, and continue discussion based on what students learned in answer to the question(s).

Reciprocal Teaching (RT)

Reciprocal Teaching (Palincsar & Brown, 1984) is an attempt to amplify and elaborate the fundamental elements of the ReQuest procedure into a more broadly based educational approach. To raise students' sense of agency, or involvement in the process, it begins, as does Ciardiello's (1998) TeachQuest noted above, with a class discussion of why we sometimes experience difficulties in reading text. The processes of *questioning, summarizing, clarifying,* and *predicting* are introduced as helpful strategies for attending, understanding, and remembering.

The next phase in Reciprocal Teaching is direct instruction in each of the four processes. This is done in isolation but through teacher modeling and examples based on a meaningful text. When students are comfortable with the four processes of questioning, summarizing, predicting, and clarifying, they and the teacher begin to take turns assuming the role of teacher. The one playing the role of teacher is responsible for leading the dialog examining the reading selection. Figure 4.6 presents an example of the questioning, summarizing, and predicting aspects of Reciprocal Teaching. This script is taken from an actual classroom dialog with a group of children that Palincsar & Brown trained in this strategy.

In this content area version of Reciprocal Teaching, students are grouped by twos in "peer dyads," and are instructed to ask each other questions about the material to be read. The content area variation has the following five steps.

Figure 4.6
Illustration of Reciprocal Teaching.

Student 1 [in role of "teacher"]:	My question is, what does the aquanaut need when he goes under water?
Student 2:	A watch.
Student 3:	Flippers.
Student 4:	A belt.
Student 1:	Those are all good answers.
Teacher:	Nice job! I have a question too. Why does the aquanaut wear a belt? What is so special about it?
Student 3:	It's a heavy belt and keeps him from floating up to the top again.
Teacher:	Good for you.
Student 1:	For my summary now: This paragraph was about what aquanauts need to take when they go under the water.
Student 5:	And also about why they need those things.
Student 3:	I think we need to clarify *gear.*
Student 6:	That's the special thing they need.
Teacher:	Another word for *gear* in this story might be *equipment—* the equipment that makes it easier for the aquanauts to do their job.
Student 1:	I don't think I have a prediction to make.
Teacher:	Well, in the story, they tell us that there are "many strange and wonderful creatures" that the aquanauts see as they do their work. My prediction is that they'll describe some of these creatures. What are some of the strange creatures you already know about that live in the ocean?
Student 6:	Octopuses.
Student 3:	Whales?
Student 5:	Sharks!
Teacher:	Let's listen and find out. Who would like to be our teacher?

1. Students convert subheadings in text into two written predictions of what they think they will read about.

2. The class discusses these.

3. Following reading of a segment of material (usually four paragraphs), students write two questions and a summary reflecting the information in that segment.

4. Students write examples of any information that require(s) clarification.

5. The class discusses their written questions, summaries, and clarifications.

Positive outcomes have been reported from studies using Reciprocal Teaching with students who were classified as good decoders but poor comprehenders (Reeve, Palincsar, & Brown, 1985). *Time* magazine (circa 1988) called Reciprocal Teaching the most important development in instructional theory in the twentieth century. Bruner (1993) further referred to it as a primary example of the cognitive psychology revolution that has taken place in instruction, and that few outside education are aware of. Ironically, Reciprocal Teaching has appeared in fewer and fewer textbooks for teachers in recent times. A possible reason for this diminished interest may be found in the fact that Reciprocal Teaching requires considerable teacher and student training prior to use, whereas its predecessor ReQuest, which Palincsar and Brown (1984) credit as RT's theoretical platform, ideally is used by uninitiated students and teachers to learn how to reciprocally interact. The only other reservation that we once had about RT was that findings on its efficacy were based exclusively on investigator-made tests based on the subject matter read. Now, however, there are findings to suggest that overall reading comprehension can show improvement on standardized tests as well (King & Parent Johnson, 1999), as is the case with primary research on the ReQuest procedure (Manzo, 1969a, 1969b).

Question-Only

The next few methods have the simplicity of a straight piece of wire twisted into the now-ubiquitous paper clip: evident once seen and said, but apparently not so easy to first imagine without prompting. See if any of these instructional ideas have ever occurred to you in some form.

To follow this simple instructional idea, it is useful to review some prior points on inhibitions to questioning. Whenever students read or listen in school, questions are being answered. The problem is that students often don't know what those questions are, and hence cannot read or listen actively. Even when they have some level of awareness of an important organizing question, students tend to be inexperienced in framing their question in such a way as to allow focused reading, or to invite appropriate help from a speaker/teacher when they are listening. In due course, natural curiosity begins to suffer and soon most inquiry grinds to a halt. The Question-Only method can almost instantly reverse this trend.

Question-Only is designed for nonfiction materials, and does not work particularly well with fiction or poetry. It can be used for a selection to be read in class, or as preparation for an outside reading assignment.

Steps in the Question-Only Method (Manzo, 1985)

Preparation: Review the reading selection to write several quiz questions covering important information, and including at least two questions that students are not likely to ask about before they read. Decide whether to use the title of the selection to introduce the lesson, or a more general statement of the topic.

Step 1	The teacher announces the title or topic of the reading selection to the class and explains that *before reading* the selection, they will have a chance to learn about it by asking questions. Then they will be given a quiz over the content of the selection. The quiz will cover all the information the teacher considers important, whether or not the students actually extract the information with their questions. Finally, they will read the selection to check their answers to the quiz questions.
Step 2	The class questions and the teacher answers fully, but without going beyond the answer to the question as asked.
Step 3	The teacher gives the quiz.
Step 4	*Do not* grade the quiz yet. Ask students to raise their hands if they think they got most of the questions right. Ask which question(s) they had trouble with.
Step 5	Have students read silently to double check their answers to the quiz questions, and to find the answer(s) the question(s) they did not ask about. If the selection is to be read as a homework assignment, write the purpose question(s) on the board or overhead for students to copy.
Step 6	After students have read, begin discussion or other followup with their answers to the purpose question(s).

Notes on Question-Only: Tips on Implementation

✦ The Question-Only quiz should be given orally. If it is prepared on a handout ahead of time, you can't adjust it based on the questions students ask. Remember, the objective is to have as many students as possible get the correct answers to all but one or two questions. Therefore, you should prepare more quiz questions than you probably will use.

✦ When answering student questions during step 2, it is a good idea to write a *brief form* of each question and a *brief form* of the answer on the chalkboard, and leave this in view during the quiz. When students ask why you are leaving it "up," you have the perfect opportunity to explain that the object of the lesson isn't really to get the quiz questions right, but to learn to ask good questions. All the information they got from questioning, therefore, is theirs to use during the quiz. It is very important, though, to use abbreviated forms, and write quickly, or the lesson will get bogged down and boring.

✦ Keep an eye on students who did not typically participate in class discussion. Question-Only gives them an excellent opportunity to participate. They don't have to answer a question, only to ask one.

✦ Many questions are likely to be about information not covered in the reading selection. To keep the lesson on track, simply tell students when this is the case. Say something like, "That's not included in this selection, but you're using good logical thinking processes to eliminate possibilities." You can also answer in ways that subtly direct students toward important questions and followup questions (see the example in Figure 4.7).

✦ Research and field experience have revealed that Question-Only helps students from kindergarten through medical school to raise incisive and systematic questions on difficult and mundane topics (Manzo & Legenza, 1975; Legenza, 1978). The enthusiasm students have shown for this method probably arises from the fact that it offers them an assertive but nonbelligerent means of "poking back" and reciprocally influencing lesson activity. It also helps students to develop a sense of agency, or to incidentally discover and provide for their own learning needs by stimulating them to ask questions about the things that most befuddle them in an upbeat and ego-protective atmosphere.

✦ Ironically, the only time this highly analytical activity may go stale is when the teacher becomes overwhelmed by the rapid pace with which material is covered. The teacher may react by slowing down the lesson and, in the process, taking the winds of enthusiasm out of the students' sails; therefore, be prepared to cover a good deal of information quickly and with considerable depth.

Cooperative Question-Only (CQO)

To increase student participation in Question-Only, try this *cooperative structure* variation. Children's knowledge construction has been found to be significantly enhanced by guided cooperative questioning (King & Rosenshine, 1993). There also is logical and anecdotal support for certain types of role-playing in learning situations (cf. Manzo & Manzo, 1993), the other ingredient in CQO.

Figure 4.7
Example of the Question-Only method with "Vaulting Vampires."

The teacher prepared the following topic and quiz questions:

Topic: Vaulting vampire bats

Quiz Questions:
[Underlined questions are questions the teacher expects that students may not ask—one should be included in the quiz, to serve as a purpose for reading]

- Do vampire bats really drink blood? (yes)
- How much blood do vampire bats drink? (half their weight per night)
- How do vampire bats launch themselves into flight? (jump from the ground)
- How high do they jump? (3–4 feet)
- How many types of bat are there? (about 900)
- What is unusual about the vampire bat's ability to move on the ground? (It is the only bat that can move as well on the ground as in the air.)
- What is the major muscle the vampire bat uses to launch itself from the ground? (the pectorals)
- How have scientists studied the vampire bat's vaulting? (force measuring platform and high speed camera)
- Why is "vaulting" an important ability for vampire bats? (they do most of their feeding on level ground)
- What are two ways in which other creatures launch themselves? (dropping from branches, and running to build up speed)

Teacher: For tomorrow, your assignment will be to read an article called "Vaulting Vampires." Right now, I'll give you a chance to find out everything you can about it just by asking me questions. Then, I'll give you a quiz over what's in the actual article.

Student 1:   You mean, we have a quiz before we read it?

Teacher: Yes, but you have 20 minutes or so, right now, to get all the answers you can.

[Writes "Vaulting vampire bats" on the chalkboard—see below for information eventually written on the board]

Student 2:   Oh, vampire *bats*. You didn't say that before.

Teacher: Yes, *vaulting* vampire bats.

Student 3:   Why do they vault?

Teacher: They vault, or jump, to launch themselves into flight.

Student 1:   Will that be on the quiz?

Figure 4.7, *continued*

Teacher:	The questions can only be about what might be in the *article.*
Student 1:	Can they really fly?
Teacher:	Yes.
Student 4:	Are there other kinds of bats?
Teacher:	Yes, and the article tells how many other kinds.
Student 1:	How many?
Teacher:	About 900.
Student 2:	Where do they live?
Teacher:	Good question—about a whole category of information—but the category of their habitat isn't included in this article. Now you've narrowed it down a lot. I'm going to use the abbreviation "NI" to mean that there's no information about the vampire bat's habitat in this particular article.
Student 5:	Do all bats vault?
Teacher:	Good question! No, vampire bats are the only ones that launch themselves into flight from the ground.
Student 6:	How do the others do it?
Teacher:	They begin their flight by dropping down from a tree branch.
Student 7:	How high does the branch have to be?
Teacher:	Ha. Good detail question, but this article is about the vampire bats, remember.
Student 8:	Do vampire bats really drink blood?
Teacher:	Yes, they certainly do; you might be surprised at how much.
Student 8:	How much do they drink?
Teacher:	They try to drink half their body weight every night.
Student 9:	How much is that?
Teacher:	Well, they're kind of small. The article doesn't say how small, but I'll guess about 3 pounds. So that would be a pound and a half of blood a night.
Student 4:	What kinds of animals do they drink blood from?
Teacher:	The article mentions cows, as one of their prey.
Student 1:	How do they hang onto the cow's neck?
Teacher:	The article doesn't mention the bats drinking from the cow's *neck.*
Student 4:	Where, then?
Teacher:	It mentions the bats drinking from the cow's *foot.*
Student 7:	Don't they get kicked?
Teacher:	They would, if they couldn't move around pretty well on the ground.
Student 9:	Can they?
Teacher:	Can they what?
Student 9:	Can they move around pretty well on the ground?

Figure 4.7, *continued*

Teacher:	Yes, in fact they're the only kind of bat that can maneuver as easily on the ground as in the air.
	You've asked some good questions: Take out a sheet of paper now, and number from 1 to 7. You can use the information you got from your questions [on the chalkboard].

Information recorded on the chalkboard:

Vaulting Vampire Bats

Why do they vault?	To launch into flight
Really fly?	Yes
Habitat?	NI
Other kinds?	Yes, about 400
Do all vault into flight?	No—drop from branches to launch
Drink blood?	Yes—1/2 body wt.—about 1/1/2 lbs.? a night
Prey?	Ex: cows
How?	Not from the neck—from the foot
Move on the ground	Yes—only kind of bat that can

The teacher then gives this oral quiz:

1. Do vampire bats really drink blood? (yes)
2. How much blood do vampire bats drink? (half their weight per night)
3. How do vampire bats launch themselves into flight? (by jumping)
4. How many types of bat are there? (about 900)
5. What is the major muscle the vampire bat uses to launch itself from the ground? (the pectorals)
6. How have scientists studied the vampire bat's vaulting?
7. What is unusual about the vampire bat's ability to move on the ground? (it is the only bat that can move as well on the ground as in the air)

Teacher:	How many of you think you answered at least 5 questions correctly?
[Most students raise their hands]	
	Which ones did you have trouble with?
Students:	Numbers 5 and 6.
Teacher:	Okay, copy these two questions on the back of the article, to read for tomorrow:
[Teacher writes questions 5 and 6 on the chalkboard]	

Preparation

✦ Prepare the quiz questions as for the regular Question-Only lesson, and decide whether to use the title of the selection or a reworded version.

✦ Form heterogeneous groups of four students each. Assign roles, such as: recorder, speaker, clarifier, and encourager.

Step 1 Introduce Question-Only in the same way as above, but tell students that they will have three minutes, in groups, to write as many questions as they can to get the information in the reading assignment.

Step 2 Call on each group in turn to ask one question, continuing around the groups until all questions have been asked. A group may only ask a question if they have it written down. If all their questions have been asked, they must "pass." Tell students that they will have one more opportunity to compose followup questions, so each group's writer may want to make some notes of ideas for these.

Step 3 Give groups an additional two minutes to form and write as many followup questions as they can.

Step 4 Call on groups in turn to ask their followup questions, again accepting only questions they have written, and continuing until all have been asked.

Step 5 Give the quiz.

Step 6 Have students read silently to check their answers to the quiz questions and look especially for the question or questions they did not ask.

Anticipation-Reaction Guide

The Anticipation-Reaction Guide (Duffelmeyer, 1994; Duffelmeyer, Baum, & Merkley, 1987) is a teacher-prepared worksheet that students use to respond to carefully crafted statements before reading and again after reading. The primary purpose of an A-R Guide is to alert students to currently held ideas and attitudes, which may differ from those presented in the reading selection. Thus, the effectiveness of the method depends upon the teacher's knowledge of the particular group of students' background of information and experience.

Steps in the Anticipation-Reaction Guide

Preparation: Review the reading selection to identify information or attitudes that may differ from those currently held by students. Write

statements with which students will be asked to agree or disagree with
before they read, and again after they have read. Use these statements to
create an A-R Guide worksheet such as the one shown in Figure 4.8.

Step 1 Distribute the A-R Guide to students, with directions to write
their responses (agree or disagree) to each statement.

Name: _____ Date: _____

Hour: _____

*Directions: Read each statement below, and in the left-hand column labeled
"Before Reading," write an "A" if you Agree with the statement, or a "D" if you
Disagree. After you have read today's assignment, you will be asked to re-
read each statement, and respond in the right-hand column labeled "After
Reading."*

*Before
Reading*

*After
Reading*

_____ 1. Vampire bats really drink blood. _____

_____ 2. Bats can jump very long distances, _____
but they don't really fly.

_____ 3. Bats are unable to move easily _____
on the ground.

_____ 4. Studying animal behavior would be _____
an interesting and challenging
occupation.

Figure 4.8
Example of an Anticipation-Reaction guide for "Vaulting Vampires."

Step 2   Students then are directed to read, and, after reading, respond again to the A-R Guide statements.

Step 3   Begin discussion by asking whether anyone changed their responses to any of the A-R Guide statements after they had read the selection.

Notes on Writing Statements for an Anticipation-Reaction Guide

✦ A-R Guide statements are based on your knowledge of your students. The statements must be written so that students have a reasonable basis for agreeing or disagreeing with each statement.

✦ Statements can be based on facts that can be verified in the selection; however, consider attitude-type questions as well, since these are more likely to elicit experience-based schema connections with the new information.

✦ As a variation on the basic A-R Guide, have students write the page number on which they found confirmation for or a difference from their prereading belief, or have students select one of the statements as the topic for a brief postreading essay.

✦ Anticipation-Reaction Guides can be used with fiction as well as non-fiction.

Using Cooperative Structures with the Anticipation-Reaction Guide

Anticipation-Reaction Guides can be used as the content for a number of cooperative structures, after students have individually completed the postreading step.

✦ Use "Find Someone Who" (Kagan, 1994) to structure peer comparisons. Give students a short time limit (about thirty seconds) to move around the classroom until they have found a classmate who agrees with their response to the first item. These pairs of students should initial each other's worksheet for that item. Call on a few students to explain their reason for agreeing or disagreeing with that statement. Continue in the same way with each of the statements.

✦ In "home groups" of four students, appoint these roles: Writer, Pro, Con, and Arbitrator. Distribute an extra copy of the A-R Guide to the Writer in each group. Give students a time limit of about two minutes, in which Pro attempts to convince the Arbitrator that one should agree with the statement, Con attempts to persuade him or her to disagree with it, and the Arbitrator attempts to document "proof" for one position or the other, or to state a compromise position. The Writer records the Arbitrator's conclusion. Continue in the same way with each statement, *shifting roles* one person to the right each time.

Prereading Graphic Organizer

The prereading graphic organizer described in Chapter 3 is another way to help students activate schema prior to reading. See Figure 4.9 for a prereading graphic organizer a teacher might help students create for the "Vaulting Vampires" article.

Reading Before Reading

The idea of *reading before reading* started as a popular movement in the 1950s with *Cliff Notes*, or book digests. In due course, comic-book versions of the classics became familiar "underground" means of making the classics more palatable and giving readers a head start on reading unabridged versions. Not surprisingly, these mechanisms received a black eye when many students began using them as substitutes for rather than supplements to the original books. Open resentment against digests and abridged materials was reversed shortly thereafter, however, when a theory called *advance ideational organizers* restored credibility to the intuitive value of some type of reading before reading.

Advance Organizers

In a now-classic study, learning theorist David Ausubel (1960) had college students read a prestructured statement (500 words), or advance ideational

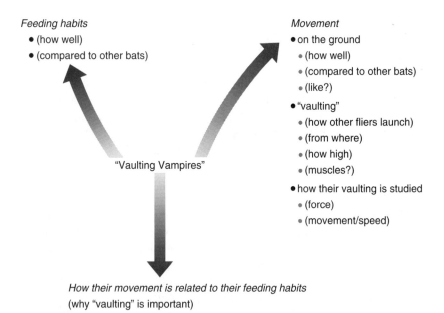

Figure 4.9
Prereading graphic organizer for "Vaulting Vampires."

organizer, before reading a longer (2,500-word) selection in science. The advance ideational organizers clearly and significantly improved student comprehension. Subsequent studies by several other researchers produced results that sometimes replicated this finding but at other times did not. The difference in these outcomes was traced primarily to the quality of the prereading passage. Ideally, an organizer had to impart a sense of structure but not be too abstract. There also were some findings to indicate that short literal accounts, usually used by the "control group" treatment, had a positive effect on comprehension as well.

Accordingly, we recommend combining abstract and literal organizers. One way to do this is to paste an *abstract organizer* to the inside front cover of a book and a *literal organizer* to the inside back cover. Then, encourage students to use both organizers as a prereading strategy and as frequently as they wish while reading the larger work. Figures 4.10 and 4.11 provide examples of each type of organizer for *The Old Man and the Sea*.

Notes on Advance Organizers: Teacher and Peer Supported
Abstract and literal advance organizers can also be made and provided for difficult chapters in content textbooks. Students can be encouraged to read these and ask questions about them before reading the text, and reminded to refer to them as needed during reading.

In a later chapter, a reading-writing method called REAP is described that teaches students how to write different types of responses to what they have read. These responses, shared via the internet, can be used as a rich resource for Advance Organizers. For an advance look at this system, go to this URL on the web: http://members.aol.com/REAP1.html.

Reiterative Reading
Reiterative reading (Crafton, 1983) is based on the proposition that students can independently acquire relevant background information through the reading process itself. In one study of this approach, it was found that simply having eleventh graders read two different articles on the same topic "dramatically improved students' comprehension of the second article and the cognitive level at which they processed it" (Crafton, 1983, p. 587). The researcher went on to say that her study supports three assertions: (1) "the common view of reading as a natural knowledge-generating activity"; (2) the belief that "text on an unfamiliar topic can serve as cognitive preparation for the next"; and (3) the observation that experimental subjects who read two forms of the same material "were more *active* during the reading process and personalized information to a greater degree than did subjects who read unrelated materials" (Crafton 1983, p. 590). Interpreting this finding into practice has been demanding, since it has not been easy to find two selections on the same topic at the same level, let

Figure 4.10
The Old Man and the Sea: Literal organizer.

> *The Old Man and the Sea* tells of an extremely poor old fisherman, SANTIAGO, who fishes along in the Gulf stream, and of MANOLIN, a boy who had fished with him until the man's luck had gone bad. The boy still had deep respect and affection for him, however, and brought him food and other things he needed.
>
> The book opens in September as the old man decides to go far out into the Gulf Stream to take advantage of a strong current. He rowed out in the dark, lowered his bait, and began drifting with the current. When the sun was high, the bait was taken by a large fish. The man tried to pull the fish up, but it was too big and simply began towing the boat out to sea. All afternoon and all night the fish pulled the SKIFF, with the old man resolutely straining against the line to ensure that the fish did not break it.
>
> About sunrise, the fish gave a lurch, which cut the man's hand. Santiago ate strips of raw tuna to keep up his strength, and he wished the boy were with him. Finally, the fish surfaced, and it was the biggest fish the man had ever seen—longer than the skiff. But it dove again and continued towing the boat the rest of that day and into the night.
>
> The old man was suffering greatly by now but was still resolved to bring the fish in. He tried to sleep, still standing and holding the line, but woke as the fish again surfaced and pulled him down into the boat, where the line cut into his hands and his back. He got up and fought the fish to try and tire it. As the sun rose on the old man's third day at sea, the fish began to circle, and the man was able to pull in some line. After several hours, feeling dizzy and faint, the old man pulled the fish near enough to the boat to harpoon it. Since the fish was larger than the boat, the man lashed it alongside, rigged the sail, and, exhausted, set sail for home.
>
> But it was too good to last. Sharks had caught the scent. From sunset until after midnight, the old man fought the sharks, first with his harpoon, then his knife, and finally a club. But it was no use—they had cleaned his fish, and he was beaten.
>
> He arrived in the harbor and managed to reach his shack before he collapsed with fatigue. In the morning, the fishermen were astounded at the 19-foot skeleton lashed to the boat. When the old man awakened, the boy heard of his ordeal and tried to console him.

alone different reading levels. However, that is being changed by the Internet.

Notes on Reading Before Reading: Supported in Terms of Efficacy and Logistics

An anecdotal validation of this idea is illustrated in Figure 4.12. Further, reading before reading today can be more easily accomplished. The Internet

Figure 4.11
The Old Man and the Sea: Abstract organizer.

> *The Old Man and the Sea* tells of a fisherman's struggle with the elements while trying to hook and kill a huge fish, only to have it eaten by sharks.
>
> The story is a testament to humankind's unconquerable spirit—to our ability to achieve dignity in the face of defeat. Humans are shown to be noble because of their willingness to struggle and preserve against the hardships in life. The man tells the fish, "I will show him what a man can do and what a man endures" [p. 66] and "Man is not made for defeat . . . a man can be destroyed, but not defeated" [p. 103].
>
> The book also shows the author's view of humankind in relation to the physical universe. The fisherman refers to both the stars and the fish as "my brother." This is taken to mean that we should respect and love our natural environment even as we strive to carve existence out of it and conquer it.

offers around-the-clock, content-rich electronic text on almost any topic. Relatedly, a monthly look at public and cable television offerings provides numerous opportunities for nontextual reiteration or previewing and reviewing of films, documentaries, and programs on topics in literature, science, social studies, and the arts.

Figure 4.12
Anecdotal evidence for reading before reading.

> The first author once taught world geography to a difficult, sometimes unruly class of low-achieving ninth graders. We had a new, slick, black-covered text that was impossible in almost every way: the print was small, information was dense, and sentence structures were complex beyond reason. In short order, we found 20 copies of a very old geography text in the district's attic. We read both books, alternating the order according to fancy more than to any deep analysis of textual value. In addition to the obvious benefits of seeing most things twice, and in different words, we often were challenged and amused by diverse perspectives, sometimes-contrary information, and changing and often bewildering facts. For example, we puzzled over how a then-obscure and backward Iran could have been the seat of the great Persian Empire. There were many times when we wished we had a third or fourth text to explain some things in even greater detail. We never could quite get a conceptual fix, for example, on how maps were made in times past when map makers could not get up high enough to see.

✦ *After Words* ✦

This chapter presented a number of ways to help readers optimize prior knowledge and experience before reading. It illustrated how students can be taught to do this for themselves through inquiry-based methods like ReQuest and Question Only, and with reiterative methods, such as parallel texts and advance organizers. The next chapter discusses several means of keeping interest and attention focused during independent silent reading and viewing. See if you can find a method for guiding silent reading that suits your subject area and teaching style.

CHAPTER 5

Methods for Guiding Silent Reading

Reading taste and ability are always tethered to past experience. But reading itself is one way of increasing this capital fund of past experience.

—Edgar Dale

✦ Fore Words ✦

The aspect of reading instruction that educators know least about is that of guiding students while they read silently. This chapter presents the techniques and methods now available for doing so. These range from methods that attempt to teach readers to internalize reading strategies that resemble antiviral software, to various types of reading guides, to restructuring or reformatting the text to readers' needs. No doubt you will find some method(s) that suit your subject specialty and personal style of teaching. For a professional experience in constructive-creative thinking, read ahead as a pioneering partner in the quest to better understand the act of silent reading-thinking and what educators might do to further facilitate it.

TEACHING STUDENTS TO THINK WHILE THEY READ

The aim of effective content area literacy instruction is not so much to teach *reading skills* as to build the *habit of skilled reading*. This is not just a play on words. It is the difference between teaching how to use a skill and teaching understanding of a skill's purpose and role, and then offering the supportive scaffolding needed as a learner struggles through the arduous process of trying it out, adjusting it, and mastering it as an intentional strategy.

In one study, students were interviewed about their understanding of this metacognitive process:

> . . . when Susan, a seventh-grade student, was asked to talk about what she had been thinking as she read a portion of text she responded: "Oh, I don't usually think while I read." Clearly, Susan misunderstands the purpose of reading and cannot be successful. (Lipson & Wixson, 1997, p. 581)

For Susan, like many students, all "reading" is the same. She makes no distinction between the easy, passive process of independent-level reading, and the challenging, active process of instructional-level study reading. Helping students to make that distinction is the point of the silent reading stage of the three-step framework for content area literacy. Even with the best prereading instruction, at some point each student goes to the printed page alone. At this point, they need something to keep the process going, and something to keep it focused and productive.

In silent reading, students must sustain attention, draw on prior knowledge and experiences, translate new information into familiar terms, identify main ideas and relevant details, monitor comprehension, use fix-up strategies when they are not understanding, and, most of all, sustain these efforts in a sea of other competing interests, needs, and distractions. Teachers cannot physically follow students on this silent incursion into print. They can, however, provide support in the form of various types of reminders to read strategically, that is, actively and purposefully.

METACOGNITIVE MONITORING AND FIX-UP STRATEGIES

Most people, adults and students alike, do more reading of independent-level than instructional-level materials. Therefore, passive reading becomes a strongly imbedded habit, and we tend to enter any reading act as if it were easy, independent-level reading. Metacognitive monitoring is like a little red flag that goes up, saying, "Uh-oh, I don't think I'm getting this," and prompting the realization that something more needs to be done here. The "something more" is the active thinking strategies for continuous

Figure 5.1
Review of metacognitive monitoring and fix-up strategies.

> **Strategies for Monitoring Silent Reading Comprehension**
> "How would I say that in my own words?"
> "What's the main point here, and why is it important?"
> "What would be an example of this?"
> "How could I cluster the ideas I've read about so far?"
> "Am I finding answers to the purpose question(s) yet?"
> "Where is this going next?"
> "Here's an unfamiliar word—what does it seem to mean in the way it's used here?"
> "Can I picture in my mind what is going on here?"
> "Does this make sense, according to my own experience?"
> "Can I trust this author's accuracy/authority/objectivity?"
>
> **Fix-up Strategies**
> "Let me reread that last part, more slowly this time."
> "Let me think about that for a minute."
> "Is there a certain word here that is throwing off my understanding?"
> "Let me read ahead a little, to see if getting the larger picture helps."

comprehension monitoring, and the fix-up strategies that act like an antiviral software program that automatically steps in as the need is detected. See Figure 5.1 for a review of the active reading strategies introduced in Chapter 3.

ENTERING STRATEGY INSTRUCTION
THROUGH A SIDE DOOR

Engagement was introduced in Chapter 3 as the single most essential element in teaching/learning. Textbook material, almost by definition, is not highly engaging. One alternative means of securing engagement long enough to provide effective strategy instruction is to *supplement* curriculum materials with interesting, real-world reading selections that help students link the abstract concepts and distant facts to the context of their own lives and concerns. These supplemental reading selections are more likely to get and keep students' attention. More importantly, they usually are written at a level closer to students' independent level, thereby increasing the likelihood that *more* students will have a *more successful* reading-based experience. More students are more likely to pay focused attention to the teacher's modeling of active reading/thinking strategies with content of this type. More students are more likely to participate in "trying out" these strategies for accurately reconstructing an author's meaning and creatively constructing personal reactions to and applications of the new information, ideas, and/or attitudes.

The short newspaper article reprinted in Figure 5.2 was used by an area social studies teacher to introduce a unit on the internment of Jewish citizens early in World War II. It is used for the examples in this chapter.

THREE TECHNIQUES FOR
COMPREHENSION MONITORING

One way to build active study reading habits is simply to require students to pause periodically while reading and use some type of monitoring strategy. This approach can be highly structured at first, fading to greater student independence as they gain familiarity with the technique. Some basic uses and variations on these three techniques are described below, but other possible variations are limited only by the individual teacher's creativity.

Guiding Questions

The wise teacher always looks for the easiest way to meet student needs. Several research findings suggest that students can easily be taught to ask

Figure 5.2

Sample supplementary reading selection. "Embracing the persecuted: Park College kept Japanese-Americans out of detention camps during war" (*Kansas City Star,* vol. 119, no. 156).

(1) Early in 1942, amid the mood of rage and fear following the Japanese attack on Pearl Harbor, the U.S. government interned more than 110,000 Japanese-Americans living on the West Coast. The great majority of those internees, some of whom were held as long as three years, were native-born American citizens.

(2) At the time, few outside the Japanese-American community had the courage or foresight to protest what many now consider one of the most shameful acts in American history. But one man who did speak out was a Presbyterian minister named William Lindsay Young, then president of Park College in Parkville, just across the river from Kansas City.

(3) Young happened to be in Los Angeles when the internment process began. And he was horrified to see thousands of people herded into a holding area behind barbed wire at the Santa Anita Racetrack. He was even more distressed to discover that the internees, rounded up solely because of their ancestry, were being shipped off to hastily constructed internment camps in Wyoming, Colorado, Arizona, Arkansas, and other states. What he was witnessing, Young thought, was frighteningly similar to fascist doctrines espoused by the nations that the United States was fighting in the name of democracy. "If we are not careful," Young said in a speech to Park students, "we are apt to do damage to those very values which we are now anxious to preserve."

(4) When he learned of a government program allowing some interned students to attend colleges away from the West Coast, he immediately set out to recruit as many as possible. "Would you like to study at Park College? All expenses provided?" he wired to prospective students. In all, he enrolled nine second-generation Japanese-Americans, or Nisei, each of whom had to be cleared by six federal agencies, including the FBI, before they could travel to Missouri.

(5) But the federal bureaucracy was not the only obstacle facing Young. His recruitment policy aroused an anti-Japanese furor in the community around his school. The response grew so intense that local newspapers called the debate the "Battle of Parkville." And into that heated atmosphere came the nine Nisei students, already traumatized by the sudden upheaval in their lives.

Dreadful Journey

(6) One of them was Masaye Nagao Nakamura, who came from East Los Angeles. She left for Park College as her family was being sent to an internment camp in Wyoming. She began her college journey

Figure 5.2, *continued*

in an Army truck. "I sat on my suitcase in the back of that open truck surrounded by three soldiers," she said. "I was going to Union Station in Los Angeles, but I felt like I was going to the guillotine." After boarding the eastbound train, she was denied a seat and forced to crouch on her suitcase in the front of the passenger car among the baggage. "You could hear a pin drop when I got on," she said. "And then, behind me, all I could hear were whispers of 'Jap, Jap'." After the conductor disdainfully snatched her ticket, he leaned down and spit in her face. "I was so shocked, I couldn't raise my arm to wipe it off," she said. "I felt his spit running down my face. I wanted a hole to open up so that I could drop through and vanish."

(7)   For two days she sat alone and terrified. She did not move. She did not eat. She did not go to the lavatory. Arriving in Kansas City, though, she was encouraged by Young's warm greeting. "The students and faculty of Park College all welcome you," he said. But then he added a warning. "You must be careful when you leave the campus," he said. "Some people in Parkville have threatened to lynch any Japanese-American student they catch."

A Hostile Town

(8)   Young had good reason to be wary. The mood in Parkville, already hostile to the Park College Nisei program, was further fueled by the Mayor, Herbert Dyer. "If the FBI is so sure that these Japs are loyal citizens, why didn't it let them remain on the West Coast instead of sending them to a concentration camp?" Dyer told the *Kansas City Star.* It was outrageous, he added, that the government chose to "dump them" on Parkville. He threatened legal action. Anonymous calls to the college threatened worse.

(9)   Dyer was supported by the City Council and by local chapters of the American War Mothers and the American Legion. Two Parkville merchants, saying they spoke for many others, announced they would not serve any Japanese-Americans.

(10)   But Young stood his ground with calm dignity. The opponents of his plan, he told the *Kansas City Times,* "apparently have lost sight of exactly those things for which this nation is now fighting." He sent a letter to 1,000 residents of Parkville and adjacent towns pointing out the irrational and racist nature of the internment policy. "What about the thousands and thousands of young men and women already in our colleges whose parents were born in Germany?" he wrote, "Is war hysteria making us lose sight of our democratic ideals?"

(11)   In September 1942, at the college's opening convocation, Young addressed the student body. "The Axis (powers) are not the only danger to our liberties as we know them," he said. "There are

Figure 5.2, *continued*

those who, because of their intolerance and bigotry, would deny to a fellow American citizen his just rights. . . . What makes this spurious loyalty so dangerous is that it is cloaked in the garb of patriotism."

(12) His words inspired students and alumni alike. "I am proud of you and proud to be a graduate of your school," wrote one alumnus living in Chicago who had read a news report about the Battle of Parkville. "What a stirring speech it was," said Harold Smith, who graduated from Park College in 1944. He later became the college's librarian, and his research was a major source for this article.

(13) "Dr. Young had already met with us in small groups," Smith said. "He told us that when the Nisei students arrived, they would need our help. And we were all receptive to the idea. I don't think there was a doubt in our minds that what was being done to the Japanese-Americans was wrong." Echoing Young, a headline in the campus newspaper proclaimed: "Welcome Nisei."

(14) But off campus, Nisei students faced threats of violence several times that year. When Nagao Nakamura walked into Parkville alone, she was harassed by a crowd that followed her through the streets. Two other Japanese-American students were chased by a mob brandishing a rope. In response, the Park College students formed groups to escort and protect their classmates. Gradually, the mood in Parkville changed. Within two years, the town, having seen reality rather than stereotypes, had embraced the Nisei students.

"You took me in"

(15) After she graduated in 1945, Nakamura returned to California, where she became an honored teacher in the Oakland school system. Retired now, she often speaks to student groups about the internment period. "It was a long time ago, but it is vivid to me yet," she said recently. "And I will remember Dr. Young's courage until the day I die."

(16) One of her classmates, William Yamamoto, became a physician and a professor at the University of Pennsylvania Medical School. In 1991, he sent a large contribution to his alma mater along with a letter. "I was declared a stranger in my own land, and you took me in . . . from behind the barbed wire that surrounded the Santa Anita Racetrack," he wrote. "At Park, many befriended me and became my campus family. All the modest success I have enjoyed, and the fullness of my days since, I owe them, the people who made up Park College."

Source: Popper, J., *Embracing the persecuted: Park College kept Japanese-Americans out of detention camps.* The Kansas City Star © 1999, reprinted with permission.

strategic questions while they read (Baker & Brown, 1984; Meichenbaum & Asarnow, 1979; Singer & Dolan, 1980). For example, these three simple questions have been taught to guide students in story-type reading:

1. What is the main idea?
2. What are the important details?
3. How do the characters feel, and why? (Meichenbaum & Asarnow, 1979)

The first two questions also can be used to guide the reading of expository textbook material. This simple approach can be structured initially by having students pause after a few minutes of silent reading and asking them these questions aloud. Depending upon the content of the reading material, other strategic questions might be added, such as:

4. Where is the author going next with this?
5. How might you organize the information you have read so far?

Students reading the newspaper article in Figure 5.2, for example, might be given about a minute and a half to read silently. This should put most students up to about the first subheading, "Dreadful Journey," a good point to pause and model strategic questioning: "Turn your papers over for a few minutes. A good first *strategic question* to ask about anything we read is, 'So far, what seems to be the main idea here?' Can someone say, in your own words, the main idea of what you have just read?" Students should be encouraged to respond with more than single words or facts, and helped to shape a main idea statement that the teacher records on the chalkboard or overhead. They should not look back to the article while trying to recall the information. The main idea statement might eventually read something like this:

> *The president of a college near Kansas City saved Japanese-Americans from being put in detention camps during World War II by offering them a special full scholarship and helping them qualify for a government program that would allow them to attend a college away from the West Coast.*

As students suggest ideas for the main idea statement, the teacher should ask, when necessary, "Is that part of the main idea, or is it a supporting detail?" Ideas that students decide are supporting details can be written to the side of the main idea statement. After the main idea has been formulated, the teacher might permit students to look back at the article for a very brief, timed, period—in this case about ten seconds—in order to locate the more important details to add to the list that has been started on the board or overhead. The list for the opening section of this article would reasonably include:

1. This happened in 1942, after the Japanese attack on Pearl Harbor.
2. Over 110,000 Japanese Americans on the West Coast were interned.
3. The camps were in Wyoming, Colorado, Arizona, Arkansas, and other states.
4. Few other Americans protested.
5. The college president's name was Lindsay Young.
6. The college was Park College.
7. Young enrolled nine Japanese-American students.
8. To qualify for the special program, prospective students had to be cleared by six federal agencies.
9. The local community was against the students coming to the college.

Then, the teacher might say, "Now, before you turn your papers back over, where do you think the author is going next with this?" Likely responses might include:

1. Real stories about some of the Japanese-Americans who went to Park College.
2. How the town responded.
3. How the college responded.
4. What eventually happened to those students.

Finally, the teacher might ask whether the "5 W's" of a newspaper article (*who, what, where, when,* and *why*) have all been answered. In this example, the teacher might emphasize what they have learned so far about the "why" question: Why did President Young put himself and his college on the line to go against public opinion? Students may recall reading in the introductory section that Young had been in Los Angeles when the internment began, and seen people herded into one of the camps. But this doesn't fully explain why he decided to personally undertake to do something to change what was happening. Urged to consider this question further, students will be more likely to take note of the message of Young's speech, which is quoted later in the article.

After several lessons in which silent reading questioning has been modeled in this way, the teacher can begin to fade out the supportive scaffolding. For example:

1. Direct students to make small pencil checks on the reading assignment at given points. When they come to these points during reading, they are instructed to write out a clarifying question of any type, and briefly record their answers.

2.   Direct students to select three points on their own, while reading, to stop and write clarifying questions and answers.

Each of these variations also is ideal for structuring student collaboration in pairs or groups of four.

About-Point

About-Point (Martin, Lorton, Blanc, & Evans, 1977) is an easy-to-remember formula for strategic reading. Students are taught to pause at logical points, such as at the ends of paragraphs or text subsections, and complete the following two phrases:

> *This section is about _____; and the point is _____.*

The simple About-Point prompt reminds readers to translate the basic meaning of the section, and then to ratchet up their comprehension to the interpretive level in order to state the author's probable intent for presenting just this information in just this way. Teach students the basic About-Point format using several short sample paragraphs. Explain that an *about* statement should be more than a single key word but less than a summary. A *point* statement should include the most important elements of the section. It is useful to demonstrate a few examples and talk through the process of expressing good *about* and *point* statements. Here are two possible About-Point statements from the newspaper article in Figure 5.2:

Paragraph 6

> *This paragraph is about one Japanese-American woman's trip from Los Angeles to Park College, and the point is that, having done nothing wrong, she was treated worse than a criminal.*

Paragraph 11

> *This paragraph is about President Young's opening of school speech in September 1942, and the point is that bigotry is a greater threat to freedom than an invading army.*

Once students have the idea, the simple format can be used in at least two ways:

1.   For a structured beginning, have students put pencil checks beside particular paragraphs in a reading assignment. Direct students to write About-Point statements on these paragraphs.
2.   For decreased structure (fading), instruct students to select their own paragraphs for About-Point statements.

Like the *guiding questions* technique above, About-Point statement writing is an ideal activity for student pairs or cooperative groups.

Comprehension Monitoring System

The *Comprehension Monitoring System* was field tested with high school teachers in home economics, social studies, and biology (Smith & Dauer, 1984). In this technique, teachers create a coding system for students to use to record their *cognitive* and *affective* responses while they read. The code will vary according to the characteristics of the material and the curriculum objectives. A coding system for social studies reading might be as follows:

B   =   Bored
C   =   Confused
D   =   Disagree
MI =   Main idea
Q   =   I've got a question about this (note the question, because you are
        not likely to remember it)

A coding system for science reading might be:

C   =   Clear
D   =   Difficult
I* =   Important
S! =   Surprising

Not every paragraph needs to be marked, but initially, the teacher should assign a minimum number of paragraphs for marked responses. If students are permitted to write in their reading materials, they can note the letter codes in the margins while reading. If not, 2-inch wide strips of paper can be distributed to insert in the assigned pages for recording responses.
    Sample markings for the article in Figure 5.2 might be as follows:

Coding System
ID =   Important detail(s)
R   =   Reminds me of something
MI =   Main point
S   =   Surprising

Paragraph 1   ID   [Sets out the basic newspaper requirements
                               for "who, what, when, where"]

Paragraph 2	R	[Reminds me of how people don't have the courage not to laugh at crude ethnic jokes]
Paragraph 3	MI	[We were doing the same thing the Nazis were doing to the Jews]
Paragraph 4	S	[Nine students doesn't sound like many, when 110,000 were arrested]
Paragraph 6	R	[Reminds me of movies I've seen about the time when blacks were supposed to sit in the back of the bus]
Paragraph 11	MI	[This seems to be the main point so far—that we were doing the same thing to these people that the Nazis were doing to the Jewish people]
Paragraphs 15 & 16	ID	[Important to note what became of these two people]

After students have been introduced to the basic technique of coding their responses to sections of a reading selection, students can work together in cooperative groups to compare their responses and/or to create their own coding systems.

The next section describes several types of guides that teachers can prepare for students to complete while they read. This fairly traditional form of reading assistance is significantly enhanced by teachers' understanding of the specific active reading processes they are attempting to encourage.

K-W-L+

Know-Want to know-Learned, Plus (Carr & Ogle, 1987; Ogle, 1989, 1996) is a popular method for implementing the full three-step framework for active reading-based instruction. It is placed in this chapter on *silent* reading because of the unique way in which it facilitates this step of the framework. In K-W-L+, students are guided in generating their own anticipation-based reading guides to prompt active silent reading. This helps them to read with greater awareness of what they already knew, what they need to know, and with the charge to carefully process and restate what they learn from reading.

Steps in K-W-L Plus

Step 1   *Know.* Students make or are given a three-column worksheet with the columns headed *Know, Want to know,* and *Learned.* The teacher leads a brainstorming session on what students already know about the topic. As ideas are given, students write them in the *Know* column of their individual worksheets. (See Figure 5.3 for an example of a worksheet that might be generated with a class for the reading selection on World War II Japanese-Americans that we have been using for illustrations in this chapter.)

Step 2   *Want to know.* The teacher then moves the discussion toward aspects of the topic that students do not know. Students are helped to state these as questions and write them in the *Want to know* column of their worksheets.

Step 3   *Learned.* As they read, students locate and write their answers to the *Want to know* questions in the *Learned* column of their worksheets. New questions and answers can be added as they read and find information they did not anticipate. The teacher leads a discussion of what was learned in answer to the original questions and what additional information was learned.

Step 4   *Plus.* The teacher leads students in categorizing the information that was learned and in creating a graphic organizer to represent this. (See Figure 5.7 ahead in this chapter for a graphic organizer format that might be used for this article in the *Plus* step.)

Notes on K-W-L Plus

The early version of K-W-L that did not contain the *Plus* step of creating a graphic organizer did not fare well in research comparisons with other methods. The Plus version, however, has been uniformly supported. Teach-

Figure 5.3
Example of a K-W-L+ Worksheet for the article: Embracing the Persecuted: Park College Kept Japanese-Americans Out of Detention Camps During War.

Know	Want to Know	Learned
Japanese-Americans were imprisoned during World War II even if they were American citizens	How did a *college* keep them out of the camps?	
Some of the prison camps were in California	How many people did the college help in this way?	
There was a lot of negative public opinion about German-Americans at that time, too	Was everyone in favor of this, or did some object?	
	How did those who were helped feel about it?	

ers especially like this method because it is well structured and students respond well to reading to answer questions that they themselves have raised.

READING GUIDES

When coaches shout commands during an athletic event, they are attempting to remind the athletes of what has always been taught and practiced in a less competitive situation. Such coaching from the sidelines would be distracting were it not for extensive prior training. The same general principle applies to written aids to text comprehension, or adjunct aids. These aids work best when students have been explicitly taught to use them and are given ample opportunity for guided practice.

The idea of *reading guides*, according to Herber (1978), their chief contemporary proponent, is to simplify difficult material. Reading guides are designed to teach reading processes as well as to improve information acquisition. Students are expected to refer to the guide while reading, then back to the text, then back again to the guide (Manzo & Garber, 1995). Often, a guide amounts to an attempt to create a written-out version of the *three-step framework* described in Chapter 3. It can contain vocabulary and concept preparation as well as guiding purpose questions. Ideally, they serve as supplementary aids in the independent processing of heavily content-laden text. The most significant advantages of guides, in our judgment, are that: (1) they permit the teacher to focus student attention on key information and concepts in a passage and (2) they require *every* student to attempt some type of active and reflective response to at least the points referenced.

Despite mixed findings on guides, their popularity is evident in the numerous versions that have been developed. Some of the most traditionally used formats for reading guides and some recent innovations are described next.

Three-Level Guides

A *Three-Level Guide* is designed to lead students from basic to more advanced levels of comprehension of textual material (Herber, 1978). Part 1 of a Three-Level Guide contains questions at a literal level: What did the author say? Part 2 contains interpretive questions: What did the author mean? Part 3 contains application questions: How can you *use* this information?

Guidelines for Constructing a Three-Level Guide
1. The Guide should alert readers to the information and ideas needed to respond to the questions or activities in part 3. Therefore, begin by

deciding which part 3 *applications* are appropriate to the material. This will help you to select which details and inferences to focus on in writing parts 1 and 2 of the Guide.

2. Next, determine what information is needed to make these applications, and whether it is explicitly stated in the text or must be inferred. Information that must be inferred to make the level-three applications is used to develop questions for part 2 of the Guide.

3. Finally, write questions for part 1 of the Guide, directing attention to the necessary literal information in the reading selection (Vacca & Vacca, 1986).

Typically, students are directed to answer the literal questions in part 1 while they are reading and to complete the interpretive and applied questions in parts 2 and 3 after reading. A useful variation is to have students complete part 1 independently, and then form cooperative learning groups to complete parts 2 and 3. See Figure 5.4 for a simple exam-

Figure 5.4
Example of a three-level guide.

Directions: Answer questions in part 1 as you read. After you have read, go on to parts 2 and 3.

Part 1: Literal Understanding

1. Who did the U.S. government imprison early in 1942?
2. Who protested this, and why?
3. What did Young do to help some of the Japanese-Americans?
4. What was the response of the townspeople?
5. What was the response of the college students?

Part 2: Interpretive Understanding

6. Why did Parkville merchants refuse to serve the Japanese students?
7. What did President Young mean by his statement that "what makes this spurious loyalty so dangerous is that it is cloaked in the garb of patriotism"?

Part 3: Applying your Understanding

8. You are a Park College student in September 1942. You have just listened to President Young's opening of school address. Write a one-page script in which you and a friend argue about the President's decision to offer scholarships for Japanese-American students to attend your college.

ple of a Three-Level Guide for the short article used for examples in this chapter.

Process Guides

Typical teacher-made reading guides focus on product, or fact identification basic inference. A *Process Guide* is intended to teach the active thinking strategies needed to construct meaning by combining text with experiences and learnings beyond the text. There is no single format for a Process Guide. The sections and questions need to be matched to students' background information and experience related to the topic and difficulty of the particular reading selection. The best way to learn how to construct one is simply to try it. Following are a few suggestions for preparing this type of guide. See an example of a simple Process Guide in Figure 5.5.

Guidelines for Constructing a Process Guide

1. Pick an important selection. Process Guides are time-consuming to construct, so you will want to spend your efforts on something of conceptual value.

Figure 5.5
Example of a process guide.

1. Read paragraphs 1 and 2. Record as briefly as possible the answers to the 5-W questions:

   Who?
   Did What?
   Where?
   When?
   Why?

2. Imagine that you are a Japanese-American in 1942, and have just learned that your family is to be sent to one of the internment camps. Write five words to describe your feeling.

3. As you read the remainder of the article, jot down your thoughts about these two general questions:

   a. What was the mood of the country that permitted this to happen?

   b. What can one person do to change the minds of an entire campus, or town, or country?

4. What more current examples of discrimination came to mind as you read or reflected on this article?

5. What parallel did Young see between internment of Japanese-Americans and the events leading to U.S. involvement in World War II?

2. Read the selection carefully, putting yourself in the students' place: "If I didn't know much about this, what would I need to do?"

3. Construct questions that engage the reader in setting a purpose for reading, and in reading actively to reconstruct information and examples.

4. Construct questions that engage students in considering possible interpretations, implications, and applications of new information.

The next type of reading guide breaks with traditional routines. It departs from the usual expectation that students need to begin at the beginning and read every word through to the end.

Reading Guide-O-Rama

The Reading Guide-O-Rama (Cunningham & Shablak, 1975) is a set of written prompts to students as to the best way to read and think about a given reading selection. In constructing a Guide-O-Rama, teachers should determine which concepts and information they expect students to learn from the reading. Next, teachers should consider how they, as an expert reader, would approach the selection. An effective Guide-O-Rama points out unimportant as well as important information and forewarns readers about what to expect in class discussion. It may direct students to read portions of the material out of sequence, such as reading a final summary first. It may instruct students to read a short section of the assignment and then summarize the key points or facts. See Figure 5.6 for an example of a Reading Guide-O-Rama.

Graphic Organizers as Reading Guides

As described in Chapter 3, graphic organizers provide another way to guide silent reading comprehension. These may be partially constructed through a whole-class brainstorming session as described in Chapter 3 or included as part of a structured reading guide. See Figure 5.7 for an example of a graphic organizer used to guide fact acquisition, interpretation, and application.

Additional Notes on Creating and Using Reading Guides

Composing any type of reading guide can be a powerful heuristic, or insightful experience for teachers. It draws one into a careful analysis of the textual material and a deeper understanding of the processes that students must call on to read in a given discipline. It also can get the creative juices flowing; teachers often are surprised at the insights into

Figure 5.6
Example of a Reading Guide-O-Rama.

Directions: Reading for information is not like reading a story. In study reading, it often helps to skip around, looking for a "hook," instead of reading straight through from beginning to end. Use this Guide to show you how this process works. Notice that you are to read paragraphs 6 and 7 first.

Read paragraphs 6 & 7	Write some brief predictions about *why* this might be happening. Briefly describe something this reminds you of.
Read paragraphs 1–5	Stop and put in your own words why the young woman in paragraphs 6 and 7 was traveling to Park College.
Read paragraphs 15 & 16	How does the story turn out?
Read paragraphs 8,9, & 14	Briefly describe ways in which the Japanese-Americans faced "a hostile town" in 1942.
Read paragraphs 10–13	Briefly describe the strategies used by President Young to encourage acceptance of the new students.

---

students' reading and learning needs that can be gained in this way. Furthermore, problems related to producing, revising, and storing guides have been virtually eliminated with the increasing availability of computers with word processing, graphics, and storage capabilities.

The final section of this chapter describes a way to give students ready access to another kind of guidance for silent reading. These are guides that are built directly into the reading selection and optimistically are a harbinger of things to come.

BUILT-IN GUIDES TO SILENT READING

A logical alternative to teacher-prepared reading guides is a textbook with *built-in* guides. These are electronic or hard-copy versions of what now is called *hypertext*. These internal guides have been called *embedded aids* (Manzo, 1977) and *marginal gloss* (Otto & Hayes, 1982). Both typically include help with word analysis, word meaning, basic comprehension, remembering, and even thinking beyond the text to greater depth, elaboration, and critical analysis. Aids can lend assistance at all levels of reading and to readers at all levels.

Figure 5.7
Example of a graphic organizer for guiding silent reading.

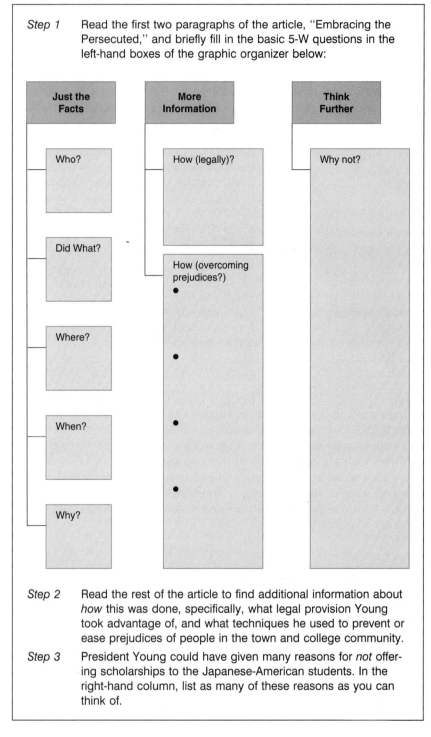

Step 1   Read the first two paragraphs of the article, "Embracing the
         Persecuted," and briefly fill in the basic 5-W questions in the
         left-hand boxes of the graphic organizer below:

Just the Facts	More Information	Think Further
Who?	How (legally)?	Why not?
Did What?	How (overcoming prejudices?) • • • •	
Where?		
When?		
Why?		

Step 2   Read the rest of the article to find additional information about
         how this was done, specifically, what legal provision Young
         took advantage of, and what techniques he used to prevent or
         ease prejudices of people in the town and college community.

Step 3   President Young could have given many reasons for *not* offer-
         ing scholarships to the Japanese-American students. In the
         right-hand column, list as many of these reasons as you can
         think of.

The idea of built-in guides is that they are woven into the actual textbook itself during the production stage. A. V. Manzo produced the imbedded aids prototype shown in Figure 5.8 for a chapter from a high school world history text, *Man's Unfinished Journey* (Perry, 1971), as part of a research and development project.

Despite the high marks that the built-in guides received from teachers and students, it was/is a hard sell to publishers to assume the additional costs involved in producing such books on a regular basis. However, books with imbedded guides are beginning to appear. This may be due to our growing collective exposure to hypertext. This software innovation, which permits additional explanatory detail by clicking on an idea or sentence, seems to be increasing our expectation that such things can be achieved in some measure with conventional print. Relatedly, a field of study called *text technology* (Jonassen, 1982, 1985a, b) at first grew rapidly, but now seems to have stalled out. It seems that the delight that many of us are experiencing in accessing vast amounts of information through intelligent search engines on the Internet has at least temporarily distracted efforts to help people better read, process, and critique it.

TEXT STRUCTURE: A HISTORICAL FOOTNOTE

Some reading educators contend that teaching students to identify text structure and expository patterns is an effective way to improve silent reading comprehension (see Figure 5.9 for a listing of the twelve most common paragraph patterns). This belief is based on a frequent research finding that there is a strong *correlation* between reading comprehension and knowledge of text structure (Meyer, 1975). This has been interpreted by some to imply that teaching poorer readers about the structure of writing will result in improved comprehension. Those who interpret the research in this way propose that recognizing the form and format of a communication are integral parts of understanding its message. However, reading specialists in one study ranked text structure instruction fourteenth of twenty-three teaching practices for comprehension improvement (Gee & Rakow, 1987), a very lukewarm level of support. Recent research in related fields, such as grammar and phonics, has concluded that elaborate instruction in classification schemes is not only unnecessary but potentially counterproductive. The reason is simple: in human learning, applications generally are acquired *before* rules. In short, when students are taught to read for meaning, their awareness of text structure increases, but when they are taught to identify text structures, comprehension growth does not follow to the same extent. That said, there is a difference between belabored isolated instruction in any system of rules, and incidental teaching of these rules as they apply in a given meaningful context. Teachers of beginning reading should know phonics rules; all teachers should know

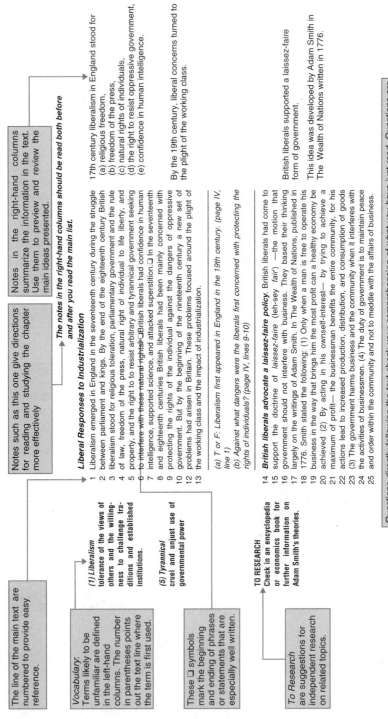

The line of the main text are numbered to provide easy reference.

Notes such as this one give directions for reading and studying the chapter more effectively

Notes in the right-hand columns summarize the information in the text. Use them to preview and review the main ideas presented.

The notes in the right-hand columns should be read both before and after you read the text.

Liberal Responses to Industrialization

1 Liberalism emerged in England in the seventeenth century during the struggle
2 between parliament and kings. By the end of the eighteenth century British
3 liberalism stood for religious toleration, parliamentary government and the rule
4 of law, freedom of the press, natural right of individual to life liberty, and
5 property, and the right to to resist arbitrary and tyrannical government seeking
6 to interfere with these natural rights. British liberals had confidence in human
7 intelligence, supported science, and attacked superstition. In the seventeenth
8 and eighteenth centuries British liberals had been mainly concerned with
9 protecting the rights of the individual against the dangers of oppressive
10 government. But by the beginning of the nineteenth century a new set of
11 problems had arisen in Britain. These problems focused around the plight of
13 the working class and the impact of industrialization.

(a) T or F: Liberalism first appeared in England in the 19th century. (page IV, line 1)
(b) Against what dangers were the liberals first concerned with protecting the rights of individuals? (page IV, lines 9-10)

14 **British liberals advocate a laissez-faire policy.** British liberals had come to
15 support the doctrine of *laissez-faire* (leh-sey fair') —the motion that
16 government should not interfere with business. They based their thinking
17 largely on the writings of Adam Smith. In The Wealth of Nations, published in
18 1776. Smith stated the following: (1) Only when a man is free to operate his
19 business in the way that brings him the most profit can a healthy economy be
20 achieved (2) By acting in his ownself-interest— by trying to achieve a
21 maximum of profit— the businessman benefits the entire community, for his
22 actions lead to increased production, distribution, and consumption of goods
23 (3) The government harms business and the community when it interferes with
24 the activities of businessmen. (4) The duty of government is to maintain peace
25 and order within the community and not to meddle with the affairs of business.

17th century liberalism in England stood for
(a) religious freedom,
(b) freedom of the press,
(c) natural rights of individuals,
(d) the right to resist oppressive government,
(e) confidence in human intelligence.

By the 19th century, liberal concerns turned to the plight of the working class.

British liberals supported a laissez-faire form of government.

This idea was developed by Adam Smith in The Wealth of Nations written in 1776.

Vocabulary:
Terms likely to be unfamiliar are defined in the left-hand columns. The number in parentheses points out the text line where the term is first used.

(1) Liberalism tolerance of the views of others and the willingness to challenge traditions and established institutions.

(5) Tyrannical cruel and unjust use of governmental power

These ◻ symbols mark the beginning and ending of phrases or statements that are especially well written.

TO RESEARCH
Check in an encyclopedia or economics book for further information on Adam Smith's theories.

To Research are suggestions for independent research on related topics.

Questions directly following the text check your comprehension of what you have just read. Questions are of two types: true/false and short answer. Write your answers on a separate sheet of paper. The page number and text line supplied after each question give you a quick reference to check you answer.

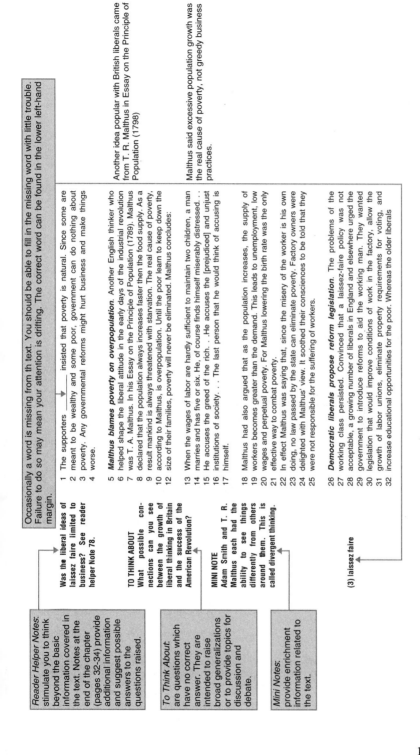

Occasionally a word is missing from th text. You should be able to fill in the missing word with little trouble. Failure to do so may mean your attention is drifting. The correct word can be found in the lower left-hand margin.

Reader Helper Notes: stimulate you to think beyond the basic information covered in the text. Notes at the end of the chapter (pages 32-34) provide additional information and suggest possible answers to the questions raised.

Was the liberal ideas of laissez faire limited to business? See reader helper Note 78.

To Think About: are questions which have no correct answer. They are intended to raise broad generalizations or to provide topics for discussion and debate.

TO THINK ABOUT
What possible connections can you see between the growth of liberal thinking in Britain and the success of the American Revolution?

Mini Notes: provide enrichment information related to the text.

MINI NOTE
Adam Smith and T. R. Malthus each had the ability to see things differently from others around them. This is called divergent thinking.

(3) laissez faire

1 The supporters ____ insisted that poverty is natural. Since some are
2 meant to be wealthy and some poor, government can do nothing about
3 poverty. Any governmental reforms might hurt business and make things
4 worse.

5 ***Malthus blames poverty on overpopulation.*** Another English thinker who
6 helped shape the liberal attitude in the early days of the industrial revolution
7 was T. A. Malthus. In his Essay on the Principle of Population (1789). Malthus
8 declared that the population always increases faster then the food supply. As a
9 result mankind is always threatened with starvation. The real cause of poverty,
10 according to Malthus, is overpopulation. Until the poor learn to keep down the
11 size of their families, poverty will never be eliminated. Malthus concludes:

13 When the wages of labor are hardly sufficient to maintain two children, a man
14 marries and has five or six. He, of course finds himself miserably distressed. . .
15 He accuses the greed of the rich. . .He accuses the [prejudiced] and unjust
16 institutions of society. . . The last person that he would think of accusing is
17 himself.

18 Malthus had also argued that as the population increases, the supply of
19 workers becomes greater than the demand. This leads to unemployment, low
20 wages and perpetual poverty. For Malthus lowering the birth rate was the only
21 effective way to combat poverty.
22 In effect Malthus was saying that, since the misery of the worker is his own
23 doing, no law passed by the state can eliminate poverty. Factory owners were
24 delighted with Malthus' view. It soothed their consciences to be told that they
25 were not responsible for the suffering of workers.

26 ***Democratic liberals propose reform legislation.*** The problems of the
27 working class persisted. Convinced that a laissez-faire policy was not
28 acceptable, a growing number of liberals in England and elsewhere urged the
29 government to introduce reforms to aid the working man. They wanted
30 legislation that would improve conditions of work in the factory, allow the
31 growth of labor unions, eliminate property requirements for voting, and
32 increase educational opportunities for the poor. Whereas the older liberals

Another idea popular with British liberals came from T. R. Malthus in Essay on the Principle of Population (1798)

Malthus said excessive population growth was the real cause of poverty, not greedy business practices.

Figure 5.8 Sample textbook passage with imbedded aids.

Figure 5.9
Paragraph patterns

1. Introductory
2. Definition
3. Transitional
4. Illustrative
5. Summary
6. Main ideas supported by details or examples
7. Chronological order
8. Comparison/contrast
9. Cause and effect
10. Problem/solution
11. Descriptive
12. Narrative

something of English grammar; and all teachers should know something of the basic paragraph patterns that lend both variety and predictability to written language.

✦ *After Words* ✦

Several options for guiding silent reading were presented in this chapter. To help yourself to decide on the one or two that you might use in your own teaching, try using one or two as you read the next chapter. Chapter 6 focuses on options for making the most of the postreading phase of learning from text.

CHAPTER 6

Methods for Postreading Schema Building

Great discoveries and improvements invariably involve the cooperation of many minds.

—Alexander Graham Bell

✦ Fore Words ✦

Successful silent reading sets the stage for verifying, clarifying, exploring, and elaborating the information and ideas encountered in print. Teachers can help students develop active postreading habits in a variety of ways. Traditional class discussion is probably the most familiar way, but orchestrating a good discussion—one with high participation and that rises above factual recitation—is not as easy as it looks. Discussion, by nature, is an unpredictable and sometimes unwieldy event. It depends on the group's willingness to pursue unplanned avenues of thought and the leader's accompanying ability to bring those avenues together toward some meaningful hub of conclusions and insights. This chapter begins with an analysis of discussion, and then lays out a variety of whole-class and small-group methods that can help both students *and* teachers to increase their competence and grace in this artful and elusive form of interacting.

CLASS DISCUSSION: WHAT IT IS, AND HOW TO GET THERE

In postreading, prior knowledge is combined with recently encountered information and transformed into usable new knowledge and opened-thoughts that are likely to cause the process to continue in students' minds and in class. The postreading step of most reading-based instruction is the point at which teachers help students to (1) check basic comprehension, (2) develop concepts, (3) connect new ideas with existing schema, and/or (4) identify misconceptions to restructure schema. The most familiar means of doing this is through teacher-directed class discussion. You can probably recall class discussions that helped you to "see" an idea more clearly, or caused you to look at something in a different way, or perhaps even changed your entire outlook on a topic. There is little done in school that is quite as "mind moving" as a good discussion, but there also is little that can be quite as numbing as a really dull one. Good, revelationary discussions are always going to be few and far between. Think how few you have heard on television or even on radio discussion programs. This is because conducting a memorable discussion is more like leading an improvisational music group than it is like conducting an orchestra that has great music on a stand before them. Of course, even improvisation only *appears* to be unplanned. Much unseen work has gone into "jamming." Keeping this in mind, let's take a closer look at some of the elements of an effective teacher-led class discussion. In this analysis, it becomes evident that teacher-directed discussion is more a culminating achievement than an inspirational moment.

Analysis of a Memorable Class Discussion

In a memorable class discussion, the teacher takes and releases control through several classical moves that are rooted in cognitive and social psychology—that is, in the way the mind works in learning, and they way people feel while they are learning and thinking out loud. Here is a quick summary of this byplay:

✦ The teacher usually begins by asking questions to determine whether students have basic comprehension of the topic.

✦ The teacher maintains a low-risk environment by rephrasing questions that students cannot answer, and through skillful handling of students' incorrect responses.

✦ The teacher uses various strategies to ensure that most students are engaged and following the discussion most of the time.

✦ Once it appears that most students have a basic understanding of the information, the teacher's questions become less literal and more conjectural. It is the compelling nature of these questions that moves the interaction to the next levels.

✦ At some point, the lines of communication shift from the pattern of teacher asks/student answers to a much looser pattern resembling informal conversations. Students interact with each other as well as with the teacher.

✦ Different points of view are welcomed, but there is a soft press to keep them relevant.

✦ Responses are longer and more elaborate than in recitation.

✦ The teacher encourages students to explore different avenues of thought, but again tries to ensure that the discussion does not wander too far astray of intended educational objectives.

✦ As conflicting perspectives emerge, a dynamic tension is created within as well as among individuals.

✦ Discussants, including the teacher, are expected to be willing to change their minds, or be transformed in response to points made.

✦ Passions are allowed to find expression, but incivility is not permitted.

Good class discussion tends to externalize the thinking strategies that characterize the internal conversations of effective learners of a given subject area. Students hear and find themselves trying out new ways of questioning and commenting that they ideally will internalize and independently employ (Calfee, Dunlop, & Wat, 1994; Tharp & Gallimore, 1989).

This is more likely to happen in classrooms where there is rapport among students and between student and teacher.

Clearly, leading a "common" class discussion is a worthy goal but an uncommonly difficult one to achieve. Consider some of the guidelines and methods for providing quality discussion and a developmental plan for achieving mastery of these as a teacher.

A Developmental Plan for Mastering Class Discussion

Following is a sequence of guidelines for emphasis and practice as you plan and implement postreading instruction.

✦ Begin on safe ground with conventional recitation-based approaches. Students have all done this before and will recognize the drill.

✦ When you anticipate that students will *not* need a great deal of review after reading, use teacher-directed recitation. Take these opportunities to practice pacing, questioning techniques, and tactful handling of incorrect responses.

✦ When you expect a greater need for basic understanding, heighten the impact of recitation-based activities by implementing them through cooperative structures in which more students are more actively involved more of the time.

✦ Use methods based on writing in response to reading to engage students in reflective thinking, building schema connections, and self-evaluation.

✦ Use cooperative structures to engage students in activities to build higher-order comprehension and to build students' confidence in offering and accepting constructive criticism.

✦ Teach explicit listening strategies, including nonverbal signals that indicate listening involvement (Barton, 1995).

✦ Use teacher-directed class discussion sparingly at first, selecting topics and crafting questions that are likely to engage student interest and lead to lively interactions.

✦ Use methods and strategies designed to teach students *how* to engage in "instructional conversation" type discussion.

✦ Alter the class discussion routine occasionally, using the guidelines for a Socratic Seminar (described later in this chapter).

TEACHER-DIRECTED RECITATION FOR CHECKING COMPREHENSION

Traditional teacher-directed recitation, or old-fashioned drill, has gone from being overvalued and overused, to being undervalued and occasionally derided. Some educators believe that postreading drill should not be thought of as teaching at all, but simply as another form of testing (Durkin, 1978–1979). We respectfully disagree. Simple literal-level questioning following reading is a reasonable way to model various essential elements of effective reading, most particularly:

+ The need to quickly check basic comprehension of what has just been read
+ The specific *kinds* of recitation questions that are useful for a given type of material

Haven (1999) describes the importance of postreading recitation even as it applies to reading fiction:

> The heart of student learning comes after the story is over and they have a chance to review and assess why the story was structured as it was and how the story achieved its effect. Before real analytical work can begin, however, it is important to cement each student's experience and version of the story in his head. Once they take full ownership of their images and interpretation of the story, evaluation and dissection of the story and of the associated writing techniques will be easier and more beneficial.

With nonfiction, there is even less room for variance in basic comprehension. After reading a nonfiction selection, it is not "each reader's experience and version of the story" that must be fixed in mind, but the basic facts and information the author has presented. This does not exclude challenges to material presented, but it does presuppose a certain clarity of understanding of what has been presented.

Guidelines and Formats for Teacher-Directed Recitation

Recitation, as defined here, consists of three general types of literal-level questions: *recognition, recall,* and *translation.* Recognition questions require *finding* information; recall questions require *remembering* information; and translation questions require *paraphrasing,* or putting the new information into one's own words. When it is used as a postreading comprehension check, it should not be an end in itself, but should bridge to further, less fact-based explorations or applications of the new information.

There are several variations on the basic teacher-led recitation routine. Here are a few reminders, however, for conducting this segment of postreading in the most effective way:

+ *Help students to differentiate recitation from discussion* by telling them that the object of the recitation is to check their basic understanding.

✦ *Keep it short.* About ten to twelve minutes is a good rule of thumb for most classes.

✦ *Keep it moving.* The point is to review the facts, not to overly elaborate on them.

✦ *Don't forget "wait time."* Students need to process the question and formulate a response; yet, the typical wait time is one second or less (Rowe, 1974, 1986). Try counting to five after asking a fact question, and to ten after a translation question.

✦ *Watch who you call on.* Try to call on all students as equally as possible.

✦ *Avoid using recitation as punishment.* Rather than calling on students who clearly are unprepared or not attending, try calling on them to answer a question you're fairly sure they can answer. This will have the effect of pulling them in rather than pushing them out.

✦ *Try versions of "Every Pupil Responds."* For example, ask yes/no questions to which, at a given signal, all students respond with thumbs up or thumbs down.

✦ *Don't forget recognition-level recitation.* Ask students to find and point to the place in the text that answers the question raised. Try using a timer; students like to race the clock.

✦ *Don't forget translation (including vocabulary).* Read aloud a short section, phrase, or key term, and ask the class to put it in their own words.

✦ *Try open-ended recitation.* Following reading, call on a student to tell any *one* thing she or he remembers from what was read. Continue to call on students to offer information, in any sequence, but without repeating any item previously stated. A variation is to permit the student who offers an item to call on another student to offer the next item. This begins to build the habit of intrastudent interaction that will support discussion.

Teachers can use these recitation routines to build their own expertise in two important elements of group leadership: modeling listening behaviors and handling incorrect responses to questions.

Modeling Listening Behaviors

Listening to one another is an important ingredient in a lively discussion. Modeling effective listening *to* your students goes a long way toward teaching them to listen to one another. During recitation, teachers can model active listening and an appreciation for students' contributions in several ways (Barton, 1995):

✦ Moving toward students as they speak

✦ Occasionally writing students' ideas on the board in their own words

✦ Returning to something someone said earlier

Handling Incorrect Responses in Teacher-Led Recitation

Given that one of the primary purposes of recitation is to get things straight, it does present some nagging social problems in how to handle incorrect responses. There are several other research-based means of turning incorrect answers into positive learning experiences (Collins, 1987; Rakes & Smith, 1987). You probably use or would use several of these techniques intuitively, but it is good to have your intuition validated when teaching is your profession.

✦ *Think again.* The most common reason for an incorrect answer is a too-hasty response. If you think this might be the case, simply ask the student to think again. Keep in mind that those moments between the time that the question is asked and an answer is given may be the most instructionally valuable time in the school day. These are the moments in which students are engaged in active thinking, self-talk and rehersal for their public response.

✦ *Give a prompt.* When a student gives an incomplete answer, or needs you to provide more structure, offer a small piece of information: "The person whose name we are looking for also died prematurely in a duel with Aaron Burr."

✦ *Differential reinforcement.* Tell what part of the answer was correct: "You're right, bears are mammals. Do you recall whether mammals are warm blooded? Are human beings warm blooded?"

✦ *Rephrase the question.* If no one seems to know the answer, yet you think that they have learned the information, change the wording of the question: "When you go west, do you gain or lose time?" "Well, is it earlier on the East Coast or the West Coast?"

✦ *Provide help but make students accountable.* If a student gives two incorrect answers to the same question, or if two students answer incorrectly, give the answer and tell them they will need to remember it. Return to the student(s) again before the period is over, and ask the same question: "Now, before you go, who can tell me again one state that borders New Hampshire?"

✦ *Permit clues.* Ask fellow students to give clues, or ask the student who missed the question to call on a classmate to help by giving either a clue or the answer: "Charlie, who would you like to ask for help in naming the other three Great Lakes?"

✦ *Incorrect "if" statements.* If you recognize why the answer was wrong, supply the question for which the answer would have been correct. For example, if you asked, "What is the capital of New Zealand?" and the student answered "Canberra," you could respond, "Canberra would be the answer if someone asked what the capital of Australia was. How about the capital of New Zealand?"

✦ *Examples of possibilities.* If students are drawing a blank, translate the question into a multiple-choice format: "Who was the first European to see the Pacific Ocean? Balboa, Cortez, or Cabeza de Vaca?"

✦ *Nonexamples or opposites.* When students have difficulty answering, tell them what the answer is not: ("Which country in South America has the oldest tradition of democracy?") "The answer is not Brazil or Chile."

Teacher-led recitation can raise attention and engagement, and lay the foundation for further, more reflective discussion. This is no small accomplishment, since one of the biggest problems in any group discussion, at any level, is just getting everyone on the same page.

PEER RECITATION FOR INCREASED STUDENT INVOLVEMENT

To get more students more actively involved in checking their basic understanding of what they have read, it helps to add a certain measure of peer involvement. Several means of structuring these interactions are described here. These methods tend to support the important element of quality teaching that has been referred to as *fading*, or withdrawing ancillary assistance so that pupils may assume more responsibility for guiding their own learning.

Recitation Led by "Home Groups"

Have "home groups" of four students each take turns leading postreading recitation sessions, using structures such as the following:

✦ *Five-question format.* A team leads the class in filling out a "who-what-when-where-why-how" outline.

✦ *Peer questioning.* One team, designated as the "answer team" tries to learn everything they can on a given section of text. The class then questions the answer team, and they try to answer as best as they can, with a short time limit for conferring when necessary. For fun a beeper or buzzer can be added. We observed one eighth-grade science teacher who gave the questioning group a child's toy that made a deep buzzing sound when a button was pushed. The class used it to signal a wrong answer. No one seemed disturbed by the competition, and several otherwise low-participating students were quite caught up in the "in-your-face" humor that young teens seem to enjoy.

✦ *Written questions.* Everyone prepares a few questions on the material. Going around the room in a certain order—up and down rows or across aisles—students read one of their questions that has not been asked, and calls on a volunteer to answer. The teacher might collect the questions and use some on future tests. This enhances students' motivation to write good questions and to listen carefully to the answers.

✦ *Have student groups work together to complete a graphic organizer*, on a large sheet of newsprint, based on the text material. This may be the final version of a graphic organizer generated as a prereading activity, and filled in individually by students as they read. Groups may be encouraged to use design elements that represent the content, or other creative twists. When finished, each group presents and explains their graphic organizer to the class.

✦ *Numbered Heads Together* (Kagan, 1994*). Have students number off within groups. The teacher asks a recitation-type question, and each group briefly confers to agree on their answer. The teacher calls a number at random (1–4), and the student with that number in each group stands. The teacher calls on one of these students to answer, then asks the other standing students if they agree. Students sit and the next question is asked.

✦ *Find the Fib* (Kagan, 1994*). Seated in groups of four, students work individually at first to write three statements: two true statements, based on the reading, and one "fib." Within groups, students take turns reading their three statements and challenging their partners to find the fib. Optionally, each group may be asked to select the best set of statements from their group, to challenge the rest of the class.

✦ *Act it out.* For fiction, and some nonfiction, a team is assigned to act out the "story" for the class. One team member tells the story as the other three act out each story element, providing sound effects, actions, and setting elements. Following the group's presentation, discuss whether the enactment helped students picture scenes, events, and characters better, and whether it changed their first impressions of the story in any ways. ("Act it out" technique from Haven, 1999.)

---

* Adapted with permission from Kagan Publishing from Dr. Spencer Kagan's book *Cooperative Learning.* 1(800)WEE CO-OP. www.KaganOnline.com

Jigsaw

One of the best-known cooperative learning activities, the Jigsaw approach (Aaronson, et al., 1975, 1978), is particularly useful for postreading recitation.

1. Divide a reading assignment into four numbered sections.
2. Set up four-student groups, have students number off, one to four, and distribute the four-part reading assignment. Each group has the entire reading assignment, with each student having a different one of the four sections.
3. Give students time to read their section silently.
4. Have all students who read the first section of the reading (one student from each group) meet in one corner of the room, all who read the second section meet in another corner, third section in another, fourth in another. In these groups, they are to check their recall and understanding of what they read, so they will be prepared to share it with their home group members. Depending on the nature of the reading selection, you may wish to have a worksheet for students to complete in these section groups.
5. Students return to four-member home groups and share, in order, the important information from their sections of the reading.

This method is especially useful for bridging to further analyses or applications in another cooperative group structure, since students already are in groups, and each group member is an "expert" on some portion cf the material.

Paired Recitation

Another approach to structuring peer recitation is to have students work in pairs. Haven (1999) suggests three "verbal reprocessing activities" for fiction; these are reworded below to extend their usefulness to nonfiction material:

✦ Allow each student about one minute to tell their partner about "what went through their mind while they read the assignment." What were they thinking about and picturing while they read? Hold a general class discussion in which students share with the class what they told to their partner (or each student summarizes what his or her partner said). Show students that most of their comments fall into the following three categories:

1. Evaluation of the reading assignment (form, content, style, etc.)
2. Comparison of the information with other versions
3. Relating the information to their own life and experience

✦ Give students about a minute to draw a quick sketch of the main point of the reading assignment. The time limit means that students can't worry about the quality of their drawing. Have student pairs compare and choose one of their drawings to share with the class. In the general discussion, help students to categorize the text elements represented in their drawings.

✦ Have each student pair "retell" the information in the reading assignment. One student begins and tells for thirty seconds. The other student continues for the next thirty seconds, then the first takes over again, and so forth. The teacher times the tellings, and calls "Switch!" at thirty-second intervals. If students can't remember what comes next, they are not excused from telling. Instead of moving forward, they repeat the last information told by their partner during their thirty seconds. If students are truly stuck, they can ask their partner for a hint. However, it is recommended that this be discouraged. Part of the value of this exercise is for each student to remember and claim his or her own version of the material.

METHODS AND STRUCTURES FOR BRIDGING TO DISCUSSION AND APPLICATIONS

Examples of techniques and methods in this section are based on the short article, "Pollution of the Caesars," found in Figure 6.1. Take a moment now to read it.

Guided Reading Procedure (GRP)

The Guided Reading Procedure (Manzo, 1975) is a highly structured method that begins with basic postreading recitation, and concludes with a test designed to convince students that they can read with much greater comprehension than they may have thought. In the course of the GRP lesson, students retrace and restructure a reading assignment in several ways, thus providing a great deal of support for understanding, organizing, and recalling the information. See Figure 6.2 for an example of a GSR lesson.

Steps in the Guided Reading Procedure

Step 1   ***Preparation:*** Select a reading assignment that is fairly short but information rich. Prepare a short-answer test of ten to twenty items on the reading assignment. (As the lesson proceeds, make sure that the test items are given fair coverage.)

Figure 6.1
Sample Reading Selection
"Pollution of the Caesars" (*Discover,* March 1998, 19:3).

The ancient Romans, for all their knowledge, didn't know that lead was poisonous. They used it to preserve food and to halt the fermentation of wines. Lead glazes coated drinking vessels and cookware. Some historians have speculated that the brain-damaging effects of lead poisoning contributed to Rome's downfall. Rome's leaden legacy survives in pottery, pipes, and other artifacts. It also survives, a physicist has now found, in Greenland's ice sheet. Kevin Rosman of the Curtin University of Technology in Perth, Australia, has detected traces of lead in Greenland's ice, evidence of large-scale pollution of Earth's atmosphere two millennia ago. And some 70 percent of that pollution can be pinned to Roman mining in one region: Rio Tinto in southwestern Spain.

Rosman wanted to trace the source of the lead found in a Greenland ice core studied by two of his colleagues. The lead concentrations in that 3,300-yard ice core peaked between 150 B.C. and A.D. 50. This matched historical records of Roman mining activity at Rio Tinto. Lead pollution levels during the Roman era were about four times greater than natural background levels of lead but were still low by modern standards. Between the 1930s and 1970s, the lead concentration in the ice was 25 to 50 times higher than during Roman times, due in large part to leaded gasoline.

Rosman was able to trace the Greenland lead to the Spanish mine because of the unique ratios of lead isotopes in the Rio Tinto ore. Lead and its isotopes form over billions of years from the decay of uranium and thorium. The ratio of two isotopes in particular—of lead 206 to lead 207—generally increases in crustal rocks over time. (The numbers refer to the total of protons and neutrons in lead nuclei.)

Unlike lead in crustal rocks, lead at Rio Tinto was trapped in a vein of silver ore and was isolated from uranium and thorium. So Rio Tinto's lead still has the lower ratio of lead 206 to 207 that it had when it became trapped in the ore billions of years ago. When Rosman found this low ratio in pieces of the Greenland ice sample dating from 600 B.C. to A.D. 300, he consulted historical records to determine which mines were active during ancient times and compared lead isotope fingerprints taken from them in recent years to isotope ratios from the Greenland core. Rio Tinto captured much of the blame.

"Greenland is quite a way from Spain, so the lead that went into the atmosphere affected the entire Northern Hemisphere," Rosman says. He also notes that hard scientific facts show the history books were right. "It's a beautiful example of the application of science using sophisticated instruments to really understand the past."

Source: Jessica Gorman © 1998. Reprinted with permission of *Discover Magazine.*

Figure 6.2
Guided reading procedure: sample dialogue.

1. **Preparation**
   "Pollution of the Caesars," is used in a ninth-grade Physical Science class. Before the lesson, the teacher prepares the following test items:

   ✦   What is the effect of lead poisoning? (brain damage)

   ✦   Why have historians thought that lead poisoning was one of the reasons for the downfall of the Roman Empire? (evidence of lead in pottery they ate and drank from)

   ✦   Where was the Roman lead mine? (Rio Tinto, Spain)

   ✦   Where did Rosman find evidence of pollution from the Roman lead mine? (in the ice in Greenland)

   ✦   How did the Roman lead get to the place where Rosman found it? (in the air, as pollution)

   ✦   How did Rosman know the lead he found in the ancient ice was from the Roman mine? (it had a different chemical structure from most lead)

   ✦   What two lead isotopes were compared to determine the type of lead Rosman found? (206 and 207)

   ✦   Which lead isotope is present in a higher proportion in most lead? (206)

   ✦   Why was the Roman lead different? (it had been trapped in a silver vein and not exposed to uranium and thorium)

   ✦   What was part of the cause of the lead pollution Rosman found in the ice dating from 1930–1970? (leaded gasoline)

2. **Purpose for Reading**
   A. "Read this article to find out how one scientist has used chemistry to find out about air pollution in ancient times."

   B. "Try to remember all that you can about this selection. You have ten minutes to read, and then I'll ask you to turn your papers over and tell me everything you remember, so I can write it on the chalkboard."

3. **Recitation and Recalling (Following Fifteen Minutes of Silent Reading)**

   Teacher: Who can tell me one thing you read about?
   Student: A scientist found lead from a Roman mine in the ice in Greenland.
   Student: It's called "Pollution of the Caesars."
   Student: The lead mining in Rome caused major pollution.
   Student: No, the lead mine was in Spain.
   [teacher records the information on the chalkboard or overhead, and places a question mark above the words "in Rome"]

Figure 6.2, *continued*

Student: The Romans used lead in the dishes they ate from.

Student: And drank from.

Student: The lead from the Roman mine had different kinds of isotopes.

Student: Not different ones, different amounts of them.

[teacher places a question mark above the words "different kinds"]

Student: The lead he found was different because it came out of a vein of silver and didn't get exposed to the air.

Student: It had different amounts of the isotopes 206 and 207.

Student: They think lead makes you brain damaged.

Student: They know it does.

[teacher places a question mark above the words "they think"]

[interaction continues; teacher records information on chalkboard, putting question marks beside any items that are challenged]

4. **Self-Monitoring/Self-Correcting (Sample Student Responses)**

Teacher: You remembered a lot. Now turn your papers over and reread the article to see if we need to change or add anything to what we have on the board.

Student: The mine was in Rio Tinto, Spain.

Student: The lead had the same isotopes, but more of the 206 than 207.

Student: Lead poisoning does cause brain damage, and more people than the Romans must have had it because the lead was in the air all the way to Greenland.

Student: We said what made the lead different was it wasn't exposed to the air, but this says it wasn't exposed to uranium and thorium.

[interaction continues, with the teacher noting corrections and additions on the chalkboard]

5. **Restructuring**

Teacher: Turn your papers face down again and let's organize our information into an outline. Take out a sheet of paper, and copy this down the way we reorganize it, so you'll have it for your notebooks. We have about ten minutes to get this all down, and then I have a short test for you. Now, what would be a good title?

Student: It's called "Pollution of the Caesars." Maybe it should be called "Rosman Rats Out the Romans."

Teacher: Okay, that will be easy to remember; now, what's the first thing the author talks about?

Student: How they think lead poisoning made the Romans brain damaged.

Figure 6.2, *continued*

> *Teacher:* Okay, the first topic will be "Lead poisoning in ancient Rome caused brain damage." Will that work?
>
> *Student:* Then under that, they got it from their dishes.
>
> *Student:* And it caused the downfall of the Empire.
>
> *[Teacher records the outline on the chalkboard:]*
>
> *Rosman Rats Out the Romans*
> I. *Lead poisoning in ancient Rome caused brain damage*
>   A. *Source*
>   1. *dishes*
>   2. *?*
>
> *[Teacher continues recording the outline for students to copy, leaving space where information or topics are missing]*

6. Teacher-Guided Correcting and Completing

> *Teacher:* Turn your papers face up now, and reread quickly for the information that we are still missing, and let's fill it in.
>
> *[Teacher completes outline on chalkboard from students' contributions]*

7. Evaluation

> *Teacher:* Put away the articles and your notes, now, and I will pass out the test.
>
> *[Students complete the test]*

8. Introspection

> *Teacher:* What did you learn from this lesson about how to "read smarter"?
>
> *Student:* I remembered a lot more than the first time we did this, just by really trying to concentrate and remember.
>
> *Student:* I still missed a lot the first time I read it, but then I knew what to look for the next time we got to look at it.
>
> *Student:* Rereading and focusing really helps. I got 100% this time. I had only 40% the first time.

9. Optional Study Step (one week later)

> *Teacher:* Today we're going to see how we are progressing in developing effective study habits. Take out your notes on *Rosman Rats Out the Romans,* and use the next five minutes to study them. Then I will put some questions on the board on that topic, and let's see how well you do. After our little quiz, we'll discuss how you studied and how to "study smarter."

Step 2	*Purpose for reading.* Give the topic of the reading assignment, a brief purpose for reading, and tell students to read to remember *everything they can* about the assignment. Tell students that as soon as they have finished reading, you will write everything they remember on the chalkboard. Tell them that if they finish reading early, they should reread to identify the most important information in the selection.
Step 3	*Reading and recalling.* Give students ten to fifteen minutes to complete their silent reading, and then ask them to tell anything they remember, without looking back at the reading selection. Record all information on the chalkboard or overhead transparency in the order given. If students question the accuracy of anything that is offered, simply record the information, and place a question mark beside it.
Step 4	*Self-monitoring/self-correcting.* Instruct students to go back to the reading selection to correct any inconsistencies that arose in their attempts to recollect and/or to add information previously overlooked. Record all changes and/or additions on the chalkboard or overhead.
Step 5	*Restructuring.* Guide students in organizing the information from the chalkboard or overhead into outline form to be recorded in their notebooks, again without referring back to the reading selection. The outline can be as simple or elaborate as age and grade level permit. Use nonspecific questions, such as "What was discussed first?" "What was brought up next?" "What seems to be the main idea?" Avoid overly specific and leading questions.
Step 6	*Teacher monitoring and correcting.* If students appear to have overlooked any critical ideas or inappropriately equated them with other ideas, raise guiding questions about these points, such as "What do you suppose is the most important of these five points made by the author?" "How does this information relate to what we studied last week?"
Step 7	*Evaluation.* Give the test prepared in step 1. A score of 70% to 80% should be required to pass the test.
Step 8	*Introspection.* After the test, ask students whether they have learned anything about their own learning as a result of the GRP experience. The point to be made is that accuracy in comprehension and recall can be greatly improved by an act of will.
Step 9	*Optional study step.* Several days later, give a second test on the same material. Allow students about fifteen minutes before the test to review material from their notes.

Notes on the Guided Reading Procedure

1. In a typical GRP lesson, students may say little or nothing on the first invitation to recall and recite what they have read. As teachers, we tend to have great difficulty with silence. If you can force yourself to wait silently for a few (seemingly interminable) seconds, the flow of language and thought will begin. The first few, hesitant, student responses will spark other recollections, which will lead to other connections, suggested corrections, and associations. This spiraling effect tends to draw in even the most reticent students.

2. When writing on the chalkboard or overhead, take the opportunity to model good notetaking. Write as quickly as you can, and use as many logical abbreviations as you can. If you write slowly and painstakingly, the lesson loses its focus: while you're writing, students are forgetting. Depending on the age and level of the class, consider selecting one or two reliable students to do the writing in the first part of the lesson.

Efficacy of the Guided Reading Procedure

The GRP has been studied by several researchers and has collected strong empirical validation (Ankney & McClurg, 1981; Bean & Pardi, 1979). Its effectiveness has been most clearly demonstrated at upper elementary and middle school levels with science and social studies material. It also has been shown to be an effective way to improve active listening (Cunningham, Moore, Cunningham, & Moore, 1983) and a particularly effective method for adolescents with learning disabilities (Alley & Deshler, 1980; Maring & Furman, 1985).

Note Cue

Note Cue (Manzo & Manzo, 1987, 1990b) is another highly structured method to scaffold students' participation in a focused class discussion. It helps to *get* discussion going, *keep* it going, and keep it *on target*. It builds the behavioral and social learnings that come from actually doing something. More specifically, it teaches students to *ask* questions and, more importantly, to *comment* on the text, as well as simply *answering* questions. It does this by relieving students of the complex burden of having to think about what to say and how to say it, leaving them only to think about *when* to say it.

Note Cue, as its name suggests, provides *cues* to students, in the form of written *notes*, that guide them through participation in a *model* discussion—model because it is prescripted by the teacher. Initially, almost the entire discussion is prescripted. Enactment of these *early* Note Cue discussions is a form of *strategic parroting* in which students are expected to participate with relatively little thinking. The potential value of strategic parroting was discovered separately by two sets of researchers working with reluctant learners (Manzo & Legenza, 1975; Palincsar & Brown, 1984).

You will be pleasantly surprised to see how this opportunity for class participation through simple parroting can provide a form of instructional scaffolding that can gradually be removed as students begin to internalize the many complex aspects of effective classroom discussion. As you read about Note Cue, notice its suitability for use with ESL students, and others who may have underexposure to typical social and language conventions.

Steps in Note Cue Postreading Discussion

Preparation: Prepare a set of "cue cards" for discussion of the material. These should be prepared as follows:

1. Write several *Questions* on 3 × 5-inch index cards (one Question per card), based on information from the reading selection. Include questions that go beyond the facts, such as translation, interpretation, inference, evaluation, and application questions.
2. Write complete but brief *Answers* to each Question on separate cards (one Answer per card). When writing Answer cards, use complete sentences that include enough context to make it clear what Question it answers (see sample below).
3. Write several *Comment* cards (one Comment per card)—relevant thoughts that might be sparked by the reading selection.
4. Label each card at the top as appropriate: Question, Answer, or Comment.

These are sample Note Cue cards for postreading discussion:

Question	**Answer**	**Comment**
How did the lead from the Roman mine get to Greenland?	The lead from the Roman mine got to Greenland by getting into the air as pollution.	I wonder what kind of brain damage lead poisoning causes.

Step 1   After students have read, the teacher places one or more of the prepared *prereading* cards on each student's desk. *A few students may be given blank cards.*

Step 2   Students are instructed to read the card(s) they have been given, and think about *when* they should read it (them) during the discussion; *students with blank cards are instructed to try to think of their own Question or Comment related to the material they are surveying, and write it on the blank card.*

Step 3   The teacher begins the discussion by asking who has a *Question* or *Comment* card to read that seems to be a good place to begin the discussion. If a *Question* is read, the teacher asks who has an *Answer* that seems to fit it. This process continues until most or all students have had a chance to participate. At this point, the teacher should ask, "Who has other personal reactions or comments?" This last question is intended to encourage personal-evaluative thinking and responding apart from the statements on the cards, but modeled after them in terms of relevance to the topic.

Step 4   (Optional) Within the same or the next class period, give a test of five to ten questions that require brief written responses. Questions should be taken directly from the note cue cards and relevant comments made during the discussion. This builds appreciation of the value of reading one's card so that all might hear and learn, and respect for independent commenting.

Fading   As a group of students becomes familiar with Note Cue (as they quickly do), subsequent lessons should include *fewer teacher-prepared cards* and *more blank cards* for students to generate their own Questions, Answers, and Comments. In this way, responsibility is gradually turned over to students as they gradually become more equal to the expectation.

Notes on Note Cue

The Note Cue system can be used to structure prereading as well as postreading discussion. For a prereading discussion, Questions should be written that will elicit students' background of information about the topic of the reading selection or that urge predictions that could be made from a quick preview of the selection. Similarly, write Comment cards that contain relevant thoughts that might be sparked by previewing the reading selection.

The second author (U. Manzo) piloted Note Cue in an inner-city middle school with low-achieving minority youngsters who had an established pattern of low participation, poor oral reading, and ineffective participation in pre- and postreading discussions. Although these early trials of the strategy were not objectively measured, when these students' participation was prompted with Note Cue lessons, their behavior seemed to be more on task for longer periods of time, and their written responses on short tests showed higher levels of comprehension than they typically demonstrated. In a set of field-based studies that *did* include objective measures, three out of four teachers obtained similar results (Educational Specialist Degree projects, University of Missouri–Kansas City, 1986–87).

There are some other incidental benefits in using Note Cue. The cards youngsters write offer insight into their thinking. Collections of student cards, and their placement in students' individual portfolios, can offer an overview of student progress in writing and oral communication.

A number of whole-class cooperative structures are useful for achieving optimal student involvement while checking and building on basic comprehension. Four such structures are described next: Inside-Outside Circle, Find Someone Who, Paired Strolling, and Postreading Three-Minute Write. These structures can be implemented in a variety of ways. The descriptions below are tailored for use as postreading recitation techniques.

Inside-Outside Circle (Kagan, 1994*)

Step 1	**Preparation:** Write half as many basic comprehension questions on cards as you have students in class (30 students = 15 question cards). The answer should also be included on the card. Opinion and evaluation-type questions may also be included.
Step 2	Move desks toward the walls to clear a large space in the center of the classroom. Have students count off by twos. Have the 1's form a circle in the middle of the room, facing *outward.* Have the 2's form a circle *outside* the 1's, facing *inward.* There now should be a double circle, with student pairs facing one another. Students are asked to greet one another by name and shake hands.
Step 3	Distribute question cards to students in the inside circle. The inside student reads the question to his or her outside circle partner. The outside circle student answers, or attempts to answer. If the student cannot answer, or gives an incorrect answer, the student's inside circle partner is to tell him or her the answer.
Step 4	At your signal (a switch of the lights, or a beeper), the outside circle students are to take a step or two to their left, so that they now are with a new partner. They are to shake hands and greet their new partner, who reads them a new question.
Step 5	The outside circle continues to shift to the left until students are back with their original partners. The inside/outside students then trade places, and the question card is traded to the new inside circle person. The new outside circle students take a few steps to the left to greet a new partner, and continue until they are again back to their original partners.

Kagan (1994) recommends adding "gambits" to structures such as this. A gambit is a phrase students are instructed to say at a certain point in

---

* Adapted with permission from Kagan Publishing from Dr. Spencer Kagan's book *Cooperative Learning.* 1(800)WEE CO-OP. www.KaganOnline.com

the interaction. For example, you might tell inside circle students that if their partner answers the question correctly, they are to say, "What a terrific answer!"—and sound like they mean it. Or, outside circle students might be instructed that if they have to be given the answer, they are to tell their partner, "I appreciate your help with that!" Gambits sound awkward at first, and students say them jokingly, but don't be surprised to hear them again when you might least expect to, and spoken appropriately and sincerely.

Find Someone Who (Kagan, 1994*)

Step 1　　**Preparation:** Prepare any type of worksheet to check students' understanding of a reading assignment. The questions and worksheets in teacher's guides for textbooks are usually perfect for this.

Step 2　　Have students clear their desks, keeping out only a pencil. Distribute the worksheets and give students five to ten minutes to complete as much as they can individually (tell them they are not expected to complete the worksheet during this time, but to skim through the questions and answer those that seem easiest first).

Step 3　　Have students stand, and tell them that they are to take their worksheets and pencils, and walk around the classroom without talking until you give a signal. At the signal they are to stop where they are, find a partner, shake hands, greet one another by name, and find the nearest two seats together. They are to compare the information they have written on their worksheets, and each should try to give an answer to the other. They are to write their partner's initials beside information they got from him or her.

Step 4　　At your next signal, students are to thank their partner, stand, and "mill around" again quietly until you signal again. They greet a new partner, find seats, and share information again.

Step 5　　The milling-and-pairing continues until most students have completed their worksheets.

Paired Strolling (Kagan, 1994*)

Step 1　　**Preparation:** Write several discussion-type questions based on the reading assignment (again, teacher's guides usually provide questions of this type).

* Adapted with permission from Kagan Publishing from Dr. Spencer Kagan's book *Cooperative Learning.* 1(800)WEE CO-OP. www.KaganOnline.com

Step 2	Clear the outside perimeter of the classroom and have students form a double parade line—each student with a partner, facing forward.
Step 3	At the teacher's signal, students are to begin walking forward, casually, while talking to their partners. Beginning with the person on the inside, they are to tell everything they remember about what they have just read. After about two minutes the teacher signals for the outside partners to speak. After about two minutes the teacher signals for the line to stop, and the inside partners to move up to a new partner in the outside line (the front person on the inside goes to the back).
Step 4	The process continues through several shifts of partners.

Postreading Three-Minute Write (Kagan, 1994*)

Several of the methods and techniques described above have included some form of writing. Writing is an especially useful ingredient in postreading instruction for several reasons:

✦ It is another way to ensure involvement of more students.

✦ Writing something down forces it into a linear string of thought—this often helps students see when they may have been fooling themselves into thinking they know something they do not yet know.

✦ Writing induces a greater sense of agency or ownership and commitment, which can be a useful lead-in to lively discussion.

The postreading three-minute write is a simple way to structure postreading writing. After students have read, provide them with a prompt for writing about what they have read. The prompt may be as broad as "Write everything you remember," or a specific question requiring analysis and/or evaluation. Let them know up front that their writing will not be collected or graded for spelling or other mechanics, but that it will be useful to them later in the lesson. Some guidelines for this technique are as follows:

✦ It works best when everyone writes at the same time (ideally, including the teacher).

✦ The only rule is that everyone must be *writing something* for the entire three minutes, even if they are writing "I can't think of anything to write," over and over.

---

* Adapted with permission from Kagan Publishing from Dr. Spencer Kagan's book *Cooperative Learning.* 1(800)WEE CO-OP. www.KaganOnline.com

The three-minute write can also be structured as a "write-pair-share," in which, following writing, students are placed in pairs and take turns, within a specific time limit, telling (not reading to) their partner what they have written.

Group Reading Activity

The Group Reading Activity (GRA) (Manzo, 1974) structures postreading recitation in a way that helps students learn to offer and receive constructive criticism. The GRA was among the first cooperative learning methods devised for classroom use that meets the requirements for effective learning as well as merely encouraging greater social interaction. It tends to be quite transformative of student classroom decorum.

Steps in the GRA

Step 1   The teacher selects the reading assignment, and writes a purpose question on the chalkboard.

Step 2   The teacher divides the text into subsections of a few pages each and assigns each subsection to a small group.

Step 3   Students read silently, and write their individual responses to the purpose question.

Step 4   Each group is given a worksheet to complete together. The worksheet should contain general, open-ended comprehension-check questions such as the following:

a. What question does this section answer?

b. Write a statement of the main idea(s) of this section. Support it with direct quotes or paraphrased facts and points found in the text.

c. Comment on the quality of the ideas and supporting statements: Do these seem true? complete? biased?

d. What other things, ideas, and facts have you learned in the past that seem to relate to what you have read here?

e. Using the information from the worksheet, the group works together to prepare a brief presentation for the rest of the class. They should choose who should present what information, in what order, and in what way.

Step 5   As each group becomes ready, a student critic chosen by the teacher from one of the other groups is sent to see and hear the group's presentation. The student critic is expected to react with constructive criticism, such as "That sounds fine," "That doesn't seem to make much sense," "Perhaps you should have. . . ."

Step 6	The group is given time to revise their presentation, drawing on the feedback provided by the student critic.
Step 7	The teacher consults briefly with each group to review their presentation plan.
Step 8	Presentations are made, and the class and teacher comment and question as relevant. The teacher or a designated student lists important information from each presentation on the chalkboard (or an overhead transparency).
Step 9	Finally, students are directed to "rapid-read" the *entire* reading assignment, watching for main points and important details.

Notes on GRA: Induces Civility and Constructive Responding

Anecdotal reports (Manzo & Manzo, 1990a) indicate that students involved in the GRA tend to assume required roles in a surprisingly adult manner. Their language, thinking, and even social graces seem to rise to the occasion. The keenest benefit seems to be that students tend to criticize each other in constructive and intelligent ways, probably to reduce the likelihood of being treated sharply when they are critiqued in turn.

FULL CIRCLE TO DISCUSSION

The sections above presented a variety of teacher-directed and peer-group approaches to checking and extending comprehension after reading. Structured experiences with these approaches help to prepare students to participate in more sophisticated forms of classroom discussion. Before turning to the next methods for scaffolding discussion, however, consider some of the ways in which teachers can anticipate and handle the student questions, answers, and comments that can lead a discussion off track or otherwise diminish its impact.

Anticipating Nonproductive Questions, Answers, and Comments

There are numerous ways for students to question, answer, and comment during classroom interactions. Some of these are facilitating and productive, and others are quirky and difficult to handle. Some typical problem situations that tend to arise, and some techniques we have seen veteran teachers use to deal with them are described below. Consider starting a personal journal of useful verbal protocols, or "things to say when. . . ."

Problem:

Students who can't seem to think without talking. They are not really disrespectful but garrulous or irrepressibly talkative. They begin to answer every question whether or not they know the answer.

Remedies:

✦ Avoid eye contact with them.

✦ Occasionally turn your back to them and ask a question while walking away from them so that they can't quite hear it, thus preventing them from answering before others can.

✦ Call a name or a row before asking a question.

✦ Strictly enforce a rule of raising a hand before talking.

✦ Find a reason to talk about the different ways people think and talk. Be sympathetic, but point out that compulsive talkers tend to disrupt the teacher, dissuade others from speaking up, overly dominate a discussion, close out opportunities to listen and learn, appear boorish, and anger others. Stress that this is a problem that can plague a person for the rest of his or her life if not curtailed early.

Problem:

The student who raises the same question that has been raised and answered.

Remedy:

Ask "Does anyone recognize this question?" If no one responds, you have strong evidence that you need to raise and probably answer the question again. If the question or the answer has more than one part, write out key words on the chalkboard.

Problem:

The student who characteristically speaks too low to be heard.

Remedy:

Begin walking to the other side of the room so that the student must project to you, and in the process speak loudly enough for others to hear.

Problem:

Disruptive sounds, such as heating or cooling systems, that prevent class members from hearing one another.

Remedies:

✦ Have students arrange desks so that they face one another.

✦ Repeat students' questions and answers (despite the usual prohibition against doing so).

✦ Explain the problem to the class, and say that you frequently will be calling on someone else to repeat questions and answers to ensure that everyone hears. This also can keep students more alert the first time.

Problem:

Students who fail to participate in responding to recitation-type questions.

Remedies:

✦ Examine your questions. You might be asking "Guess what I'm thinking" questions. All teachers occasionally lapse into this routine.

✦ Provide more wait time: count to five mentally before saying another word, then ask students if they want the question repeated or explained further.

Problem:

Students who do not pay attention or participate in discussions or other class activities.

Remedies:

✦ Reassess what you are asking students to do. Is it meaningful, clear, and doable in the time you are allowing?

✦ Use a *polling* technique to warm up your "audience" and get them involved. The most popular method is to ask questions that require one of two choices, such as those asked in television polls in which one calls a given phone number for each choice. You can also offer more elaborate, content-related choices. Here is an example: "Some people think *The Merchant of Venice* is a put-down of Jews, others think it is a put-down of Christians. Who thinks it is a put-down of Jews? who Christians? Who is undecided? Who has no idea? Let's continue to analyze this play and see whether Shakespeare tips his hand one way or the other."

Problem:

The student who asks a question, gives an answer, or makes a comment that is "out in left field."

Remedies:

✦ Simply say, "I don't quite see the relevance of that. Can you explain further?" Where such responses clearly are characteristic of a certain student and it is clear to the class that you are not being arbitrary, omit the request for further explanation.

✦ Ask if another student can help explain or clarify the question, answer, or comment.

✦ Try to get things going in another direction by simply accepting the response and saying, "Okay, does anyone else have a different point of view or way of answering this question?"

✦ When such a response seems to be intentionally irrelevant, don't forget the power of a stare—or simple silence in response.

The next techniques and methods provide further scaffolding to assist students in actively participating in more traditional forms of class discussion.

Fishbowl*

The Fishbowl technique (Baloche, et al., 1993) is a useful way to raise students' awareness of their own and others' classroom discussion behaviors. Students are seated in two concentric circles (both circles facing inward), with approximately the same number of students in each ring. Students in the inner circle are given a discussion topic and a given time limit. Students in the outer circle are given an inner circle member to observe and a teacher-designed worksheet for recording their observations. When the discussion time is up, outer circle members each give constructive feedback to their "fish." Feedback should focus on discussion behaviors rather than the topic of the discussion or specific points made.

This technique should be structured according to the sophistication level of the group. For optimal structure, assign students to one of the two circles, provide specific discussion prompts for the inner circle, and very specific items on the observation worksheet provided to the outer circle. For more sophisticated groups, and as students become familiar with the technique, participants can be permitted to choose which circle they will be in, and discussion and observation prompts can be more openended. Some ideas for structuring the observation checklist include:

✦ Place a check beside the appropriate item each time the person makes a verbal contribution to the discussion: states a new idea, paraphrases another person's idea, supports or agrees with another person, states an opposing or alternate point, summarizes, makes a humorous remark.

✦ Place a check beside each nonverbal behavior observed: smile, laugh, nod, frown, disinterested expression.

U-Debate**

Some postreading discussion lends itself naturally to a debate-type format. The U-Debate (Athanases, 1988) is a useful structure for teaching students

---

* Baloche, L., Mauger, M. L., Willis, T. M., Filinuk, J. R., & Michalsky, B. V., *Fishbowls, Creative Controversy, Talking Chips: Exploring literature cooperatively.* English Journal © 1983 by the National Council of Teachers of English, reprinted with permission.

** Athanses, S., Developing a classroom community of interpreters. English Journal © 1998 by the National Council of Teachers of English, reprinted with permission.

to engage in this type of discussion. The technique begins with the teacher stating two opposing ideas. Classroom seats are then moved into a "U" shape, with one side representing each opposing idea, and seats in the middle representing a neutral position. Students are directed to find a seat that best represents their opinion. The teacher facilitates the discussion in a typical way, with the difference that participants' views are readily observable to the teacher and one another. Students who select seats at the top of either side of the "U" usually are the most willing to begin the discussion. A lively camaraderie springs up among students seated in each of the opposing positions, and they begin to defer and/or appeal to one another as they attempt to express their points. As students change their opinions or the strength of their views, they are permitted to change their seating position.

Socratic Seminar

The Socratic Seminar is the primary instructional tool of Mortimer Adler's Paideia Proposals for educational reform (1982). Its intent is to engage students in meaningful postreading discussion by minimizing the teacher's direction and maximizing student participation. This is done by laying out a set of specific guidelines for participants, and by the teacher/discussion leader following another set of guidelines for opening the discussion and moving it along. Any text selection may be used, including standard textbook selections. It is helpful to number the lines in the text for easy reference. After everyone has completed the reading, the group is seated in a circle (or around a large table) and the basic ground rules for the discussion are explained (or reviewed).

Socratic Seminar: Guidelines for Participants

1. The purpose of the seminar is understanding of the author's message and the group's interpretations and analysis of it.

2. Every comment or question must be based on a specific portion of the text. The discussion leader may open with a text section to respond to, or may ask for a volunteer to identify a starting point.

3. You do not need to raise your hand; simply take turns as in a casual conversation.

4. Talk to each other, not the teacher.

5. You may make comments, ask questions of the group as a whole, or ask a question of a person by name.

6. You may "pass" when called on.

7. At any time, you may ask participants if they are ready to move to a different portion of the text. If they agree, identify the section you

wish to respond to, read it aloud, and then ask your question or make your comment.

8. Stick to the point. Make notes of ideas you want to come back to.

9. Listen carefully, and ask for clarification when needed.

Socratic Seminar: Guidelines for Teacher/Discussion Leader

1. Identify a portion of the text to begin the discussion. Read the selection aloud, and ask a relevant clarifying question. (With experienced groups, you may ask for a volunteer for this opening step.)

2. Maintain an unintrusive role, communicating through body language the expectation that participants should share responsibility for moving the discussion along. It may help to intentionally avoid eye contact with the person speaking, to encourage him or her to look at and speak to the other participants, rather than you.

3. Watch participants' body language to invite them in ("You don't seem to agree. Can you explain why?"; "Can you give an example to support what she is saying?"). Remember that those who aren't speaking are thinking.

4. Correct all misreadings on the spot.

5. Supply key factual information when needed (but attempt to keep this to a minimum).

6. Coach students on seminar behaviors when needed.

7. Model effective discussion strategies, such as asking for clarification of a question or statement, paraphrasing the text, distinguishing between fact and opinion, identifying conflicting views, and drawing out the reasons for or implications of an answer or a comment.

8. If overly argumentative or nonparticipating members fail to respond to subtle approaches, speak with them privately after the discussion.

9. Conclude the seminar by going around the circle asking each participant to comment briefly on the seminar.

The final step in the Socratic Seminar is a writing prompt based on the text and the points raised in the discussion (steps and guidelines amalgamated from Paley, 1986; Gray, 1988; and Sizer, 1984).

In our view, *Socratic Seminar* is an unfortunate misnomer. The method described above bears scant resemblance to the method practiced by Socrates and his teacher, Plato, in which the teacher's role was that of a "grand inquisitor," posing a question, and responding to questions and answers with ever-more sharp and stinging questions intended to expose faulty assumptions and misinformation. This latter, more genuine version of the Socratic Method, as it has been most familiarly practiced in schools of law, has been referred to as "ritualized combat" (Guinier, Fine, & Balin, 1997).

✦ *After Words* ✦

This chapter underscored the importance of postreading recitation when this traditional practice is part of a program that includes additional means of comprehension development and application. These additional means include a number of teacher-directed and cooperative group activities for bridging to traditional discussion, which is perhaps better referred to as "instructional conversation."

CHAPTER 7

Methods for Vocabulary and Concept Development

The most powerful thing that can be done is to name something.

—Albert Einstein

✦ Fore Words ✦

From the first time one beholds a beach at sunset to the next time your computer or your aspirations experience a megaflop, new images get formed into clearer ideas and ways to think, write, and speak. Improving a student's access to this communication "source code" does not merely facilitate learning, it *is* learning. This chapter is about increasing expertise in teaching the language with which we organic computers interface, store, feel, express, and self-transform.

WHAT'S IN A NAME?

Einstein's comment aptly captures the power of vocabulary acquisition and development. As children learn the words that name the basic elements of their environment, they gain the power to express their needs and wishes. As we learn the words for the more abstract and subtle aspects of experience, we gain the power to reflect on these and to begin to shape our personal value systems and world view, or life filters. The power of words is deeply engrained in every culture. In Judeo-Christian and Muslim cultures, for example, words such as the following slow the heart and evoke a sense of reverence: "And out of the ground the Lord God formed every beast of the field, and every fowl of the air; and brought them unto Adam to see what he would call them: and whatsoever Adam called every living creature, that was the name thereof."

Words are the brain's shorthand system for encoding experience without having to turn its full attention to every item and nuance of sensory experience. Try looking around you—wherever you are at this moment. Imagine that you are experiencing (seeing, hearing, smelling, feeling) every aspect of your current environment for the first time, and try labeling everything you can. Would it be difficult to come up with 100 words? 500? The brain doesn't have to be conscious of each of these things, because it has words for them: the words we know form a lens through which we see (and hear, and read, and sense) the world. Thus, every person, whether scientist, historian, artist, musician, or new-age candlestick maker, experiences the world in a unique way, through a lens fashioned out of a system of naming called *vocabulary*.

Clearly, mastering the information and ideas of any discipline is largely a matter of mastering its vocabulary. Traditional approaches to vocabulary instruction, however, are based on faulty assumptions about word learning, and fail to hook into the enormous innate word-learning capacity of the human brain. This chapter tells of several methods to introduce new vocabulary in ways that teach words and strategies for word learning. The chapter is divided into four main sections: (1) what we know about vocabulary learning and teaching; (2) introducing new words in ways that teach strategies; (3) building silent reading strategies for vocabulary development; (4) postreading vocabulary/concept development, and practice formats for long-term retention.

WHAT WE KNOW ABOUT VOCABULARY LEARNING AND TEACHING

The standard approach to teaching vocabulary is one of the most consistent things about school. On Monday, a list of words appears on the chalkboard. Students copy the words, use a dictionary to look up and write the definition of each word, and write a sentence using it. The words are then to be studied for a test on Friday. While this approach does work for some students some of the time,[1] better vocabulary instruction proves more effective for more students more of the time.

A Metaphor for the Process

Earlier in this text, we introduced the image of a fishing net as a metaphor for schema—the intricate web of information and experience each person has constructed from his or her unique history of experience. Think of vocabulary as the substance from which that net is constructed. Ideas, information, and experience are coded in words, represented by the knots in the fishing net, each connected to all the others by cords of meaning. This is a useful metaphor to keep in mind as we consider the following summary of what is known about the process of vocabulary acquisition.

How We Learn Words

To examine the process of word learning, consider the following characteristics of an *expert* word learner, comparing these to characteristics of a *novice* word learner. Keep in mind that each of these is a learned habit or strategy. Expert word learners:

---

[1] To prove for yourself how ineffective this approach is, say to students one Monday morning that you need to give Friday's test again, since you have misplaced the papers from Friday. Do not allow any cramming for the test. Then, compare Monday's results to Friday's scores and you'll have an index of how foregtful this kind of learning can be.

✦ Notice new words when listening and reading

✦ Are interested in learning new words

✦ Are especially likely to learn words that are encountered in situations marked by strong emotion

✦ Use the situational or textual context to predict possible meanings of the new term, and make a mental note of the word and its predicted meanings to check against future encounters with the word

✦ Connect shades of meaning with personal experiences, images, and examples

✦ Use their knowledge of elements of word meaning (prefixes, suffixes, root words) to predict, confirm, and anchor new word meanings

✦ Mentally "rehearse" the personal connections they have created to link a new word with its meaning.

Now consider the extent to which the traditional word list approach helps to teach these habits and strategies.

✦ The teacher provides the words for study: students are not helped in recognizing and noticing new words.

✦ Traditional approaches rely on the extrinsic motivation of the weekly test, rather than building intrinsic motivation and interest in words and word learning.

✦ Dictionary work rarely generates excitement, enthusiasm, or emotion.

✦ Words are presented in isolation, so there is no opportunity to learn to make use of context.

✦ While some students may expend the extra effort to compose a sentence that actually connects, for the most part students' sentences are vague or inaccurate applications.

✦ Although the word's history is included in the dictionary, few students pay attention to it, and it is not usually required.

✦ When students study word lists for an upcoming test, they usually do so by memorizing the word-for-word definitions and spellings they have looked up, rather than trying to make any personalized, meaningful connections to the ideas represented by the words.

On this view, it is fairly clear that the traditional word list approach does little to teach students how to learn words. Its purpose is to have students memorize definitions. Its expectation is that students will, on their own, make the comparisons, connections, evaluations, applications, and exclusions that will firmly affix the words as solid elements of operational schema—tight knots in their own personally constructed net. But will they?

Do We Need to Do It Better?

It could be that vocabulary instruction comes under the category of "if it ain't broke, don't fix it." However, sound research indicates that the vocabulary level of college-bound 18-year olds has dropped sharply in recent years. In 1940, these students typically knew the meanings of 80% of the words on a standardized reading test. By the mid-1990s, the typical student scored only 30%, which is just a little better than random guessing (Johnson O'Connor Research Foundation, in Dortch, 1995). These figures are likely due, in large measure, to self-selection, the fact that there are far more students today than in 1940 who have declared themselves to be college-bound. Be that as it may, it is evident that students are not being well served by whatever approaches to vocabulary instruction they have experienced. This picture is even more distressing when one considers the implications for thinking, reading, writing, and learning. A measure of a person's vocabulary provides the single best prediction of general (academic) IQ, scholastic aptitude, level of reading comprehension, and grade point average.

Vocabulary acquisition, like improvement of reading comprehension, is an ongoing, lifelong process. To teach someone effective vocabulary learning strategies is to establish a trust account that earns daily compound dividends. Unlike most factual knowledge, vocabulary terms are like self-generative energy packs that unlock doors, offer insights, and automatically grant interesting perspectives, when heard, read, thought, or expressed in speech or writing,

Principles to Guide Vocabulary Instruction

There is an extensive body of research on how words are learned and how to best promote that learning. The next section provides a summary derived from several reviews of this research (Baumann & Kameenui, 1991; Kibby, 1995; Manzo & Manzo, 1990a; Manzo & Sherk, 1971–1972; Nagy, 1988; Stahl & Fairbanks, 1986):

+ Students develop a lifelong interest in learning new words primarily through observation and interaction with others. Intentionally or un-intentionally, teachers communicate their personal attitudes about the importance of word learning and their interest in words.

+ It is far more beneficial to show students how to use strategies for learning word meanings than to require rote memorization of definitions. Only about 20% of an average adult vocabulary of approximately 20,000 words are learned through direct instruction. The rest are learned incidentally, through reading and listening.

✦ Vocabulary is best taught at the "teachable moment"; that is, when the need to know arises. However, it also must be taught regularly and systematically for significant growth to occur.

✦ When a student encounters a new word in everyday experience, he or she will remember it by associating its meaning with the actual or vicarious experience in which the word was encountered. The most effective word learning strategies to teach students are those that most closely resemble natural word learning strategies.

✦ The familiarity of vocabulary in text is one of the most important determinants of students' ability to comprehend. Preteaching selected words from a reading selection before students read greatly improves their comprehension of the material.

✦ Simply noticing unfamiliar words in print and oral language is a fundamental vocabulary learning habit, one that can be developed during silent reading.

✦ Transformation of superficial word knowledge into concept knowledge requires multiple encounters with a word, and analysis of its shades of meanings in a variety of contexts.

✦ Once a student learns a word at the *definition level*, repeated practice and use of the word will solidify its meaning.

✦ The meanings of many unfamiliar words can be predicted based on knowledge of morphemes—prefixes, suffixes, and roots. It is useful to teach word learning strategies based on morphemes, the meaningful elements that constitute words. Just as words combine to form sentences and sentences combine to form paragraphs, morphemes (mainly prefixes, roots, and suffixes) combine to form words. Word = prefix + root + suffix is the general formula for a word in English.

✦ The most important step in improving students' vocabulary is to foster a rich "community of language" within each classroom and across the school to encourage continued vocabulary reinforcement and use outside the classroom.

Selecting Words for Instruction

How many words should you teach each week/month/year? Which words should you teach? The answers, of course, depend partly on your students, partly on your subject, and partly on your instructional emphasis. In general, as they plan each course unit, teachers should identify key terms for concept development. Then, in previewing materials students will read during the unit, vocabulary for preteaching should be identified. Of course, there will be more words that *could* be taught than there will be time. Ruddell (1999, pp. 148–149) offers suggestions for selecting words for prereading, guided reading, and postreading instruction:

1. Select a word for prereading instruction when it is central to the meaning of the selection, and you anticipate that many of your students do not know the meaning of the word as used in this context, and the context does not convey the meaning.
2. Select a word for emphasis in a silent reading format when students are likely to know the word in general, but not in this specific context, or when the context clearly conveys the meaning.
3. Select a word for postreading emphasis when it is central to the knowledge and concept base of the unit, and, because of students' limited background knowledge related to the word, small group and/or whole class discussion is needed to connect the new ideas to prior learning and experience.

METHODS FOR VOCABULARY INTRODUCTION

Introducing key terms from a particular reading selection often is an essential element of prereading instruction. When it is judged to be needed, vocabulary preteaching should meet three basic criteria:

1. To quickly introduce students to words that are likely to be unfamiliar to them
2. To do so in ways that not only provide the word meaning, but permit the teacher to model strategies for learning new words (in doing so, the teacher also models an interest in words and word learning)
3. To establish a low-risk environment in which students can try out and experiment with these word learning strategies

We know of only a few methods that satisfy these criteria. Before we introduce these methods, consider some of the general components that they have in common:

1. They introduce a maximum of five words for a given reading selection.
2. They limit this part of the lesson to a maximum of fifteen minutes.
3. Each method puts the words in display as each is introduced (not the entire list at once).
4. In each case, the word is spoken, written, and defined. This is a crucial component of vocabulary preteaching for several reasons. First, the meaning is given in the simplest terms possible. To see the importance

of this translation step, look at the dictionary-like definitions of these words, and try translating them into "student" language:

Potential: "Capable of being but not yet in existence; latent."

Expansion: "The act or process of expanding."

This component is also crucial because it is contrary to one of the most basic "teacher scripts" we have internalized through years of traditional classroom experience: after the teacher writes a word on the board, she or he next asks, "Can anyone tell me what this word means?" What this question does, in effect, is eliminate a large portion of the class—all those who don't have a clue as to the word's meaning. When the teacher says instead, "This word is _____, and it means _____," everyone is still able to participate.

5. The teacher then introduces a strategy for connecting the new word with its meaning, and invites volunteers to try out the strategy. At this point, the teacher should watch for and encourage contributions from students who might not have known the meaning of the word, and who might not otherwise have been able to participate.

6. As suggested above, the teacher tries to keep the interactions brief and to the point.

7. When possible, time should be given for students to at least begin the reading immediately following the vocabulary preteaching. When it is not possible to have them do the entire reading in class, be sure to have students write the pretaught words and keep them with the reading assignment to be done later.

The word learning strategies used in the methods in this section represent different ways of connecting the new word with some schema element that is related to the new word meaning. In the Keyword Vocabulary method, the schema element is a visual image, in the Subjective Approach to Vocabulary, it is an image of a personal experience, and in Motor Imaging, it is a gestural pantomime that suggests the new word meaning. The fourth method in this section, Incidental Morpheme Analysis, is different in nature from the first three. It is a kind of guided guessing game that teaches students to draw on what they already know about the structural elements of words (prefixes, suffixes, and roots), in the form of other words they know, and to apply this knowledge to predict the meaning of the new word. Incidental Morpheme Analysis, as its name implies, can be used only incidentally—when the word to be used is composed of familiar word elements. It will be used fairly infrequently, but when the opportunity arises, it is a powerful way to teach students an important independent word learning strategy.

Keyword Vocabulary Method

The Keyword Vocabulary method is based on an ancient memory technique that dates back to the time when unschooled messengers had to recall long and explicit details. In this application, a new word is linked to a mental image that it suggests, and that in turn is connected in some logical way to the actual meaning of the word. The object is to create mental images that are easy to recall because they are easy to visualize, and even odd or amusing.

Steps in the Keyword Vocabulary Method

Step 1   Write the word on the chalkboard, pronounce it, and tell what it means.

Step 2   Ask students to come up with a visual image that will help them remember the word meaning. For example, *plateau* (a large grassy flatland) could be linked to the image of a huge upside-down green dinner plate. *Collage* (an artwork created by random combination of bits and pieces of other pictures and/or objects) could be linked to the image of a bulletin board filled with pictures of different colleges. *Amulet* (a charm worn around the neck to ward off evil forces) could be linked to the image of an arm bracelet with an odd charm on it.

Step 3   As an optional step, students can be directed to write each word and its meaning, and draw a simple line drawing or stick figure to represent their visual image connector. Another option is to have students record the words in a form that can be used for later review by writing the word and drawing their picture representation on the front of a note card, and writing the meaning on the back. This is a useful technique for studying lengthy word lists in preparation for standardized tests such as the SAT.

Notes on Keyword Vocabulary

The Keyword Vocabulary method has been reported to be effective in learning content material (Konopak & Williams, 1988; Levin et al., 1986) and with learning-disabled students (Condus, Marshall, & Miller, 1986; Guthrie, 1984). Those who have studied Keyword the most extensively maintain that it helps students to learn how to form connections and to develop elaborations on concepts (Pressley, Johnson, & Symons, 1987; Pressley, Levin, & MacDaniel, 1987; Pressley, Levin, & Miller, 1981).

A Keyword Vocabulary lesson usually sparks an interesting instructional conversation in which the teacher and students come to the "word workbench" together in an attempt to capture and represent word meanings in memorable ways. It also tends to incidentally reveal students' thought processes, thus making it a useful diagnostic teaching tool.

The next method has long been popular for concentrated vocabulary study. It is shown here for use on those occasions when key subject area vocabulary terms are composed of familiar prefixes, suffixes and/or roots.

Subjective Approach to Vocabulary (SAV)

The Subjective Approach to Vocabulary (Manzo, 1983) builds on what students already know by urging them to find personal experiences or other associations with which to anchor the sometimes ethereal definitions of new terms found in dictionaries. The method helps students remember meanings of important content-related terms while illustrating how they might use the same strategy in self-directed word learning. In the Subjective Approach to Vocabulary, the teacher engages students in a highly inter-active "talk-through" designed to have them learn how to use their own and other students' experiences and tellings as a foundation for acquiring new word meanings. In this way, the biographies of individual lives become connected to the stories of the words and ideas offered in school. SAV can be particularly useful for providing multicultural outlooks and for working with second-language students. It gives teacher and students access to the alternative ways students may be processing and interpreting the world around them.

Steps in the Subjective Approach to Vocabulary

Step 1   Write the word on the chalkboard, pronounce it, and tell what it means. Direct students to write the word and its *objective* meaning on their own paper.

Step 2   Ask students to try to think of a personal experience they are reminded of by the word meaning. (The teacher should have an example or two in mind for each word, in case students are especially slow in coming up with their own. Usually, once they have heard one example, they will quickly begin to come up with their own). Call on several volunteers to tell their *subjective* associations. Tell students to try to picture their association as clearly as they can, and to think about how it connects to the new word meaning.

Step 3   Tell students to record their subjective association for the word underneath the objective meaning. They can record an association they volunteered in class, or one that they thought of but did not state, or one offered by another class member. See Figure 7.1 for a sample SAV lesson.

Step 4   *Optional:* Distribute or guide students in preparing a work-sheet consisting of a large square divided into four smaller

Figure 7.1
Subjective Approach to Vocabulary:—sample lesson.

The word "arboreal" was in a seventh-grade science text. The teacher wrote the word on the board and gave the meaning: "The word *arboreal* means 'having to do with trees or living in trees.'" A few examples were given: "Monkeys are arboreal animals; the word *arboreal* comes from the word *arbor,* as in Arbor Day, the day put aside to plant trees." The subjective-based aspect of the lesson began at this point. Explaining her question, the teacher added, "It will be easier for you to learn and remember this new term if you can think of some personal images or experiences which you can picture with it."

One student suggested, "The word reminds me of how my mother killed my peanut tree that we brought home from Georgia by overwatering it." To this, another student added, humorously, "That sounds like a 'tragic arboreal' experience." In that same humorous vein, another student asked, rhetorically, "Did you say that *arboreal* means 'living and swingin' in trees(?),' cause I think my little brother is arboreal!"

The teacher then asked if anyone had formed a new meaning for *arboreal.* "It sounds to me like 'anything to do with trees,'" one student volunteered. The teacher then directed the class to record the word *arboreal* in their notebooks with the objective meaning she had provided and a parenthetical note on their initial and subsequent personal associations with the word.

---

squares. There should be one four-section square for each word introduced. Have students write the word in the top-left section of a larger square, its objective definition in the top-right section, their subjective association in the bottom-left section, and a line drawing or stick figure illustration in the bottom-right section.

Notes on the Subjective Approach to Vocabulary

It is hard to tell how readily a class will take to an SAV lesson on its initial presentation. Group size may be an important factor. For example, the second author once used SAV with a tenth-grade English class of only nine students. When asked for associations with five words (*adipose, adage, accrual, agape, alimentary*), the students stared at me blankly. The very next hour, with a little trepidation, I trotted out the same five words and another tenth-grade class of fifteen students was off and running. Soon they were composing as well as associating: "I picture Royal Stadium [home of the Kansas City Royals] when we were down but not out and came back to win the pennant and the Series; it's not over til the 'adipose' lady sings." A large group sometimes may be necessary to increase the chance of at least one extrovert stirring the class's imagination and responding.

In a study with sixth-grade subjects (Casale & Manzo, 1983), SAV was found to be considerably better than traditional (dictionary "look-up" and sentence-writing) approaches to vocabulary instruction. However, it was slightly less effective than the approach described next, which urges teacher and students to employ physical, or motor, associations to a greater extent than is usual in the sedentary context of schooling.

Motor Imaging

Motor Imaging (Casale [now Manzo], 1985) draws on the physical-sensory as well as cognitive and affective domains of learning. The underlying principle of this method is akin to an expression that says, "Nothing is in the intellect which was not first in the senses."

Developmental psychologists have observed that infants learn to represent meaning with gross motor movements. Over time, these motoric representations, or *motor meanings* are increasingly refined until they are internalized as *symbolic meanings*, in Piaget's terminology. Apparently our initial ways of learning consist almost exclusively of tactile and sensory-motor experiences. While this is no great surprise, since that is all babies can do, we seem to have overlooked the fact that this aspect of learning may remain active long into human development.

Steps in Motor Imaging

Step 1   Write the word on the chalkboard, pronounce it, and tell what it means.

Step 2   Tell students to imagine a simple gesture, or pantomime for the word meaning that you might use to "show" the word meaning, or that you might use when speaking the word in context.

Step 3   On the teacher's signal, students "do" their gestures, or pantomimes simultaneously.

Step 4   While observing the student's pantomimes, choose one of the most common ones, show this gesture to all the students, and tell them that when you point to the word, they are to do the selected gesture while saying the word aloud.

Step 5   Introduce each of the words to be pretaught in this way. As words are added to the list, when you point to the word for students to say and pantomime, go back to earlier words to quickly review these word/pantomime connections.

Step 6   Now that each of the new words has been connected to a pantomime, tell students that this time, when you point to a word, they are to do the pantomime and say the meaning. Practice the words in this way, in mixed up order, for several minutes.

Figure 7.2 presents some examples from a Motor Imaging lesson.

Notes on Motor Imaging
The same comparison study cited above, of a cognitive (dictionary), affective (subjective association), and this physical-sensory, motor approach to vocabulary, showed the Motor Imaging method to be significantly better on four out of five vocabulary measures (Casale [now Manzo] & Manzo, 1983). It appears that the highest forms of learning have a most humble, if not primitive foundation.

The promising implication of this point is that students at every level of intellectual ability seem to share a common capacity for physical-associative learning. This makes Motor Imaging, and possibly other motor-based methods yet to be devised, especially promising possibilities for heterogeneously grouped students.

Morpheme Analysis

A teacher identifies core concept words in the text—words like *ecology* in science, *quadrangle* in math, *millennium* in social studies, *participle* in grammar, or *prologue* in literature—that are composed of elements likely to be familiar to students.

Figure 7.2
Motor imaging examples.

New Word	Language Meaning	Motor Meaning
Appropriate	Right or fit for a certain purpose	Both palms together, matching perfectly
Convey	Take or carry from one place to another	Both hands together, palms upward, moving from one side to the other
Woe	Great sadness or trouble	One or both hands over the eyes, head tilted forward
Dazzle	Shine or reflect brightly	Palms close together, facing outward, fingers spread
Utmost	The very highest or most	One or both hands reaching up as far as possible
Abode	Place where you live	Hands meeting above the head in a triangular "roof" shape

A graphic organizer for vocabulary acquisition such as that shown in Figure 7.3 is helpful for analyzing the morphemes from which unfamiliar words are constructed. The target word, correctly spelled, is written in the center of the graphic by the teacher and copied by the students. The teacher asks the students to use their knowledge to identify possible prefixes, roots, and suffixes that are embedded in the word. Students then define the target word as best they can, using clues from their knowledge of the parts of the word. Next, they share their definitions with a partner or in a small group. To conclude this first step, the pair or group composes one definition and writes it on the chalkboard. Groups compare their definitions and begin to discuss similarities and differences. When the root of the target word begins to emerge in the discussion, the teacher shares the dictionary etymology with the students, inserting this in the section of the graphic labeled "roots."

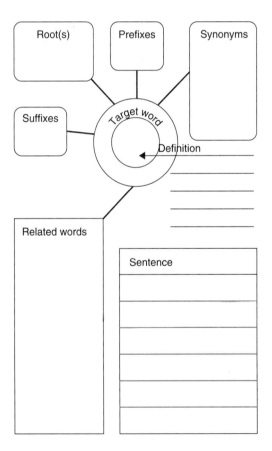

Figure 7.3
Graphic organizer for morpheme analysis.

Then, the teacher writes the prime dictionary definition in the appropriate space on an overhead transparency copy of the graphic. The students compare their definitions with that written by the teacher. They discuss similarities between definitions, with emphasis on why the word means what it means and why it is spelled as it is. Often, the students are very close in their definitions, and since learning what a thing is *not* can be very helpful in understanding what it *is*, the discussion of differences between the conventional and unconventional definitions helps everyone get closer to actually knowing the word.

The teacher and students create an exemplary sentence using the target word, based on what they've found together to that point. The teacher refers the students to the actual definition, as the context of the discussion requires. This keeps the focus on the actual target of the lesson.

Next, students brainstorm synonyms for the target word. If a word can be substituted in the sentence and still make the same sense, it must be a synonym. Sometimes, slight changes in the sentence are necessary to retain sense, but often the substitute word will not fit at all. Then the question becomes, "Is this a related word or a discard?" (Related words are words similar in meaning, though not synonymous, or words with the same root.) When the morpheme graphic is complete, students have a picture of the meaning of a word and, more important, a clear idea of how the word means what it does.

METHODS FOR DEVELOPING STRATEGIES FOR HANDLING VOCABULARY DURING SILENT READING

An important goal of vocabulary instruction is to teach students to notice unfamiliar words when they are reading, and to develop a variety of strategies for predicting and confirming the meanings of these words. One way to do this is the straightforward strategy approach represented in the name of the Context, Structure, Sound, Reference method described first below. The next method in this section, Contextual Redefinition, focuses on the process of using context to predict word meanings. The next three methods, the Community of Language Approach, the Secret Language Police and the Vocabulary Self-Collection Strategy, focus on developing the habit of realizing that a word is unfamiliar when it is encountered in print or oral language.

Context, Structure, Sound, Reference: The Basic Strategy

Context, Structure, Sound, Reference is a good basic strategy for handling unfamiliar words encountered while reading (Gray, 1946; Ruddell, 1997).

1. Read to the end of the sentence. Can you guess the meaning? Are there any clues in the surrounding sentences or paragraphs that help

you? Now do you have a pretty good idea of the meaning? Does it make sense? If so, keep right on reading.

If not,

2. Look at the parts of the word. Are there prefixes or roots that you know? Do the suffixes or inflections (plurals, past tense, etc.) help you? Combine this information with context information to arrive at a meaning. Does it make sense? If so, go right on reading.

If not,

3. Try to pronounce the word. When you hear it, does it sound like a word you already know? If not, are there letters or letter combinations that help (e.g., the 'ct' in *tract* as opposed to the 'ck' in *track*)? Combine this information with information from context. Does it make sense? If so, go right on reading.

If not,

4. Look for footnotes or margin notes. Check the glossary or a dictionary. Ask someone for help: a friend, or me, or anyone else. Combine this information with information from context. Does it make sense?

Contextual Redefinition Strategy: Using Context to Predict Word Meanings

Typically, new words are encountered in the following sequence: context, isolation, context (Putnam, Bader, & Bean, 1988). What this means is that when readers encounter an unfamiliar word in context, they try to figure out its meaning from the context, and then, if unsuccessful, seek meaning from another source, such as a dictionary or another person. Finally, they return to the original context to make better sense of both the word and the context. The Contextual Redefinition Strategy (Cunningham, Cunningham, & Arthur, 1981) applies this natural process to a simple format for classroom instruction (Tierney, Readence, & Dishner, 1990). Although this method is used before reading, it's goal is to model and provide practice in an important "during reading" vocabulary strategy.

Steps in Contextual Redefinition

To prepare for using this method, first select target words from the reading selection. Then, for each word, write one or more sentences that provide reasonable clues to the word meaning. The sentences may come from the selection itself, if these provide reasonable clues.

1. Write each target word on the chalkboard or overhead and ask students to guess the word meaning. Students should be encouraged to discuss

their ideas, and try to come to a reasonable consensus on their predicted meaning for each word.

2. Present each target word in the context sentence(s) you have prepared.
   Have students revise their predictions for each word's meaning, again
   encouraging them to provide the reasons for their ideas, and building
   on one another's thoughts to come to a consensus.

3. Ask a volunteer to look up the word in the dictionary, and to compare
   the dictionary definition with their predictions. This step can stir a
   very productive instructional conversation, since dictionary definitions
   can sometimes be too abstract for easy interpretation, or the word
   could have been used in some unusual or ironic way.

Notes on Contextual Redefinition

This method teaches youngsters that context can provide clues to word
meaning (Gipe, 1978–1979), but cannot be relied upon to fully reveal word
meanings in all cases. Teaching students to over-rely on context clues is
one of the great errors that tends to be made in vocabulary strategy instruction. A less-structured approach to calling student attention to context
clues is to provide a list of words for students to watch for while reading
an assignment. When they come to each of the words, they are to write a
predicted meaning and tell what clues they used to make the prediction.

Community of Language Approach: Attending to Language in the Environment

One of the easiest and most effective things that can be done to improve
reading, word learning, and oral written language is to elevate the vocabulary used in a class, subject, or ideally, the entire school. We know of at
least one situation in which all of the teachers in a junior high school
adopted a list of thirty very difficult words from a test-preparation manual.
Rather than teaching these words explicitly or assigning them to students,
each teacher made a conscious daily effort to use the words whenever
and wherever possible. Teachers watched for opportunities to use the
words in appropriate contexts and sometimes even created contexts as
an excuse to use the words. Throughout the spring semester, students
heard these thirty words in math class, science lab, shop, art, gym, and
even on morning announcements. In only a few weeks' time, students
could be heard using the words in casual conversations in the hallways
and cafeteria. The teachers effectively had created an elevated community
of language (Manzo & Manzo, 1990a).

The impact of a simple incidental learning plan like this one cannot be
exaggerated. It builds student respect for teachers as models of language,
reinforces reading vocabulary, raises word consciousness and precision
in thinking, and boosts standardized test scores. This seemingly incidental
approach can have an even more important and far-reaching effect: stu-

dents will take their new oral language home and, in turn, incidentally share it with their family and friends. This can elevate the levels of language and precision in thinking in students' families and in the community at large, thereby reaching children who have not yet started school as well as parents who have long since left it.

The Secret Language Police: Weaving New Words into the Environment

The *Secret Language Police* (Baines, 1998 pp. 209–210) is an effective approach to teaching students to pay attention to words around them:*

Steps in the Secret Language Police

Step 1   Designate two students in class to serve as the secret language police.

Step 2   The secret language police have the job of communicating the words and definitions of two bonus vocabulary words to other members of class.

Step 3   The secret language police cannot directly state, "These are the bonus words and they mean. . . ," but they should use the words in their own comments during class.

Step 4   The secret language police are encouraged to spread the words around to the principal and to other teachers. If the secret language police convince the principal (or whoever makes the school announcements) to use their words over the public address system, they receive five extra points on the exam of their choice. If they spot one of their words in a newspaper, magazine, book, or web site and highlight it for the class before the day of the exam, they receive another five points.

Vocabulary Self-Collection Strategy (VSS): Developing Independence in Identifying Unfamiliar Words and Predicting and Clarifying Meanings

The Vocabulary Self-Collection method (Haggard, 1982, 1986) is a cooperative structure that provides practice in identifying important terms and using context to predict meaning. Although it takes place after students have read, its goal is to teach students to identify important key terms as they read, and to access appropriate sources—from context, to dictionary, to other people—to obtain meaningful definitions.

---

* Excerpts from "The future of the written word," by L. Baines, in J. Simmons and L. Baines (Eds.), *Language Study* in middle school, high school and beyond: Views on enhancing the study of language. Newark, DE: International Reading Association. © 1998 by the International Reading. Reprinted with permission of L. Baines and the International Reading Association.

Steps in the Vocabulary Self-Collection Strategy

Step 1   **Preparation:** Use this method with concept-rich reading selections that contain several important vocabulary terms. Identify the terms you would expect students to have difficulty with. When using VSS for the first time with a group of students, prepare an example (described below) to use in introducing the method. After students have completed the reading assignment and some type of comprehension check, form small groups (nominating teams) of two to five students.

Step 2   Small-group work: Each group's task is to identify and nominate one vocabulary word from the reading assignment for further emphasis. When the team has agreed on a word, they prepare the following information for the team spokesperson to present to the rest of the class. (When this activity is new to a group, the teacher gives a previously prepared example.)

Step 3   Read the word in context.

Step 4   Tell what the group thinks the word means (they may use context and/or any other resources available in the classroom).

Step 5   Explain why the group thinks the word should be emphasized.

Step 6   Whole-class reporting: Each group's spokesperson provides the information their groups have prepared. The teacher facilitates by writing the words and meanings on the chalkboard, along with any additional information and clarifications provided by the class.

Step 7   Recording: Students record the information from the chalkboard in their vocabulary notebooks or journals.

This method provides a natural link to the next level of postreading vocabulary/concept development.

METHODS FOR POSTREADING VOCABULARY/CONCEPT DEVELOPMENT

Once a new word has been noticed and its meaning has been either predicted or superficially determined, it can be thought of as clinging lightly to the appropriate schema location. To more fully learn the word, it needs to be more tightly affixed. This is achieved through cross-referencing it with numerous other bits of information and experience, and through repeated exposure. Word knowledge is transformed into concept understanding by means of inclusion, exclusion, subordination, and superordination:

1. *Inclusion:* What other words belong in the same category with this word? What are its relevant characteristics or properties? What are some specific examples/applications of the word?

2. *Exclusion:* What similar words do not belong in the same category with this word? What are some related but inappropriate examples/ applications? What are some non-relevant characteristics?

3. *Subordination:* What are some words that would fall into subcategories of this word?

4. *Superordination:* What broader category does this word fall under?

This section deals with the deepening of understanding that converts word meanings to concept knowledge. The following section provides activities for repetition and practice.

Typical to Technical Meaning Approach

Common words often have special, technical applications in a particular content area. For example, the word *true* is used in mechanics to indicate that gears are well synchronized, hence, *not-true* means poorly synchronized. Today this phenomenon occurs most with tech terms like *cookies* and *spam*. In the Typical to Technical Meaning Approach (Welker, 1987), the teacher prepares a worksheet exercise that provides practice in using a term in both its typical and its technical meanings. While these practice sheets require considerable preparation time, once students have become familiar with the format, the teacher simply can ask, "Do we have any terms in today's material for which there is a common as well as a technical meaning?" and the rest of the lesson will unfold from previous practice.*

Steps in the Typical to Technical Meaning Approach

Step 1   Discuss a term's common meanings, then introduce its technical meaning.

Step 2   Have students complete a word-to-meaning exercise, matching each term with both its common and its technical meaning (see part 1 in Figure 7.4). Then have students complete a cloze-type exercise, filling in the blanks where the terms are used in either the typical or technical sense (see part 2 in Figure 7.4).

Step 3   Briefly discuss students' responses prior to presenting information based on technical uses of the terms.

---

*Excerpt from "Open to suggestion: Going from typical to technical meaning," by W. A. Walker, *Journal of Reading* 31. © 1987 by the International Reading Association. Reprinted with permission of W. A. Walker and the International Reading Association.

Figure 7.4
Typical to Technical Meaning exercises.

Part 1
Directions: For each term below, write the letter of its common meaning, and its technical meaning under the headings given.

Terms	**Common Meaning**	**Technical Meaning**
acute		
supplementary		
complementary		
angle		

Meanings

A. A person's point of view

B. Making whole, or completing something

C. Something additional to the basic requirements

D. Space between two lines or surfaces that meet

E. Having a sharp point

F. Either of two angles that combine to equal 90 degrees

G. An angle which is less than 90 degrees in value

H. Either of two angles that together form exactly 180 degrees

Part 2
Directions: Select the best word from the word bank to complete each sentence below. Each word will be used twice.

Sentences

1. The sword had a very _____ cutting edge.

2. The _____ angle for a 50-degree angle is a 40-degree angle.

3. Our reading textbook comes with _____ materials such as workbooks and ditto sheets.

4. If an angle is 53 degrees, it is called an _____ angle.

5. A black tie with a white shirt would be considered a _____ match.

6. Now that I have gotten my thoughts on the subject, what is your _____ (or opinion) on the matter?

7. A pie can be sliced into pieces with many different _____.

8. Two angles that together equal 180 degrees are _____ angles.

Word Bank

complementary   acute   angle   supplementary

Source: "From SAVOR the word to reinforce vocabulary in the content areas," by E. L. Stieglitz and V. S. Stieglitz, *Journal of Reading* 25, pp. 46–51. © 1981 by International Reading Association. Reprinted with permission of E. L. Stieglitz and the International Reading Association.

Subject Area Vocabulary Reinforcement (SAVOR)

Learning is a process of placing new information into existing categories until a special feature that does not fit is encountered. Then a new category must be created to expand schema. Semantic Feature Analysis (Johnson & Pearson, 1984) is a method designed to permit students to engage in this process in a conscious and focused way. A variation on this method, called Subject Area Vocabulary Reinforcement (SAVOR) (Stieglitz & Stieglitz, 1981), is designed specifically for content area use.

Steps in SAVOR

Step 1 Identify a category of words. Then have students brainstorm words that fit in this category, and list these examples in a column on their own paper.

Step 2 Then have students brainstorm specific features of the words they have listed. These features are listed as column headings across the top of their paper (see Figure 7.5 for an example of how the chart is constructed).

Step 3 Next, have students fill in the charts individually, using plus (+) or minus (−) signs to indicate whether each word has a particular feature.

Step 4 After students have completed their charts, the teacher encourages discussion about the patterns of pluses and minuses and to discover the uniqueness of each word.

As students gain experience with the Semantic Feature Analysis format, the teacher may wish to switch from a plus/minus system to a numerical

Figure 7.5
Semantic Feature Analysis in mathematics.

Shapes	Four Sided	All Curved or Rounded Lines	Line Segment	Sides Equal in Length	Right Angles
Triangle	−	−	+	+	+
Rectangle	+	−	+	−	+
Parallelogram	+	−	+	+	+
Circle	−	+	−	−	−
Trapezoid	+ −	−	+	−	−
Semicircle	−	+	+	−	−
Square	+	−	+	+	+

system (0 = none, 1 = some, 2 = much, 3 = all). The method is viewed as a culminating activity for reinforcing and expanding concepts introduced in the conventional content area lesson or following reading. It is particularly suitable for clarifying frequently confused terms.

Notes on SAVOR

Semantic Feature Analysis has been found to be significantly more effective than traditional methods for this purpose (Johnson, Toms-Bronowski, & Pittelman, 1982). It also has been shown to effectively improve content area reading vocabulary and comprehension in learning-disabled adolescents (Anders, Bos, & Filip, 1984).

Cultural-Academic Trivia

The title of this method, Cultural-Academic Trivia (CAT) (Manzo, 1970b, 1985), refers to common cultural learnings and associations that are found in our language as frequently used metaphors and allusions to explain feelings, facts, and concepts. In initial field tests of this method, students felt it was quite appropriate that the word *trivia* appeared in the title. In time, however, as their connections and fund of academic information, vocabulary, and allusions grew, they concluded that it is minds that can be trivial, not information. This prompted the idea that the game should be called *Cultural-Academic Treasures*.

Steps in Cultural-Academic Trivia

Step 1   The class is divided into two groups. A chairperson is assigned to each group and given a set of index cards initially prepared by the teacher and subsequently added to by students and the teacher. On the front of each card is a word or phrase with a number from 1 to 3 designating its relative difficulty. On the reverse side is an explanation or definition of the word or phrase.

Step 2   The chairperson of one group chooses and writes a word or phrase on the chalkboard and then asks students in the other group if they know that word or phrase. All the information gained from the members of a group constitutes that group's total response. If that information amounts to merely an identification or recognition of the word or phrase, only the number describing the level of difficulty (from 1 to 3) is awarded to the group. If any worthwhile elaboration, as determined by the teacher, also is contributed, the score is doubled. Conversely, if the students on one team cannot respond successfully, the opposing team is given the opportunity to win points.

Example.   In a high school class, the word *utopia* might be assigned a difficulty level of 2. If one team volunteers that the word means "a perfect political and social system," they gain the two basic points. If team members add that *utopia* is also the title of a book by Sir Thomas More, or that it came from Greek, they receive two additional points. After the first round of the game, students are asked to submit terms they have selected from their reading, viewing, and living environments.

Notes on Cultural-Academic *Treasures*

Students' contributions are essential if students are to be resensitized to the language they encounter about them but tend to block out because the unfamiliar can cause undue dissonance. In the particular setting in which this game was first played, the first author treated the cards as admission tickets to class. Students who arrived without one were sent scurrying to the library to find an appropriate term. Today, we would urge students to browse the Internet for new and poignant terms. See Figure 7.6 for some indications of this phenomenon.

Of course, not all words are created equal. The success of this game-like method hinges on the terms used. Well-selected words and phrases

Figure 7.6

Tech talk—new members to our community of language and allusions.

Technology is the language du jour. It permeates our style of speaking/writing and is an analogical, or metaphorical means of thinking and hence communicating. Vocabulary knowledge itself could be likened to a computer's random access memory (RAM). The human equivalent of RAM pretty much defines the type and sophistication level of the learning software, or content and concepts, that a mind will be easily able to recognize and run. Of course, this need not be the case. RAM is mechanical, fixed, unreflective, and indeed bogs down with demand. Minds are organic, have no apparent limitations, and can reflect on and, with proper stimulation, restructure themselves in ways that actually permit them to grow greater, wiser, and more efficient with each additional word and concept that is strategically added. If there is a limit to the mind's capacity to learn, we have yet to discover it; thus far it seems to expand further with each breakthrough means of teaching it.

In any case, once it was trains that captured human imagination with images like "building up a head of steam"; now we speak of someone's "bandwidth" to describe their capacity, or ask ourselves if we have enough "cycles" to get something done. New dictionaries are listing between 300 and 400 new and new-meaning words.

By the way (or BTW, in e-mail lingo), if you need a dictionary before one is available for terms like *digerati* or *cookie* or *Netiquette,* try WWW.Whatis.com.

should key students to central, or schema-enhancing, academic ideas and allusions (e.g., hieroglyphics, Communist Manifesto, citizen's arrest, Chaucer). If the teacher intends to develop students' sophistication in just one area, the name of the game can be altered accordingly, for example, BAT (Biological-Academic Trivia) or HAT (Historical-Academic Trivia).

Themed Vocabulary Study, Webbing, and Semantic Clustering

One of the most rational means of vocabulary enrichment is based on grouping words by themes. *Themed vocabulary study*, also called *webbing* and *semantic clustering* (Marzano & Marzano, 1988), permits students to take well known, partially known, and barely recognized words and link them together into a semantic web that will catch and hold yet-newer words as well as nuances of meaning and connotation for familiar words. Paradoxically, it helps students understand that words do not always have precise, distinct, and unchanging meanings (Anderson & Nagy, 1989). Most importantly, themed vocabulary study imparts an effective strategy for lifelong word learning.

Steps in Themed Vocabulary Study

Step 1 Identify a theme. For example, the theme "talk" is used in Figure 7.7. As shown in this example, the inner cluster reflects words as might be known by a second grader, the outward cluster words known by most sixth graders, and the outermost cluster as should be known by college students.

Step 2 Ask students to state words they think are related to the theme.

Step 3 If necessary, use dictionaries to check word meanings and to find additional synonyms, antonyms, and subtly different meanings.

Step 4 Link the relevant words to one another (with brief definitions) in the form of a semantic map or web as shown in the figure.

Step 5 Reinforce and evaluate by testing students' recall of word meanings and distinctions by having them write sentences or descriptive pieces designed to elicit the new words.

Notes on Themed Vocabulary Study

Themes for vocabulary study can be selected based on the guiding concept of instructional units: the possibilities are as broad as one's imagination. Here are some themes to consider for general word study that we have found to be of particular interest to middle and senior high school students:

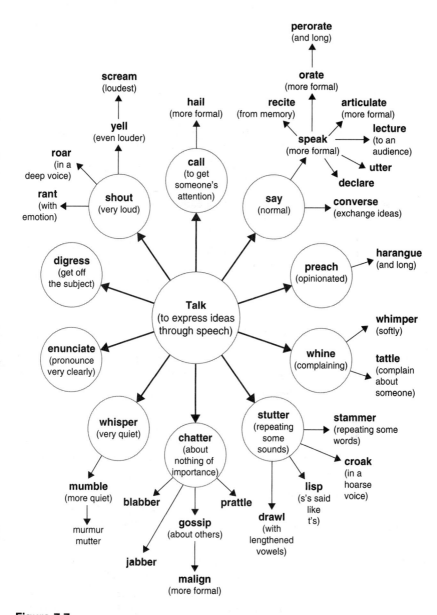

Figure 7.7
Themed vocabulary study—semantic cluster web for *talk.*
Source: Baines, L., Language study in *middle school, high school and beyond: Views on enhancing the study of language.* International Reading Association © 1998.

+ Noncomplimentary but nonvulgar terms (pesky, brusque, prissy, scattered, antsy, bawdy, addlebrained)

+ Behavior-related terms (manners, antsy, comportment, deportment, inappropriate, maladaptive, poised, irascible)

+ Character traits (endurance, restraint, perseverance, reflection, tolerance)

+ Thinking terms (abstract, concrete, rational, irrational, creative, critical, cognitive, diffusive, constructive, coherent)

+ Temperament labels (sanguine, industrious, hyper, choleric, mercurial, pensive)

+ Attitudes (positive, negative, hostile, aggressive, assertive, constructive)

The impact of themed vocabulary study can be greatly amplified by combining it with other vocabulary methods previously described. It also can be linked to the next method as an incidental means of building word power.

Multimedia Vocabulary Review

Two formats are suggested by Baines (1998) for transforming vocabulary worksheets into a multimedia experience. The first has students working in pairs to create "word posters":

1. Place students in pairs.

2. Give each pair of students the responsibility for one vocabulary word.

3. Give students ten minutes to illustrate their word. Students may draw, cut out pictures in magazines, use computer clip art, or use images from the Internet. After the images have been selected (printed and cut out), students should paste them on a large piece of posterboard and beside it write their own brief definition in large letters. Encourage students to use mnemonic devices.

4. Have the students explain their posters, then perform a live thirty-second skit that illustrates the meaning of their word.

5. Give an extra point on the next vocabulary test to the first student each day to use one of the vocabulary words in class in "everyday conversation."

6. If more than one class has the same vocabulary words, place all the posterboards with the same words in the same area. Hang the posterboards conspicuously around the room until the exam is given.

The second format is the *vocabulary chain e-mail* (pp. 208–209):

1. Create a flowchart with PowerPoint, Persuasion, or another presentation software package. If you do not have access to these, use a ruler. Draw a flowchart in which one green box is at the top, five red boxes are under the top green box, and five more blue boxes are under each of the red boxes. This is a flowchart for 31 students that is easily modifiable for more or fewer students.

2. Give the student whose name is in the top green box the vocabulary list a day before you hand it out to the rest of the class. The student should write definitions of the words, be able to pronounce them correctly, and use them in a sentence.

3. The next day, speak individually with the student whose name is in the top green box. Answer any questions he or she might have about the vocabulary. Then, hand out the list of vocabulary words to the rest of the class.

4. A day or two before the vocabulary test, the student whose name is in the top green box e-mails or calls the students whose names appear in the five red boxes and helps them review for the vocabulary test. Then, each of the students whose names appear in the five red boxes e-mails or calls each of the students whose names appear in the five blue boxes. By the day of the exam, everyone in class has received an e-mail message or a telephone call and has reviewed for the exam.

5. Shift responsibilities weekly. At the end of the term, give a prize to the individual whose name was in the top green box when the class scored the highest on the exam.

QuestMagnet for Pioneering Minds—Join the Revolution

Where vocabulary/concept development is concerned, there are two interacting issues. First and foremost, few educators seem to understand just how important vocabulary acquisition is (not one principal in a recent literacy leadership institute expressed any interest whatsoever in the topic, nor in a doctoral-level literacy course did any student choose it for a focus topic). Relatedly, while there are solid methods, there are no integrated, wraparound approaches to ensure that it occurs—that is, "surroundsound" strategies that are equal to the several different and overlapping ways by which kids acquire concepts, content, and language proficiency. Each of the methods presented in this chapter has strengths, but individually they have some weaknesses as well. Weaknesses range from methods that some teachers would find too mechanical, to others that may be too much of a digression from the content, to yet others that require school or department leadership, planning, and cooperation. See if you can envision a cohesive, wraparound program that would make school a place where vocabulary and concept acquisition occurs more soundly, systematically, and effectively. Since we already know a good deal, much of what needs to be done may require little more than skillful synthesis of off-the-shelf parts and procedures.

✦   *After Words*   ✦

This chapter laid out a technology for building better thinking—one word and concept at a time. Methods were described for teaching potentially difficult words before students begin to read a selection. Other methods were described for helping students deal with unfamiliar words encountered while reading. Followup methods were outlined for helping students revisit, practice, and reflect on new word meanings. The next chapter tells how to create active, expressive ways to use new words and concepts in writing to further build critical/constructive thinking in the disciplines.

SECTION III

Higher-Order Literacy and Assessment in the Disciplines

You have now been exposed to the rudimentary tools for helping students to *read the lines* and in some measure to *read between the lines*. The next section addresses the knowledge and skills that teachers will need to also promote *reading and thinking beyond the lines*. Chapter 8 focuses on critical-constructive reading, writing, and thinking. Chapter 9 introduces assessment techniques for achieving the objectives of the previous chapters. Chapter 10 is designed to reground us in one of the more inescapable elements of school life—the development of powerful reading/study habits.

CHAPTER 8

Critical-Constructive Reading, Writing, Thinking, and Telecomputing

Izzy, did you ask a good question today?

—from D. Sheff's account of the life of Isodore I. Rabi, Nobel
laureate in physics

✦ Fore Words ✦

The thoughts in this chapter are aimed at the improvement of critical-constructive or creative thinking at all levels of reading proficiency. This type of teaching is given lip-service but little real support in school or common culture. Achieving this aim implies the need for instructional approaches designed to *transform* rather than simply inform. This chapter focuses on three interlocking approaches to transformation. One is aimed at converting inert knowledge to dynamic knowledge, an objective that has been described as moving the simple thinking of "ungeared minds" to the more complex thinking of connected minds (Chase, 1926). This is accomplished largely through brief, multiperspective writing and exchanges with other reader-writers. The second approach is to stress "knowledge making" or original thought as well as the more traditional goal of "knowledge taking." Ironically, this is accomplished by reeducating minds to patterns of thought that could make creative thinking part of school tradition (Manzo & Manzo, 1997b). The third approach is to connect students to virtual communities of learners whose knowledge quests and idea exchanges match the most idealized campus environments of the past.

PREFACE TO CONSTRUCTIVE THINKING:
AIMING HIGHER

Chances are that you already know something about *critical* reading-thinking. However, your own schooling and teacher education probably have not tended to address issues in *constructive-creative* thinking: it is a fairly new development in school programming. Despite its newness, teaching for constructive-creative outcomes does have some lore associated with it. Knowing some of this will help you to be ready to learn more. So, here is a quick summary of some of the key ideas that should make your reading of the content area literacy contributions to constructive thinking more profitable. First, we will briefly address the role of *text* in constructive reading, then the relationship of constructive reading to "constructivism" and conventional critical thinking, then the affective side of this process, and finally, some general guidelines for promoting constructive-creative thinking outcomes in the classroom. Think of this initial information as *frontloading* for reading the remainder of this chapter, which in turn is front material for personally joining this very exciting new devel-

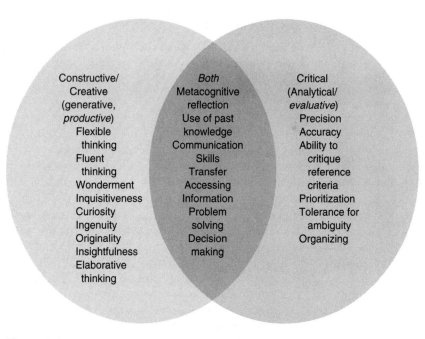

Figure 8.1
Cognitive map of similarities and differences between creative-constructive and critical thinking.
Source: Fogarty, R., and McTighe, J., *Educating teachers for higher-order thinking: The three-story intellect.* Ohio State University © 1993.

opment in professional education. See Figure 8.1 for a cognitive map of similarities and differences between creative-constructive and critical thinking.

The Role of Text

An English teacher in Brookline, Massachusetts, wrote an article on her remarkable three-month effort to teach to students *To Read Beyond the Plot* (Metzger, 1998). She used her own variations on Socratic Seminars and other elaborate techniques to foster such in-depth thinking. Along the way, in reading *Romeo and Juliet, The Great Gatsby,* and the poem *Ozymandias,* the class she led and tutored in discussion techniques did something else that can be easily forgotten when reaching "beyond the lines"; they read "the lines" again, and again.

At the beginning of each discussion, we read the passage two or three times, each time more slowly. Therefore during a single class period, the same page was read four to six times. . . . The act of re-reading helped students focus and notice details . . . (and) words. . . . It was no longer enough to skim over an assignment and consider it finished. (From *Teaching Reading: Be-*

yond the Plot, by Margaret Metzger, PHI DELTA KAPAN, November 1998, p. 246. © 1998 Phi Delta Kappa International.)

This teacher's words and experience tell how important the *words* are in teaching thinking beyond the text. Literal understanding is essential, although it need not all be achieved before there is any discussion; which is to say that it is necessary but not sufficient for promoting higher literacy.

Constructive-Creative Thinking and Constructivism

By constructive thinking, we mean thinking that is grounded in critique more than criticism and that is pointed toward building alternative perspectives. This approach is not quite the same as *constructivism*, a philosophy advocating the importance of learners figuring things out for themselves. *Unlike* constructivism, teaching for constructive-creative outcomes does not contradict the value of old fashioned lecture, recitation, and factual learning—three potentially powerful forms of "verbal learning" (Ausubel, 1960). What it does do is emphasize inquiry and personal responsibility for one's own knowledge and for the state of human knowledge. It raises this seemingly abstract responsibility to a conscious goal for teachers and students (Manzo, 1998). In so doing, it should help to increase internal motivation, grasp of larger concepts, and appreciation for existing knowledge that has been painfully accumulated. Done properly, efforts to teach about the *limits* of knowledge can implicitly impart ways to respond to the irritation of uncertainty, that ever-present feeling that can either immobilize the will, or stir its quest for new knowledge.

Affective Disposition

The way in which a person typically deals with problems is the key to whether and how they will address problems in reading, writing, thinking and knowledge acquisition. There are five characteristic *dispositions* for responding to a barrier, conflict, or paradox:

1. Ignoring it
2. Saying it is unsolvable
3. Working harder at the same solution hoping for a different result
4. Trying for more inventive solutions
5. Considering the possibility that the wrong questions are being asked.

The first three are counterproductive. The latter two—looking for inventive solutions and reconsidering the question, are the focus of this chapter.

Guidelines for Teaching for Creative Outcomes

Successful teaching for creative outcomes tends to require creative teaching. Some guidelines for inviting creativity include:

✦ Believing students are capable of creative production

✦ Simply asking for creative responses

✦ Providing critical-constructive feedback

✦ Inviting and welcoming expressions of curiosity

✦ Illustrating and underscoring new twists on old patterns

✦ Teaching students how to give as well as receive critical-creative critiques

✦ Reading students for a much greater level of error or mistakes than most of us are used to experiencing

✦ Inviting contrary or opposing views

✦ Finding ways to grapple with authentic as well as academic issues (Manzo, 1997)

In addition to these classroom-based considerations, there is a need to build systemic support in the society at large for inventive thinking, especially for procedural and social solutions, for which society provides few incentives such as patents or royalties.

Much of what you will be reading and thinking about from this point forward is one of the *quests* or pioneering realms of content area literacy and professional education. Try to think both critically and constructively about how this might be done better in schools and, by extension, in society.

The NAEP Indicators of Higher Literacy

The National Assessment of Educational Progress (NAEP) is one of the major tools for documenting the efficacy of schooling in the United States. It samples students' academic progress in several areas and at several levels.

The 1998 NAEP results in the area of literacy are being heralded as showing significant progress over 1994. Actual scores, however, are not up in any meaningful way. For example, scores that are reported on a 500-point scale are up at fourth-grade level to 217 in 1998, but that is only a 3-point gain. Similarly, the mean score of 264 for eighth-graders is only a 4-point gain, and the 291 for seniors also is only a 4-point gain. The good news is that this is the first across-the-board gain at all levels tested in thirty years. The not-so-good news is that these 1998 gains, which come on the heels of huge expenditures and political focus, largely are rebounds from 1994 and about the same as 1992; with the exception of eighth-grade scores, where some new highs are being seen. The fourth-grade results are the ones being most carefully watched since they should reflect changes instituted at first-grade level. Those results, while encouraging, are not much to cheer about, since 38% of youngsters are below the basic level, 33% are at the basic level, 25% are at the proficient level, and *only about*

4% are at the advanced level. If we used a "normal distribution curve" as a guide, there should be about the same proportion of students in the lowest category as in the highest, but there are nearly ten times as many in the lowest than the highest. It should also be noted that many who are in the "proficient" and "advanced" groups may have areas of need that these conventional tests do not measure and that therefore go unattended.

Unattended Needs of Even the Most Proficient Readers

Educators carefully note that there are subgroups of readers who are *dyslexic, remedial,* and *corrective*. However, when discussing *developmental readers*, or those on grade-level and above, the implicit belief is that these students are a homogeneous group who are progressing as expected and need no further examination or assistance. Lack of attention to this issue masks several reading-thinking problems that need to be acknowledged before they can be addressed. Recent research is raising this veil of denial.

Four subtypes of otherwise proficient readers seem to be emerging. Each subgroup has strengths and weakness that content area literacy, and specifically the critical-creative thrust of this chapter, could be addressing. A recent study found that only one of the four subgroups was making real progress toward reading maturity, and even this group had a weakness in what could be called "entrepreneurial literacy," arguably one of the strongest needs in contemporary life. (See Figure 8.2 for descriptions of the four subgroups identified; for more on this topic, see the hypertext chapter, twenty-first-century Trends in Content Area Literacy, on our web site.) Two other subgroups of proficient readers had a decided gender-dominated bent, and the fourth appeared to have mastered the mechanics of language but not much of its subtleties and complex implications (Manzo, Manzo, Barnhill, & Thomas, in press). These subtypes, or *reading personality profiles*, were deduced from a 148-item self-report inventory given to college level. We do not yet know for certain when the characteristics identified had their developmental onset. However, one point seems logically supportable: students are more likely to be "transformable," or guided toward a critical-constructive disposition, when younger than when older. Therefore, efforts to promote higher-order reading, writing, and thinking probably should be cultivated for all students, from the earliest grade levels, no matter how proficient they might appear on conventional measures of reading comprehension.

The Need to Cultivate Multiple Literacies as Opposed to Merely More Reading

Jane Fell Greene in a conference title for a presentation we have yet to hear, unpacks much of what concerns us in this tag line: "We Confused

Figure 8.2
Proficient-reader subtypes.

SUBTYPE I: DEVELOPMENTALLY MATURE ANDROGYNOUS READERS

These most highly optimized subtype readers report that their reading is characterized by concentration, critical analysis, concept formation, inference, and interpretation. They think creatively with minimum prompts, and write fairly well. They have eclectic reading interests and seem confident and comfortable with traditional schooling. Since they did not have the strong, conventionalized male or female schema orientations noted in other subtypes, they are characterized as androgynous, or in touch with both their male and female sides. The only hypothesized characteristic of mature readers that these individuals lack is the entrepreneurial spirit that has become so necessary in contemporary life (more on this in Chapter 14).

SUBTYPE II: CONVENTIONALIZED NONFICTION MALE ORIENTATION

This subtype tends to have a conventionalized orientation that is most often associated with males in western cultures. They have an action stance and a fair transfer-of-training (the application level of thinking), and are disinclined to self-examination. They have conventional male interests in sports, outdoor life, business, gambling, social studies, and the mechanics of how things work. However, they indicated that they do not enjoy reading for pleasure, and even report some physical discomfort in doing so. They further indicate that they have trouble paying attention while reading, and suspect that they may be "learning disabled," to the point of being unable to stay attentive without active, pencil-in-hand, reading. They indicate that they are only moderately creative, and prefer repetitive tasks. Yet, they are critical and reflective: they engage in a great

---

Literature With Literacy. . . . So What Do We Do Now?" Higher-order literacy is not likely to be achieved merely by *more* story reading, nor by reading that is totally limited to one's narrow field of interest. Becoming more informed in a variety of fields and topics, or achieving multiple literacy, as in computer literacy and financial literacy and historical literacy, is the most basic and traditional way to enrich schema and broaden orientation. These *multiple literacies* amount to ingraining implicit questions, or quests, that engender the interests, motivation, and ability to use metaphors, and analogical thinking ("Oh, this is like that . . .") to comprehend and reason beyond the lines. Real experts in any field are those who leverage their primary interest area to find more universal meanings and levels of meaning in various other knowledge areas. Further,

Figure 8.2, *continued*

deal of active questioning while reading, attempting to convert what is read into action plans. Overall, they prefer to read in short spurts, and for pragmatic purposes.

SUBTYPE III: CONVENTIONALIZED STORY-READING FEMALE ORIENTATION

This subtype tends to have characteristics traditionally associated with females in literate cultures. They enjoy reading fiction, and report little interest in thinking deeply about what they read, and *no* interest in self-examination. They have virtually no interest in things mechanical, political, functional, or pragmatic. They have narrow, traditionalized female interests in fashion and children. They read for pleasure and escape with a self-declared tendency to be too literal, and to lack confidence in their understanding of what they read. Contrary to the image of the female diary keeper, they do not feel as if they learn from writing, and they find it very taxing. Overall, they are story-readers with solid literal comprehension and strongly expressed enjoyment of reading, but who see little connection between what they read and their own lives. Since it is the nature of fiction to unveil the complexities in understanding "relationships," it is possible that this is a desired, pragmatic goal.

SUBTYPE IV: DETAIL-DEPENDENT RULE FOLLOWERS

This subtype tends to be passive reader-learners with apparently good mastery of the mechanics of language, such as grammar and spelling, but who feel that they tend to get lost in details when they read or write. They have an expressed interest in magic, which suggests less emotional maturity and relatively unsophisticated patterns of thought for otherwise capable minds.

they return from forays into other knowledge areas with new metaphors and analogies that excite clearer thinking in their areas of expertise. However, this transfer does not seem to occur naturally (Kirshner & Whitson, 1997). A study of mathematics majors had results similar to one found in the proficient-reader study referenced above. It showed that among those college students who had considerable experience with mathematics there was not a commensurate improvement in thinking that even vaguely resembled that of mathematicians (Stenger, 1999). The primary reason to study in any field is often said to be to learn how to "think in that subject." Current schooling does not seem to be accomplishing this objective to the extent that modern teaching and ancillary technologies suggest we could and should. The next section suggests some possible reasons for the difficulty of teaching toward this "transfer of learning," and some viable class-room solutions that would be within the reach of content area teachers in middle and secondary schools.

The Problem of Inert Knowledge: The Value of Connective Teaching-Learning

Traditionally, two of the highest objectives of literacy education have been to keep learning continuous or ongoing (Bruner, 1971) and to help students to more successfully transfer learning from one situation or context to another—sometimes called the *evaluation/application level of thinking* (Bloom, 1976; McKeough, Lupart, & Marini, 1995). Fundamental to these interrelated objectives is the need to have knowledge rise above the level of the *inert*. The way this is done can be represented in a single word: *connections*. New experiences, ideas, and facts become usable, or transferable, only when they are connected with prior experience and knowledge. We have discussed several ways to do this in previous chapters under the labels of *schema activation, frontloading*, and *reading between the lines*. Now we will address several other reasons and ways to *excite* acquired knowledge, making it more active and potentially attachable to other sources of incoming information.

It is now commonly held that the conversion of *inert* to *dynamic* knowledge is not best done merely through conventional *transmission* education—where information and knowledge is transferred from those who are "in the know" to those who are ignorant. Nor is it done merely through *transactional* education—where the object of teaching/learning is the individual's unique perceptions of experience and information. Achieving dynamic learning requires a certain level of *transformative* education—where learning and thinking are intended to change the learner's attitudes and dispositions, providing a more solid preparation for tomorrows that cannot be predicted. This form of learning is based on extensions of cognitive modeling or *cognitive apprenticeship* approaches that have been illustrated earlier in this text. These apprenticeships can be conducted in a variety of settings and from a variety of perspectives (Rogoff, 1990). Aiming these approaches toward transformative goals tends to require:

✦ Problems that are stated in evocative ways
✦ Reciprocal interactions that shape the thinking of learners and the offerings of teachers
✦ Frequent, brief writing
✦ The environmental impact of *telecomputing* on information sharing and our social images of literate people

To overlook the wraparound effect of telecomputing is to miss a developing opportunity to capitalize on its benefit to influence learning and thinking around the clock, around the home, in the community, in classrooms, and around the globe.

Writing in response to reading is a traditional means of teaching comprehension and developing thinking strategies. The types of responses students are guided toward reflect the teacher's theory of teaching-learning. The next section summarizes the primary schools of thought in this area.

Reader-Response Theories: Toward Transformational Teaching

For some educators, the primary purpose of reading in school is to achieve cultural and historical *transmission* (Hirsch, 1987), or the *orderly* transfer of knowledge from those who have it to those who would then be sufficiently informed to do likewise. For others, response to text largely should be a *transaction* (Harste, 1994; Rosenblatt, 1938), or a personal construction of meaning that is highly subjective and unguided by the teacher or some other higher authority. This can be somewhat disorderly, since it seems to imply that there are no limits to the number of different ways that text can be interpreted. For a growing number of educators, such as the previously mentioned English teacher from Brookline, Massachusetts, response to text has many, but not an infinite number of possible interpretations. As such, it should be, at least in school, based on certain grounded outcomes that are both informative and transformative. That is, students should become more willing to reformulate as well as formulate ideas through what have been called "reflective turnabouts" (Santa, Dailey, & Nelson, 1985) and "tiny rebirths" (Burke, 1950; 1969), or changes, in personal view. Such change may follow from receiving sound arguments and evidence contrary to their initial views (Manzo, Garber, Manzo, & Kahn, 1994; Manzo & Manzo, 1995), and from exchanges of different perspectives. In some cases, the change may come as an epiphany triggered by new experience, but it is more likely to be a gradual transformation to more qualified thinking. These enlightenments seldom come about through argument. They tend to culminate from stories as much as from statistics. The challenge seems to be to impart a balance of intentional information that is "suasive," though not blatantly persuasive (more on this later), along with a continuing supply of stories and perspectives that encourage deeper sensitivity to the incongruities in language and common conceptions. Salibrici (1999) refers to these as "Burkean moments," a reference to the writings of Kenneth Burke on what we would characterize as the "implosive effect" on learning and thinking that can come from attempting to reconcile incongruities and paradoxes, or seemingly conflicting stories and statistics.

A comparison study of the effects of each of these three approaches on measures of complexity of thinking and socioemotional adjustment

Figure 8.3
Theoretical perspectives on guiding students' responses to reading.

TRANSMISSION MODEL PERSPECTIVE

Role of the Text: The text is a means of transmitting society's dominant historical, literary, and cultural canon. It has fixed meanings and values irrespective of the reader. The text remains virtually static over time.

Role of the Reader: The reader is expected to acquire the precise facts and ideas being conveyed by the author and reproduce these in the same formats in which they were presented. Little attention is given to the reader's personal or critical examination of the text. The reader is simply responsible for reconstructing the author's ideas.

Role of the Teacher: The teacher focuses classroom discussion on the author's biography, the historical and political context of the author, and the traditional literary elements.

TRANSACTION MODEL PERSPECTIVE

Role of the Text: The text means unique things to different readers regardless of what the author may have intended to communicate. There is no static or inherent meaning incorporated within the text itself. Instead, the text is viewed as dynamic and subjective.

Role of the Reader: The reader brings a host of associations and inferences to every reading experience. These reader-based conceptions are a chief consideration as the reader attempts to build meaning from the written words. The reader makes fresh and unmediated interpretations, which may reflect the emotional and aesthetic needs of the reader.

Role of the Teacher: The teacher focuses classroom discussion on the reader's feelings, associations, and personal interpretations of texts.

---

showed that *transmission-type* teaching was the least effective, *transactive* was next best, and *transformative* teaching was by far the most effective (Garber, 1995). This finding is being supported in a second pilot study with college students (Jackson-Albee, 2000). For a rhetorical picture of the distinctions among these three perspectives in terms of the role of the text, the reader, and the teacher, see Figure 8.3. For a more personal

Figure 8.3, *continued*

TRANSFORMATION MODEL PERSPECTIVE

Role of the Text: The text is a tool for critical and constructive thought. It not only reflects the ideas and contexts of the author but also invites the thoughts and feelings of the reader. The text is a stimulus for critical-evaluative, or formative, thinking.

Role of the Reader: The reader examines the text critically with the goal of becoming a constructive thinker and solution-creator/implementer in the context of the surrounding society. The reader approaches each text consciously, separating what the author says from the reader's own thoughts and feelings. The reader suspends final judgment until the reader has developed legitimate and rational positions through a process of rigorously examining multiple interpretations. The reader sometimes reformulates thinking and/or becomes a producer of new knowledge and new texts as a result of this examination.

Role of the Teacher: The teacher focuses classroom discussion on generating and supporting varied interpretations with examples of multiple reader-response options. The teacher may ask students to make judgments about the author's intent, purpose, accuracy, logic, reliability, and literary form, or about others' responses to the same text.

Source: From K. S. Garber (1995), *The Effects of Transmissional, Transactional, and Transformational Reader-Response Strategies on Middle School Students' Thinking Complexity and Social Development,* unpublished doctoral dissertation, University of Missouri, Kansas City. Adapted by permission.

account, consider Mary Salibrici's (1999) anecdotal report. She describes how her students reacted to a unit of reading, writing, and discussion of the Rosenberg trial of the early 1950s. Julius and Ethel Rosenberg were the only Americans ever executed for treason during peacetime. They were instrumental in helping the then–Soviet Union to gain access to secrets on how to build an atomic bomb. That which started as a topical unit in literature soon became almost indistinguishable from a unit in social studies on the mass psychology of fear. In this case, what would have been a mildly interesting story of an earlier era is converted to a potentially transformative reminder to think clearly about whatever time we are in just as you would try to rise above the preoccupations of a particular clique. (By the way, the Rosenbergs have been confirmed to have been communist spies by recent releases of previously secret Soviet files.)

In simplest terms, the key element in transformative theory is a commitment to providing youngsters with some basic values, such as those associated with democratic life, without preaching or serving up unnecessarily biased views of life's options. Needless to say, this isn't easy and we will all do it poorly sometimes. Therefore, we should judge ourselves by our long-term commitment more than our occasional lapses into preaching and pedantry. Writing and encouraging writing can be very useful in clarifying one's thoughts and message.

CRITICAL READING-WRITING-THINKING: A TRADITIONAL AND EVOLVING GOAL

With a background now in place on the general idea of *constructive* reading, writing, and thinking, and the transformational approach to teaching toward these ends, we turn to a review of *critical* thinking, including some new concepts and challenges in this field. We then will recombine critical-constructive reading, writing, and thinking into one more or less unifying concept and speak to several concrete methods for promoting this highest level of literacy. By the end of the chapter, you will have recapitulated much of the evolution of knowledge and art on these topics, from "critical" to "critical-constructive" to "constructive-creative" reading, writing, and thinking. Ideally, this exposition should be orderly, unambiguous, and without redundancancies. In fact, it will be more like an effort toward this end that readers probably will need to finish constructing as part of their contribution to the science and art of professional education.

Critical reading-writing-thinking clearly is one of the most written and talked about topics in modern history. Nonetheless, it remains one of the least well understood. Critical reading is merely the use of critical thinking in the act of reading (Ennis, 1962). Hence, almost anything said about one is likely to be true of the other. David Russell, writing over forty years ago, provides a most basic way for educators to understand critical reading and thinking. He says, essentially, that it is best defined as a three-factor ability, to which most contemporary educators would add a fourth, as shown here. Critical reading is:

✦ An attitudinal, or dispositional, factor of effective questioning and suspension of judgment

✦ A functional factor of logical inquiry and problem solving, sometimes known as *dialogical* or *dialectical thinking*

✦ A judgmental factor based on some set of norms growing out of consensus, now called *cultural imperatives* (Russell, 1961)

✦ A matter of being able to imagine alternative perspectives often not represented (Paul, 1993; Lenski, Wham, & Johns, 1999), and which now we would generically call *constructive-creative thinking*

There are several paradoxes to overcome in teaching for and even talking about critical reading-thinking. For one, it is a *process*, the merit of which people tend to acknowledge based on whether or not the *product*, or conclusion reached, pleases them. In general, the term *critical* is only applied when the facts are incomplete or in dispute, and therefore where "right-thinking" people are likely to disagree. In other words, to teach critical thinking one must broach some controversial and even sensitive topics.

Critical Reading-Writing-Thinking Objectives

There are certain functions that sketch out the teacher's and students' rhetorical processes in achieving progress toward this higher level of literacy. Notice how these ideas begin to lean toward a more holistic concept of critical-constructive thinking rather than some kind of step-by-step process:

✦ Growth past reductionist thinking, or the tendency to oversimplify complex matters to black and white, either/or choices

✦ Overcoming the tendency to be deceptive and self-deceptive, as when sound information is disallowed because it does not suit one's purpose

✦ Learning to unpack one's own and a writer's intentions/motivations

✦ Learning how to read-write-think in ways that are not immediately comfortable to us, since various domains of learning and influence have their own characteristic ways of conducting discourse (e.g., science-talk, literature-talk, business-talk)

✦ Achieving a certain measure of the goal of "critical pedagogy/literacy," which is to increase insight into the ways in which one's reading-writing-thinking are bound to our cultural perceptions of race, gender, representations of self-image, and hence power

✦ Recognizing that language is "symbolic action" (Burke, 1950/69), which implies a need to interrogate one's own and a writer's choice of words and positions in terms of their consequences to others

✦ Belief that one is responsible in some ways for the production or creation of knowledge and insight as well as for its consumption

There probably is no better, though no more disquieting, way to become a better critical-constructive reader-writer-thinker than to start with a thorough examination of one's own assumptions. This is especially urgent for teachers, ministers, administrators, and lawyers, since assumptions guide the way we implicitly teach others to think critically.

Watch Your Assumptions

Most faulty conclusions can be traced back to faulty or unexamined assumptions. Of course, these seldom seem unexamined at the time. Some assumptions go unexamined because they are traditionally accepted "givens." For example, the conclusion that one needs to have a college education to be successful in life is based on employment practices and cultural expectations that are changing rapidly. Other assumptions go unexamined because they ride into town as innovations or movements that reveal the error or outdatedness of the old or traditional ways of thinking and/or acting. The other side of the example above is the conclusion that the cost of a college education may now have exceeded its value. This conclusion, being reached by many young people who in prior times would never have raised the question, can be justified by numerous facts. However, it is based on the assumption that the primary benefits of a college education are financial in nature.

Examining assumptions involves a set of thinking strategies that form the core of insightful critical-constructive analysis, for example:

✦ Asking a lot of relevant questions, even when the answers may seem self-evident.

✦ Acquiring and objectively dealing with available information, whether or not it is personally "pleasing."

✦ Avoiding good/bad dichotomies.

✦ Recognizing the persuasive effects of emotionally laden language.

✦ Examining the author's motivation. (Reformers' identities can get so tied up in the struggle that perpetuation of the cause becomes more important than its achievement.)

✦ Examining one's own motivation. (This may involve coming to grips with that egoistic voice inside each of us, and recognizing self-serving myths and convenient distortions of the truth; in other words, internalizing the spirit of the old saying, "If the truth is getting in your way, chances are that you're going the wrong direction.")

These habits of thought are fairly self-evident. Teaching them, however, requires some heuristics to stir them to action. The next subsection provides a set of questions for modeling critical thinking strategies on any issue.

Helping Adolescents Think More Critically

✦ Has this been proposed before, and under what label or name?

✦ What are the credentials, background, and interests of the major advocates and adversaries?

✦ What assumptions are nested in the competing proposals?

✦ What factual evidence and logic supports and refutes this proposal?

✦ What other issues or matters are affected by accepting or rejecting this proposal?

✦ How might critics label or name this proposal?

✦ How do the choices affect me, and can I think clearly about this?

✦ Is there something of value and something needing correction in the competing proposals? Can these be reconciled?

✦ Is there more here than meets the eye? A useful metaphor for critical reading/thinking is *pentimento*—a term used in art restoration to refer to finding an (sometimes more valuable) oil painting underneath another one (due to the fact that canvasses were expensive and artists often painted over their own works).

Exercise your critical-constructive powers of analysis on some issues that are current in literacy and general education (see Figure 8.4). Realize as you do this that the above is a set of thought-stimulating guidelines, and not a step-by-step formula. Nonetheless, as with any set of ingredients, each may need to be folded in to achieve an optimal outcome. There also

Figure 8.4
Examples of evocative and critical issues in literacy education.

✦ Never teach or drill anything in isolation.

✦ Graded books (written to be at a given difficulty level) are inauthentic and hinder learning at every level.

✦ The only way to improve reading is to read, read, read.

✦ Youngsters need to be taught to love reading.

✦ Education should be conducted so that it is a liberating force, rather than an indoctrination.

✦ Literature is literacy.

✦ Lecturing is bad teaching.

✦ Any subject can be taught through literature.

✦ Diversity is good, core culture is bad.

✦ Teaching declarative facts and consensual interpretations is bad.

✦ Teacher talk is bad, student talk is good.

✦ Constructivist philosophy is good for learning, traditionalist philosophy is bad for learning.

✦ Teaching phonics rules is bad.

✦ Teaching context clues is good.

See discussion of these issues on the textbook web site.

is an open invitation to add, though not to delete, considerations as long as the additions do not have the effect of altering something beyond recognition. For example, you cannot take the seafood out of paella, nor add a jar of peanut butter to the recipe for linguini with clam sauce, without altering the basic character and purpose of the dish. However, even this is allowable if it is declared that a new purpose or mission is being proposed, or a new target raised. In fact, fertile minds regularly raise and hit targets that others have yet to identify. Being able to do this is almost a definition of the elevation of critical thinking to critical-constructive thinking.

Critically Reading a Writer's Intent

In most print materials intended to inform, the writer has attempted to build an orderly progression of thought and information toward an unambiguous conclusion. Relevant examples and details are interwoven to add clarity and support. Depending on the author's intended or unintended purpose, however, the "facts" may be more or less complete and verifiable, and there may be more or less acknowledgment of alternative perspectives. Some theorists would argue that virtually everything written, from the Declaration of Independence to a cereal box, is intended to convince the reader of something, thereby shaping the reader's views and behavior. In the end, it is up to the reader to determine what to believe. There are several sets of "lenses" that can heighten critical analysis of a writer's intent and credibility.

The first aid in critical reading is to determine whether the author is attempting *knowledge-telling* or *knowledge-making* (Flower & Hayes, 1981). *Knowledge-telling* typically is the attempt to articulate something one knows, or presumes to know, in the clearest and least ambiguous way possible. *Knowledge-making* is an author's plunge into the murky unknown in an attempt to discover what he or she is thinking or how he or she really feels about something. This also is the most transformative mode of writing. It tends to induce deeper thinking, and result in more conclusions that influence, if not radically change, a great deal of subsequent reading, thinking, attitudes, and human behavior.

Another set of critical reading lenses involves recognizing and analyzing the nature of the claims used by the author to support a conclusion. A *claim* is a statement presented as truth when in fact it is open to question. Unrau (1997) details six types of claims that should alert critical readers to consider alternative propositions:

✦ What the writer believes to be true (*knowledge claims*)

✦ What or how something causes something else (*causal claims*)

✦ What is likely to result from current conditions (*predictive claims*)

✦ What is good and noble (*evaluative claims*)

✦ What is right and wrong (*moral claims*)

✦ What should be done (*policy claims*)

A final set of lenses for critical reading is awareness of the classical propaganda techniques that have evolved from marketing and politics. These techniques, detailed in Figure 8.5, provide a useful language for talking about critical reading as well as persuasive writing, debate techniques, and oral presentation.

Impediments to Critical-Constructive Thinking

A final consideration in melding a new focus on constructive reading-thinking with traditional and emerging concepts of critical analysis is to more carefully articulate why this is not already being done more systematically. Careful articulation of a problem is one way to overcome the human instinct to deny problems, avoid problems, or simply say that a problem is unsolvable. Furthermore, stating the question or problem often translates into 50% of the solution.

The human instinct to avoid problems is so deeply rooted that at one point in the late 1980s it reached national concern. This led to an announcement by the Education Commission of the States of a large "Higher Literacies" project to look into state policies that either "constrain or promote" schools' efforts to teach "writing, problem-solving, critical thinking, argument, analysis, synthesis, interpretation and evaluation" (Tchudi, 1988). Here is a partial list of likely impediments to acknowledging and hence addressing problems:

✦ Textbooks tend to be inane and therefore fail to evoke critical thought.

✦ The printed word generates a "halo" effect: because it is in print, it is true and therefore not worth questioning.

✦ Many school administrators and teachers are afraid to broach controversial subjects with students.

✦ There is a general emphasis on conformity in almost all aspects of life.

✦ Personal emotions and prejudices often tend to disrupt clear thinking.

✦ Critical reading-thinking is not routinely assessed, and therefore is assumed to be less important than basic objectives.

✦ There is a lack of models (persons and programs) that epitomize or focus on constructive and critical thinking.

✦ Curriculum requirements generally do not include addressing or teaching specific critical reading-thinking strategies.

Figure 8.5

Propaganda techniques.

> Critical reading often involves recognizing an author's use of propaganda, or selling techniques. These techniques are designed to convince, persuade, or move the reader/listener to action.

Bandwagon: Everyone is doing a certain thing, so jump on the bandwagon and go along with the crowd. ("More kids want _____ than any other toothpaste.")

Testimonial: A well-known person endorses a certain product or course of action even though he or she is not an authority on the subject. ("Take it from me, _____, this is the niftiest video game you can buy for the money.")

Plain folks: People who appear to be "just plain folks," or "just like you and me," suggest that we think or act in a certain way. ("My family has been in farming for fifty years; you know I won't forget you when I get to Washington.")

Snob appeal: The opposite of plain folks. ("These beautiful designer jeans were created for the with-it girl.")

Name-calling: Applying a currently unpopular put-down to a person or movement without seeing if it really applies. ("That teacher is a geek—look at those ancient-looking clothes.")

Glittering generalities: Words or phrases with favorable suggestions that lead us to favor a person or movement without examining the evidence (can also be used with unfavorable words). Such abstract words or phrases (e.g., "public spirit," "time for change," "patriotic duty," "fiscal responsibility") are used to make us support some person or idea with little further analysis. ("We need a leader who will guide us to greater fiscal responsibility, an improved standard of living, and a more fair system of taxation. It's time for a change.")

Transfer: A commercial symbol that trades off our respect for something to which it really is not connected. ("Buy Red Cross shoes.")

Scientific slant: Use of scientific terms and phrases to persuade us to accept something as being more than what it really is. ("The titanium light bulb burns for 7,000 hours"; "Four out of five dentists surveyed . . .")

False analogies: Use of an analogy or comparison situation that is not really parallel, or simply is divergent on a critical point. ("Learning to read; is a language process; it is no different from learning to speak.")

Confusing correlation with cause: This deception amounts to attributing causation to things which may be related, but are not necessarily related in a cause-and-effect way. ("In the two years that I have been president we have had nothing but prosperity").

✦ There is a pervasive fear among students and teachers that criticism of *anything*, including introspective self-appraisals, ultimately unleashes criticism of *everything*, including schools, teachers, society, and self.

✦ It is a paradoxical fact that classroom questioning is used on the one hand to stimulate curiosity, reinforce knowledge, and ignite discussion and on the other to scold, embarrass, and test.

✦ Great ideas often are conceived and forged in passion, and we haven't quite figured out how to endure, let alone allow, passion in our schools and policy-making arenas.

The methods described next were designed to expose, circumvent, or even build on these innate human dispositions. *Intra-Act*, for example, capitalizes on adolescents' natural interest in predicting the opinions of their peers and in informal small-group interaction.

Alternate Sources of Content: Critical "Media Literacy"

The act of reading is no longer limited to the printed page, nor are texts perceived in the narrow sense of traditional print media. Virtually all systems of signing, from that employed by musicians and artists, to choreographers and television dramatists and comedians, are sending signals about what one might feel, believe in, or live by. This has led to two relatively new fields of study: *semiotics*, or the study of the history and impact of different signing systems, and *Critical Media Literacy*, or the use of popular-culture texts and symbols in teaching, such as advertising and even storyline suasion techniques, where the story, such as Pearl S. Buck's *The Good Earth*, sends a penetrating message.

The idea of using everything from *Ally McBeal* and the *Power Rangers in Space* to any recent "fad ad" as a poignant frame of reference for discussion in school is sensible and resourceful, but not without hazards. Lewis, in a forward to a new book on the topic by Alvermann, Moon, and Hagood (1999), makes several interesting points to consider as one ventures out in the direction of popular cultural references and studies, say in English and social studies. She says,

✦ Popular cultural studies is inherently interdisciplinary.

✦ Popular cultural studies allows youth to self-examine the pop culture that may be strongly influencing their lives.

✦ Popular cultural studies tends to create a more student-centered classroom.

In a more recent article, Alvermann and Hagood (2000) make two additional points in favor of *critical media literacy*:

✦ Engaging students in multiple interpretations of popular cultural texts "may be a way to get students interested in school literacy practices" (p. 445).

✦ "Welcoming certain aspects of adolescent fan culture into the school curriculum . . . may bring about insights into how students construct meaning from their personal interests and provide teachers with a window through which to view students' constructed identities" (p. 437).

There is a certain degree of contradiction in teaching kids more about what they are expert in and about which we are relatively naïve. *Pop culture*, by its very name, is ephemeral, that is, quickly passing and hard to keep track of. There also is a strong likelihood that kids don't really want us in their world. This may be one of the reasons that they carefully craft it to look, feel, and be different from whatever it is that their parents are embracing. During the greatest period of divorce and "youth" orientation in modern history, kids turned to the sedate, traditional, and innocent, watching rerun shows like *The Brady Bunch* in record numbers. Therefore, it is probably best to monitor pop culture carefully, but to use this resource sparingly.

WRITING-BASED METHODS FOR GUIDING CRITICAL-CONSTRUCTIVE READING

One of the most effective ways to teach students to respond critically and constructively to what they read is through various forms of written response. This is traditionally done in the form of the "research paper," a lengthy process in which students collect information from various sources and then synthesize it in their own words and toward their own points and conclusions. This process of "transforming text," according to Moffett (1989), is the highest level of writing. By translating information from the words of various authors to their own choices of words and phrases, the ideas and information become integrated into the students' personal knowledge bases. In this more personal form, it is less likely to be forgotten, and more likely to grow into more sophisticated language and thought.

The challenge always has been in just how to teach the multiple perspectives and attitudes necessary to enable such transformation of text and student thinking. The methods in this section provide various ways to do this with reading materials of any type, of any length, and in any discipline. The first method is something of a template for eliciting students' thoughts and reflections on a variety of possible topics, whether they be in pop culture, traditional literature, or wide-ranging ideas. It involves prompting students to make evaluative responses, predict the responses of their peers, and discuss the reasons for their judgments.

Intra-Act: Values-Guided versus Values-Driven Reading-Thinking

The challenge to educators, and virtually all thinking people, is in how to be reasonably guided by a set of values, but not so driven by these as to lose clarity and objectivity. One way that has been suggested by reflective educators is to provide more experience in school with the examination of authentic critical issues, and hence more experience with *evaluative thinking*, the cognitive psychology name for value-based reasoning. *Intra-Act* (Hoffman, 1977) is a teaching method that is representative of this class of methods, and one that is especially compatible with content area literacy.

Intra-Act was designed to develop readers' ability to draw upon their personal values base that permeates and colors their sense of what they read and what they do with what is read. Intra-Act was influenced by the earlier work of Raths, Harmon, and Simon (1978) on "valuing process" and of Manzo and Sherk (1978) on "languaging," the process of using language to more deeply process complex issues. It involves group problem solving and cooperative learning. A study of the efficacy of the Intra-Act activity conducted by Hoffman (1977) concluded that the method was an effective means of teaching basic comprehension, that students were willing and able to "go beyond the material in projecting and perceiving personal values related to the content of the selections," and that "given an appropriately structured learning environment, . . . students can and do learn from one another" (p. 63).

Steps in the Intra-Act Procedure

Preparation: Create two worksheets based on the reading selection. One is a set of non-fact-type questions that could be answered, and argued, from several perspectives. The second is a set of related values-based (agree–disagree) statements (see the example in Figure 8.6).

Step 1	Students read the assigned selection and individually answer the comprehension questions on the first worksheet.
Step 2	Form cooperative groups of four students each. A chairperson is appointed. (The chairperson's role is rotated each time the activity is performed.) Students compare their answers to the questions within their groups and *discuss the reasons* for their answers.
Step 3	The second worksheet is distributed, and students individually record their own responses to the values-based statements, and predict the responses of the other members of their group (see Figure 8.6).
Step 4	The chairperson reads the first statement, tells his or her response, and asks each group member to share his or her

Figure 8.6
Sample valuing statement exercise sheet for Intra-Act.

Your Name: _____   Date: _____
Group Chairperson: _____   Hour: _____

Directions: Circle A for "agree" or D for "disagree" to indicate your own
responses to each statement. Then circle A or D to indicate how you
think each other member of your group responsded to each state-
ment.

		Group Members			
		Me	*Mary*	*Jack*	*Helen*
1.	Men are usually better bosses than women.	A/D	A/D	A/D	A/D
2.	Once elected, a legislator should vote according to the wishes of the people he or she represents, not according to personal feelings.	A/D	A/D	A/D	A/D
3.	I would have voted the way the main character did in this story	A/D	A/D	A/D	A/D
4.	I probably would have reacted as negatively to the main character as her "constituents."	A/D	A/D	A/D	A/D

---

response. Students "check" their own predictions of their classmates' responses as the chairperson guides them through each item.

Step 5   The teacher leads a whole-class discussion of students' personal judgments about the valuing statements and the accuracy of their predictions of the other students' judgments.

Extended Anticipation-Reaction Guide

An extension of the Anticipation-Reaction Guide described in Chapter 4 is an effective way to encourage critical-constructive reading and responding. After students have recorded their responses to the A-R Guide statements before and after reading, they are directed to write an essay elaborating on their response to any one of the statements on the worksheet. Figure 8.7 presents an example of an A-R Guide and a related student essay from a class in economics.

Active interaction of the type generated by Anticipation-Reaction Guides promotes several key ingredients of critical reading-thinking:

- ✦ Conflict identification and resolution (Frager & Thompson, 1985)
- ✦ Metacognitive awareness of the strategies one is employing while reading (Brown, 1980)
- ✦ Connections between one's knowledge of the world and comprehension of text (Waern, 1977a,b)

Regarding the last point, Ericson et al. (1987) point out that in the California Academic Partnership Program, in which professors used A-R Guides in working with teachers and junior high school students, students often would leave class at the end of the period still arguing the relative merits of their various points of view. This act of carrying the classroom out into

Figure 8.7
Anticipation-Reaction Guide: Supply-side economics.

Directions: Before reading, check Agree or Disagree for each statement. After reading, write a brief essay on one statement of your choice.

Agree	Disagree		
————	————	1.	Supply-side economics favors the wealthy.
————	————	2.	You cannot be a Republican and be against supply-side economics.
————	————	3.	You cannot be a Democrat and be for supply-side economics.

STUDENT ESSAY

I think that supply-side economics favors the wealthy because it says that when profits go up, the number of suppliers will increase. This also is supposed to increase competition, and therefore reduce prices, since there would be more supply than demand.

The government, under this approach, is dedicated to helping create greater profits for suppliers. This, however, would tend to make the rich richer and leave the poor and middle class to be the perpetual shoppers, looking for oversupplies. In fact, though, whenever supply begins to exceed demand, the rich simply move their assets elsewhere, quickly reducing supply and competition.

Of course, supply-side thinking is basic to free enterprise. Without a profit motive, investors would not take risks. The role of government, however, needs to be balanced carefully so as to avoid unnecessarily crimping profits, but also avoiding measures that virtually guarantee profits. These include big tax breaks for industry or freedom to exploit the environment. When large corporations are legally permitted not to pay tax and/or to leave behind their industrial wastes, this amounts to a hidden surcharge on all the products bought and one that the rest of us, including future generations, eventually must pay.

---

the student's world may be the most powerful influence of all on learning and thinking. It extends the school day by increasing student time on task and reducing the sharp line of demarcation that often separates school learning from home and life experiences.

Opinion-Proof

The Opinion-Proof method (Santa, Dailey, & Nelson, 1985) requires students to engage in four important aspects of higher-order literacy:*

- ✦ Evaluative thinking—forming an opinion
- ✦ Verification—supporting the opinion
- ✦ Persuasive articulation—writing about the opinion convincingly
- ✦ Forming a consensus, or cooperative critiquing and reviewing of opinion

Steps in the Opinion-Proof Method

Step 1   Provide students with an Opinion-Proof guide, either written on the chalkboard or as a handout (see the example in step 2).

Step 2   Have students write an opinion and supporting evidence for it from the text. Following is a guide for the short story "Old Horse," a popular selection about an elderly algebra teacher by Oliver Andersen:

Example:

- ✦ *Opinion Statement:* Old Horse was sensitive.
- ✦ *Evidence to Prove My Opinion:*

   Old Horse was sensitive.

   He was patient with Rabbit.

   He wanted Rabbit to belong.

   Old Horse forced Rabbit to dislike him.

   He put himself down for the sake of Rabbit.

Step 3   Students write a connected essay using their opinion and evidence as topic sentence and supporting details, respectively.

Example:

Old Horse was a very sensitive teacher. One reason I feel this way was because of his ability to understand Rabbit. Rabbit was not

---

* Excerpt from "Free-response and opinion proof: A reading and writing strategy for middle grade and secondary teachers," by C. M. Santa, S. C. Dailey, and M. Nelson, *Journal of Reading* 28, pp. 346–352. © 1985 by the International Reading Association. Reprinted with permission of C. M. Santa and the International Reading Association.

liked by the other students in his class because he was a friend of Old Horse's. In addition, Old Horse understood Rabbit's need to become a part of a group of friends, and Old Horse knew that he was part of the problem. Finally, Old Horse forced Rabbit to dislike him so much that he could become accepted by the other students. Therefore, Old Horse was a very sensitive man. He even sacrificed himself for the sake of his student.

Step 4   The final step is peer editing. In this step, students (1) develop specific criteria for evaluating their writing, asking such questions as "Does my paragraph contain a main idea statement?" and "Do I have evidence to support my main idea?"; (2) divide up into pairs or small groups and read and react to one another's paragraphs; and (3) edit and/or revise their own paragraphs before submitting a final draft for teacher evaluation.

In addition to its role in reading and thinking, the Opinion-Proof process provides a useful sequence for organizing persuasive speeches, another important language art. It accomplishes this by having students state opinions and write out supporting and nonsupporting points. This often leads to the reflective turnabout that makes Opinion-Proof a good framework for teaching in the transformative mode.

Read-Encode-Annotate-Ponder

The Read-Encode-Annotate-Ponder (REAP) method (Manzo, 1973; Eanet & Manzo, 1976) was shown to be an effective tool for transformational teaching in two recent studies (Garber, 1995; Jackson-Albee, 2000). At its most basic level, REAP is a way to teach students to write (and think) from a variety of perspectives. It also was among the earliest strategies developed for students to use to improve study-type writing, thinking, and reading. The basic REAP formula is as follows:

Read to discern the writer's message.

Encode the message by mentally translating it into your own words.

Annotate, or make written note of, your brief responses from several perspectives.

Ponder, or further reflect on what you have read, thought, and written, through discussion of your own and others' responses to the selection and/or your and their annotations.

REAP introduces students to a variety of brief and poignant ways to critique or *annotate* what they have read. Annotation types range from simple summaries to highly challenging critical-constructive responses.

Research on writing suggests that efforts to improve this type of critiquing, when taught concurrently with analytical reading and discipline instruction, result in enriched factual knowledge, conceptual development, writing improvement, vocabulary growth, and personal-social adjustment (Applebee, 1981; Bromley, 1985; Cunningham & Cunningham, 1976; Doctorow, Wittrock, & Marks, 1978; Eanet & Manzo, 1976; Garber, 1995; Tierney, Soter, O'Flahavan, & McGinley, 1989).

Reap-Share

Today, critiquing, annotating, and discussing are part of several on-line services whereby readers can exchange views on a variety of subjects and books. This can be done asynchronously (on-line, but at different times) or through chat groups (on-line, in real time). In either case, the exchanges tend to be open-ended and hit-and-miss in terms of pedagogic value. REAP-Sharing is more disciplined. As indicated above, it is a structured system designed over a generation ago to guide and teach reading and thoughtful reacting in a pedagogically sound way. Students are introduced to the concept and value of writing from different perspectives in class. They then are led to discuss the merits of posting their annotations where they would be accessible to one another. Students easily spot one basic value, namely that they can read each others' critiques of certain works before they read the longer work, and/or following reading. Through guided discussion, they come to appreciate other values in sharing annotations. Benefits include having multiple representations of different perspectives on a variety of materials to guide higher-level thinking; having model critiques to guide the craft side of writing; and having the option to reread or further read annotations during the time they are reading a difficult, longer work like *Tale of Two Cities*, where it is easy to lose the thread of the plot. See http://members.aol.com/ReadShop/REAP1.html for some web sites that are based on REAP-SHARE, also called REAP ANX, for REAP Annotation Exchange. This basic system now is serving, too, as the basis for efforts to extend curiosity and creative thinking. More on this presently. There also is a technological innovation, ThirdVoice.com, that will allow for the annotation of web sites for subsequent viewers. Some have called this unwanted graffiti; others see it as a major breakthrough in reducing the power of publishers and authors over what the reader-viewer gets to see. It becomes on-the-spot criticism. Check it out and see what you think.

Stages in Using REAP as a Teaching Tool

The first stage in using REAP is to teach students how to write several of the annotation types described below and illustrated in Figure 8.8. Note that the annotation types represent a hierarchy from basic to higher-order levels of thinking, with the first four categorized as *reconstructive* level, requiring literal-level responding, and the next ten as *constructive* level, requiring reading and thinking between and beyond the lines. It is best to

Figure 8.8
Examples of REAP annotations.

"Travelers and the Plane-tree: A Fable"

Two travelers were walking along a bare and dusty road in the heat of a mid-summer's day. Coming upon a large shade tree, they happily stopped to shelter themselves from the burning sun in the shade of its spreading branches. While they rested, looking up into the tree, one of them said to his companion, "What a useless tree this is! It makes no flowers and bears no fruit. Of what use is it to anyone?" The tree itself replied indignantly, "You ungrateful people! You take shelter under me from the scorching sun, and then, in the very act of enjoying the cool shade of my leaves, you abuse me and call me good for nothing!"

Reconstructive Responses:

1. Summary response
   Travelers take shelter from the sun under a large tree. They criticize the tree for not making flowers or fruit. The tree speaks, and tells them that they are ungrateful people for taking shelter under her leaves and then criticizing her.

2. Precise response
   Travelers stop for rest and shade under big tree. Travelers say tree is useless. Tree tells them off.

3. Attention-getting response
   In this story, a tree talks back to people. The tree says, "You ungrateful people! You come and take shelter under me . . . and then . . . abuse me and call me nothing!"

4. Question response
   What tales might be told if inanimate objects could talk?

Constructive Annotations

5. Personal view responses

   (a) We use resources like coal without thinking. Then we criticize the resource for damaging our lungs and dirtying our air

   (b) Kids sometimes use their parents the way the travelers used the tree—and then criticize them for letting themselves be used.

6. Critical response
   Not every word spoken in criticism is meant that way. The travelers were just a little grumpy from the long hard trip. The tree is being too sensitive.

7. Contrary response
   The travelers could be right. There are other trees that could produce something, as well as just providing shade.

8. Intention response
   The author wants us to be more sensitive to the people and things we depend on—especially those we see and use most often.

Figure 8.8, *continued*

9. Motivation response
It sounds like the author may have felt used, after having a bad experience with friends or family.

10. Discovery response
I wonder how many of us know when we are being "users." It would be interesting to take an anonymous poll to see how many people secretly feel that they have been used, and how many honestly see themselves as users.

11. Moral-ethical response
I think we should ask how some of history's enlightened moral thinkers would respond to this, say Jesus, Confucius, Augustine, Thomas Jefferson.

12. Discipline-connective responses
    (a) A poet would easily write an ode to such a tree; are there any?
    (b) A scientist might ask, "how does this tree manage to thrive where others cannot even manage to survive?"
    (c) A mathematician likely would want to calculate the probability of this tree's having rooted and found water before it was consumed by heat and drought; can that be done?

13. Creative response
[Teacher guidance: What are some analogous situations this fable reminds you of?]
    (a) This fable reminds me of how Dobie Gillis uses and then abuses that nice, but plain girl who always hangs around him.
    (b) This fable made me think that teachers are sometimes used unfairly. They give us so much, and then we put them down if they make little mistakes. They're only human!
    [Teacher guidance: Having gotten the point of this fable, what should we do?]
    (c) We should put this fable on the bulletin board where it will remind us not to be ungrateful "users."
    [Teacher guidance: How would you retitle this fable if you were writing it?]
    (d) I'd call this fable "Travelers in the Dark," to show that we go through life without appreciating the many small "gifts" that come to us, while we're busy grumbling about what we don't have.

14. Reading awareness (metacognitive) response.
    (a) I feel like I'm beginning to better understand what the word "indignant" means from reading this, but I don't think I could define it yet
    (b) This fable is too short. My mind feels like it needs more words, or something to really get this.
    (c) I keep wondering how a fable is different from a parable.

introduce students to three or four annotation types initially, provide practice with these, and then add additional annotation types gradually. Experience suggests that a good cluster to begin with is summary, heuristic, and critical.

Reconstructive Responses

1. *Summary response.* States the basic message of the selection in brief form. In fiction, it is the basic story line; in nonfiction, it is a simple statement of the main ideas.

2. *Precise response.* Briefly states the author's basic idea or theme, with all unnecessary words removed. The result is a crisp, telegram-like message.

3. *Attention-getting or heuristic response.* Restates a snappy portion of the selection that makes the reader want to respond. It is best to use the author's own words.

4. *Question response.* Turns the main point of the story or information into an organizing question that the selection answers.

Constructive Responses

5. *Personal view or transactional response.* Answers the question "How do your views and feelings compare with what you perceive the author to have said?"

6. *Critical response.* Supports, rejects, or questions the main idea, and tells why. The first sentence of this type of response should restate the author's position. The next sentence should state the writer's position. Additional sentences should explain how the two differ.

7. *Contrary response.* Attempts to state a logical alternative position, even if it is not one that the student necessarily supports. This is an especially important way to represent a minority view that can easily be overlooked.

8. *Intention response.* States and briefly explains what the responder thinks is the author's intention, plan, and purpose in writing the selection. This is a special version of the critical response that causes the reader/responder to try to think like the author or from the author's perspective.

9. *Motivation response.* States what may have caused the author to create or write the story or selection. This is another special version of critical responding. It is an attempt to discover the author's personal agenda and hence areas of writing or unwitting biases.

10. *Discovery response.* States one or more practical questions that need to be answered before the story or facts can be judged for accuracy or worth. This type of response to text is the mode of thinking that

leads to more reading and research and occasionally to a reformulated position or view.

11. *Moral-ethical response.* Requires reference to values and beliefs that guide, or one believes, should guide attitudes and behavior; and hence, both reflects and influences character development and complexity of thinking.

12. *Discipline-connective (or interdisciplinary) response.* This is a conscious search for relevant ideas, facts, and factors that may seldom appear related to a topic because schooling, as opposed to learning, tends to have subject boundaries whereas ideas do not.

13. *Creative response.* Suggests different and perhaps better solutions or views and/or connections and applications to prior learning and experiences. Students usually need some guidance and/or examples to produce this type of response. Once they begin thinking in this way, however, the results can be remarkably constructive.

14. *Reading awareness (metacognitive) response.* Identifies or comments on a problem one may have had in reading and understanding a specific piece.

After students have had some practice in writing various types of annotations, these can be used in a variety of ways:

✦ When giving a reading assignment, assign three annotation types for students to write and turn in.

✦ As students become more skilled at annotation writing, the assignment can be given with the requirement that, after they have read, students themselves decide which three annotation types to write in response.

✦ Assign each member of cooperative groups a different annotation type to write. When groups meet, encourage group members to offer constructive suggestions by offering extra credit points to the group with the best annotation of each type (judged by the teacher or the class as a whole).

✦ Introduce a new reading assignment by having students read annotations written by students in a previous year (or from a different section of the class).

✦ Provide incentive to read and write reflectively by posting exemplary annotations, signed by the author, on a bulletin board or Internet system.

✦ Encourage students to write from different disciplinary perspectives ("Write an annotation on *The Rainman* the way Mr. Kezlan your math teacher might or like Mr. Willson your English teacher might write one.") Expect some of these to be humorous, because they will be. (See item 12 (discipline-connected responses) in Figure 8.9 for some representations that reduced the probability of humorous responses, should you wish to avoid these.)

REAP Responses as an Evaluation Rubric

To monitor student progress toward higher-order literacy, the teacher can use the preceding annotations listing as a rubric for reviewing student writings. The rubric can serve as a means of appraising the characteristic way in which a student or group of students respond to text. To use the REAP annotation types in this way, simply compare a student's writing to the preceding descriptions, and decide which annotation type it most closely resembles, keeping in mind that the annotations, as listed and illustrated above, already are roughly in order of difficulty: lower numbers indicate more concrete thinking, and higher numbers more personal and abstract patterns of responding.

Further Thoughts on Encouraging Higher-Order Responding

One of the simplest ways to teach students to write constructively is to elicit quick personal responses to a piece they have read. Then, the teacher

Figure 8.9
Encouraging higher-order responding.

Following silent reading of a selection on the exploits of Hernando de Soto, an eighth-grade teacher, rather than first seeking a summary of facts, asked the class, "What did you think of de Soto?" Reactions included "sick," "cruel," and "loser." When asked to explain why they felt this way, students recited a litany of facts and events that amounted to a summary. Then the teacher asked them to get together in groups and form their reactions and reasons into personal comments on the selection. The following critique was typical of the results:

> *Hernando de Soto was a loser. After bringing gold back from Peru, the Spanish king encouraged him to go back to the New World by making him governor of Florida in 1539. He and 550 men looked for more gold. Even though some of them were priests, they mutilated and killed Indians in their search. After three years of this, de Soto died with nothing, and his men returned to Spain empty-handed.*

In this case, students' visceral and somewhat "cranky" responses seemed to help them distinguish de Soto from other explorers of his time and recall important information. In this way, the purpose of writing following reading was well served: information was carefully processed, personalized, and stored for long-term recall. Further, the concept of "de Soto" and the context of the times replaced a collection of random facts about a vague historical figure named de Soto.

should work with the class to form these initial highly subjective responses into more thoughtful critical and constructive ones. One way to do this is simply to ask students to give support for their positions. That is, to reconcile, or attempt to balance, their initial responses with the ethical and values-based positions that are fundamental to their communities and to higher ideals, such as liberty, as well as more practical ones such as how would this be paid for or made workable. Again, students should not be forced to conformity here but should be encouraged to reprocess the rationale for societal goals and expectations. Where students' responses differ markedly from one another, divide them into groups that produce critiques of their varied viewpoints. See Figure 8.9 for an anecdotal example from an eighth-grade social studies class we observed.

Letters to the Editor
Another means of stimulating cogent writing in response to text is to refer students to good approximations of it in the form of model letters to the editor in newspapers and magazines. Notice how the sample letters to the editor in Figure 8.10 help one get a better grip on one's own thoughts and feelings about problems in China. This is a good place to invite interesting perspectives as may come from trying to write a letter as if it comes from a famous person, say Benjamin Franklin, one of our first foreign ambassadors (see "Ben Franklin on Tiananmen," also in Figure 8.10).

Less Can Be More
Brief response-type annotations, like letters to the editor, offer a challenge to sift through information and feelings and to struggle to take a thoughtful position. To this extent, such critiques can be more valuable than formal

Figure 8.10
Letters to the editor exemplify cogent response to text.

"How tragic it is that to cope with change, China's leaders felt they needed to kill their young."

"The people of China will triumph. Deng Xiaoping and followers have forgotten their own history. It is impossible to repress an idea whose time has come!"

"China had to crush the democratic resistance. The blood spilled in Tiananmen Square is a small price to pay to prevent a civil war that would consume thousands, if not millions."

Ben Franklin on Tiananmen:

"China is a sovereign state whose internal affairs we cannot intercede in under international law. However, if we trade with them, we will be their customers, and merchants always try to please their best customers."

term papers and conventional book reports because they align more closely with student experiences and the faster pace of modern life.

Additionally, this type of writing, because it is brief, provides more frequent opportunities for students to read, react, and write. On a very pragmatic level, such annotations can more easily be read and shared with peers and occasionally reviewed by a secondary teacher with an average load of more than 135 students per day, per semester.

A FORMULA FOR PROMOTING CRITICAL-CONSTRUCTIVE THINKING

When the formula for teaching constructive reading, writing, and thinking is finally written, there is a good chance that it will contain at least these three factors: (1) respect for the past; (2) problem-based teaching; and (3) a collection of ways to invite creative production. See if the thoughts in the sections that follow meet these criteria.

Exploring Ideas—Past, Present, and Evolving

Once we heard a popular futurist speaker at an educational conference say that when you are traveling at the speed of light, as we are now in the modern age, you don't need a rear-view mirror. We respectfully disagree. The past is always important. It is the way we are able to escape the limitations of personal experiences and connect to the continuum of efforts and solutions that have proven workable. The challenge of course is to recognize the difference between a road and a rut. A problem-solving orientation is one way to deal with this challenge.

Engagement with problem-solving teaches respect for the past, or what has been learned. Tussling with problems also can be empowering because it helps us to tackle the daunting task of trying to have original thoughts, which it turns out we are more capable of than we ever realized. Teachers need to help students to discover that they are capable of being *ideators*, that is, idea makers and problem identifiers and solvers. Our collective tendency as teachers to almost never ask for creative production becomes a repeating, confirming lesson that this is hardly possible, let alone doable. For this problem, we are discovering some remarkably simple remedies with powerful implications for how kids will read, write, and learn subjects, and otherwise think.

The "Just Ask For It" Hypothesis

The simplest way to open the door to creative thinking is to put question marks where there are premature periods, in other words, to explicitly *ask for* new twists, innovative approaches, original thinking, saying, and expressing. Ollmann (1996) compared seven formats for promoting higher-level thinking. Reflecting on the results, she noted, "I could see clearly that if I wanted a particular kind of thinking, I needed to *ask students for it*" (p. 581). "Asking for it" begins with the teacher displaying his or her own enthusiasm for reading, learning, expressing, and inquiry; a sentiment nicely captured in this Indian bromide: *One who learns from one who is learning drinks from a running stream.*

There are some convincing clinical accounts and field studies suggesting that there is a great dormant force of creative energy waiting to transform the way in which we read and write in school, if teachers would "just ask for it." The question seems to impel the thinking and actions that follow.

One account, for example, tells of a professor of engineering's action research with his students. Students were randomly assigned to two groups and given identical plans to critique. However, one group was told to "critically" critique the plans, and the other to "constructively" critique them. The results showed that the "constructive" critiquers produced better criticisms and several very plausible, even creative, alternative solutions. The "criticisms" group offered weaker and more picky criticisms and virtually no constructive alternatives (in Baker & Schutz, 1972). Apparently, the capacities of the students in the "criticism" group to be constructive-creative simply remained dormant with no trigger mechanism to activate them.

If you are inclined to celebrate the wonders and unique capabilities of the human mind from such stories, you may need to consider deleting the words *unique* and *human* after reading this next account. Louis Herman, director of a marine mammal laboratory, had taught dolphins to respond to directions communicated through hand gestures. In some way, not explained in the news account, he taught them, or they learned, to comprehend a gesture meaning "creative." In any case, one day he signaled to two of them to perform in tandem, and to do "something creative." With only that prompt, the dolphins submerged for a few moments, then swimming in tandem leaped into the air and simultaneously spit out jets of water before plunging back into the pool. On another occasion, given the same command, they performed a synchronized backward swim culminating in a simultaneous wave of the tails (*Time*, March 22, 1993, p. 54). Of course, almost as amazing as the creative nature of this feat is the wonder about how these sea mammals were able to comprehend the concept of creative, and to communicate intentions to one another for a tandem effort.

Nonetheless, these anecdotes and some related empirical findings discussed in the following seem to give considerable creditability to the proposition that asking for critical-constructive (i.e., creative) production is a solid way to begin to stimulate it. The simple, logical explanation for this is the fact that higher levels of thinking tend to be *as much a matter of orientation and disposition* (Bereiter, 1995)—or attitude, inclination, and focus—*as of aptitude*—or innate capacity and skill.

Inviting Creative Production: Expressive-Artistic

A group of inner-city, once-failed-English, tenth-grade students were asked as part of a *death and dying* literature theme to try and create their own "communal poem"(Manzo & Martin, 1974). What they produced was called very worthy by several professors of literature, including the poet, Dan Jaffe, who led this particular session. See Figure 8.11 for the *communal poetry process and poem.*

The communal poetry process is an excellent way to build group cohesiveness and collaboration. Importantly, the topic and mood are easily set with just a few words. For example, on another occasion, we observed a teacher leading a session where she had conveyed a more humorous, in-your-face mood, and the class came back with a brief, rollicking poem that ended with a satisfying "Hurrah" for their effort (Manzo & Manzo, 1990a). While we have not tried it yet, it seems as if it could be convened and conducted on-line in real time or asynchronously. Please let us know if you pilot this possibility, and we will share your efforts on our web site.

Inviting Creative Production: In the Realm of Idea Making (QuestMagnets)

Recently, we have begun to experiment with QuestMagnets (QM), a more wraparound, or surround-sound form of just asking for it. QuestMagnets

Figure 8.11
Communal poetry process and poem.

Communal Poetry Process

1. The teacher asks questions designed to elicit fresh language and personal sensory responses about a chosen subject (e.g., "If death walked through that door, what would it look like?" "Who knows death best?").

2. Responses are recorded on the chalkboard. Clichés and other prosaic or hackneyed phrases are edited out as they occur.

3. Once the board is filled with raw material, students are asked to choose a beginning line from the material on the board.

4. The teacher writes the line and then aids students in selecting other phrases, helping them to establish rhythm and/or continuity of thought.

5. The teacher reads the recorded lines aloud again and asks students for additional choices from the board, allowing changes as the group indicates need.

6. When students are satisfied with the product, the leader reads the finished poem aloud.

7. A final copy is prepared with the names of the student participants, and copies are presented to the class.

Figure 8.11, *continued*

Communal Poem

Somebody's Missing

Take a look around.
somebody's missing
> *the dogs are howling*
> *somebody's going to sleep.*

The grandfathers know
> *what's going on:*
> *the air is polluted with grief.*

Down on the corner, in the grocery store,
he's about to touch you on the arm
> *with a silver knife*
> *a black guillotine*
> *a .38 pointed at your head.*

Even the tough people are scared.

There I was slipping in the dark,
smelling the dumpyard,
> *the wrinkled dirt,*
> *feeling so low I felt like getting high.*

It's time
> *to let life into this poem!*
Time to take a bath,
> *to pay death back with babies,*
> *to make even a policeman cry.*

It's true
> *not only an undertaker knows bodies.*
Let's touch one another
> *and send Death Nowhere.*

---

are heuristics, or specific self-discovery mechanisms that evoke fresh thinking and writing. They are served up as an inviting variety of questions, problems, factoids, ideas, and musings that interrupt mundane thinking. Essentially, QMs amount to open-ended questions and dialogues about a wide variety of things encountered in and out of school; they are one way to begin to convert periods to question marks and question marks to wonder and original thinking. The goal is to enrich students' inner-speech with reminders of the mysteries and questions that anchor much of what is taught in school, and of how much more needs to be discovered. For example, in science one might ask the question, "How does gravity really work?" If you have ever thought about this, and who hasn't, you will be interested to discover that the answer is "We haven't but a clue." Ironically, discovering this seems to benefit attention and learning better than a lecture on the byplay between centripetal and centrifugal forces, words that more describe than explain how it is that the oceans don't empty into space.

There is no single way to stir and support higher-level reading, writing, and thinking, and yet there seem to be many ways. Clearly, doing so must involve turning the attention of both teachers and students to the things about them that are worth pondering before being ingested as givens. Kristin Weissinger, a Manzo granddaughter, e-mailed us after a conversation on this subject with the contents of a poster she had told us was on the bulletin board of every classroom in her middle school:

+ *What if . . . ?*
+ *How would it change if . . . ?*
+ *Is there another way to solve, write, or say this?*
+ *What's wrong here?*
+ *Why can't we do that?*

Her e-mail with these potentially stirring questions also contained a note that has us wondering, "What's wrong here?" Her note continued:

> . . . but no one really pays attention to them. I think they're mostly there for the teachers. Love, Kristen

Though these questions contain the basis for imaginative thinking, creative writing, innovative problem-solving, problem identification, and plausibility testing, they appear to be impotent when merely posted on classroom bulletin boards. QuestMagnets are designed to be more participatory and to occur in a variety of ways and places. They are intended to "rouse minds to life" (Tharp & Gallimore, 1989).

Questmagnets: Permission to Interrupt

To optimize the positive effects of QuestMagnets, the first and most important thing to do is to explain to pupils and parents, in a note home, the value and purpose of these to learning, thinking, and discussion. In other words, ask for permission to interrupt, much as modern advertising is based on "permission marketing" (Godin, 1999), a means of not only gaining attention to a product but interest in hearing more about it because of the personal value that it brings. To extend the critical-constructive, reading-writing-thinking "ad campaign," QuestMagnets could be:

+ Posted on classroom bulletin boards, but also where one might not expect to find them, such as in locker rooms and on cafeteria walls

✦ Made into printed notes for the home refrigerator, where families can enjoy engaging and discussing them

✦ Invited from students, faculty, and parents (to further encourage thoughtful contributions, create blank postcards addressed to the school's Quest Learning Manager, and post names of submitters)

✦ Treated as brief critical/constructive writing assignments in classes where they might tie in with a curriculum topic

✦ Entered and dialogued on a class's or a school's web site

✦ Possibly submitted to global web sites, such as the Registry for Better Ideas (http://members.aol.com/csholumkc/RBI.html), a site that is raising funds to make awards to incisive new questions as well as solutions

Consider some examples of QuestMagnets that might be used to stir REAP-like response writing, and to generate additional submissions of like kinds. The categories below are not mutually exclusive.

QuestMagnets: Writing the Future

✦ Why are eyeglasses not engineered to more easily adjust to the facts that most people's ears are of unequal height, and that long hours of pressure on any skin surface, such as the nose, is irritating?

✦ Why aren't we developing something like a web-based universal voting system to complement and balance the influence of lobbyists on our current political system?

QuestMagnets: Factoids

✦ Deduce this: On what day are more take-out pizzas purchased than any other? (The day before Thanksgiving.)

✦ Southern California has for fewer flying and crawling bugs per cubic foot of ground and space than the rest of the United States. Could this be the reason they also have less topsoil? Is topsoil largely bug guana and dead bug bodies?

✦ Females tend to see and remember more about what is in a room than do males; what can this mean?

✦ Single males are living home with their parents many years longer than single females, 29 years old versus 22.

✦ We're probably not all alike, and that may be our collective, adaptive advantage.

✦ Each U.S. acre contains an average of 400 lbs. of insects, compared with only 14 lbs. of people.

✦ The number of teen drivers killed in auto accidents is four times greater than that of urban teens killed by guns (*Time*, August 1999).

QuestMagnets: From the Heart

There are certain essential humanistic feelings that are not covered by law, but that help us to keep our moral-ethical bearings. Sometimes these gurgle up within us as an urge or counterurge, that says "This doesn't feel right." On a purely cognitive level, observing, thinking, and puzzling over these "gnarlies" is a fundamental way to build higher-order thinking, interdisciplinary problem-solving, and a sense of moral rectitude. Here are some examples:

- ✦ Isn't there some more humane way to kill and cook lobsters than to slowly boil them alive?

- ✦ Shouldn't we think twice about adopting pets that require more care and attention than we are ready to provide?

- ✦ Should there be a web site where one can post and date the license plate numbers of reckless drivers?

QuestMagnets: By Subjects

(Math)	Why did it take such a very long time for humankind to discover and create zero (0)?
(Math)	What's all this business about "magic 9's"?
(Science)	Does anyone know how gravity really works? (Again, no they do not. For a fascinating new theory, see http://amoureternal.com/oti/gravity/phen.htm).
(Science)	How do electronic waves pass through the air and then recollect themselves in a radio or television set in the same patterns as they were sent?
(Social Studies)	If everyone has some money and they keep getting more, where did it first come from, and how does it continue to grow?
(Social Studies)	Why do some countries (like the U.S.) have "states" (which means independent countries, within the country as a whole) and doesn't this result in different laws and punishments in places that are separated only by an imaginary line?

QuestMusings: Wit and Wonder

School can be too serious and therefore a bit too confining. It can be liberating of the mind and spirit to think unseriously, ideally, wittily, and amusingly. Invite such thoughts, more so than reactions, by sharing the wit and musings of some of the masters. Avoid heavy moralizing here; it's all in fun.

How come abbreviated is such a long word? (Steven Wright)
Why do scientists call it "re-search" when they are looking for something new? (Steven Wright)

QuestFinancial: Investing and Entrepreneurism

Making and keeping money is a fundamental need for almost everyone. Help students to prepare for this life venture by orienting them early on to its obligatory demands. One way to do this is by raising it as a target, or orientation for reading. writing, and learning. (Read more on this topic in a hypertext chapter, *The Twenty-first century*, on our web site.) Minimally, however, have students read and react to articles and statements such as might be gathered under a title such as *$QUEST*, or *FinancialFutures*. Here are some evocative statements from a series of recent articles in a financial advisory magazine. Let students chew on some of these before, during, and/or after reading such articles.

$Quest

✦ The key to having money is not in making a lot of it, but in not spending so much of what you earn.

✦ You can be young without money, but you can't be old without it.

✦ The key to success in Internet selling, according to one entrepreneur, is simply to be there first with a simple idea, such as he was with ⟨golfball.com⟩, a company that started by just selling and shipping golf balls, but now is selling lots of related paraphernalia.

In general, questing is more a "search" than a "re-search" approach to reading-writing-thinking. It is the conscious effort to see what others are seeing but to see it freshly; to more clearly detect the signal through the static.

CRITICAL-CONSTRUCTIVE DISCUSSION TECHNIQUES

Many teaching methods have a step called "discuss." Following are two classical methods and one newly developing method for promoting discussions that "rouse minds to life."

Developmental Discussion

The Developmental Discussion (Maier, 1963) and a rediscovered version called Guided Conversation (Gauthier, 1996) are intended to teach students about the full process of problem solving by involving them in all of its parts: identification and partitioning of the problem, collection of relevant data or information, generation of solutions, and appraisal of solutions. Most importantly, it places heavy emphasis on going beyond existing knowledge. As such, it should be basic to any program to improve creative thinking and problem solving. Needless to say, much of this process can be shifted to an asynchronous system such as a web site with a bulletin board and/or an e-mail list serve.

Steps in Developmental Discussion/Guided Conversation

Step 1 The teacher instructs students to try to identify certain conflicting points (rather than views) or problems inherent in material presented in text and lecture.

Step 2 The teacher initially provides examples that can serve as models of problem identification (this usually requires comparing textual information to prior knowledge and experiences).

Step 3 The teacher assists students in narrowing and partitioning the problem into manageable segments.

Step 4 Students are divided into cooperative learning groups to solve the smaller parts of the problem. Each group is asked to jot down notes on individual and group members' answers using questions such as the following to guide their analysis:

    a. What do we know about this problem part?

    b. Which parts of the information we have are relevant to the problem?

    c. What more do we need to know to construct a possible solution?

    d. What are some possible solutions given what we now know?

    e. What additional information can we collect (and how) to formulate better solutions?

Step 5 A large-group discussion is held to illustrate the different ways the problem can be viewed and solutions sought. The teacher reminds students to add to their notes during this discussion.

Step 6 The class decides on a solution (usually a synthesis) or—in a significant departure from conventional school practices—may choose to table the matter until the class can collect additional information (see Figure 8.12 for an anecdotal account).

Step 7 Students individually write out the solution as they see it and in the most convincing way possible. Then students exchange papers and give one another feedback on their essays. The teacher invites students and reviewers to read aloud phrases or sections that they feel were particularly well stated.

Devil's Advocate

One simple and direct way to encourage students to consider an issue from alternate perspectives is to get students into a discussion that evokes

Figure 8.12

Anecdotal account of Developmental Discussion.

Mr. Freeble, a high school civics teacher, works with a group of average ability students for fifty minutes each morning. In a previous class session the students had read a five page textbook assignment and had completed the accompanying study guide. The assignment covered information about the Supreme Court—what it is, its purpose and charges, and its relationship to the entire governmental system.

Freeble began the developmental discussion by reviewing the previous textbook assignment for five minutes. From the review, students were reminded of the following key concepts: the Supreme Court is the highest court in the land, the individuals sitting on the Supreme Court are charged with interpreting the Constitution, and members of the Supreme Court may change a previous ruling by another branch of the government.

Next, Freeble asked the students to supply current information about events in the news concerning recent Supreme Court rulings. Elicited were facts about prayer in school and nativity scenes set up on public property. Freeble noted that the seasonal influence (it was close to Christmas) play [sic] a large role in students' interest in a local newspaper story about a controversial nativity scene. After ten minutes of discussing that story and its implications for local residents, the class decided on a problem that was text based but of immediate interest to them—should religious groups be allowed to erect nativity scenes on public property?

The teacher guided the students in breaking the larger problem (separation of church and state) into three smaller problems: (1) Does setting up a nativity scene on public property violate the rights of individuals who do not have the same religious beliefs?; (2) What information could the class add that would help solve the problem?; (3) What would be a reasonable way to share what was learned with the people involved in the controversy?

The students broke into smaller groups and began to work on the first part of the problem. Freeble supplied each group with a one page summary of the Pawtucket case involving a Supreme Court ruling on the display of nativity scenes on public property. Freeble circulated among the groups, observing and offering assistance when requested.

During the last fifteen minutes of the period, students participated in a large group discussion in which they reported on their reactions to the Pawtucket case and whether they believed the case had any implications for the local controversy.

Over the next two days, the students worked in small groups to tackle the remaining problem parts. Solutions to the overall problem included working with community leaders to foster improved communication among the dissident groups and writing letters to the editor of the local newspaper on the topic of how the Pawtucket case compared to the local one.

Source: From Donna E. Alvermann, Deborah R. Dillon, & David G. O'Brien (1987). *Using Discussion to Promote Reading Comprehension,* IRA. Reprinted with permission of Donna E. Alvermann and the International Reading Association. All rights reserved.

this type of reasoning. *Devil's Advocate* is an issues-based discussion that has a rich heritage (Alvermann, Dillon, & O'Brien, 1987; Roby, 1983). It was used by Socrates and Plato and is a common convention at synods of several religions around the world.

One of three things may happen in a Devil's Advocate discussion: positions may be strengthened, modified, or abandoned. In any case, students involved in such a discussion tend to have a great many experiences with reflective turnabout. They learn about the enormous complexity of issues that initially appear clear-cut. They learn about the paradoxes involved in trying to solve a problem only to find that the best solution can sometimes be more disruptive than the existing problem. Finally, they learn to use language not merely to state what they believe but to discover what they *might* reasonably believe.

Steps in Devil's Advocate Method

Step 1	The teacher poses an issue to the class.
Step 2	Students are paired but asked to individually prepare written arguments using the text for essential information. Sometimes there are more than two positions.
Step 3	Students are instructed to describe to their partners their best arguments for each position. They should discuss each argument to determine whether it contains faulty reasoning.
Step 4	Still in pairs, students are asked to discuss with their partners whether the positions they originally supported have changed as a result of this activity and, if so, why and in what way. Then they revise their individual written statements accordingly.
Step 5	A class discussion follows based on students' arguments for each side of the issue, any changes in attitude that occurred as a result of the activity, and sources of further information related to the issue.
Step 6	Students are offered a final opportunity to revise and prepare a final form of their position statements.

See Figure 8.13 for an example of the Devil's Advocate method. Notice how this method emphasizes critical examination of the issue with the possibility of changing one's mind, or reformulating a position, rather than winning a debate.

Regression Equation Technique (RET)

The *regression equation technique* is a method under development for increasing the likelihood that the discussion will detect the "truth" signal through the haze of social and semantic static, this enabling participants

Figure 8.13
Example of devil's advocate method.

> Mr. Tennyson, a ninth grade social sciences teacher, used the Devil's Advocate strategy to structure a class discussion on banning nuclear testing. His students had read a section of their text that dealt with the horrors of nuclear warfare. As the discussion opens, Tennyson has just finished assigning the students to pairs.
>
> "All right now, you and your partner find a place where you can talk quietly. Each of you should jot down why you believe the United States should stop testing nuclear weapons. Be sure to support your beliefs with evidence from the text. Then take the opposite stance (why the United States should not stop testing nuclear weapons) and again support your beliefs with evidence from the text."
>
> (The students, working individually in pairs, take about ten minutes to complete this task.)
>
> "Okay, now we're ready for the next step. Choose your best arguments and present them to your partner. Be certain that you discuss your beliefs with your partner; for example, seek your partner's ideas and evaluations of the pros and cons that you took on the issue. Is there evidence of any faculty reasoning on either one's part?"
>
> (After approximately fifteen minutes, the noise level in the room drops, an indication that students have finished presenting the arguments they had with themselves.)
>
> "May I have your attention. . . . There are two more things I would like you to do: (1) Think about how your ideas have changed on banning nuclear testing. For example, has your position shifted from your original one? If so, why? (2) Decide whether you have strengthened your original position, abandoned it completely, or only modified it. Then tell your partner your decision and see if he or she agrees."
>
> (After approximately ten minutes, Tennyson drew the students into a whole class discussion by asking them to share some of their ideas on both sides of the issue.)

to move more expeditiously toward sensible solutions. The method, actually two versions at the moment, is being studied by Anthony Manzo, Julie Jackson-Albee, and Matt Thomas. It is based on a principle used in a statistical procedure with a similar name, the *multiple regression equation analysis.* The technique also draws on group process methods that encourage personal development of evaluative thinking, such as Hoffman's (1977) Intra-Act, and newer methods, such as Moller and Bohning's (1992) *participatory ranking,* that are designed to get the best decision making out of diverse groups. These methods are built around some form of guided value voting, tallying, discussing, and revoting. Here is the useable core of RET as it now is conceived.

Steps in the Regression Equation Technique (RET)

Step 1   Set-up an equation that represents an item, or "independent variable," that you wish to explore or better understand. Start by simply writing the entity or factor to be examined on the left side of an equal sign.

Step 2   Place all other factors or "dependent variables" that seem to explain that factor on the right side of the equal sign. Be sure that one of these dependent variables is titled "unexplained portion." Invite the group to add or restate any factors, except the one to be examined. (Rewording the independent variable changes the exercise, and should only be undertaken advisedly or as another comparative exercise.)

Step 3   Have everyone in the discussion group independently distribute percentage weightings for each dependent variable to the right of the equal sign, including the "unexplained portion" (to total 100%).

Step 4   Tally and record the range and average percent score for each factor.

Step 5   Attempt to explain findings with briefly written personal notes, and to reconcile differences through discussion.

Each time the researchers have used this basic discussion design in a domain in which the participants had real-life experience, they seem to have uniformly found their way back to some clearer signal (truth), and away from whatever static interference had been building around it. For example, the independent variable, or factor being analyzed, could be "academic success for inner-city youth" and the dependent variables or explaining factors could be elements like: structured classrooms; direct instruction; reading of core literature; reading of nonfiction material; vocabulary study; academic aptitude; recitation; transactional (subjective) reacting; self-esteem; family reading habits; and multicultural curricula. In such cases, the results often come out sounding as they did in a radio ad for a new Charter school that has emerged in a district that was recently disaccredited for failing to meet every one of its state's eleven criteria. It had experimented for thirty years with almost all of the above dependent variables, though often by misassigning their respective weightings as explaining outcomes on conventional standardized tests (arguably one of the basic means of quality control of schools and learning). The Charter school ad essentially said the following:

What insures school success? Is it diversity, attention to differences between boys and girls, campaigns to end violence, efforts to increase social responsiveness, attention to learning styles, cooperative grouping practices? Not really. Important as each of these may be to someone or even everyone, success in school is determined in greatest measure by a focus on reading, writing, and content area teaching and learning.

If you think you would like to join the effort to further develop this critical-constructive discussion technique, look in on our web site for details as they develop. And, ideally try using the method either in a professional discussion or in a classroom situation where the independent variable can range from such traditional fare as "Rise of Labor Unions" or "Elements of Tragedy in Hamlet" to more contemporary issues such as "The Likely Power of Telecomputing in Modern Life" or " Factors Influencing Violent Behavior in Young Adults."

As you can see, this evolving technique is rigorous yet open-ended. It brings several subtle points into focus that need to be better understood and dealt with in order to promote effective critical and constructive reading, discussion, and learning in school and in society. Some of these points are not immediately evident. For example, the person or group who gets to state the agenda or problem for review also has the greatest control over the discourse and hence the conclusions; therefore teaching youngsters how to articulate problems may be as important as teaching them how to solve problems. At least half of the solution to any problem can be found in its identification and statement.

The critical-constructive value of RET is amplified by telecomputing. An equation can be electronically published as a standing quest to which value can be added by each class and individual who reads, thinks, and writes about it over time. The equations would stand as QuestMagnetes of their own, attracting relevant positive and negative experiences in life, literature, and varied content areas. This ongoing discourse should help teachers and students to make better sense of the overly compartmentalized structures of school curricula and the near-chaotic flow of information on the web. The process of framing the equations and the posting of them can serve as the shared quests that help solve the timeless educational problem of "ungeared minds" (Chase, 1926). These public quests can serve as the *motive ideas that call the will to action* (p. 196), and especially assists those who are able to read and write but are somehow ever bewildered by answers to questions that they have not learned to raise.

✦   *After Words*   ✦

A new target was raised in this chapter for content area literacy and education in general. It is to promote the constructive-creative process, as well as critical reading-thinking. Proposed as the basic means to achieve this is building content, reading, and writing instruction around a sense of wonder or quest to understand the questions as well as the answers that constitute the disciplines. The next chapter describes a variety of means and methods to assess and monitor specific educational needs, including the need to read, write, and think beyond the lines, although you will not be surprised to learn that achieving the latter turns to out require more of a change of attitude than some breakthrough in psychoeducational testing.

CHAPTER 9

Interactive Assessment for Active Self-Monitoring

The examiner pipes and the teacher must dance—and the examiner sticks to the old tune.

—H. G. Wells, 1892

✦ Fore Words ✦

Interactive teaching is characterized by interactive assessment. To achieve this, it is essential that assessment techniques are selected that invite a reasonably high level of student involvement. This chapter details several such techniques that are both timely and have withstood the test of time. These include an Informal Textbook Inventory designed to assess and teach students about the parts of their books, a rationale for portfolio evaluation of student progress, and a rubric system for easy evaluation of student writing. The chapter then addresses several simple ways to estimate the difficulty level, or readability, of textual material. Appropriate shortcuts and computer-based alternatives are noted along the way.

INTRODUCTION TO STUDENT ASSESSMENT

The Power of the Examiner

The power of the examiner is a long-standing and deeply rooted issue in education. In fact, the influence of testing may be greater now than at any time in our prior history. There are a variety of assessment movements with puzzling titles throughout the nation. In the past ten years, most states have first instituted and then dropped or redirected assessment procedures with names like *basic competencies, mastery learning, criterion-referenced* testing, and more recently, *holistic, authentic, outcomes-based,* and *performance-based* assessment. One measure, however, remains a constant since it is mandated by federal law.

National Assessment of Educational Progress (NAEP)

The NAEP is the major literacy benchmark. It was mandated by the Congress in 1969, and is carried out on a mixed subject schedule every two or three years. Students in grades four, eight, and twelve receive fifty minutes to read graded passages and answer questions, both multiple-choice and written. There are four possible levels of competency that one can achieve : *below basic, basic, proficient,* and *advanced.* Three sets of data are relevant: for 1992, 1994, and 1998. The 1994 data were the most shocking to the national conscience.

In that year, about 60% of adolescents, according to NAEP performance indicators, were able to read at a basic level. They could gather details, identify a main idea, and recognize connections among textually explicit ideas. Fewer than 5% of youngsters surveyed, however, were able to perform at *advanced* levels where they were required to examine, extend, and elaborate meanings from representative fiction and nonfiction materials (Campbell et al., 1996). Results of an NAEP *writing* assessment (Applebee et al., 1994) revealed that *almost all* students in grades four, eight, and twelve had difficulty with writing tasks that required higher levels of coherent thinking and the important capacity to provide details to support points made. Some have called this a national crisis (Vacca & Alvermann, 1998). We tend to see it as a growing awareness of one of the challenges inherent in the field of content area literacy: in addition to the need for systematic, direct *instruction* in reading-thinking strategies across the disciplines, we need systematic ongoing *assessment* and feedback at the classroom level. Several basic formats for classroom assessment are described next.

Higher-Order and Performance-based Assessment

Of the many recent efforts to reform educational assessment, the movement toward higher-order thinking and performance-based assessment, or the representation of real-life tasks in assessment, may be the most welcome (see Figure 9.1). The logic of mastery learning, which so strongly influenced teaching and testing in the past, now finally is being replaced with assessment more firmly grounded in interactive and integrated performance. Where mastery learning stressed the passive acquisition of facts and skills, newer interactive assessment models tend to emphasize the active role of readers and learners in using print to construct meaning and

Figure 9.1
Performance-based, or authentic, assessment: The current trend.

> The goal of traditional assessment is to evaluate acquisition of information. The goal of performance-based assessment is to evaluate the processes for acquiring and using information. To do this, performance-based assessment is expected to have several of the following characteristics:
>
> + Is problem-centered
> + Requires use of facts rather than recall of facts
> + Requires higher-order thinking along inferential and evaluative lines
> + Is more constructive in format than reconstructive
> + Does not necessarily have a single correct answer
> + Involves more hands-on doing than conventional knowledge testing
> + Is more authentic, or real-life
> + Reflects more fairly the diversity of perspectives in American cultures

Figure 9.2
Local high school excels in knowledge but lags in reading.

The following standardized test score information was reported for a local high school in a major city. Of thirty-four high schools recently tested in the state, this high school was

First in mathematics

First in social studies

First in science

Second in narrative (story) reading

Sixth in expository (content area) reading

These data suggest the following conclusion. If the youngsters in this school are first in the three traditional areas of knowledge acquisition but sixth in ability to comprehend (i.e., think) in these subjects, then a program to further maximize application and content area reading in the disciplines is in order.

solve problems. Thus, there is a decreased emphasis on product outcomes of learning, such as information acquisition, and an increased emphasis on how well students are internalizing the thinking processes they will need to learn both in and out of school.

As more states move away from use of standardized test scores as the primary approach to evaluation of schools and school districts, it is expected that educators will feel less obliged to concentrate on simple fact acquisition and more committed to engaging students in authentic learning activities. Of course, this does not mean that standardized test scores are without value. See Figure 9.2 for an example of how such data can be used to suggest programmatic decisions.

For a more authentic and interactive means of assessing students' needs, consider the Informal Textbook Inventory (ITI). It is a means of introducing a textbook to a class, having students tell the teacher about their preparation for using it effectively, and seamlessly teaching them how to use it to full advantage. This technique sometimes is referred to as a Classroom Reading Inventory (CRI).

TOOLS FOR ASSESSMENT OF STUDENT READING

The Informal Textbook Inventory

An Informal Textbook Inventory (ITI) essentially is a special type of open-book test designed to familiarize students with using one of education's most basic learning tools: the textbook. This "new idea" is over seventy-five years old. We have seen an excellent ten-question version of the ITI in a 1924 edition of a fifth-year reader (Walker & Parkman). Since most texts on the market do not contain such a ready-made inventory, you probably will need to construct your own. There are several good reasons for creating and using an ITI at the beginning of the school year:

+ It is easily administered in group, paper-and-pencil format.
+ It tests and teaches simultaneously.
+ It draws the teacher's and students' attention to the processing strategies involved in using text parts, text aids, and related resources.
+ It provokes active awareness and discussion of text features.
+ It lends itself well to computer (hypertext) presentation and scoring.
+ It is purposeful and well structured but nonthreatening.
+ It reflects the highest current standards of performance-based assessment.

When used early in the school year, while student attitudes and expectations are still being formed, the ITI provides an excellent means of establishing a disciplined, well-managed classroom tone. By simply tallying the results of the inventory, the teacher can obtain a record of each student's ability to deal with the textbook as well as indications of some of the potential benefits and shortcomings of the textbook itself.

Such assessment can take time to prepare, but it also stores well and improves with age and use. It is the type of activity that is the mark of a professional teacher. Students appreciate the help, and supervisors rarely fail to take note. The second and subsequent times you use the ITI, you will be even more pleased because you will have refined it and will know what to expect and how to better orchestrate the full activity.

Constructing the Informal Textbook Inventory

The following outline illustrates the general form of the ITI:

I. Organization and Structure of the Text

    A. Understanding the Textbook Organization
        Develop three to five straightforward questions about how the text is structured and how to use the comprehension aids provided within the text.

    B. Using the Text Organization Effectively
        Develop three to five questions that students can answer by referring to the index, table of contents, glossary, appendices, or other text sections and/or aids.

II. Basic Comprehension

Select a short portion of the text that contains an important concept with supporting details and at least one graph, chart, or picture. (The same selection can be used in the following section on applied comprehension.)

A. Comprehending the Main Idea
Develop one or two fill-in or multiple-choice questions that direct students to state or select the main idea of the material read.

B. Noting Supporting Details
Develop three or more fill-in, multiple-choice, or matching questions about specific facts or ideas in the selection.

C. Understanding Vocabulary in Context
Develop three or more fill-in, multiple-choice, or matching questions that direct students to state or select a definition for key terms used in the selection.

D. Understanding Information Presented in Graphic or Pictorial Form
Develop one or more questions requiring students to state or select an interpretation of a graph, chart, or picture that adds information not explicitly stated in the selection.

III. Applied Comprehension

Questions in these sections can be based on the same text selection used in Part II.

A. Drawing Conclusions and Critical Thinking
Develop one or more questions that require students to draw valid conclusions based on the information presented.

B. Evaluating and Judging
Develop one or more questions that require students to evaluate and apply information from the text in terms of their own experiences, values, and existing knowledge base.

IV. Specialized Options

A. Assess special requirements of the discipline. This could mean understanding geographical directions in social studies, a section on understanding style or mood in literature, or a section on applying symbols in mathematical formulas. Examples are found in Chapter 11, on content-specific applications.

B. Assess pupil abilities to deal with the linguistic features of the text with a Standard Cloze Passage test (described later in this chapter).

Administering and Evaluating the Informal Textbook Inventory

Before asking students to tackle the inventory, explain some of its features and purposes: it is not a test in the usual sense of the word; every text differs slightly from every other, and this is a way to find out how. Point out further that although answers will be discussed as a group, each student will need to independently complete the inventory as thoroughly and accurately as possible.

Once all students have completed the inventory, collect and score the results. For diagnostic purposes, any error is taken as a sign of need in that category.

Much of the diagnostic value of the inventory comes from the group discussion of the items when the tests are returned to the students. Compare and contrast student strengths and weaknesses among the various categories of questions. Review and discussion of the inventory with the class can take from one-half to two full class periods depending on individual students' abilities, the difficulty of the text, and the objectives the teacher may wish to achieve.

The next assessment instrument, the Standard Cloze Passage test, also can be constructed from a class textbook. It is much easier to construct, but it yields a more general account of a pupil's ability to handle a given textbook at the linguistic, or language and syntactic, level.

Standard Cloze Passage Test

The term *cloze* refers to a written passage with certain words blanked out to be filled in by the reader. Early studies of this task revealed that it is closely related to reading comprehension across age and most grade levels (Bormuth, 1965). Subsequent studies, however, indicated that cloze was not a direct measure of reading comprehension. Instead, it was a fairly accurate measure of one of the factors that contributes to comprehension, namely, familiarity with the language redundancy patterns, or repetitive sentence structures and phrases in prose (Culver, Godfrey, & Manzo, 1972; Weaver & Kingston, 1963). Technically speaking, this means that cloze and reading comprehension have relatively little in common with one another, but both are strongly related to a third thing (probably verbal reasoning), and therefore either can be used to infer the other.

This and related work added several points to our understanding of the potential values and possible shortcomings of cloze passage testing. These points are summarized as follows:

✦ Cloze is a good, quick assessment strategy for sampling students' ability to handle the language patterns common to different types of content material—and therefore is a good complement to an ITI.

✦ Cloze will tend to underestimate the comprehension abilities of students with weak standard-English backgrounds, since comprehension is inferred from familiarity with English-language patterns.

✦ Cloze tends to penalize students who are divergent thinking, impulsive, or perfectionistic, since the task is rather tedious, with an error rate higher than what students are used to.

✦ Independent practice on cloze tasks does not contribute to improvement in reading comprehension; however, guided discussion of which words work best in each blank, and why, does result in improved comprehension.

The general cloze task can have many forms and purposes. The specific form of the cloze task described next, the Standard Cloze Passage test, is a useful assessment tool for content teachers.

Purpose of the Standard Cloze Passage Test

When constructed, administered, and scored as described next, the cloze test provides a fair indication of how a particular group of students will be able to read and understand a particular piece of reading material. Students' individual scores can be categorized to indicate whether the reading material used is at their own independent, instructional, or frustration level.

Preparation of the Standard Cloze Passage Test

To prepare a Standard Cloze test, select a passage of about 300 words from a textbook. The passage should be one that students have not yet read. Copy the first sentence with no deletions. Then select a word at random in the second sentence. Delete this word and every fifth word thereafter until fifty words have been deleted. Finish the sentence containing the fiftieth blank, and copy the next sentence with no deletions. The blanks should be typed as lines five spaces long and numbered from one to fifty. Students record their responses on numbered answer sheets.

Administration of the Standard Cloze Passage Test

To administer the Standard Cloze test, first talk through a few sample cloze sentences. See Figure 9.3 for suggestions about how to do this. Tell

Figure 9.3
Pointers on demonstrating cloze testing.

Two elements must be considered for proper word replacement, *semantics*—or meaning—and *syntax*—or grammatical function. Demonstrate these by making choices available on the first two examples that make this point. Then increase the difficulty level of the examples to the actual testing task with two or three more deletions that offer no choices.

Example

Germany today is reunited, but its people still feel the differences from the period of Soviet domination. West Germans are highly (industrious/frivolous), in the tradition of (ancient/old) Germany. The East (Germans) feel less industrious and (are) given to reliance on (government) for their support.

---

students that the task is more difficult than what they may be used to, but that even if they miss half of the items they will have done very well (actually, 40% correct is still instructional level). You may also wish to assure students that their scores will not be part of their course grades but are an important means for teachers to better understand and provide for their reading needs. This introduction should encourage most students to do their best while reducing the problem noted earlier with this type of task.

Scoring the Standard Cloze Passage Test

To score the Standard Cloze Passage test, simply count the number of words filled in correctly. Count only exact words; do not count synonyms as correct. Multiply this number by 2 (since there are fifty items) to get the percent correct. Scores below 40% mean the material is at the students' frustration level: it is too difficult for them to read and learn from even with instructional support. Scores from 40% to 60% mean that the material is at these students' instructional level: They can read and learn from the material with some assistance and guidance. Scores above 60% generally indicate ability to read and learn with no special assistance, or the independent level.

Why Synonyms Won't Do

An understandable concern of teachers is the fact that only exact replacement words are counted correct in scoring the standard cloze test. Synonyms are not counted in such testing for three reasons. First, the assessment format was standardized according to exact-word scoring; therefore, the evaluation criterion cannot be used if synonyms are accepted. Second, the rank ordering of students does not change appreciably when synonyms are accepted; everyone simply has a higher score. Finally, if synonyms are allowed, scoring for the teacher becomes a much longer and more tedious process. You may, nonetheless, wish to use a more interactive version if you feel that the standard form is inappropriate for your students.

Interactive Cloze

For a more interactive version of cloze testing, consider these guidelines for a nonstandard form. Have students score their own papers with an allowance for synonyms based on class discussion of reasonable alternatives to the exact word deleted. Increase the independent-reading-level score to 70%.

To further encourage self-evaluation and strategic reading, ask pupils to write a sentence or two telling what they think their score indicates about their ability to read the material and what they think they should do to read better in the particular textbook from which the passage was taken.

Next, we turn to the topic of writing. Of all the things we attempt to evaluate in school, writing is one of the more difficult to assess satisfactorily. Nonetheless, it is an area of considerable interest in modern education.

EVALUATION OF STUDENT WRITING

Teachers' enthusiasm for activities that involve student writing often is dampened by the prospect of piles of papers to be painstakingly graded. Fortunately, the recent renovation of an old idea called *rubric* evaluation of student writing cuts down on the paper load. As a result, it is making student writing a more attractive option for more teachers. Two types of rubrics are discussed next, one done essentially by teachers and one done by students.

Using Rubric Evaluation to Enhance Writing Activities

A writing rubric is a set of guidelines for holistic scoring of compositions. It is a teacher-constructed list of characteristics for ranking the quality of student papers, generally on a number scale or simply as *high, medium,* or *low.* The teacher uses a rubric to grade student compositions by simply determining which rubric level each composition best matches. Grading compositions thus becomes a speedy process of categorizing papers by level rather than a tedious chore of red-penciling each and every error and composing brief but time-consuming written comments on students' papers.

Ideally, the teacher gives the rubric for a writing assignment to students along with the topic. This encourages students to participate in self-evaluation and to internalize high standards. A student's working drafts are read by a partner student, using the rubric to make editorial suggestions. As teachers drop in on these peer editing sessions, their suggestions become more meaningful to these works in progress than conventional written comments on a final-product paper. Used in this way, rubrics are a valuable way of stimulating individual and peer revisions of school compositions.

Depending on the importance of the objective of the writing assignment, the rubric may be simple or quite complex. Figures 9.4 and 9.5 provide two sample rubrics: one addressing a specific writing objective, and the other addressing content objectives of a particular writing assignment.

Figure 9.4
Sample rubric 1: Using examples and illustrations.

3	The topic sentence is clearly written and strongly supported by lucid and interesting examples. Transitions tie the paper together in a fluid manner. Mechanical errors are slight.
2	The topic sentence is present, but support from the examples needs to be stronger and better organized. Transitions are used but need polishing. There are some mechanical errors.
1	The paragraph lacks a clear topic sentence. Examples are few in number and inadequately explained. Transitions are lacking, and mechanical errors are frequent.

Source: Adapted from P. Behle (Ed.) (1982), *The Double Helix: Teaching the Writing Process,* Florissant, MO, Ferguson-Florissant Writers Project. Copyright 1982 by Ferguson-Florissant Writers Project.

Evaluating Expression and Concepts

A persistent problem in evaluating student writing is that some compositions will be organizationally, structurally, and mechanically perfect but lack originality and richness of thought, while others may have distracting errors in form but contain striking expressions and/or fresh conceptual approaches. A popular solution to this problem has been a dual-grade system—one grade for ideas and one for mechanics. A rubric that combines mechanics and content, such as sample rubric 2 in Figure 9.5, provides guidelines for students to assist one another in working toward an effective combination of both aspects of a quality composition.

The initial planning time spent in preparing a rubric tends to enhance the quality of student products as well as to simplify grading. A rubric-guided writing assignment at the beginning of the school year can provide a valuable addition to the ITI.

Self-Analysis of Writing (SAW) Checklist

Recently, rubrics have been evolving into means of urging students to pay adequate attention to a chosen set of objectives in writing. The *Self Analysis of Writing* (SAW) (Figure 9.6) is a checklist-type rubric that is intended to guide students in reviewing their own work prior to submission.

Next, we discuss another form of assessment that is growing in popularity. It is a means of incorporating and organizing many possible forms of assessment, called *portfolio collection and analysis.*

Figure 9.5
Sample rubric 2: A specific content assignment.

PAPER TOPIC: 1960s APPROACHES TO CIVIL RIGHTS IN THE UNITED STATES

High-Quality Papers Contain:

✦ An overview of civil rights or their lack during the 1960s, with three specific examples

✦ A statement defining civil disobedience, with three examples of how it was used and Martin Luther King, Jr.'s role

✦ At least one other approach to civil rights, with specific examples, and a comparison of this approach with King's civil disobedience that illustrates differences or similarities in at least two ways

✦ Good organization, well-developed arguments, few mechanical errors (sentence fragments, grammatical errors, spelling errors)

Medium-Quality Papers Contain:

✦ An overview of black civil rights during the 1960s with two specific examples

✦ A statement defining civil disobedience, with two examples of its use and Martin Luther King, Jr.'s involvement

✦ One other approach to civil rights, with examples, and a comparison of it with King's civil disobedience by their differences

✦ Good organization, few mechanical errors, moderately developed arguments

Lower-Quality Papers Contain:

✦ A general statement defining civil disobedience with reference to Martin Luther King, Jr.'s involvement and at least one example

✦ One other approach to civil rights and how it differed from civil disobedience

✦ Fair organization, some mechanical errors

Lowest-Quality Papers Contain:

✦ A general statement on who Martin Luther King, Jr. was, or a general statement on civil disobedience

✦ A general statement that not all blacks agreed with civil disobedience

✦ A list of points, poor organization, many mechanical errors

---

Source: From D. L. Pearce (1983), "Guidelines for the Use and Evaluation of Writing in Content Classrooms," *Journal of Reading, 27,* p. 215. Copyright 1983 by the International Reading Association. Reprinted with permission of Daniel L. Pearce and the International Reading Association.

Figure 9.6

SAW (Self-Analysis of Writing) checklist.

Conventions (mechanics)	____	My work has been edited and proofread; it is easy to read.
	____	I used capital letters and punctuation correctly.
	____	I checked my spelling.
	____	You'd have to look hard to find mistakes in my paper!
Word Choice (vocabulary)	____	My reader will enjoy the words I chose.
	____	My words paint a descriptive picture.
	____	I think this is the best way to say it.
Ideas (topic)	____	It all makes sense, from title, to topic, to details.
	____	My reader will learn a lot.
	____	This is what I wanted to say.
	____	Details are adequate, but not overwhelming
Organization (sequence)	____	I love my beginning.
	____	I know where I am going; the middle nicely connects to the start.
	____	You can follow me.
	____	My ending is interesting and pulls things together.
Sentences (fluency & variety)	____	My sentences make sense.
	____	My paper is easy to read out loud.
	____	Some sentences are long and some are short.
	____	My sentences begin in several different ways.
Voice (overall impression)	____	This is what I feel, or believe.
	____	It makes you laugh, or cry, or even be angry.
	____	If you read my paper and it did not have a name on it, you would know that it is mine!
Rich Thinking (critical/	____	This is why I believe what I do.
	____	The paper rises above my personal feelings and beliefs.
	____	The paper gives a fair representation of other points of view.
	____	The paper seems to connect with certain other things we have learned.
	____	The paper raises some interesting questions that I will think about and perhaps write more about sometime.
	____	I'll bet I can find or think of a better idea or way to look at this.
Overall rating:		1 2 3 4 5 6 7 8 9 10

Source: Modified from a workshop handout of the Northwest Regional Education Laboratory, Shawnee Mission, KS, School District, May 1998.

PORTFOLIOS: RATIONALE, FUNCTIONS, PROMISE, PROBLEMS

A *portfolio* is a collection of works intended to illustrate a range of abilities and possible special talents over time. The idea of a portfolio is to show what one can do and how one has progressed through various stages and periods.

Portfolios for students, in effect, are based on the proposition that pupils should be involved in assessing their progress and actively selecting and keeping samples of their best work for periodic review. There are two popular types of student portfolios: show portfolios, which include only a few selected samples of work, and working portfolios, which include a wide array of works in progress (Farr, 1992). Periodically, students should be helped to select pieces from their working portfolios to place in their show portfolios. The show portfolio should include the pupil's best current works, as well as some works that are representative of earlier stages of learning. The teacher's role is largely to serve as a consultant who counsels students on the works that seem to reflect their progress in reading, writing, thinking, and content learning. The process of collecting, reviewing, and maintaining student portfolios tends to create interactions between teachers and students that can lead to greater empathy and a sense of common purpose.

Contents of Portfolios

Depending on the teacher's purposes, student portfolios may include any or all of the following types of entries:

- ✦ Quarterly writing samples from a variety of perspectives across genre: journal writing, personal narrative, fiction, nonfiction, poetry
- ✦ Evidence of progress in aspects of communications from phrasing to grammar and spelling
- ✦ Evidence of progress in comprehension and content knowledge
- ✦ Results from informal inventories
- ✦ Taped oral readings and presentations
- ✦ Drawings and other expressive works
- ✦ Photographs of special projects too bulky to store
- ✦ Year-to-year photographs of self, the teacher, and other students
- ✦ Periodic anecdotal accounts and comments from teachers

Teacher and student comments give the portfolio depth and dimension. Here are some sample comments:

Jack, your account of the religious basis for the civil war in Bosnia is enlightening. I read it to my wife at dinner the other night.

Mr. Ahkim 10/23/99

Tamica, this algebra homework assignment tells me that you can read and follow word problems quite well. However, I think you should recheck your calculations.

Ms. Toma 11/10/99

Students can be asked to write short explanations of why they chose certain entries for their show portfolios. For example:

I included this report on "Russia Today" because I think it includes my best work so far on using citations and references.

Mark 11/10/99

This is a tape recording of me in the spring play. I was the narrator, and I thought I was pretty good. I'd like to listen to it again next year, and see how much I have changed.

Nina 5/12/99

The single most important value of portfolio assessment is that it shifts the emphasis away from the errors and the false starts students make while acquiring knowledge and skill. Instead, the emphasis is placed on preserving, and periodically reviewing, completed pieces that youngsters value. Unlike grade books and permanent record files, which few have access to, the portfolio collection may be kept in an easily accessible part of the room for others to view, with proper permission. Importantly, maintaining portfolios is something youngsters do for themselves as well as for others. As such, the portfolio system helps to build and expand interests that lead to further reading (Ediger, 1992).

Disadvantages of Portfolios

The most serious disadvantage of portfolios is that they can quickly become quite complex and cumbersome. Portfolios were originally intended to provide a means of balancing other more standardized forms of assessment with a concrete record of a student's actual work. The student portfolio itself, however, is only the raw data on which this balancing is based. Evaluating these data should be a simple, subjective, and self-evident process. It can, however, be turned into a tedious, overly objectified, time-consuming one. According to one research report, some teachers view student portfolios as too demanding, and "yet another means of increasing

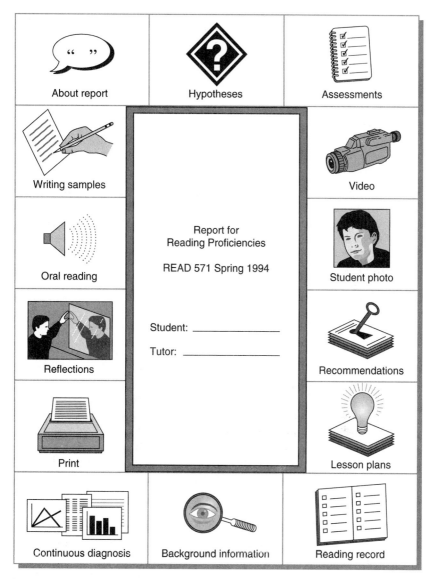

Figure 9.7
Assessing literacy through hypermedia portfolios.

and controlling teachers' work while appearing to empower them" (Gomez, Graue, & Bloch, 1991, p. 621). On the other hand, electronic technology is making portfolio collection and analysis somewhat easier. Computer programs are being written that guide collection, assessment, and interpretation, all with a click on an appropriate icon. See Figure 9.7 for an example (Duckworth & Taylor, 1995) of a computerized portfolio.

Now that you know about several means of estimating students' abilities and progress in reading and writing about materials at different levels of difficulty, learn next how to estimate the difficulty level of the textual material they are asked to read. This, too, is a "new" technology that is about seventy-five years old.

ASSESSING TEXT DIFFICULTY

Readability Formulas

The difficulty level of a text is referred to as the text's *readability*. Historically, junior and senior high school texts have been written with more concern for content than for difficulty level. A tenth-grade American history text, for example, might have a readability of grade twelve. This has begun to change in recent years as members of school district text selection committees have started including readability as a major criterion by which to evaluate potential textbook purchases.

Readability depends on a number of factors, including the influence of print size, number and quality of graphic aids, and an individual's level of interest and prior knowledge in the topic area. The greatest influence by far, however, comes from two simple factors: average length of sentences and word difficulty, which largely is a function of the frequency of use of a word in popular print. The most commonly used procedures for estimating readability are formulas that employ these two factors in one way or another.

One of the more commonly used readability formulas is detailed next. It is presented here to illustrate the process of estimating readability level rather than to suggest that teachers should regularly undertake even these abbreviated analyses by hand. However, it can be enlightening to do a text analysis by hand, especially if no other means is available.

Raygor's Readability Graph

The Raygor procedure, illustrated in Figure 9.8, uses the number of words containing six or more letters and the average sentence length of three passages of 100 words each to estimate a text's difficulty. Baldwin and Kaufman (1979) found the Raygor formula faster than and as accurate as the original Fry formula (1968, 1977), on which it is based.

Computer Programs for Readability Checking

Even simplified formulas for estimating readability are time-consuming to do manually. Fortunately, a wide variety of computer software now is available for obtaining readability estimates on textbook excerpts. This is much more realistic in terms of time and elimination of the human error

Figure 9.8
The Raygor procedure for estimating readability.

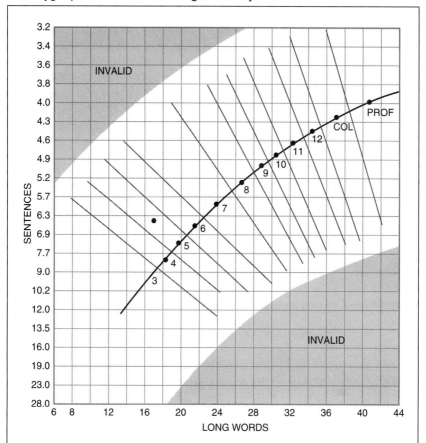

1. Count out three 100-word passages at the beginning, middle, and end of a selection or book. Count proper nouns but not numerals.

2. Count sentences in each passage, estimating to the nearest tenth.

3. Count words with six or more letters.

Average the sentence length and word length over three samples, and plot the average on the graph.

Source: From A. L. Raygor, "The Raygor Readability Estimate: A Quick and Easy Way to Determine Difficulty," in *Reading: Theory, Research and Practice. Twenty-sixth Yearbook of the National Reading Conference* (pp. 259–263), edited by P. D. Pearson, 1977, Clemson, SC, National Reading Conference.

inevitable with lengthy syllable/word counting and calculating. Microsoft Word 5.0 or higher has two readability formulas built in. For more information on commercially available computer readability programs, ask your local software dealer or school librarian.

There is another approach to evaluating readability that any veteran teacher can use effectively and that new teachers can use to increase their sensitivity to factors in a text that will influence the level of difficulty for students. It is called a *readability checklist*.

Readability Checklists

Checklists to guide readability estimates are totally subjective and do not necessarily yield a grade-level readability estimate. They do, however, indicate whether a given book is appropriate for a particular group of students. Checklists are most effective when several teachers rate the same material and then average (or otherwise compare) their judgments. A group of teachers from a given content area may wish to develop their own checklist that addresses specific content concerns.

One list includes the following items, to which the rater responds with a particular group of students in mind:

1. Are the concepts far beyond the students' direct experiences?
2. Are abstract concepts linked to examples and situations that are familiar to students?
3. Are technical terms defined in context as they appear?
4. Does one idea lead logically to another?
5. What does the author assume about the students' previous learning experiences?
6. Are textbooks aids provided?
7. Is the material appealing, or does it look too "textbookish"?
8. Is the writing brief, concise, and to the point? (Harker, 1977)

Readability checklists can even be adapted for use by students. To help students to become more independent and strategic readers, they need a greater capacity for self-appraisal of text difficulty, text aids, and personal ability to negotiate a given textbook. One way to help them to do this is the FLIP inventory, described next.

FLIP: For Student Analysis of Text Difficulty

FLIP (Schumm & Mangrum, 1991) invites students to judge how well they will be able to read and learn from a particular reading assignment by analyzing its *f*riendliness, *l*anguage, and their own *i*nterest and *p*rior knowledge, using a FLIP chart (see Figure 9.9). Students are instructed to FLIP

Figure 9.9
FLIP chart.

Title of assignment _____ # of pages _____

General directions: Rate each of the four FLIP categories in a 1 to 5 scale (5 = high). Then determine your purpose for reading and appropriate reading rate, and budget your reading/study time.

F = Friendliness: How friendly is my reading assignment?

Directions: Examine your assignment to see if it includes the friendly elements listed below.

Friendly text features

Table of contents	Index	Glossary
Chapter introductions	Headings	Subheadings
Margin notes	Study questions	Chapter summary
Key terms highlighted	Graphs	Charts
Pictures	Signal words	Lists of key facts

1————2————3————4————5

No friendly text features	Some friendly text features	Many friendly text features

Friendliness rating = ___

L = Language: How difficult is the language in my reading assignment?

Directions: Skim the chapter quickly to determine the number of new terms. Read three random paragraphs to get a feel for the vocabulary level and number of long, complicated sentences.

1————2————3————4————5

Many new words; complicated sentences	Some new words; somewhat complicated sentences	No new words; clear sentences

Language rating = ___

I = Interest: How interesting is my reading assignment?

Directions: Read the title, introduction, headings/subheadings, and summary. Examine the pictures and graphics included.

1————2————3————4————5

Boring	Somewhat interesting	Very interesting

Interest rating = ___

Figure 9.9, *continued*

P = Prior knowledge: What do I already know about the material covered in my reading assignment?

Directions: Think about the title, introduction, headings/subheadings, and summary.

1———————2———————3———————4———————5

| Mostly new information | Some new information | Mostly familiar information |

Prior knowledge rating = ____

Overall, this reading assignment appears to be at:

____ a comfortable reading level for me

____ a somewhat comfortable reading level for me

____ an uncomfortable reading level for me

Source: Flip chart from Jeanne Shay Schumm, & Charles T. Mangrum, II (1991, October), "FLIP: A Framework for Content Area Reading," *Journal of Reading,* 35(2), pp. 120–124. Reprinted with permission of Jeanne Shay Schumm and the International Reading Association. All rights reserved.

through the reading assignment and use the chart to record their judgments.

By adding the FLIP elements rated, students are able to evaluate the general level of the assignment. They then proceed to interpret their assessment to determine an appropriate reading rate and to budget reading and study time (see Figure 9.10).

Following is a valuable closing thought on readability. It uses the idea of student input in a way that may have occurred to you when you first read about cloze testing.

Matching Student Abilities With Text Difficulty Through Cloze

The Standard Cloze Passage test described earlier is as much a readability strategy as it is a measure of students' reading ability. It does not yield a grade-level estimate of the difficulty of a given text, but it does predict how well a particular student or group of students will be able to read and learn from it. Hittleman (1978) pointed out that cloze measures readability, whereas other means predict text difficulty. He also noted that the cloze procedure is the only available procedure that can take into account, in a natural setting, the constraints of the language system of the reading matter, the reading ability and other characteristics of the reader, and the background information needed by the reader. In other words, there are two ways to compare your students' reading levels with your textbook's

Figure 9.10
FLIP follow-up.

My purpose for reading is (circle one):

A. Personal pleasure

B. To prepare for class discussions

C. To answer written questions for class assignment or for homework

D. To prepare for a test

E. Other _____

My reading rate should be (circle one):

A. Slow—allowing time for rereading if necessary

B. Medium—careful and analytical

C. Fast—steady, skipping sections that are about information I already know

Active reading time:

Chunk 1, pages _____–_____, estimated time: _____ minutes

Chunk 2, pages _____–_____, estimated time: _____ minutes

Chunk 3, pages _____–_____, estimated time: _____ minutes

Chunk 4, pages _____–_____, estimated time: _____ minutes

Total estimated time: _____ minutes

Source: Flip chart from Jeanne Shay Schumm, & Charles T. Mangrum, II (1991, October), "FLIP: A Framework for Content Area Reading," *Journal of Reading,* 35(2), pp 120–124. Reprinted with permission of Jeanne Shay Schumm and the International Reading Association. All rights reserved.

readability level. One is to compare some form of student reading test score to a formula-based readability estimate in the text. Another is simply to give a Standard Cloze Passage test constructed from a representative portion of the text. Hence, the Standard Cloze Passage test permits a direct comparison using a single measure. To improve the quality of the match, you have only to construct more than one sample for the text.

AFFECTIVE ISSUES AND MEASURES

It is an axiom of professional education that to know others, you must first know yourself. To reach this island of self-knowledge, however, one must navigate through the reefs of self-doubt and self-examination. This can be particularly formidable because, as the German writer Herman Hesse put it, "Nothing . . . is so distasteful to man as to go the way which leads him to himself."

When you are up to facing this process, you might wish to look into some of the personality and temperament inventories that are available for popular consumption in most bookstores. These may not always have the same level of accuracy as norm-referenced personality tests, but they tend to be sufficiently accurate for getting a look at yourself, since most of them essentially are made up of the more telling items of traditional measures like the Minnesota Multiphasic Personality Inventory (MMPI). See our web site for one such inventory, the Impulsivity/Stability Index, which is easy to administer, score, and interpret.

✦ *After Words* ✦

This chapter offered a broad range of options for considering and conducting assessment in the context of the content area classroom. It described traditional and emerging options for assessing students' reading, text management, and writing. Finally, the chapter turned from student assessment to text assessment and provided a tour of available means for assessing the difficulty level of printed material.

CHAPTER 10

Reading, Learning, and Remembering: Study Methods and MindTools

Study without reflection is a waste of time; reflection without study is dangerous.

—Confucius

✦ Fore Words ✦

The term "study strategies" refers to the efficient use of time spent in learning and remembering. As such, it includes an array of diverse topics such as time management, techniques for active reading and listening, note taking, and test taking. Study strategies may be taught in minicourses or as units in a regular class and/or integrated with the content of various classes. Each approach has merit. The content class approach is gaining in popularity as more teachers learn about the methods for imparting these strategies in their primary teacher training and in-service programs.

FROM SKILLS TO STRATEGIES TO MINDTOOLS

The techniques and objectives that have been known until quite recently as *study skills* have tended to reflect the educational trends of the times. McMurray wrote the first study skills text for classroom teachers in 1909. It was a no-frills book called simply *How to Study and Teaching How to Study.* Its approach reflected the early twentieth-century assumption that reading was a bottom-up process of mastering and applying a series of discrete subskills.

This skills-based approach continued through the popularization of self-directed study techniques during World Wars I and II. Armed services inductees needed quick training in how to read and master the contents of the manuals that accompanied increasingly sophisticated weapons and machines. Later, returning veterans willingly enrolled in study skills courses to improve their reading efficiency and grades in technical schools and colleges. By 1930, skills-based books with names like *Outlining as a Study Procedure* (Barton, 1930) were available at the college level.

The open-admissions policies initiated in many colleges in the 1960s created a further need to assist underprepared students in meeting college-level reading, writing, and study requirements. By this time, many educators were realizing that effective study, like reading, was not something done to one, but something that one did. The emphasis on imparting study skills gradually evolved into the new emphasis on the learner as an active doer and strategy user.

Today, a new era is opening, one that is offering MindTools to students at every developmental level, and is customizeable to a variety of different learning styles and needs. These are being offered largely over the Internet,

265

but they have their origins in the reading-thinking-study guides popularized by Herber (1978). MindTools take many forms. They can be formats for outlines, incomplete outlines, graphics, and even guides to thinking creatively such as the semantic/conceptual maps, charts, and graphs depicted in previous chapters. They also can be like formulas that guide investment, in this case, of human capital in dividend-rich reading and learning. The Internet offers the capability to search huge, worldwide databases for information and chat rooms on topics of interest and research. There also is a new search engine, ScholasticSearch, that provides easy access to research portfolios created by others on the same and similar questions—a remarkably efficient means of reading and learning. Let's go back now for a historical look at one of the first and still most widely known MindTools for effective reading and study.

SQ3R: A Story unto Itself

The Survey-Question-Read-Recite-Review (SQ3R) technique is the acknowledged granddaddy of study formulas or MindTools. It was developed by Francis Robinson (1946), who traced its roots back to 1923. Robinson developed it in response to a need expressed by the U.S. Department of Defense during World War II (Stahl & Henk, 1986). As noted earlier, U.S. troops had a great deal of technical information to learn and little time in which to learn it. They needed a rigorous, self-guided technique that they could use with minimal instruction in field-training situations. SQ3R stresses meticulous, step-by-step analysis of text, followed by repeated reviews to overlearn textual material to the point where key information can be recalled and recited with minimal cueing.

Steps in SQ3R

Step 1   *Survey.* Survey a chapter before reading it closely.

a. Read the title, and think about what it says or implies.

b. Read the headings and subheadings.

c. Read the summary if there is one.

d. Read the captions under the pictures, charts, graphs, etc.

e. See if there is a bibliography or a list of books related to the chapter.

Step 2   *Question.* Ask yourself questions about what you are going to read.

a. What does the title of the chapter mean?

b. What do I already know about the subject?

c. What did my instructor say about this chapter when it was assigned?

d. What questions do the headings and subheadings suggest?

Step 3   *Read.* Read actively.

a. Read to answer the questions you raised while doing the survey/question routine.

b. Read all the added attractions in the chapter (maps, graphs, tables, and other illustrations).

c. Read all the underlined, italicized, or boldface words or phrases extra carefully.

Step 4   *Recite.* Go over what you read in step 3 by either orally summarizing what you just read or making notes of some type.

Step 5   *Review.* Periodically survey what you read and learned.

a. Use your notes or markings to refresh your memory.

b. Review immediately after reading.

c. Review again periodically.

d. Review again before taking an exam on the subject.

Efficacy of SQ3R for Independent and Content Class Use

The balance of opinion among specialists regarding the efficacy of SQ3R is positive but by no means unanimous. Several studies (Diggs, 1973; Donald, 1967; Gurrola, 1975; McNamara, 1977; Willmore, 1967; Wooster, 1958) found no significant differences between SQ3R and control (i.e., placebo) treatments. Thus, despite the popularity of SQ3R, evidence of its effectiveness as a self-guided reading–study formula still is uncertain.

We continue to endorse SQ3R for content classroom use, especially when each step is practiced under teacher guidance. Used in this way, SQ3R parallels the Directed Reading–Thinking Activity (DR-TA), which has been proven effective. There are several additional obstacles, however, to study strategy instruction in general, which are discussed next.

Obstacles to Study Strategy Instruction

Teaching study strategies presents several unique challenges. At a basic managerial level, study strategy instruction is an additional layer of *content* to be taught and learned on top of existing demands.

The second challenge is the quite lofty goal of this type of instruction. The intent is to teach information, processes, and even beyond this, to change habits of mind. And habits are notoriously difficult to change. Teaching students to use study strategies like SQ3R is analogous to teaching teachers to use instructional methods like the DR-TA. In each case, what is taught is a set of steps that teachers and students are expected to understand, remember, and then apply *on their own*. This requires

Figure 10.1
Pauk's eight learning principles.

---

1. **Principle of Motivated Interest.** We remember what interests us. Develop your natural interests, and try to create new interests by reading (e.g., magazine and newspaper articles) in diverse areas. If you find a subject boring, or irrelevant, try to find something in it of personal interest or use, and you will find it easier to learn.

2. **Principle of Selectivity.** Information must be grouped into units of a manageable size for efficient recall. In the nineteenth century, Hermann Ebbinghaus, one of the world's earliest experimental psychologists, found that it took fifteen times as many trials to memorize twelve nonsense syllables as the number of trials needed to memorize six nonsense syllables. One would predict that it would take only twice as many trials.

3. **Principle of Intention to Remember.** Prerequisites to efficient learning include careful attending, getting the facts right the first time, and striving to understand. Recall that this is the basic principle underlying the guided reading procedure, a total reading and study lesson design covered in Chapter 4. Active reading the *first* time saves time in the long run.

4. **Principle of Basic Background.** What we perceive (see, hear, taste, smell, feel, and read) depends in large measure on what we already know. Whenever you are trying to learn something new, connect it to something you know.

5. **Principle of Meaningful Organization.** George Miller, the eminent Harvard psychologist, found that the immediate memory span of the general population seems fixed at approximately seven bits of information, plus or minus two. For effective recall, therefore, information should be categorized into meaningful groups of no more than seven bits. The telephone company heeded this research when developing the telephone numbering system. The U.S. Postal Service, on the other hand, has challenged it by implementing a nine-digit Zip Code system.

6. **Principle of Recitation.** Study reading must be an active process. Recitation is analogous to exercising a muscle: it builds and embeds information in long-term memory. Pauk reminds us of how H. F. Spitzer's classic study compared the amount of information recalled by students seven and sixty-three days after learning. Students who reviewed immediately after learning remembered 83% after seven days and 70% after sixty-three days. Those who did not review immediately after learning remembered 33% after seven days and 14% after sixty-three days. Control groups of students who also did not review immediately after learning remembered approximately 55% after one day, 22% after fourteen days, 18% after twenty-one days, and 1% after twenty-eight days. Obviously, recitation-study works!

Figure 10.1, *continued*

---

7. **Principle of Consolidation.** Information must be harbored in the mind for a certain period before a temporary memory can be consolidated into a more permanent one. Numerous records of accident victims show that a period of unconsciousness can erase the memory of events that occurred from fifteen to five minutes before the person lost consciousness. Spitzer's study, described in principle 6, further illustrates the effectiveness of an immediate review of new information.

8. **Principle of Distributed Practice.** A number of brief reviews are more effective than one long review session. Short sessions prevent physical and emotional fatigue and help sustain interest and motivation.

Source: From Walter Pauk (1989), *How to Study in College* (2nd ed), Boston, Houghton Mifflin. Copyright 1989 by Houghton Mifflin Company. Adapted with permission.

preparation, guidance, and lots of practice. Even if students become convinced of the usefulness of a particular study strategy, they are likely to slip back into more accustomed patterns. To be effective, study strategies need to become new habits. Francis Robinson himself observed that SQ3R cannot possibly be effective until it becomes automatic and "subordinate to the task of reading" (1946, p. 21).

Another complicating factor is that people tend to resent being given advice, and most study strategies amount to advice. This problem persists even though the strategies and techniques are quite effective.

Finally, teachers tend to believe that what we do when we study is highly individual, and that no one strategy will work for everyone. While it is true that each of us tailors a particular strategy to our own personal style, fundamental principles of learning apply regardless of individual differences. In one of the early textbooks designed for college students with weak academic skills, Walter Pauk (1989) summarized much of what is known about effective learning and study in his "eight learning principles." These research-based principles, shown in Figure 10.1, provide an excellent orientation to the field of developmental studies and a basis for evaluating any study strategies program.

CONTENT AREA STUDY METHODS FOR IMPROVING LECTURE NOTE TAKING AND LISTENING

Palmatier's Unified Note-Taking System

Students need instruction in how to learn from lecture as well as from text. Palmatier's Unified Note-Taking System (PUNS) urges students to review lecture notes immediately after class and supplement them with text information. The note-taking format also provides a built-in study system by separating key words from the body of the notes. PUNS is one of the few note-taking methods that has been validated through empirical research (Palmatier, 1971, 1973; Palmatier & Bennett, 1974).

Steps in PUNS

Step 1   *Record.* In a loose-leaf binder, use only one side of $8\frac{1}{2}$-by-11-inch notebook paper with a 3-inch margin on the left side. (Many college bookstores now stock this type of paper for this purpose.) Record lecture notes to the right of the margin. Use a modified outline form to isolate main topics. Leave space where information seems to be missing. Number each page as you record the notes.

Step 2   *Organize.* As soon after the lecture as possible, add two sections to the notes. First, place labels inside the left margin. These should briefly describe the information in the recorded notes. Second, insert important text information directly into the recorded notes. If you need more space, you can use the back of the notebook paper.

Step 3   *Study.* Remove the notes from the loose-leaf binder, and lay them out so that only the left margin of each page is visible. Use the labels as memory cues to recite as much of the information on the right as you can recall. The labels can be turned into questions stems, "What do I need to know about [insert label]?" Verify your recall immediately by lifting the page to read the information recorded to the right of the label. As you master the material on each page of notes, set that page aside in an "I already know" stack. For objective tests, the labels can be approached at random, simulating the format of multiple-choice, true/false, and matching tests. For essay tests, group information into logical units, formulate predicted essay questions, and practice writing answers. Figure 10.2 presents a sample PUNS format.

The notes students take during lectures are influenced as much by listening habits as by note-taking strategy. The next sections suggest ways to improve attention and active listening.

Enabling Questions

The Enabling Questions procedure is a student-initiated strategy that we developed. It is a prepared set of questions that students can use to tune in and reduce distraction during lectures. Using Enabling Questions puts

Step 1: *Record.*
Use the right-hand side of a specially divided page, leaving space to add text notes.

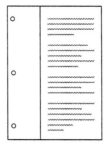

Step 2: *Fill in labels.*
Write key word labels in the left margin and text notes in the space provided for lecture notes. Use the back of the previous page if you need more space.

Step 3: *Study key words.*
Lay out pages so that only key words show, and try to recite information from your notes. Remove each page as you master its contents.

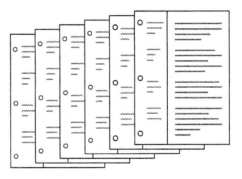

Figure 10.2
PUNS note taking

the listener into an active, evaluative thinking mode and invites the teacher or speaker to talk a little less and welcome more interaction. Students should be urged to translate these questions into their own words.

Set 1: Questions that Help the Listener Organize and Clarify Information

1. What is/are the main *question(s)* you are answering by your lecture (or lesson) today?

2. Which key terms and concepts are most important for us to remember from what you have said (or will say) today?

3. What is most often misunderstood or confusing about the information or position you are presenting today?

Set 2: Questions that Help the Listener Get a Mental Breather

1. Could you please restate that last point in some other words?

2. Would you please spell _____ and _____ for us?

3. Would you please say which points you especially want us to note at this time?

Set 3: Questions that Invite Give-and-Take with the Speaker

1. How does what you have said compare with positions others have taken, and who might these others be?

2. Is there convincing evidence to support your position that you can share with us?

3. What do you think is the weakest part of the position you have taken?

4. How do you think this position (or new information) affects previously held beliefs?

5. What do you suppose would happen if you extended this point another step or two?

6. Would you mind pausing for a moment to see if there are other views on this in the class/audience? This would help us better understand and follow your points.

Any one of the latter set of questions likely would put the listener back into an active, evaluative thinking mode and reduce the sometimes excessive dominance of the speaker. It is important that the listener who wishes to use these types of questions does so with an eye toward using them for enriching comprehension, learning, and mature interaction, and not as a counteroffensive. One way to help students learn the value and become regular users of Enabling Questions is to write these questions on index cards and distribute a few to each class member. Then urge students to try to use the questions on their card(s) intelligently over a two- to three-day period. Schedule a day to discuss what happened and what students learned and what might need to be modified to make the Enabling Questions even more enabling.

Guided Lecture Procedure

The Guided Lecture Procedure (GLP) (Kelly & Holmes, 1979) is a teacher-directed method for improving listening. It is the listening counterpart of the Guided Reading Procedure (Manzo, 1975).

Steps in the GLP

Step 1   Students are directed to take no notes as they listen carefully to the lecture.

Step 2   The teacher writes the objectives of the lecture on the chalkboard along with key technical terms.

Step 3   The teacher lectures for about half the class period, then stops.

Step 4   Students attempt to write down everything they can recall from the lecture.

Step 5   Students form small cooperative learning groups to review and discuss their notes. This discussion, or language component, helps build related speaking, writing, and thinking strategies.

The GLP has been used effectively with classes from middle school to college levels (Kelly & Holmes, 1979). The small-group activity that forms the latter part of the lesson is an excellent cooperative learning activity.

CONTENT AREA STRATEGIES
FOR TEST TAKING

Taking Multiple-Choice Tests

It is difficult to overstate the effects of test taking on the body and the ego. If test taking were a pill, it probably would never pass the Food and Drug Administration guidelines for benefit-to-risk ratio. The growing emphasis on writing and performance-based assessment has begun to decrease the use of multiple-choice tests in the classroom. However, most schools still use standardized multiple-choice tests for evaluation of their overall program. Students' scores on multiple-choice tests can be more a reflection of their test-taking savvy than their knowledge acquisition. See Figure 10.3 for a brief list of helpful hints for taking multiple-choice tests.

PORPE: A Strategy for Taking Essay Tests

Predict-organize-rehearse-practice-evaluate (PORPE) was developed in response to students' anxiety about taking essay examinations (Simpson, 1986). The method evolved from a review of the research literature to find practical ideas about how proficient readers prepare for essay-type tests. PORPE's five steps guide students to behave like "effective readers who have some awareness and control of their own cognitive activities while they read and study" (p. 408).

Figure 10.3
Tips for taking multiple-choice tests.

- ✦ Block out a rough time plan for timed tests. Note what time it will be when half the time is up, and how many items you should have completed by that time.

- ✦ Read slowly and answer quickly. Focus on the question instead of the answer choices. This prevents the frequent and irritating problem of misreading the question.

- ✦ Answer the easy questions first, and skip the hard ones. Spending time on difficult questions raises anxiety and may cause you to forget information you knew when the test began. As you go through the test, you may find information that will help you remember answers to earlier difficult items.

- ✦ Don't assume that the test is loaded with trick questions. This will cause you to read too much into the questions and spend too much time in needless internal debate. Read each question carefully, but concentrate on the main point rather than the details.

- ✦ Avoid anxiety reactions that break concentration: glancing frequently at the clock or the instructor, polishing eyeglasses, examining fingernails, gazing at the wall or ceiling, excessive yawning or stretching.

- ✦ Use all the time allotted. If you finish before the time is up, always check your work. Make sure you answered all the questions, but don't waste time reviewing the answers to easy questions. Change your answers if you have reason to. Research shows that contrary to common belief, three out of four times your changes will be correct. This may be because during a final check, the tension begins to lessen and thought processes are clearer.

Steps in PORPE

Step 1   *Predict.* Students are asked to predict essay questions that they might be asked. Teachers should make every effort to help students at this stage to raise synthesizing, analyzing, and application questions as well as more literal *what-* and *when*-type questions. One way to do this is to introduce students to a glossary of the most common words used in essay questions, such as *explain, criticize, compare, contrast, react, support,* and *elaborate.* As follow-up, teachers should model the thought process they go through in preparing (predicting) and phrasing essay questions on a previously studied body of information. Students then should prepare and share their predicted questions with classmates.

Step 2   *Organize.* Students are encouraged to organize the information needed to answer predicted questions. Students are encouraged to use semantic maps and outlines for this purpose. Again, teachers should model this strategy.

Step 3   *Rehearse.* This is the conventional study or recall-and-recite step. Students should be encouraged to use appropriate memory devices.

Step 4   *Practice.* In this step students practice composing or answering essay-type questions. They should be reminded of the following in doing so:

a. Work from an outline.

b. Make sure your opening sentence rephrases the question and/or takes a clear position.

c. Make the structure of your answer clear by using transitional words and phrases like *first, on the other hand, furthermore,* and *finally.*

d. Give examples of major points.

e. Reread what you wrote, and make appropriate editorial corrections.

Step 5   *Evaluate.* This step continues logically from the latter portion of the last one but should occur after a brief pause. The idea simply is to consider how a teacher might evaluate your answer. It may be necessary to conduct several sessions where students listen to, read, and discuss the relative merits of various essay answers before they acquire the ability to get outside of themselves and review their own work.

Notes on PORPE

PORPE has been found to be significantly more effective than question–answer recitation in improving comprehension and essay writing (Simpson, Hayes, Stahl, Connor, & Weaver, 1988). PORPE also makes a great deal of sense at an intuitive level. It incorporates attention to metacognitive development, content mastery, effective predicting, organizing, and test writing. Structurally, it progresses in logical movements from teacher instruction, modeling, and guidance to total student independence and control—the purpose of all study strategies instruction.

Study Journals

Keeping a study journal can make students more aware of their present study habits and attitudes. A study journal is simply a written record of thoughts and feelings about studying and about school. Students should be encouraged to make four or five brief journal entries each week, without undue concern for form or style. Guiding questions should be "What am

I doing when I study?" and "How do I feel about it?" Some categories for consideration include the following:

✦ *Classes:* participation or lack of it, difficulty paying attention, confidence level

✦ *Homework:* difficulty concentrating or getting started, organization of materials, strategies for studying

✦ *Tests:* thoughts before, during, and after tests; controlling anxiety

✦ *Time management:* difficulty getting everything done; setting priorities

✦ *Symptoms of stress:* fatigue, headaches, worry, apathy, guilt, problems in interpersonal relationships, insomnia, excessive snacking, and so on

Following are some sample study journal entries:

9/10: Algebra class always begins in English, but it soon becomes Greek. There must be something I can do to keep from getting lost about midway???

9/14: When I get home from school, I can't stand to face homework. Soon it's dinnertime, then the good programs are on, then I'm too tired. When are you supposed to do homework anyway?

9/25: I hate tests. I never seem to study the right things.

10/2: I've been having trouble falling asleep, and I wake up two hours early thinking about that darn paper due next week. I also find it impossible to stay awake after lunch.

After students have made several entries in their journals, they should be encouraged to look back over what they have written. Are there noticeable patterns? Are there certain kinds of situations that tend to precipitate stress? What coping strategies did students try? How effective were these? We have found that study journals are more likely to be kept when they are combined with the next strategy, which offers a place and time for their use and reinforcement.

Problem-Solving Approach to Study Skills

The *Problem-solving Approach to Study Skills* (PASS) (Manzo & Casale, 1980) is an interactive method designed to communicate the attitude that school, learning, and living present a series of typical study problems that generally are quite manageable and often solvable by critical, constructive analysis and personal resolve.

Steps in PASS

Step 1 *Count.* The teacher presents students with a list of common study problems and asks them to check those that apply to them (see Figure 10.4).

Step 2 *Characterize.* The teacher guides students in defining selected problems, and themselves, in specific terms. The teacher urges students to take inventories of learning style, temperament, skills, abilities, and attitudes in an effort to reach a firmer sense of themselves as learners. (The learning styles inventory called the Core Functioning Inventors found in Appendix C, can be helpful here.)

Step 3 *Consider.* Students consider how they typically have dealt with their particular needs and problems and the possible merit in these intuitive coping strategies.

Step 4 *Collect.* The class discusses and judges standard techniques for dealing with reading/study problems on the basis of their compatibility with each student's style and character. Where

Figure 10.4
Checklist of common study problems.

—1. Taking good notes in class

—2. Completing reading assignments

—3. Finding the main ideas when reading

—4. Remembering details when reading

—5. Figuring out what the author/teacher means

—6. Staying relaxed when studying

—7. Concentrating while reading

—8. Paying attention in class

—9. Asking questions in class

—10. Vocabulary meanings

—11. Writing answers to questions

—12. Writing personal opinions about class topics

—13. Writing research papers

—14. Planning and completing class projects

—15. Taking notes while reading/studying

—16. Finding reference materials in the library

—17. Participating in class discussions

Other: _____

these appear incompatible, the procedures are dismissed as inappropriate.

Step 5   *Create.* Students seek inventive alternatives that match their personal styles. This step is best handled initially in small groups and then in larger group discussions.

Notes on PASS

PASS was evaluated in a case study approach and found to be a very sound means of improving study habits and positive attitudes toward learning (Casale & Kelly, 1980). The content teacher's efforts to teach students how to study will be time well spent. Learning is as much attitudinal as it is intellectual. Teaching students how to study tells them that they are as important as the content.

✦ *After Words* ✦

This chapter suggested some ways in which the content area teacher might help students to build needed study strategies, attitudes, and habits. It focused on the things students do most: listening, note taking, personal problem solving, and test taking. The next chapter addresses some discipline-specific problems that students may encounter and the specific help that each subject teacher might contribute to a schoolwide content area literacy effort.

SECTION IV

Issues in Literacy Applications, Leadership, and Futures

Even now that you have established a solid understanding of how to promote reading/writing/thinking of, between, and beyond the lines, there is much more to learn about. The chapters in this section might be considered optional, or as reference material for you going forward. Chapter 11 contains examples of applications of content area literacy in specific disciplines, Chapter 12 addresses special needs students, and Chapter 13 is designed to help you begin the process of becoming a literacy leader. Chapter 14 is for fun and further preparation for the events and multiple literacies that seem to be shaping our futures. It addresses interdisciplinary learning, e-commerce, and "other mooga-mooga," or things that sound foreign at the moment, but could be essential literacies in the new millennium.

CHAPTER 11

Discipline-Specific Applications of the Content Area Literacy Technology

Too much new information can drive knowledge out of circulation.
Knowledge is orderly and cumulative, an enduring treasure.

—Dan Boorstin

✦ *Fore Words* ✦

At this moment, schools are interviewing for enlightened educators to join their efforts to integrate the teaching of reading, writing, and thinking into the disciplines. Soon, perhaps by the time you graduate and/or have some more teaching experience, they will be asking for thought-leaders to work with them to achieve these ends. This is a matter of acquiring certain professional knowledge in the particular. This knowledge base is a technology that is just as refined and precise as any in the medical, legal, or computer science fields. Here is your chance to read the past, or what we have learned about how to do this, and to write the ways in which we will do so in the future.

DISTRIBUTED AND UNIVERSAL RESPONSIBILITY

For some time, it has been the practice to educate teachers to the belief that it is each discipline's role to teach virtually all of the literacy skills that could possibly be employed in each subject area. This "everyone is responsible" approach sometimes tends to result in no one being responsible. To counter the downside effects of this unsuccessful policy, we would suggest that you consider taking responsibility for some very specific skills that you would teach by special application. In addition, let all who teach also continue to feel responsible for imparting all literacy skills and strategies. To launch this relatively new approach we have identified some basic skills to be distributed to at least four subject areas (See Chapter 13, Figure 13.2). We will add to these on our web site based on the reactions and suggestions received from you and your course instructor.

QUAINT OLDE ENGLISH

The English curriculum is the focal point for teaching language mastery. The term *English* is a quaint reminder of our colonial and cultural past. In fact, our language is Anglo-American and the discipline is Language Arts, or effective listening, speaking, reading, and writing. English clearly is the current language of choice on the World Wide Web, at major airports throughout the world, and at global financial centers. The language may still be a little quaint and quirky, but it also is viable, and for those born speaking it, a great gift that keeps giving.

Reading and English

Student progress in reading receives its greatest emphasis in the English curriculum. English is the only discipline that traditionally has designated reading and writing improvement as a key objective. It also has traditionally provided direct and systematic instruction in vocabulary, writing, cultural literacy, and literary appreciation. Lately, it has taken to teaching "mass media," and "communications" as well. As such, the English curriculum lays the classical and modern foundations for effective comprehension of text, and for interpreting the contemporary experience. The English curriculum, however, remains primarily dedicated to ensuring that at least some explicit attention is given to receptive and expressive language in school. There are sound reasons for continuing this focus on language and literature up to and through graduate education. The most obvious, is the fact that aural, written, and spoken language, along with reading, are developmental processes that can be refined and enhanced throughout one's lifetime. They are the mechanisms through which learning, as well as the capacity to learn, can be grown.

The English curriculum has some special requirements. The most difficult of these for pupils is the requirement to read anthologies of prose and poetry that often span hundreds of years in origins, context, and style. Finding value and meaning in story was and is the center of English class. To this end, we have discussed several means and methods in previous chapters, from plot mapping to character study. To this, we now shall add a basic set of questions to guide literature study. Notice that the questions raised reveal a good deal about author craft, and therefore can serve as aids in teaching creative writing. Keep in mind while reviewing this guide that it is just that, a *guide*. Literature is art, and art, like the life it imitates and the imitation of itself it evokes in life, does not lend itself to easy categorization and dissection. Realize too, that this same guide can be used to unpackage a film or television presentation. It also can be used for general literature study, that is, as a postanalysis of several previously read and viewed pieces of fiction.

Guide to Literature Study[1]

Character Study

Who is the protagonist, or main character and why?

Who is the antagonist, and why?

---

[1] Liberally modified from Patricia O. Richards, Debra H. Thatch, Michelle Shreeves, Peggy Timmons and Sallie Barker (1999), "Don't Let a Good Scare Frighten You: Choosing and Using Quality Chillers to Promote Reading," *Reading Teacher, 52*(8), pp. 830–840.

Does the author use common stereotypes, or some inventive ways to introduce and picture the main characters?

Are there any minor characters who seem to have special appeal, or possibilities for future development?

Setting

Does the story take place in a real or totally imagined place?

How does the author create mood through setting?

How do the characters react to the setting?

Plot

How does the author tell the story—through a narrator, a character, or some other way?

How does the point of view help readers relate to the characters and buy into the plot?

What information is given and when?

What information is held back from the reader for dramatic effect?

Theme

What type of conflict is depicted (e.g., person against person, person against nature, person against self)?

Can you detect some idea or attitude being conveyed through the story?

Are there subplots, and do they convey the same or different themes?

How do characters grow or change?

How do they deal with problems?

Style and Tone

Does the story contain elements of the unbelievable, and how is it made believable?

How are facts, images, and words used to hook readers?

How is tension/humor built?

How is tension relieved?

What sensory images are used, and toward what effect?

Universal Truths

What ideas and values underlie the story or piece?

In your judgment, are the ideas and values mature or immature?

Are the ideas and values central to the piece or simply a mechanism for telling an entertaining story or tale?

Genre Comparisons

How would you characterize the story by literary type (e.g., fantasy, mystery, survival, science fiction, biography)?

What are the genre features of a given story?

How would you compare stories of a similar genre for distinguishing characteristics?

Author Comparisons

What are some of the distinctive style features of authors working in a similar genre?

What are some of the distinctive style features of authors working in the same theme but in different genre?

Can you describe different audiences that likely would be attracted to different author styles?

Which is/are your favorite authors/styles/genre and why?

Illustrations and Camera Work

Can you describe the style characteristics of the illustrations/camera work?

Are illustrations/camera work realistic or impressionistic?

What tends to be in focus, out of focus?

Beyond Literature Study to Technical Language

A newer view of the English/Language Arts curriculum says that a good job is being done with prose and poetry reading, but that students need to be taught more about how to read technical writing, something nineteen other industrialized nations already do. School reformer William Doggett maintains that America has moved on from being an industrialized society to one based on technologies, and that our curricula are yet to catchup.

Much of the catchup being called for, we believe, is occurring and will continue to occur at a lively pace largely due to the influence of the content area literacy movement, which emphasizes such, and the Internet, which is bringing terse, content-laden, hi-tech language into schools and homes via electronic text. For these reasons, our sense is that there is little reason to panic and "revolutionize" this aspect of education; rather we should just stay a bit ahead of it and let the process continue to evolve. In this way, new technologies will be folded into the core curriculum without another overswing of the educational pendulum.

While almost all of the methods presented thus far would serve the English/Language Arts curriculum, two are highlighted here: specifications for English textbooks that could be added to the Informal Textbook Inventory (see Figure 11.1); and *cloze-plus* (Blanc, 1977), a method designed to improve poetry comprehension and appreciation more directly than do the reading guides previously described.

Cloze-Plus for Poetry

Cloze-plus enhances comprehension of the meanings and techniques of poetry by dealing directly with the poem, using a cloze-type worksheet. Cloze techniques are most effective when they serve as the basis for an interactive discussion about language choices and forms. Used in this way, they also encourage peer teaching, urge students to generate their own guiding questions, and serve as a readiness step for poetry-writing activities.

Steps in Cloze-Plus

Step 1   The teacher prepares a worksheet by writing the poem, deleting every fifth word beginning with the title (see Figure 11.2 for an example).

Step 2   The teacher tells students that although they have not read to poem, they are to try to recreate it by filling in the deleted words as closely as possible to the exact words of the original. The teacher points out that the activity will be difficult and students should rely on whatever clues they can find. Students then complete the poem individually.

Step 3   Next, students work in small groups to discuss their word choices. The teacher stands back and lets it happen.

Step 4   Once the groups have reconciled their choices, the teacher resumes a leader role, explaining terms such as context, syntax, and rhyme and asking students to express how they might have used these to fill in the blanks. (Further class discussion might include comments on poetic license, grammar, vocabulary, and style.)

Step 5   The teacher reads the poem aloud, pausing at the previous blanks to give students time to correct their initial responses.

FOREIGN LANGUAGE

No matter how the teaching of foreign languages is approached, its ultimate success depends on two rudimentary principles of learning: thinking about and in the language, and practice outside of scheduled lab and class times. For this reason, foreign language teachers have worked hard to network with English language teachers from around the world. In this way they have arranged for student pen pals and for students to visit one another's countries. This has been marginally successful. Now there is a new tool, the Internet.

Figure 11.1
Informal Textbook Inventory questions for English.

I. Use of Text Aids to Locate Information
Construct 10 to 15 questions that assess student's ability to use parts of the textbook, such as:
A. What is the title of the book?
B. When was it published?
C. Who wrote the book?
D. How are the chapters arranged or grouped?
E. On what page does Chapter 8 begin?
F. In which chapter can you find something about Langston Hughes?
G. In which chapter can you find "Types of Humor in Modern American Literature"?

II. Rate of Reading and Levels of Comprehension
Choose a passage from the textbook that has not been read by students. Have students read the passage and record the time when they finish it. Help them to compute their rate of reading, or words per minute (number of words read divided by number of minutes spent = words per minute). Have students answer questions about the passage that require comprehension at literal, interpretive, and applied levels.

III. Vocabulary Development
A. *Contextual Analysis:* Choose sentences from the textbook that contain words that may be difficult for students. List these sentences, with the difficult words underlined. Have students predict the meaning of the underlined words, using clues from the context to make reasonable predictions (evaluate student responses in terms of "reasonableness" of prediction rather than accuracy of definition).
B. *Structural Analysis:* Select words from the textbook that are made up of affixes and recognizable English root words. Have students identify and explain the meaning or function of the root word, prefix, and/or suffix in each of these words.
C. *Dictionary Use:* Choose sentences from the textbook that contain a word or words that have multiple meanings. List these sentences, with the multiple-meaning word(s) underlined. Have students check a dictionary to select and write the appropriate meaning of each underlined word according to its use in the sentence. (From a term paper by Fengfang Lu, UMKC, 1986.)

IV. Use of Reference Sources to Locate Information
A. In our classroom dictionary, locate the origin of the word ("bonfire").
B. Using the library card catalog, find the names of two books written by (Judy Blume). Who is the author of (*The Great Gilly Hopkins*)?

Figure 11.1, *continued*

C. In the *Reader's Guide to Periodical Literature,* locate the journal and the year and month in which you find the short story entitled ("Down the Down Staircase: A Sequel").

D. In the *Essay and General Literature Index,* find the titles for three stories related to the theme of (family conflict).

E. In the *Current Biography,* locate information about (Ernest Hemingway's life).

F. In *Bartlett's Familiar Quotations,* locate the person credited with having written: ("One thorn of experience is worth a whole wilderness of warning.")

G. A thesaurus is a book of words grouped by ideas and used to locate precise words to express your idea. In *Roget's International Thesaurus,* locate at least three nouns that could be used instead of (*cheerfulness.*)

V. *Use of Graphic Aids to Interpret Meaning*

A. Study the cartoon on page ____ of your text. Describe what you believe to be the message of the cartoon.

B. Examine the timeline of major English literary periods on page ____ of your text. What years are considered to encompass the neoclassical literary period? List three prominent writers for this period.

C. The diagram on page ____ depicts the plot structure of Jackson's "The Lottery." After reading the story, briefly discuss the conflict, rising action, climax, and denouement of "The Lottery."

Source: Sections IV and V from Criscoe and Gee, Content area reading: A diagnostic/prescriptive approach. Copyright © 1984 by Allyn & Bacon. Reprinted with permission.

Newby et al. (1996) describe the new dimension through the story of a Spanish teacher whose students now regularly chat by e-mail with a classroom in Seville, Spain. The future of foreign language education will be in cultivating the many dimensions and values in this new, rapid, and easy-access means of writing, reading, and "speaking" in the vernacular(s) of other languages. Foreign language education will never seem tedious again. To further advantage this chat environment, foreign language teachers could develop some common pieces of material for students to read and react to, such as in the REAPANX program described in Chapter 8. Every part of REAPANX seems to meet some part of learning a foreign language.

MATHEMATICS

Reports of the National Assessment of Educational Progress (1988–1998) repeatedly reveal dismal facts about the state of mathematics proficiency

Figure 11.2
Example of cloze-plus.

Richard Cory
Whenever Richard ___ 1 ___ went down town,
We ___ 2 ___ on the pavement looked ___ 3 ___ him;
He was a ___ 4 ___ from sole to crown,
___ 5 ___-favored and imperially slim.

___ 6 ___ he was always quietly ___ 7 ___.
And he was always ___ 8 ___ when he talked;
But ___ 9 ___ he fluttered pulses when ___ 10 ___ said,
"Good-morning," and ___ 11 ___ glittered when he walked.
___ 12 ___ he was rich,—yes, ___ 13 ___ than a king—
And ___ 14 ___ schooled in every grace;
___ 15 ___ fine, we thought that ___ 16 ___ was everything
To make ___ 17 ___ wish that we were ___ 18 ___ his place.

So on ___ 19 ___ worked, and waited for ___ 20 ___ light,
And went without ___ 21 ___ meat, and cursed the ___ 22 ___,
And Richard Cory, one ___ 23 ___ summer night,
Went home ___ 24 ___ put a bullet through ___ 25 ___ head.

                                        —Edwin Arlington Robinson

---

1. Cory; 2. people; 3. at; 4. gentleman; 5. clean; 6 And; 7. arrayed; 8. human, 9. still;
10. he; 11. he; 12. And; 13. richer; 14. admirably; 15. In; 16. he; 17. us; 18. in; 19. we;
20. the; 21. the; 22. bread, 23. calm; 24. and; 25. his.

in the United States. What they show can no longer be referred to as findings, but as themes.

✦ More than 25% of thirteen-year-olds cannot handle elementary school arithmetic.

✦ One-third of eleventh graders agree that they don't even know what their math teacher is talking about.

✦ Only 6% of seventeen-year-olds can handle algebra or multistep math problems.

✦ Scores for blacks and Hispanics, despite modest gains, lag 7% to 11% behind those of Caucasians.

✦ The average Japanese and Taiwanese high school student does better at math than does the top 5% of American high school students.

The difficulties students experience in dealing effectively with "word problems" and related mathematical concepts is unparalleled among current educational dilemmas. Clearly there are more "math illiterates" than there are people who cannot read. Until recently, however, this problem has been among the lowest-ranked national priorities. Weakness in dealing with math concepts, computation, and word problems is so pervasive that it tends to pass for a fact of life.

Mathematics as a "Second Language"

Improvement of mathematics and reading instruction has finally begun with the reconstruction of math books to conform more closely to conventional conversational language. See Figure 11.3 for examples of the more conventional language found in modern math texts. Math itself is a system of reality coding that benefits from this more conversational approach.

Working within this theme, MacNeal (1994) referred to this need in a book he called *Mathsemantics: Making Numbers Talk.* Students can be taught to listen to and speak the language of mathematics in settings and situations that closely parallel the ways in which people successfully learn language, but more especially second languages. Using the principles of second-language instruction, the reason, purpose, and value of mathematical systems can be more easily imparted, reinforced, and internalized. The simple idea is to *preteach* mathematics incidentally by making it a more common frame of reference in conversation. This allows the repeated exposure of previously unfamiliar terms to create a contextual lesson and an inclination to be attentive when direct instruction is offered on one of these terms. Another principle involves use of artifacts. An artifact is some concrete thing that is identified with a culture or activity; such as a baseball glove is with baseball and sport. One often-overlooked way to introduce the "second language learner" to the "culture" and tools of the new language is through its literary artifacts, or books and writings. Math books are artifacts that represent math culture, and serve as a math learning tool. Ideally, it should become a point of conversation and comfort, rather than fear and anxiety. To be sure math, for all but a few, is an acquired taste: hence it may be necessary to create an interesting room and environment of other math artifacts, such as of pictures and objects reflecting the past and present contributions of math to human history. The Internet, of course, is the place to do some electronic-archeological digs. It also contains stories of modern efforts to do and teach math inventively.

CAUGHT IN THE NET

Math and Physics in Motion

Ed Zobel, high school math teacher, has created ZONA LAND, a nifty site that animates physics and math concepts in VRML and Java programming languages. He hopes to make this site an on-line interactive textbook, probably by the time you will be looking in (<id.mind. net/~zona>).

Figure 11.3
Mathematics Informal Textbook Inventory.

---

1. **Locating Information**
   Directions: Terms used in the book can be found in one of several places; preface, contents, appendix, and glossary/index. You will be able to locate each term on the right in one of the places on the left. Locate the term and then mark the place where you found it. Do this as quickly as you can.

Book Section	*Term*
A. Preface	_____ Using your income
	_____ Axes
B. Contents	_____ Individual differences
	_____ 4 pecks = 1 bushel
C. Appendix	_____ Cubic units
	_____ Objectives
D. Glossary/Index	_____ Tables and graphs
	_____ 1,760 Yds = 1 mile
	_____ Dividing fractions
	_____ Hourly wage
	_____ Measure your progress
	_____ Inch
	_____ Lesson organization
	_____ Overtime
	_____ Review

2. **Reading the Mathematics Textbook**
   Directions: Read p. 69. When you have finished reading, close your book and answer the following questions. Remember, once you have closed the book you may not open for any answers.

   Vocabulary: Mathematical and General

   a. Define *prime* first in the words of the text, then in your own words.
      What the text said: _____
      Your Words: _____
   b. What did the author mean when he said, "a simple hunting and fishing existence . . ."?

      _____
   c. What does the term *signified* mean?

      _____

   Main Ideas

   d. How did the author explain that early humans needed a method of counting things?

      _____
   e. Why did the author include information about early counting methods in this chapter?

      _____

Figure 11.3, *continued*

3. **Interpreting Graphs**
   Directions: Turn to p. 259 and read the section entitled "Reading Bar Graphs." Study Figure 199 and answer the following questions:

   a. How many students (total number) are represented on the bar graph? _____

   b. Circle the two categories below in which the same number of students is found:

      Poor   Fair   Good   Excellent   Superior

   c. Use the graph to determine an approximate answer to each of the following questions:

      How many students received "poor" grades? _____

      How many students received "good" grades? _____

      How many students received "excellent" grades? _____

      How many students received "superior" grades? _____

   d. Would you say that this test was a good test or a poor test? (Explain your answer.)

4. **Seeing and Using Text Markers**
   Directions: Read pp. 119–121. When you finish, close your book and fill in the missing parts of the following outline. Do this in pen.

   I. Units of Measurement
      A. Direct: measuring height with ruler
      B. _____
         1. Measuring temperature—thermometer
         2. _____—_____
         3. _____—_____
         4. Measuring air pressure—barometer
   II. Ancient Measurement Devices
      A. _____
         1. thumb
         2. foot
         3. hand
         4. forearm
         5. _____
      B. Difficulties of Ancient Measuring Devices
         1. _____
         2. _____

   Directions: Now that you have written in your first set of responses in pen, open your book and try to complete the outline in pencil.

Figure 11.3, *continued*

---

5. **Summarizing**
   Directions: You are going to read the section "The Metric System of Weights and Measures," p. 202. When you have finished this section about the consistency of the metric system, close your book. Write a summary of what you have read in four complete sentences.

   _____

   _____

   _____

   _____

6. **Where I Need Help!**
   Directions: Think back to all that you just read and the answers you gave. Indicate in no fewer than two sentences where you think you need help in understanding the information presented.

   _____

   _____

7. **What More?**
   Directions: Think again about what you have read. What are you most curious about? Write at least one sentence telling what you would like to learn more about.

   _____

   _____

Informal Textbook Inventory:
Book as Traveling Companion

Math is a trip—for some a good and for others a bad trip. Introducing students to their textbooks is a simple, sensible way to have them get to know and draw comfort from this well-informed travel companion. The math teacher should plan on spending a minimum of three days on this activity and giving two one-day refresher and extender sessions about two months apart. As students' skills and knowledge base in mathematics grow, so will their perceived need for, and therefore receptivity to, the "helping" features and value of the text.

The teacher should make an extra effort to conduct all sessions in a relaxed and supportive atmosphere. The Informal Textbook Inventory experience can be a nonthreatening, math-teacher-generated means of desensitizing and counterconditioning math anxiety. The examples of Figure 11.3, especially questions 2, 5, 6, and 7, offer useful ways to help students converse in conversational terms about mathematical systems. Note especially question 7 for its possibilities for making math something to be curious about and interested in.

The next method for teaching mathematics and reading also imparts something more of the culture that is part of thinking and talking about math. The method addresses the persistent problem of reading and comprehending word problems. There have been many efforts to make math more friendly, such as with the lively and loosely connected quote and colorful names and problems. (See Figure 11.4, from a recent mathematics textbook, for examples of both of these.) Nonetheless, word problems remain complex—the one shown from the math book in the figure has five major parts, and is difficult to translate into computational steps, which most students know how to do.

The Dahmus Method for Word Problems

The Dahmus method for teaching word problems (Dahmus, 1970) emphasizes the translation of English statements into math statements. Recall from previous chapters that translation questions provide a bridge from literal to higher-order thinking skills.

Steps in the Dahmus Method

Step 1 The statements and their parts in the translation must be in the same order as the verbal form.

Step 2 No operations or substitutions should be performed until the translation is completed.

Step 3 Students should read slowly and translate each idea and fact in the verbal form as it appears before reading. Dahmus recommends that students not read the entire problem beforehand.

Step 4 All other facts suggested by the verbal form and required for the solution should be stated mathematically on students' papers. There should be no verbal forms of translation, only math notation.

Step 5 Students should use deductive reasoning on the translated and implied facts to obtain a solution.

Figure 11.5 provides an example of the Dahmus method.

BIOLOGICAL-PHYSICAL SCIENCES

For over forty years, science education has called for science to be taught as a "narrative of inquiry" with emphasis on self-discovery and hands-on learning. In point of fact, science education remains largely textbook dominated. On the plus side, a good deal of the influence of this revisionist view is now being reflected in published science materials and in a revised

What's Ahead

• Finding area and perimeter of rectangles and squares

WHAT YOU'LL NEED

✓ **Square tiles**

✓ **Graph paper**

Problem Solving Hint

Drawing diagrams may help.

 In 600 B.C. Nebuchadnezzar had the Hanging Gardens of Babylon built. They were so beautiful and complex that they became one of the seven wonders of the ancient world.

Source: Encyclopedia Britannica

6-2 **A**rea of Rectangles and Squares

T H I N K A N D D I S C U S S

Moses is planning a garden. He decides to use 12 square garden plots that measure 1 m on each side. He wants to arrange them in a rectangle. After he lays out the plots, he will put a fence around the outside of the garden.

1. **a.** How could Moses arrange the plots so that he would have the least perimeter and use the least amount of fence? **in a 3 m by 4 m rectangle**

   b. How could Moses arrange the plots so that he would have the greatest perimeter? **a 12 m by 1 m rectangle**

2. **a.** What is the area of the arrangement with the least perimeter? **12 m²**

   b. What is the area of the arrangement with the greatest perimeter? **12 m²**

   c. Will the area change if Moses arranges the plots in a nonrectangular shape? Why or why not? **No; no matter how he arranges the plots, there are 12 with area 1 m² each.**

In the garden-plot problem you can count the square plots to find the area of the rectangular arrangement. When you do not have squares to count, you can find the area A of a rectangle by multiplying the length l and the width w. You can find the perimeter P by adding $l + w + l + w$ to get $2l + 2w$, or $2(l + w)$.

Area and Perimeter of a Rectangle
$A = l \times w$
$P = 2(l + w)$

A square is a rectangle in which the length and the width are equal. You can find the area A of a square by squaring the length s of a side. The perimeter P is $4s$.

6-2 Area of Rectangles and Squares **233**

Figure 11.4

Aids in modern mathematics textbooks.

Source: From S. H. Chapin, M. Illingworth, M. S. Landau, J. O. Masingila, and L. McCracken (1995), *Middle Grades Mathematics: An Interactive Approach* (p. 233), Upper Saddle River, NJ, Prentice Hall. Copyright 1995 by Prentice-Hall. Reprinted by permission.

Mark is twice as old as John. In two years, the sum of their ages
M $\quad = 2\times$ J. $\quad (M + 2) \quad + \quad (J + 2)$
will be five times as much as John's age was four years ago.
$= \quad 5 \quad \times \quad (J - 4)$
How old is each now?
$M = ?$ $\quad J = ?$

Figure 11.5
Example: The Dahmus method.
Source: Dahmus, M. E., *How to teach word problems*. School Science and Mathematics Association © 1970.

and more socially sensitive science curriculum in teacher-training institutions. Accordingly, the stated goals of science education now include understanding self, appreciating (i.e., reading and following) technology, preparing for college, advancing modern culture, and understanding local issues.

Contribution of Science to Reading

The typical science curriculum, whether textbook or experiment based, already contributes naturally to growth in reading. Simply by teaching science well, the science teacher helps students to better grasp the fundamentals of systematic observation, scientific thinking, problem solving, science vocabulary, science concepts, and the physical world. These elements promote progress in reading by enhancing student schemata, as well as important related linguistic and thinking processes. For these reasons, science and reading have been called a "harmonic convergence" (Johnson, 1995).

The characteristics of an "expert reader," such as described in prior chapters, strongly resemble and therefore are greatly compatible with the characteristics of a "scientifically literate person" as defined by the National Science Teachers Association:

> The scientifically literate person has a substantial knowledge base of facts, concepts, conceptual networks, and process skills which enable individuals to continue to learn and think logically.

Problems in Reading Science

The problems students encounter in reading science material stem in large measure from five problem areas:

✦ Inadequate background of information
✦ Misconceptions about the physical world

✦ Inconsiderate or assumptive and inadequately explained text

✦ Difficulty in handling esoteric or technically overwhelming terms

✦ Inadequate preparation and orientation of teachers, particularly at the elementary level, in the basic sciences

Consider some solutions to these problems as they bear on effective reading and study in science.

Using New-Generation Science Texts

Recently, science textbooks have been roundly criticized as being inadequate (Bradley, 1999). However, this criticism belies the fact that there is a new generation of science materials that offer great promise despite some rough spots that are not easily overcome because they are inherent to the discipline. The promise of the newer materials lies in their being better grounded in compellingly interesting issues, their attempt to stress scientific thinking, and the opportunities they offer for developing integrated reading, writing, and science skills. The inherent problem they pose is that "issues-based" materials tend to exceed the mental and social maturity levels of most students and can be quite controversial in some communities (e.g., the perceived conflict between theories and findings for evolution and beliefs nested in conservative religious views). Additionally, from a purely pedagogic perspective, real issues cannot easily be disassembled and reassembled to meet a typical learning sequence. These problems aside, the new materials do tend to do a better job of engaging students.

One of the reasons for higher levels of engagement in science texts may be traced to the casual use and reference to prose, poetry, and common experience as a known ground on which to build a sense of familiarity and a basis for new, less familiar knowledge (see Figure 11.6). Admittedly, these connections sometimes are a bit strained, but our sense is that students would rather have them than not.

Use of Science Texts

One ready means of learning how effectively students are using their science text while helping them improve their use is to prepare an Informal Textbook Inventory on the basic text. See Figure 11.7 for examples of science-oriented items to add to an ITI.

Using Media, Magazines, and Computers

One effective way to build your own as well as students' background knowledge in science is to read lay science magazines, watch public television, and access a multimedia encyclopedia and texts on CD-ROM and the

5–2 The Excretory System

When the sixteenth-century English poet John Donne wrote that "No man is an island, entire of itself," he was actually talking about the human mind and spirit. However, this phrase can also be used to describe the human body: No human body can function without help from its surroundings. For example, your body must obtain food, water, and oxygen from its surroundings and get rid of wastes that may poison you. In order to do this, three body systems work together to provide a pathway for materials to enter and leave the body.

You have already learned about two of these systems: the digestive system and the respiratory system. The digestive system is the pathway for food and water to enter the body. The respiratory system enables oxygen to enter and carbon dioxide and water vapor to leave the body. The third system is the excretory (EHKS-kruh-tor-ee) system. **The excretory system provides a way for various wastes to be removed from the body.** These wastes include excess water and salts, carbon dioxide, and urea (a nitrogen waste). The process by which these wastes are removed from the body is called **excretion.**

You have just read about one of the organs of the excretory system: the lungs. Because the lungs get rid of the wastes carbon dioxide and water vapor, they are members of the excretory system as well as the respiratory system. The remaining organs of the excretory system are the kidneys, the liver, and the skin.

A**CTIVITY**
READING

Reading Poetry

The first line of John Donne's poem entitled "Meditation XVII" was quoted in this chapter. Find a copy of this poem in the library and read it. Is there another line in this poem that is familiar to you?

①

The Kidneys

Have you ever made spaghetti? If so, you know that you have to use a strainer to separate the cooked spaghetti from the cooking water or else you will be eating soggy spaghetti! The strainer acts as a filter, separating one material (spaghetti) from the other (water). Like the spaghetti strainer, the **kidneys** act as the body's filter. In doing so, the kidneys filter wastes and poisons from the blood.

The kidneys, which are the main organs of the excretory system, are reddish brown in color and

Figure 11.6

Poetry and the excretory system.

Source: From A. Maton, J. Hopkins, S. Johnson, D. LaHart, C. W. McLaughlin, M. Quon Warner, and J. D. Wright, (1994). *Human Biology and Health* (p. 118), Upper Saddle River, NJ, Prentice Hall. Copyright 1994 by Prentice-Hall. Reprinted with permission.

Figure 11.7
Sample items for an informal Textbook Inventory for a science text.

Using Resource Materials

The book *Through the Magnifying Glass* will tell you many ways to use scientific tools:

- ✦ How could you find who wrote the book?
- ✦ What is its library call number?
- ✦ Where in the library could you locate the titles of filmstrips that deal with ecology?
- ✦ In what library index could you locate the title of an article by Asimov?
  Applying Theoretical Information
- ✦ How can the law of "centrifugal force" be proven?
- ✦ Describe an example of inertia that you might see every day.

Formulas and Symbols
- ✦ List the meaning of the symbols F and C.
- ✦ What do cm and ml stand for in measurement? (Criscoe & Gee, 1984, pp. 124–125)

Using Graphics and Visual Aids
- ✦ What does the illustration on p. 202 (see below) say about the current flow in electricity?

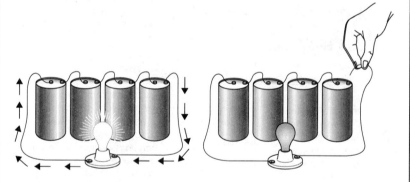

(Answer: Current flow requires a closed path)

Internet. A new breed of lay-technical writers are turning out articles on such mind-boggling topics as quantum physics and string theory in crystal-clear language—which is not to say that these topics are easily comprehended even then. *Discover* and *Omni* are among the best written of these publications. There are also a multitude of project activities in progress on the Internet in the fun and collaborative ways inspired by the web.

Caught in the Net

Mars 2030

Originally created by the White House Millennium Council, the United States through NASA has created a project for students of all ages and grades to design a community for Mars for the year 2030. Kits are available (<www.Mars2030.net>).

Adaptations of the Guided Reading Procedure for Science

Two adaptations of the Guided Reading Procedure (Manzo, 1975) are especially appropriate for pre- and postreading activities using science material (Spiegel, 1980). The GRP-based *prereading procedure* has students identify clear purposes for study, become aware of specific gaps in their knowledge, and build the scaffolding necessary for forming new concepts. This is achieved by having students bring to mind what they already know about a topic and then organize this information into an "advance outline" prior to reading. Then students read to test their preconceptions.

Steps in the Prereading GRP

Step 1   The teacher identifies a unit or topic of study that is fairly narrow in scope, such as photosynthesis or spiders.

Step 2   The teacher has students tell peer recorder(s) at the chalkboard everything they know about the topic prior to lecture or reading.

Step 3   The class identifies conflicting information and areas in which no information has been provided ("Hey, we don't know what spiders eat!"; "Are very large spiders insects or animals?").

Step 4   Students construct an outline with conflicting information listed side by side ("Spiders have six legs/eight legs[?]"). Areas in which no information is known are listed by headings in the outline.

Figure 11.8
GRP Prereading outline.

Spiders

I. How they look
?A. Have six legs/eight legs
  B. Have two body parts
?C. Antennae

II. How they live
?A. What they eat
  B. Spin webs
    1. Made of silk
    2. Lots of different kinds of webs
    3. Sticky
      ?a. What makes them sticky
      ?b. Why doesn't the spider get stuck?

Step 5   The outline is displayed in the classroom throughout the unit of study.

Step 6   The class is told to read to fill in or alter the outline (see Figure 11.8).

✦ *Other Science Application Methods* ✦

Several other methods covered in previous chapters have excellent application to science. Chief among these are the Question-Only Strategy, which offers an effective means of inquiry training; the Oral Reading Strategy for giving direct assistance with science words and phrasing; and Mapping for imparting a "conceptual set" for numerous easily confounded details.

SOCIAL STUDIES

Executive Training

The Constitution gives enormous executive power to every citizen. Social studies is the fundamental school-based source of the executive training that every citizen needs in order to read, interpret, and vote on the streams of raw and prepared information emanating from newspapers, magazines, broadcast media, and now the Internet. The awesome responsibility facing all citizens with such executive power increases the responsibility of those of us who must agonize over what and how to teach them. Accordingly, today's social studies consists not merely of traditional fields like history, government, and geography but fields such as psychology, sociology, and philosophy and several conceptual approaches that can be applied across these fields, such as social inquiry, moral education, and values clarification (Peters, 1982). Indeed, one of the more welcome changes in the teaching of social studies is that it is more about people. Look, for example, at a page from a contemporary text (Figure 11.9) to see how immigration has been reduced to human scale in the story of Sacco and Vanzetti; it's not *People* magazine, but it's also not the antiseptic and decontextualized social studies of just a generation ago.

Contribution of Social Studies to Reading

The principles, precepts, and actual content of social studies underlie almost everything written. This may explain why social studies as a discipline is so highly correlated with general reading comprehension (Adams, 1982; Artley, 1944). Also for this reason, the social studies teacher is especially well situated to enhance students' understanding of how best to read and think about nearly all things written. This is done naturally as the teacher and textbook report to students how others think and feel about a variety of issues such as economics, politics, and culture and the consequences of these beliefs for individual liberties. Most important from the standpoint of reading process, social studies imparts a rich fund of general information, a specialized vocabulary, refined critical-relative thinking strategies, and the rudiments of cultural literacy, both about the core culture and the many diverse cultures within the American mainstream. It also is students' main source of information on our growing global awareness.

Obstacles to Reading and Studying in Social Studies

The major problems students encounter in reading in social studies stem in large measure from the very elements to which social studies ultimately contributes in general reading. Reading in social studies often requires conceptual and informational preparation. It also requires considerable assistance with objective reasoning and in connecting loose factual elements into a structure that subsequently can be used to read, grasp, and interpret still more.

Reasoning Guides

Reasoning guides were developed and popularized in direct response to the above concerns. A reasoning guide is a specialized form of reading guide that strongly emphasizes interpretive and applied levels of reading and thinking (Herber, 1978). See Figure 11.10 for an example of the format and question types in a reasoning guide. Steps for using the reasoning guide are given below.

Sacco and Vanzetti
Millions of Americans mourned when Nicola Sacco and Bartolomeo Vanzetti were executed. They believed the immigrants were victims of prejudice. In this painting by Ben Shahn, the two men are shown handcuffed together as they await their fate. **Citizenship** *How did the Sacco and Vanzetti case fuel anti-immigrant feeling?*

Middle-class Americans worried that communists and anarchists would invade the United States.

Congress responded by passing the Emergency Quota Act in 1921. The act set up a quota system that allowed only a certain number of people from each country to enter the United States. "America must be kept American," said Calvin Coolidge.

The quota system favored immigrants from Northern Europe, especially Britain. In 1924, Congress passed new laws that further cut immigration, especially from Eastern Europe. In addition, Japanese were added to the list of Asians denied entry to the United States.

Immigrants From Latin America

Latin Americans and Canadians were not included in the quota system. In 1917, the Jones Act made Puerto Ricans American citizens. Poverty on the island led to a great migration to the United States. In 1910, only 1,500 Puerto Ricans lived in the mainland United States. By 1930, there were 53,000.

Farms and factories in the Southwest depended on workers from Mexico. By 1930, a million or more Mexicans had crossed the border. Most came to work in the vegetable fields, orchards, and factories of the Southwest. The pay was

low and the housing was poor. Still, the chance to earn more money was a very powerful lure. During the 1920s, more and more Mexicans began to settle in the large cities of the Midwest, too.

Solo in Chicago

Just before World War I, exciting news began filtering across the border into Mexico:

❝ In the early days . . . one heard only of the states of Texas and California. The few Mexicans that left Mexico went there and wrote back from there. After a while we heard of New Mexico and Arizona, but beyond that there was no more United States to us. I remember distinctly with what great surprise we received a letter in our pueblo from a Mexican who had gone to Pennsylvania. 'Oh, where can that be! That must be very, very far away.' ❞

As news about jobs in the United States spread, young Mexican men made their way to El Paso or Laredo, Texas. There, they

Figure 11.9
Putting the story back in history.
Source: From J. W. Davidson and M. B. Stoff (1995). *The American Nation* (p. 700). Upper Saddle River, NJ, Prentice Hall. Copyright 1995 by Prentice-Hall. Reprinted by permission.

Figure 11.10
Sample reasoning guide for social studies.

Directions: Reread the sentences below taken from John F. Kennedy's inaugural address, which you just read in its entirety in your textbook. Then complete the exercises called for below.

A. The world is very different now.

B. For man holds in his mortal hands the power to abolish all forms of human poverty and all forms of human life.

C. . . . (T)he rights of man come not from the generosity of the state but from the hand of God.

D. United there is little we cannot do in a host of cooperative ventures.

E. To those people in huts . . . we pledge our best efforts . . . not because the communists are doing it, . . . but because it is right.

F. We dare not tempt them with weakness.

G. So let us begin anew, remembering on both sides that civility is not a sign of weakness . . .

H. Let both sides explore what problems unite us instead of belaboring those problems which divide us.

I. And so, my fellow Americans, ask not what your country can do for you, ask what you can do for your country.

Directions: Now consider each of the statements below, and decide based on the statements above whether JFK would have approved or disapproved of each. In column A, answer yes or no. In column B, write the letter indicating the quotation from JFK that influenced your decision. For number 10, write an original statement that you think JFK might have made. Quote some part of the address (in your text) other than the quotations listed above as evidence.

A   B

____ ____   1. The problems we are facing today are not much different than those that faced our forefathers.

____ ____   2. The oriental world is immensely different from our own.

____ ____   3. Our rights are given to us out of the goodness of humans' love for humankind.

____ ____   4. If we are to win over the threat of world communism, we must give money, supplies, and help to underdeveloped nations of the world.

____ ____   5. Let us demonstrate our goodwill to the world by disarming.

____ ____   6. Only the federal government can solve the complex problems of our society.

____ ____   7. We will never resort to violence.

____ ____   8. The events of the past have helped us to realize the truth of Washington's policy of isolationism. We should continue to heed the advice of our president.

____ ____   9. The greatest threat to humankind is not famine and sickness but the threat of world communism.

____ ____ 10. _____
                _____
                _____

Steps in Using a Reasoning Guide

Step 1   The teacher constructs a guide that draws focused attention to the key portions of a longer section (see Figure 11.11).

Step 2   Students read the longer selection first before using the guide.

Step 3   Students complete the reasoning guide, rereading the key portions of the text as necessary.

Step 4   A class discussion in which students compare their answers and their reasons follows.

Step 5   Students further discuss what they learned about their own thinking and about thinking in general, for example:

   a. In what way(s) can we discover what attitudes we and others hold other than by what we/they say? (By our/their actions)

   b. Is there really any value in trying to form generalizations without all the facts? (Life requires that we do, but any new piece of information may change all previous thoughts and conclusions)

Building Good Judgment

No one is born with good judgment. It is painstakingly acquired. An interesting format for promoting good judgment, or critical-evaluative thinking, in social studies was borrowed from experimental tests (Manzo & Manzo, 1990a) and further developed by ninth-grade teachers Susan Tarwater and the late Phyllis McConnel. McConnel and Tarwater used these formats in a team-taught core curriculum program combining social studies and English. The team approach permitted team members to relieve one another from classroom teaching duties to enable them to develop the necessary materials.

In the Critical Judgments Exercise, students first decide and then discuss their judgments of the relative *value* of certain pieces of information. The format can be used with general or background information or with items selected from a section of text that students read in class. Figure 11.11 presents examples of both general-information and text-based items.

CONTENT AREA READING IN THE SUPPORT SUBJECTS

Physical Education, Vocational Technology, Art, Music, and Speech

The contemporary forces that have led to the information explosion in the core areas of the curriculum have profoundly influenced the support subjects as well. The evidence for this is readily apparent in even a casual

Figure 11.11
Critical judgments exercise.

PART 1: GENERAL INFORMATION ITEMS

Directions: Using your best judgment, decide what you think would be the value to society in knowing each of the statements listed below. Consider each statement to be true. We shall discuss these momentarily.

$$
\begin{array}{lll}
1 & = & \text{of no use} \\
2 & = & \text{of little use} \\
3 & = & \text{of moderate use} \\
4 & = & \text{very useful} \\
5 & = & \text{extremely useful}
\end{array}
$$

_____ 1. Mary Queen of Scots inherited the throne at the age of six days.

_____ 2. Simplicity and elegance in writing are more desirable than length or vocabulary.

_____ 3. The first European to sail into New York Harbor was Henry Hudson.

_____ 4. The tomato is not a vegetable but a fruit.

_____ 5. Left-handedness is a recessive genetic trait.

_____ 6. Mary Goddard was the only woman to have her name on the Declaration of Independence.

_____ 7. Diamond dust is black.

_____ 8. Red meats are high in fat content.

PART 2: TEXT-BASED ITEMS

Directions: Indicate your judgment of the relative values of the statements below taken from your text. Use the five-point scale—1 = lowest, 5 = highest value—that we have used previously.

A. _____ 1. The Nobel Prize is given at least once every five years.

_____ 2. The Nobel Prize is awarded for important discoveries or inventions in the five categories of knowledge.

_____ 3. No Nobel Prizes were given in 1940–1942.

_____ 4. The Noble Prize was founded by Alfred Nobel, a Swedish chemist and philanthropist.

_____ 5. Women as well as men have been awarded the Nobel Prize.

B. _____ 1. Oliver Cromwell was called "The Protector."

_____ 2. Cromwell was born in 1599.

_____ 3. Cromwell was a violent and persuasive speaker.

_____ 4. Cromwell expanded England's territories and increased her commerce.

_____ 5. Cromwell's court was frugal but dignified.

inspection of any support area syllabus. In music, students now study jazz and rock as well as choral, orchestral, and symphonic works. Physical education now encompasses physiology and less-popular sports such as badminton and soccer. In industrial arts, particularly automotive technology, there now is a strong emphasis on electronics. Home economics now addresses complex issues in nutrition, parenting, and diverse family relationships. Business education, which formerly meant typing and shorthand, now means word processing, inventory control, networking, and purchasing. In short, the traditional separation between academic subjects and what once were known as "minor" area subjects has all but vanished. These support areas involve complex technologies and require considerable and ongoing reading, research, and critical analysis. In some very real sense, the *support area subjects* are our best hope for a curriculum that is both authentic, in the sense of real, and interdisciplinary.

Today's teachers of these subjects rarely need to be convinced that their subjects contain a heavy academic component. Thus, the support area teacher now has a heavy investment in, and commitment to, nourishing reading, writing, studying, language, and thinking strategies.

PHYSICAL EDUCATION

"Reading is sport," wrote Gentile (1980). "It requires mastering the fundamental skills, sufficient practice, a well-balanced diet of literary experiences, and a lifetime of development" (p. 4). The artificial separation of physical and academic education that exists in most schools is unfortunate, unnecessary, and uncaring. Plato placed gymnastics at the highest level for training his philosophers.

The Physical Domain—Linking Physical and Academic Development

The relationship between physical and academic development is more than coincidental. As we noted in earlier chapters, all learning enters through and takes place in the body as well as in the mind. The linking of motor involvement with language and academic learning can be a "natural" for the physical education class, as illustrated in a recent news report that went something like this:

In the gymnasium at the Jackson Avenue Elementary School of Mineola, New York, 8-year-olds ran through the pathways of a human circulatory system drawn on the parquet floor.

Pretending they were blood cells, they grabbed oxygen molecules (bean bags) from a bucket, raced through the heart chambers (red and blue Hula-Hoops) and completed the circuit by exchanging the oxygen for carbon dioxide (crumpled waste paper). Their warm-up finished, the panting pupils checked their pulse rates.

Watching them, Kathleen Kern, the school's physical education teacher, said, "You can't teach kids about aerobic fitness until they understand the circulatory system."

In the same vein, Gentile (1980) suggests an interesting metacognitive activity involving reading, appreciation of the physical domain, and provocative discussion. In gym class, have students read and discuss statements, such as one from Michener's *Sports in America*, which says, in effect: "If I had a child determined to be a writer, I'd expect that child to take two courses: one in ceramics so that he or she could feel form emerging from inchoate clay and a second in eurythmic dancing so that child could feel within his or her own body the capacity for movement, form, and dramatic shifts in perspective."

The highest goal of the reading curriculum, as noted several times previously, is not merely to teach youngsters to read but to promote language, thinking, and social-emotional maturity. Here, in slightly paraphrased form, are a few methods recommended by Maring and Ritson (1980), professors of reading and physical education, respectively, for fostering content area literacy in gym classes.

Method 1: Reading to Reinforce Instruction
Make up one-page handouts that summarize and reinforce the physical education content and skills that have just been taught via lecture-explanation, demonstration, or charts and diagrams. Type key terms in all-capital letters, and underline portions of the text that explain their meanings. On the bottom or back of each handout, include a set of questions that relate to the main ideas in the lesson. After students have read the handout, have them form small groups to answer the questions (see Figure 11.12).

Method 2: Read and Do
Prepare "Read and Do" instruction sheets so that students will learn required content and at the same time improve their ability to follow written directions (see Figure 11.13).

Method 3: Book Checkout
In the locker room or near your office, place a revolving book rack displaying high-interest paperbacks with checkout cards pasted inside the back covers that relate to aspects of your physical education curriculum. Consult the school librarian and reading specialist for assistance in book selection. Have the class or team elect a librarian to be responsible for the lending and returning of the books.

Figure 11.12
Reading to reinforce instruction.

THE BASIC RULES OF BASKETBALL

Directions: Review the underlined information about the capitalized key terms below. Then answer the questions that follow.

Key Terms

1. Each team is composed of five MEMBERS who play the entire court area.

2. A team scores 2 points when the ball passes through the hoop during regular play (FIELD GOAL).

3. A team may score additional points by means of free throws when a member of the opposing team commits a PERSONAL FOUL (hacking, pushing, holding, etc.).

Questions

1. Where on the court do team members play?

2. Explain in your own words what a field goal is.

3. Name two kinds of personal fouls.

Method 4: "Testlets"

Evaluate students' performance skills and knowledge by giving short tests that require students to read and follow directions (see Figure 11.14). Each test can be presented on an individual card. Students should be familiar with this format before being tested.

Method 5: Student Reports

Have students read and write a brief (half-page) report on any person making news in sports. Invite different students to give these reports in the opening five minutes of class. Tack up the best reports on a cork display board (Gentile, 1980).

Figure 11.13
Read and do.

MOTOR DEVELOPMENT EXERCISE

Single-heel click: Jump into the air, click heels together once, and land with feet apart (any distance). This can be turned into an amusing exercise in which students try to write out totally unambiguous expository directions for their peers to follow. You might invite an English teacher to cooperate with you on this project.

Figure 11.14
Testlets.

Grapevine Test
Stand with heels together. Bend trunk forward, extend both arms down between legs and behind ankles, and hold fingers of hands together in front of ankles. Hold this position for five seconds. Failure: (a) to lose balance; (b) to not hold fingers of both hands together; (c) to not hold the position for five seconds.

Three-Dip Test
Take a front leaning-rest position. Bend arms, touching chest to the floor, and push body up again until forearms are in a straight line with upper arms. Execute three performances in succession. Do not touch the floor with legs or with abdomen. Failure: (a) to not push body up three times; (b) to not touch chest to floor; (c) to touch the floor with any part of the body other than hands, feet, and chest.

Full-Left-Turn Test
Stand with feel together. Jump upward, making a full turn to the left. Land at approximately the same place from where the test was started. (Feet may be separated when landing.) Do not lose your balance or move feet after they have touched the floor. Failure: (a) to not make a full turn to the left, (b) to move feet after they have returned to the floor; (c) to lose your balance.

VOCATIONAL TECHNOLOGY

Problems and Goals

One of the nagging issues in vocational and technical education is whether conventional schooling transfers to work environments. Apparently it does, to a degree, but on-the-job training seems to be necessary initially and periodically thereafter (Gerber & Finn, 1998). Federal Public Law 98-524, also known as the Carl D. Perkins Vocational Act of 1984, anticipated this need. One of its main purposes is to improve the academic foundations of vocational technology students. Simply put, the objective is to create a work force able to adjust to the changing content of jobs. This act contains provisions to support schools willing to develop quality programming in reading, computing, and vocational areas.

The justification for such programming is well supported by several studies that have shown that the average workday for nonprofessional workers requires between 24 minutes and 4 hours of reading per day (Rush, Moe, & Storlie, 1986). Related research indicates that workers themselves underestimated by an average of 45% the amount of time they spent reading (Mikulecky, 1982). Furthermore, job-related reading is by no means easy. The materials essential to job competency in 11 fields, ranging from account clerk to welder, have readability levels that rarely dip as low as ninth grade and typically reach as high as the sixteenth grade level. Secretarial reading is the most difficult, ranging from sixteenth to college graduate levels (Diehl & Mikulecky, 1980).

Not surprisingly, one of the nagging problems of vocational technology has been the difficulty level of school texts, and the information and schematics that come up on computer screens. While this situation is changing, there still are plentiful examples of "inconsiderate" text. Derby (1987) offers examples from one vocational technology textbook:

✦ *This chapter is devoted to a study of the various ways in which the basic engine theory and parts are utilized to produce multicylinder engines of several types.* This, Derby explains, is an awkward way of saying *This chapter is about the different kinds of engines that are used in today's cars.*

✦ In a second example, the same textbook states: *Although a number of three-rotor and four-rotor experimental engines have been built, common usage at this time employs* either *a one-rotor or a two-rotor engine.* A more "considerate text" version would read: Although *a number of experimental engines have been built with three or even four* rotors, *most engines being built today have just one or two rotors.*

Here are some services and functions vocational technology teachers can offer to help promote literacy in this domain.

Six Services Vocational Technology Teachers Can Provide

1. Work with students to use, and where necessary create, text aids such as advance organizers, pivotal questions, glossaries of terms, and concept maps.

2. Follow the simple steps of the Listen-Read-Discuss method so that students will be better empowered for reading dense and often inconsiderate text.

3. Using the Informal Textbook Inventory, give students practice and instruction in using basic texts and reference books. For students of electricity, teach the use of the National Electrical Code; for health assistants, demonstrate the Physician's Desk Reference on diseases; and for automotive students, develop familiarity with the Chilton Repair Manual and other motor company services manuals.

4. Use the Question-Only procedure as a prereading and prelecture method. Instead of merely announcing a topic, show the class a vital engine part and have them conduct a systematic inquiry into its nature, functions, and most frequent failure points.

5. Vocational technology subjects offer abundant opportunities to use the Typical to Technical Vocabulary Approach (Walker, Walker, 1987). This strategy also can be used to concurrently improve abstract thinking. Here are some examples of automotive terms, suggested by Piercy (1976), for which students might have culled meanings from everyday life:

   ✦ *Differential*—a set of gears that permit rear wheels to revolve at different speeds
   ✦ *Differential*—peculiarity; distinction; feature; earmark
   ✦ *Governor*—a device for automatically controlling the speed of an engine by regulating the intake of fuel
   ✦ *Governor*—the elected head of any state in the United States
   ✦ *Distributor*—a mechanical device for distributing electric current to the spark plugs of a gas engine
   ✦ *Distributor*—a business firm that distributes goods to customers

6. Guiding a pre- and postreading analysis of diagrams and illustrations is a powerful way to promote strategic reading. This can be done in a survey fashion prior to reading and in a very careful way following silent reading. Where this procedure is followed routinely, students will be keyed into the supportive graphic material as they begin to read and anticipate further analysis following reading. This combination should increase the probability that they will use the illustrations, like the one in Figure 11.15, to grasp and clarify meanings when they read silently. It also should help them become better strategic readers for the time when they must read independently in school and on the job.

Career-Oriented Literature (COL)

Quite apart from textbooks and manuals, the vocational technology teacher needs a ready and readable supply of career-oriented literature (COL). Career-oriented literature refers to articles and stories about jobs and career areas. It tends to reflect how real people feel about their jobs and vocations.

COL materials tend to touch on matters that textbooks and manuals rarely address, such as apprenticeship programs and various employee benefit options. For publishers who offer other special, hard-to-find, human elements, see Figure 11.16.

Language Experiences

Most activities undertaken in career and vocational education can be performed better with student input. Language Experience Activities (LEAs)

Figure 11.15
Using illustrations to grasp and clarify meaning.

Text and Picture*

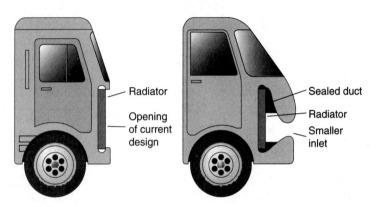

Current truck radiator installation design (left) requires flat front. Air resistance can be reduced by a streamlined design (right) where ducts bring sufficient cooling air to the radiator.

Source: From R. Timothy Rush, Alden J. Moe, & Rebecca L. Storlie (1986), *Occupational Literacy Education,* Newark, DE, IRA. Reprinted with permission of R. Timothy Rush and the International Reading Association. All rights reserved.

*Through design improvement, over-the-road trucks can function with radiator openings one-third as large as those used currently. Seating of ducts is necessary so that all cooling air is directed to the radiator. Applications of such truck designs have existed in the aircraft industry for many decades. Automotive engineers should examine aeronautical engineering practices in their quest for aerodynamic efficiency.

Figure 11.16
Career-oriented literature.

The Globe Book Company has two books (*All in a Day's Work* and *It Happened on the Job*) containing true, brief anecdotal accounts of work situations which are unusual and sometime humorous.

Pitman Learning offers *Pacemaker Vocation Readers,* a set of ten high-interest, controlled-vocabulary books describing young trade-type people in challenging situations.

Scholastic Magazine has an Action Series that has a number of job-related storybooks like the *Plumber's Line, Rosina Torres, L.P.N., Demolition Man,* and *Paramedic Emergency.*

Vocational Biographies, Inc. offers *Project Earth* and *Project Explore,* describing jobs and careers in the context of scientific principles and actual vocational biographies highlighting real individuals.

Career World (formerly *Real World*) is a color newspaper, written in the vein of *USA Today.* It addresses the work-a-day world and contains actual reading-skill exercises (Derby, 1987).

provide such opportunities. Here are a few LEA-type activities that are especially suitable for the vocational technology class.

1. *"Celebrity" interview:* Have students interview working people as though the latter were celebrities. Ask concerned questions such as might be asked of celebrities: "How did you first get into this business?"; "Has this work been fulfilling for you?"; "Have you ever wished that you could have done something else?"; "Can you tell me an interesting or amusing experience that you have had in this line of work?" Students could be instructed to watch television interview shows to get some ideas for "people questions." Discuss the questions they might ask before they ask them.

2. *Dialogue journal:* As previously noted, have students keep a journal in which they write a sentence or two every other day regarding their career interests and experiences. Periodically, read and write a brief reaction to these: "Charlie, I didn't realize that your father is an electrician!"; "Mary, if you will see me after class, I can tell you where to get more information on summer jobs with the city."

3. *Vocabulary from the workplace:* To help build respect and support for the vocational program throughout the school, have students interview friends and family about words and expressions that they use on the job but lay people would be unlikely to know. Ask English teachers, for example, to use the *vocabulary self-selection strategy* (Haggard, 1978) to include some of these words on English vocabulary lists. Vocabulary collections of this type can contribute to students' sense of accomplishment and make English teachers realize that many students who might not know what onomatopoeia means probably do know what a rocker-panel is (the name for the narrow shelf beneath all car doors). Terms such as these, which the English teacher probably doesn't know and which rarely can be found in most standard dictionaries, constitute a wider and richer language system than most academically oriented teachers have considered.

4. *Magazines:* Have students subscribe to a few quality news and trade magazines. These can be read in class or for homework. Assign groups to give well-organized reports on different articles.

5. *Computer networks:* Browse the Internet for home-page sites that correspond to specific vocational technical interests.

ART, MUSIC, AND SPEECH

Pleasure and Elevated Expression

Art, music, and speech teachers are important advocates and shapers of cultural literacy in the schools. Studies in art, music, and speech contribute to progress toward higher literacy in a variety of ways. Art and music raise students' level of cultural literacy; speech raises "phonemic awareness" (discussed below); and together they contribute to effective decoding and comprehension. Further, art, music, and speech offer a sheltering and enriching alternative to the sometimes harsh sounds and challenges of life. As such, they enhance emotional well-being and simple joy in living. Art, music, and speech also tend to reflect diverse perspectives, dialects, and historical periods, and therefore contribute to a broader and more multicultural outlook. They also provide pleasure and offer an outlet for more elevated expression. For these reasons, it is important to consider ways to gently weave together content area literacy and the art, music, and speech curricula, since each benefits the other.

The Challenge

Writing in art and music almost by nature tends to be esoteric and difficult to read. Sentences often contain complex syntax, unusual phrasings, assumptive references, sophisticated ideas, and names and words of foreign origin. It has been said that "One does not really read a music theory book . . . one grapples with it" (Duke, 1987). A typical passage from a popular library book on music reads like this:

> In all of art's best periods, creative people were brought together, and thus we had Pericles' Athens, the Medici's Florence, Elizabeth's London, Goethe's (and later Liszt's) Weimar, Beethoven's (and later Brahms') Vienna, Emerson's Concord, Lowell's Boston and Monet's Paris. These were by no means smooth waters, but they were lively. (Bacon, 1963, p. 130)

One would need to be quite well informed in the areas of art, music, literature, and history and in the characteristics of several different cultures to take in the full significance of this almost casual observation by pianist and teacher Earnest Bacon.

Meeting the Challenge

The art, music, and speech teacher can help students meet and profit from the challenge of "inconsiderate text" in several ways. Some of these are specified below. Consider a suggestion to be applicable to all three subjects unless otherwise specified.

1. Use the Oral Reading Strategy to familiarize students with syntax, phrasing, proper breathing, enunciation, and pronunciations.
2. Ask frequent translation questions: "Can you say this in your own words?"

3. Add information as needed to enhance schema, or background knowledge: "Have you read or heard about the Medici family in world history class yet? They were a wealthy and influential Italian family in medieval Florence—a thriving seaport city in Italy. They were great patrons of the arts."

4. Use the Listen-Read-Discuss method and Note Cue to guide reading and discussion in art, music, and effective speaking.

5. Have students use the Subjective Approach to Vocabulary with illustrations. Divide a page into quarters, and have students write the new word in quadrant I, write its dictionary meaning in II, draw a pictorial representation in III, and write out the subjective association in IV. Then the class discusses these and stores them in their notebooks.

6. The ambitious speech/theater teacher or speech pathologist can incidentally help youngsters to become better decoders of words by raising their phonemic awareness, or sense of the speech sounds represented in print. In fact, there is an approach to reading by the Lindamoods (1975) that is based on such training. The program, used largely with adults, teaches students to feel and label various speech sounds, which are the basis for phonics in reading. The terms used for the speech sounds are descriptive, rather than the technical terms used in linguistics (e.g., fricatives, continuents, etc.). See Figure 11.17 for sample descriptive speech sounds that increase phonemic awareness. For

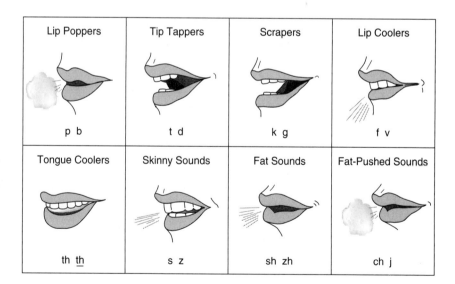

Figure 11.17
The Lindamood approach to reading. *Source:* From *The A.D.D. Program, Auditory Discrimination in Depth* (Books 1 & 2) by C. H. Lindamood and P. C. Lindamood, 1975. Austin, TX: Pro-ed. Reprinted by permission.

more precise information on this technique, see Manzo and Manzo (1993).

7. Work with science, literature, and social studies teachers to have students produce various forms of artistic representations of significant ideas.

8. Work with the school principal to use music in appropriate settings. Music has been shown to facilitate creative writing, mathematics, spelling, and art (Greenhoe, 1972; Maor, 1979; Taylor, 1980). While music sometimes can be distracting during reading, classical music has been found to be conducive to comprehension gains (Mulliken & Henk, 1985). The classical music played in the latter study was Pietro Mascagni's *Cavalleria Rusticana*, "Intermeggio." A no-music condition produced better performance than did rock music, which is to say that rock is disruptive. Apparently, something soft, slow, and with methodical cadence is necessary to foster reading and thinking. The second author found this to be true while using taped music during sustained silent reading time with urban junior high school reading classes. Music was played during the first ten minutes of class, during which time students who were caught up with classwork had the privilege of reading anything of their choosing. I began the year with a few classical and "easy-listening" instrumental selections that I used for free reading time. Not knowing about Mulliken and Henk's finding, I succumbed several times to students' pleas to use rock music instead. It never worked: with a rock music background, students were more distracted than they would have been otherwise. When I eliminated rock music, however, they appreciated the more traditional melodic pieces enough to hush one another rather than lose the privilege.

9. Outstanding television shows are dramatized with music. Work with the English teacher to have students think through and try to score selections of literature with appropriate musical pieces and/or poignant oral readings. This takes a good deal of thinking and analysis. If you feel daring, ask students to select or compose theme tunes for the school and/or individual teachers.

IN CONCLUSION: BE CREATIVE AND ENCOURAGE CREATIVITY

The last suggestion, to invite students to be creative, seems a good note on which to tie up this chapter. We urge you to encourage creative thinking and problem solving, *and* to be encouraged to be creative in your own thinking and teaching. Again, the three main ingredients encouraging creativity are to:

1. Connect your students and yourself to creative thinkers whenever and wherever you can. Again, you might look up the web page of the Foundation for Better Ideas on the Internet. It is one way to provide exposure to creative questions, creative answers, and even monetary and social incentives for creative production in a variety of disciplines and across disciplines.

2. Teach students to formulate appropriate guiding questions, or purposes, for which to read and listen.

3. Request and expect expression and creative production from your students, and they will not disappoint you.

✦ *After Words* ✦

This "reference" chapter was intended to provide you with further possible in-depth knowledge of content literacy in your own area of specialization, and with an overview of the specific values and problems of the other disciplines. Logically, you may wish to know a bit more about how to attend to students with specific or special needs in these same situations. The next chapter should equip you to better understand and provide for such needs.

CHAPTER 12

Literacy Support for Special-Needs Students in the Content Classroom

A helping word to one in trouble is often like a switch on a railroad track—an inch between wreck and smooth-rolling prosperity.

—Henry Ward Beecher

✦ Fore Words ✦

There is a lot to reflect on, if not agonize over, in this chapter. We write from the perspective of over forty years of work on some of the issues ahead. But don't take that to mean that we are certain of the best directions. We are, however, ready to take some stands. Your professors may disagree. Keep an open mind and tell us and them what you are thinking. Maybe together we can get this right. This chapter opens with a note on its guiding principle, *compensatory education*. A discussion follows of some concerns that touch several areas of special needs, especially the gap in achievement test scores traditionally found among different racial and ethnic groups. It then addresses some underlying issues in remediation and diversity. The chapter urges that we reclaim some modest solutions that have lost favor in recent times, but perhaps for the wrong reasons. Ideally, this admittedly provocative discussion will encourage you to think through what your professional positions eventually will be on these critical issues. The remainder of the chapter details very specific teaching methodologies ranging from means to improve basic word analysis (phonics), to techniques for enhancing comprehension, thinking, writing, and classroom discussion. Considerations are given also to youngsters with *limited English proficiency* (LEP).

SPECIAL-NEEDS STUDENTS: GUIDING PRINCIPLE

The term *special needs* is used here to refer to youngsters who are at risk of underachieving for a variety of reasons that are not typically provided for in a regular classroom setting. The chief approach is *compensatory*. This refers to methods, materials, and means of helping students with such needs to make up, or compensate, for some deficit or difference that may be putting them at increased risk to underachieve. Reasons might include limited English proficiency (LEP), different cultural orientation, learning disability, or simply a lack of motivation or opportunity to learn.

Keep in mind as you read that there are other categories of concern that may require extraordinary attention, including the special developmental needs of almost every normal child. As an example, Gurian (1998) writes insightfully about the tensions in every male that arise from five to seven hormonal surges per day. In many ways, safe schools and eventual success in dealing with the needs of all youngsters are tied to our commitment to better understanding and managing the very challenging nature of such normal development. The underlying idea here resembles this book's theme of "inverse teaching." It is to pay more attention to kids' needs on the *front end*, before trouble erupts. For an example of how we might begin to better address such needs, see the forming Quest Literacy Curriculum in Chapter 13 on schoolwide programming and on our web sites. This more discovery-based approach to literacy and learning draws heavily on many of the highly *interactive* methods that have been described. These methods, in our judgment, are more aligned with the needs of most boys to be in a more active environment, and for most girls to become more comfortable and practiced in the action-oriented nature of life outside of school. But, let's turn now to the special problem referred to as the *achievement gap*.

The Minority Student Gap

Before attempting to fix anything, it is best to determine what is broken and how seriously so. The problem that is commanding the most concern in American schools is the gap in standardized test scores between Caucasians and Asians on one hand and African-Americans and Latinos on the other. The differences are considerable and despite many experimental programs and large scale efforts to narrow margins, has remained fairly constant over time. For example, Iowa Tests of Basic Skills (ITBS) reading scores recently reported for the Kansas City, Missouri Public Schools for grades three, eight, and eleven show white kids in the same district to score in about the fiftieth percentile, while black kids score in the thirty-fourth percentile and Latino kids in about the thirty-fifth percentile. Math scores are similarly disconcerting: whites about 53, blacks about 36, and Latinos about 37 (*Kansas City Star*, August 16, 1999). In general the black–white gap is about 12 percentile points in the early grades, and grows to 18 percentile points in the upper grades. This is a national crisis with implications for how society is, and likely will continue to be, stratified. It requires unrestricted dialogue, and reevaluation of almost everyone's pat answers and especially of certain socially driven educational experiments that may be exacerbating the problem. This is not to say that the things that have been tried to date are of no value. Each prior effort has taught us much about what to question and possibly eliminate as a solution. One thing that the experiments of the last thirty years seem to be saying clearly is that programs, consultants, and strategies should not be put to social litmus tests, but determined by substantive changes on instruments like the ITBS, and ideally other more enlightened tests as well. The past may even be telling us to think more deeply about social issues and answers, but not to overburden the educational system. Good intentions, such as jobs programs for African-Americans, have led to "mission creep"—or trying to do more than the school situation and resources will allow. This tends to nullify even that which could have been achieved with a clearer mission focus. Several leading black educators, such as Thaddeus Lott, speaking to the Kansas City, Missouri school board, are saying things like: "[Educators] are hooked onto the latest classroom fad at the expense of methods already proven successful. They may even avoid things that they are opposed to philosophically even though they work" (*Kansas City Star*, November 6, 1998). The Missouri State Board of Education recently voted for disaccreditation of the Kansas City Public Schools. This follows over twenty-five years of federal court–ordered desegregation efforts and a billion dollars in federally mandated state aid. That state board also has voted to do the same to St. Louis, effective in the year 2002. The problems here are massive, complicated and not limited to Missouri. One problem, however, is clear: efforts to end segregation are not the same as making provisions for quality education. Let us see now what seems to work, philosophically and practically. After nearly thirty years of backsliding, it appears that board members, school administrators, community groups, and courts may finally be ready to seriously address this core school issue.

What Fleas Can Tell Us

Try this: put some fleas in a glass jar with a lid, and observe. At first the fleas will try eagerly to get out, jumping all around and up and down in the jar. After just a few minutes, however, they will no longer hit the lid. Now take the lid off. The fleas will still jump now and then, but they never will jump out of the jar.

The lesson in this is obvious, but bears stating. The content area teacher must be especially careful about inadvertently creating a glass ceiling of literal-level expectations for students, particularly those whom one might presume to be "too slow" to learn. It is just as important to "teach up" (Estes, 1991) for remedial-level learners as for those who are average and above. Several studies have definitively shown that teaching weaker students to read between and beyond the lines actually boosts their ability to read the lines, or at the literal level (Collins, 1991; Cooter & Flynt, 1986; Haggard, 1976). However, this is not the same thing as saying that those labeled slow are not slow, or that they can do anything if teachers would only challenge or teach them properly. Everyone does better when they are treated as if they are whole and unique, rather than totally defined by a given deficiency, or for that matter, even by a high proficiency, as in the cases of those who are academically gifted but may nonetheless have areas of specific need. Now prepare to tackle two related and intermingled messages that have come to be overstated and may need a modification of perspective, if we are to do what is best, rather than what pleases us philosophically.

Two Overstated Perspectives: "Diversity Should Be Encouraged and Perpetuated," and "Remedial Reading Doesn't Work and Is Oppressive"

Two important aspects of schooling have taken an unfortunate turn where at-risk students are concerned. One is that cultural diversity and language differences necessarily need to be perpetuated by being formally structured into the school curriculum, and the other is that remedial reading programs don't work and may even be oppressive. Our conclusions on both accounts are somewhat different.

Should Cultural and Language Differences Be Encouraged?

Efforts to bring about greater tolerance of differences are always proper and reasonable. However, efforts to underscore cultural and language differences may be countereffective to the natural evolution of both and may be a serious disservice to individuals who may wish to be equipped to conduct most of life and business in a dominant culture and language different from their own. Importantly, too, the dominant culture is ever evolving. It regularly shifts to be more like those who accumulate power to influence it; whereas excessive efforts to represent different cultures can perpetuate stereotypes that often have no life outside the representations presented in staged multicultural situations.

It is further notable that parents from America's diverse backgrounds overwhelmingly expect schools to prepare their children to speak, write, and acclimate to the mainstream as a means of becoming an influential part of it. The methods suggested throughout this text, and in this chapter, tend to have this as a goal. Of equal importance, the methods described below have the goal of empowering youngsters to influence culture and language by being highly competent and effective in telling their individual and collective stories. It is largely in this way that they can reasonably be expected to form the literary and intellectual bases from which to win empathy for their particular ways of thinking, speaking, behaving, and conducting business. This is the way diverse cultural and linguistic orientations traditionally have come to be considered legitimate entries into the competition for the conduct, curriculum, and character of the ever-evolving mainstream, or dominant, culture. Other means of fostering cultural equity may be more "fair" or philosophically preferable but they are not proven. And, frankly, no means yet devised, short of creation of a new, hybrid culture and ethnic group, have been totally successful in integrating even people who are indistinguishable, as are the northern and southern Irish and the factions in Bosnia who have been warring for 1,200 years, much less folks who look and sound differently. Nonetheless, America takes pride in its multicultural differences and hence in efforts to be tolerant of one another, unlike some countries who sing the praises of homogeneity, such as do Japan and Korea. Nonetheless, it does not seem wise to press these differences, since intellectual enlightenment often runs ahead of baser instincts, but it cannot outrun them.

Should Remedial Reading Continue in a State of Neglect?

The evidence is overwhelming that most remedial reading programs work quite well, although you might never know this by the criticisms and faint praise leveled at them even by certified literacy experts (Johnston & Allington, 1991; Ruddell, 1993). Remedial reading programs are proven to help many youngsters achieve at approximately twice the average rate in reading per semester and four times the prior pace of these same students (Manzo & Manzo, 1993; Spache, 1976). The fundamental reason that this goes unnoticed is because there have been an almost irreducible number of students who do not make progress even with remedial assistance. Ironically, this number would be even smaller if remedial and early prevention programs and efforts were more fully supported, rather than reduced and maligned, which has been the case now for over twenty years.

The disrepute into which remedial reading has fallen is part of a complex set of dynamics that have little bearing on the real efficacy of such programs. There appears to be a confluence of at least three forces mitigating the potential values in remedial reading. Understandably, middle-class parents wanted a way to get help for their underachieving children without social stigma. In response, they seem to have created *learning disabilities* (LDs), a condition that clearly has some bases in reality, though no educationally sound definition. In any case, some 80% of LD problems seem to be reading related (Alley & Deshler, 1980). These facts aside, legislative bodies have designated an LD as a physically handicapping condition that otherwise is not the result of a socioeconomic deficit, cultural difference, or any apparent emotional problem. This entitled students with learning disabilities to receive special and personalized help in a least-restrictive environment (i.e., in a socially acceptable fashion), with services to continue through college. Accordingly, students so designated receive a great deal more in support than remedial readers ever did, including the right to have tests read to them and other such personalized accommodations. This gain for students with learning disabilities has been at great cost to taxpayers and has overburdened teachers and systems. These considerations for LD students are not unjustified. Many do need help. However, in a world of limited resources, they have resulted in the loss of support for remedial reading programs that previously served a much larger population of those in need. Many colleges are now beginning to "jettison all remedial courses" (Cronholm, 1999), while the number of students claiming learning disabilities at the college level continues to multiply each year.

A second trend that has weakened belief in and support for remedial reading, ironically, has been the overgeneralization of an argument in favor of content area literacy. The argument was that content teachers should provide a certain measure of help (i.e., instructional scaffolding) to all youngsters, especially those with special needs, and in a regular classroom setting. By a twist of fate, this regular class accommodation of readers came to replace remedial reading because the reading specialists who taught the remedial sections felt overburdened by the responsibility both to guide the school's content area literacy program and to teach the separate remedial groups. Of course, the logical thing to have done was to hire more reading specialists, but the funds went to create and hire more LD specialists, so that now there are very few literacy specialists in schools at any level.

Finally, important social activists, such as Paulo Freire (1985, 1987) and Ira Shor (Shor & Freire, 1987), have had their messages of *liberation education* convoluted by some to mean that remedial reading is oppressive. They have argued, as have most enlightened educators, that school should empower individuals to compete in society where the playing field often is not level. However, these social activists noticed that schooling, largely in the third world, seemed to be designed to educate individuals only sufficiently to have them function as cogs in someone else's machine, but not to aspire to be, or to run, their own economic engines (see more on efforts to reverse this trend in the final chapter of this book). This message became erroneously attached to remedial and corrective reading programs in the United States, which due to a high percentage of enrollment of African-American students became viewed as another symbol of oppression. This connection was intensified by the concerns expressed about this by some very well-meaning American educators and humanists, many of whom were "whole-language" enthusiasts who do not believe in heavy doses of direct instruction in any form. They further felt that underachievement was almost exclusively the result of social policies, lowered expectations, and poor self-esteem. Further, since whole language is largely based on an incidental learning model and an abhorrence of all testing, it was quick to condemn remedial reading, which is based on a direct and intensive teaching with lots of diagnostic and followup achievement testing. In fact, of course, the two positions—are not in opposition to one another, but are complementary.

In any case, even the most old-fashioned remedial/corrective reading programs tend to work quite well, with many youngsters achieving at two to four times their prior average rate per unit of time. However, we must avoid becoming delusional in the sense of visualizing "remedial students in a kind of seamless progression, moving through their remedial classes, into college-level work, on to graduation, and then profitable postgraduate careers" (Cronholm, 1999, p. B6). Remedial/corrective reading programs are sensible and necessary because content area teachers cannot reasonably provide explicit and intensive instruction to youngsters who are several grade levels below expected norms and hence unable to independently learn from most print sources. Ironically and sadly, efforts to make classroom teachers responsible for such dramatic differences in instructional need, without remedial/corrective reading support, may well have been the impetus for causing some of them to further lower their expectations for many students and to quietly pass and graduate youngsters who hardly read at all.

One way in which this is subtly communicated is by the number of mind-numbing ways that we try to avoid academic competition and to treat everyone as if they are so fragile that they will break if we were to emotionally challenge them.

Reconsider the "Pain" of Competition, Especially for Boys

Traditionally, 80% of remedial readers have been boys and about 80% of their teachers have been women. This inversion of gender-cultures, along with the prevalence of the currently popular victim philosophy, may require some serious rethinking. Popular author Michael Gurian puts it this way:

> Boys need to compete . . . to feel tested in the physical and interpersonal world. . . . Understanding boy society and its love of competition and performance ultimately requires us to give less weight to our victim-based relationship philosophies. The victim-based relationship philosophy says, "I'm set up to be a victim, so let's train everyone else not to victimize me." . . . This I've-been-abused philosophy impedes our ability to raise sons. It forgets that each of us care for ourselves. Especially as I grow up, no one else is responsible for me." (Gurian, 1997, p. 32)

A discussion on the CNN Book Channel by women authors Diana Furchtgott-Roth and Christine Stolba of their new book, *Women's Figures* (2000), confirms that an end may be in sight for the overgrowth of the "victim syndrome." They argue convincingly that women are no longer victims. They show that the statistical difference in income compared with men is less than 6% when even the most superficial factors are taken to account, such as comparing men and women in the same profession or doing the same work. Other differences are explainable by free decisions women make to work less and spend more time on personal matters such as raising children or simply living less-harried lives.

Consider now just a few of the methods that can be used to help youngsters with special needs. Frankly, most of these require more energy, effort, and directiveness than the methods in previous chapters. But, then, with few remedial/corrective programs still operating, it necessarily falls on content teachers to do whatever they reasonably can to accommodate special-needs youngsters in the regular classroom.

Teaching Methods for Special-Needs Students

The methods presented next focus on the needs of students who are said to have reading/learning disabilities, those with limited English proficiency, those with personal-social adjustment problems, and/or those who are culturally different.

Fortunately, most of the methodology and ideas developed for special-needs students are of benefit to most typical students as well. This is because people are more alike than they are different from one another. And, almost all students, at one time or another, are likely to need some of the same kind of extraordinary thought, concern, and assistance that tend to be reserved for the different, the reluctant, and the chronic underachieving.

Throughout we have tried to select methods that are conducive to both teacher and student discovery and learning. Many of the ideas and practices advocated also are valuable in promoting tolerance, a multicultural outlook, and diversity in education.

We have not directly addressed the gifted as a category of special-needs student in this chapter, because many further issues confounding the definition of *giftedness* are well beyond the scope of this text. Also, you probably already have noticed that many of the methods presented in previous chapters, especially those on writing and higher-order literacy, serve the gifted quite nicely.

MOTIVATING THE UNMOTIVATED: "KIDS ON THE CUSP"

An earlier chapter defined and developed the role of engagement theory in motivation. This section adds a few more thoughts and devices for reaching the reluctant, and occasionally resentful, reader. It begins with ideas for encouraging reading, discusses means and methods for dealing with disruptive behavior in the classroom, and concludes with techniques for improving basic word attack, comprehension, personal-social adjustment problems, and content-based mainstreaming efforts.

Encouraging Reading

Here are fourteen methods designed to encourage reading. If you were to view this section as a checklist and commit yourself to doing half of what is suggested for one full year, you would help weak readers and contribute to creating a school environment conducive to higher-literacy and content learning.

1. *Establish a Sustained Silent Reading (SSR) program.* Once or twice a week, have students read anything they choose that is content related. Increase the time from seven to twenty minutes over a few months. This lengthening period of SSR can become an effective management tool as well as a means of teaching students how to read in an increas-

ingly sustained manner. To be sure that everyone has something to read and to allay students' sense that this is an idle-time activity, it is best to store SSR materials in class and to periodically invite individual students to discuss what they are reading. This classroom-based activity can be broadened to include the entire school. It is most conducive if teachers, administrators, and all other personnel read for the sustained period as well.

2. *Keep interesting newspaper and magazine articles,* and make them available in the classroom for students to read before or after class or during downtime.

3. *Have students fill out a reading interest inventory, indicating the types of books they enjoy reading.* Invite the school librarian to help you select an appropriate inventory and to develop a list of suggested book titles related to areas of interest.

4. *Encourage students to join a book club and/or subscribe to magazines in areas of special interest.* Concerned members of the business community often will pay for these.

5. *Become a reading motivator.* Almost everyone likes to be read to. Set aside a few minutes of classroom time to read a poem, newspaper, magazine article, or portion of a cherished book to the class.

6. *Let two or more students read the same book for a book report to the class.* Encourage them to discuss the book with one another.

7. *Use technology to encourage reading.* The school can buy multimedia CD-ROM disks or borrow them from libraries and hook up to the Internet to encourage reading for pleasure and expanded knowledge.

8. *Cut out and display the weekly book review section of the newspaper.*

9. *Ask students to see a movie or television program* either before or after reading a book on which one or the other is based.

10. *Have student groups create a book- or article-of-the-week poster.* Display books and articles with the caption "Read All About It." Invite students to share their books or articles with the class, noting the titles, authors, and sources of critiques.

11. *Invite local authors or poets to class to discuss and read their works.*

12. *Give students incentives to read.* Students who read three or more books during a quarter or a semester can be rewarded with a donated gift certificate from a bookstore, record store, clothing store, or food store.

13. *Conduct reading conferences with students.* Personalized discussion and interest in a student's reading can be deeply motivating.

14. *Teach students to use the closed caption option on television to incidentally work on their own reading effectiveness* (Koskinen, Wilson,

Gambrell, & Jensema, 1987). Similarly encourage weak readers to listen to books on tape while they follow along; however, this may have a slightly negative effect with above-average readers (Cloer & Denton, 1995).

The next section offers insights into dealing with behavioral as well as literacy problems. The thrust of each of these methods is to help teachers and students deal with the sometimes corrosive effects of daily teaching and learning situations more than the explosive ones—a need poignantly expressed by the playwright Chekhov's observation that "Any idiot can face a crisis. It is this day-to-day living that wears you down."

Personal-Social Adjustment Through Story, Biblio-Support, and Dialogue Journals

Story

Stories are one of the world's oldest tools for imparting values, guideposts, and enrichment of analogical thinking, the means by which minds establish parallel structures and understand the new from the previously learned. The archetypes of hero stories are not stereotypes, but animated representations of good and bad in palpable, digestible form. Archetypes exist in relation to one another, serving as a map or record of the inner life of a single human and a society (Gurian, 1998).

Biblio-Support

For students who are inclined to read, biblio-support (Manzo & Manzo, 1995) can be an effective means of aiding with personal-social adjustment. Biblio-support is based on bibliotherapy, which essentially means healing through reading (Edwards & Simpson, 1986). Generally, it entails redirecting students' perceptions and attitudes in a healthy direction by getting the right reading material to the right student at the right time.

The sources of problems students encounter as they grow and mature are varied: cultural differences, family relationships, moving, divorce, peer pressure, physical handicaps, racial prejudice, death of loved ones, gender identification, and many others. Biblio-support is merely a means of becoming more broadly informed on and dealing with these personal-social dilemmas so that schooling does not suffer irreversibly.

Whenever possible, the teacher or counselor who recommends a book to a student should invite the student to retell the story, highlighting incidents and feelings that are relevant to the central situation. Changes in behavior, feelings, and relationships should be looked at closely to permit reasonable identification and empathy with the textual characters (Heaton & Lewis, 1955). Most important, the reader should have an opportunity to form a conclusion about the consequences of certain behaviors or feelings to determine whether these behaviors or feelings improve the human condition, as well as one's self-centered concerns or personal situation.

Reading and discussion are most fruitful when they are built around two questions, one of which almost everyone can answer easily, "What have you read that reminds you of someone you know?" and another that few of us can answer easily, "What reminds you of yourself?"

Dialogue Journals

Biblio-support can be greatly enhanced by the addition of a writing component. The easiest way to do this is to have students keep personal journals in which they write brief reactions—at least one sentence—to whatever they read. Be careful not to overdo this, however; the majority of boys and girls really do not like to write, and certainly not continuously in pensive, reflective terms (Manzo, Manzo, Barnhill, & Thomas, in press). That which is written can be stored in a box in the classroom or in a word processor, where, with students' prior approval, the teacher may read through them and write back personal notes and thoughts. Of course, notes and dialogue need not be limited to textual material; they can be extended to anything a student wishes to write or to anything a teacher may be interested in communicating. The idea of dialogue journals (Staton, 1980) is as old as conversation between caring friends. Teachers who use this approach regularly report touching insights revealed and warm relationships formed with students who at first appeared apathetic, hostile, or otherwise reluctant to learn (Kirby & Liner, 1981). In time, a teacher who uses this interactive means of teaching will learn a great deal about how to respond to many common complaints and potentially seething concerns of pre- and early adolescents. One teacher we know, for example, reminds teens, who frequently complain about the material things that they do not have, that even the poor today live better then the rich did 100 years ago, and infinitely better than did many kings and emperors 1,000 years ago. To dramatize the point, he has them list ten things that most of them have that the Czar of Russia did not have in 1900.

As classroom disruptions begin to diminish and participation starts to rise, it is necessary to simultaneously begin closing gaps in the literacy levels of underachieving students. Failure to do so can inhibit progress and even foster a more embittered and hopeless attitude. The methods described next are particularly useful for helping to make quick-paced progress.

IMPROVING DECODING AND WORD LEARNING

The most essential facets of effective reading are decoding, or phonics, and comprehension. Poor readers, by definition, have difficulty with either or both. Here is a way for nonexperts to help with phonics and word learning.

Glass Analysis Approach: Phonics Training, Not Rules

Glass Analysis (Glass, 1973) is a simple procedure that enables virtually anyone who knows how to read to teach others how to do so. It can be used at opportune times as a whole-class method when introducing or reinforcing difficult content terms. Moreover, it takes some of the mystery out of dealing with the lowest readers. Teachers need not know about diphthongs, digraphs, and other phonic elements and rules. Teachers simply provide occasional assistance, based on their own ability to decode, as time and circumstances permit.

Glass Analysis is fairly directive method that boys especially can be induced into following as if it were a cadence for marching. It is based on two verbal protocols, or cadence-like scripts. The scripts are designed to teach students to focus attention on the word and increase their familiarity with the sounds of the most common letter clusters in the English language. Ideally, youngsters internalize this cadence and exercise it as a mediational system, or self-spoken strategy, for unlocking unfamiliar words. The sound for *ing*, for example, has a high frequency of occurrence and is more easily learned as a cluster than as three separate letter sounds that then must be synthesized. Following are some general guidelines and steps for teaching with Glass Analysis.

Guidelines for Teaching Glass Analysis

Students should continuously look at the word. Never cover part of the word or point to letters when presenting the word. Do not include definitions of words in the instruction unless a student asks. Reinforce students for correct responses. If a student cannot answer a word attack question, state the answer and return to the same question before finishing with the word.

Steps in Glass Analysis

Step 1 Write the word to be taught on the chalkboard or a large card.

Step 2 Pronounce the word. Then teach it using as many combinations of letter clusters as are sensible.

Step 3 Use the following questions or verbal scripts:

"What letters make the ⟨ch⟩ sound?"

After you have used this question with the possible combinations, ask

"What sound do the letters ⟨c/h⟩ make?"

Figure 12.1 illustrates how Glass would use this approach with a new word before silent reading. See Figure 12.2 for a listing of common letter clusters, grouped according to difficulty level.

Uses of Glass Analysis

Glass Analysis can be used in three ways to create an effective schoolwide remedial/corrective decoding program:

1. Content teachers can incidentally use this simple letter-clustering approach each time a new technical or content word is introduced: "The

Figure 12.1
Example of Glass Analysis.

The teacher writes the word *forgetfulness* in large letters on the chalkboard. Then the teacher uses the Glass analysis script as follows:

In the word *forgetfulness*, what letters make the *for* sound?

The *or* sound?

What letters make the *et* sound?

The *get* sound?

What letters make the *forget* sound?
In the word *forgetfulness*, what letters make the *ful* sound?

The *forgetful* sound?

What letters make the *fulness* sound?

What letters make the *getfulness* sound?

(Notice how many structures can be learned in just one word—all transferable to other words.)

In the word *forgetfulness*, what sound do the letters f/o/r make?

What sound do the letters e/t make?

The g/e/t?

The f/o/r/g/e/t?

What sound do the letters f/u/l/ make?

What sound does g/e/t/f/u/l make?

What sound does e/s/s make?
n/e/s/s?

In the word *forgetfulness*, what sound do the letters f/u/l/n/e/s/s make?

If I took off the letters f/o/r, what sound would be left?

If I took off the *ness* sound, what sound would be left?

What is the whole word?

Figure 12.2
Letter clusters (by difficulty level).

Starters	Medium 1	Medium 2	Harder 1	Harder 2
1. at	1. ed	1. all	1. fowl	1. er
2. ing	2. ig	2. aw	2. us	2. air
3. et	3. ip	3. el(l)	3. il(l)	3. al
4. it	4. ud	4. eck	4. ite	4. ied
5. ot	5. id	5. ice	5. es(s)	5. ew
6. im	6. en	6. ick	6. om	6. ire
7. op	7. ug	7. if(f)	7. oke	7. ear
8. an	8. ut	8. ink	8. ore	8. eal
9. ay	9. ar	9. ob	9. tow	9. tea
10. ed	10. em	10. od	10. ast	10. ee
11. am	11. up	11. og	11. ane	11. care
12. un	12. ate	12. ub	12. eat	12. deaf
13. in	13. ent	13. uf(f)	13. as(s)	13. oat
14. ap	14. est	14. ush	14. ev	14. ue
15. and	15. ake	15. able	15. ind	15. oo
16. act	16. ide	16. ight	16. oss	16. ou
17. um	17. ock	17. is(s)	17. oem	17. ound
18. ab	18. ade	18. on	18. ost	18. ure
19. ag	19. ame	19. or	19. rol(l)	19. ture
20. old	20. ape	20. l(l)	20. one	20. ur
21. ash	21. ace	21. ac	21. ate	21. ir
22. ish	22. any	22. af(f)	22. ave	22. ai
23. enk	23. ook	23. ove	23. Au	
24. ong	24. tion	24. folly	24. Oi	
25. age				

word is *photosynthesis.* What letters make the *photo* sound? What letters make the *syn* sound? the *thesis* sound? What is the whole word again?"

2. Content teachers also can occasionally preview textual material assigned for reading and use Glass Analysis to teach other challenging words, especially foreign-language terms, that occur in text. "This is the Italian word *ciao.* Which letters make the *ch* sound in Italian? Which make the *ow* sound? How is the whole word pronounced again?"

3. All students with serious decoding deficiencies can be scheduled for one to five fifteen-minute sessions per week in which Glass Analysis tutoring is provided. Decoding stations can be set up in convenient, unobtrusive places throughout the school. These can be staffed by teachers serving a duty period and/or by volunteer paraprofessionals. (Glass Analysis letter-cluster kits for such intensive training are avail-

able from Easier-to-Learn, Inc., P.O. Box 329, Garden City, NY 11530, 516-475-3803.)

Incidental Morpheme Analysis: Using Known Word Parts as Analogs to Predict Word Meanings and Build Vocabulary

Eighty percent of the words in the English dictionary contain Greek or Latin prefixes, suffixes, or roots. These word parts, called morphemes, are units of language that cannot be further divided without losing meaning. Some morphemes have meanings only when attached to other word parts. Examples of such "bound" morphemes include *ed*, *ing*, *tele*, and *cide*. Other morphemes, such as *cover*, *graph*, and *stand*, called "free" morphemes, can stand alone, that is, are words in themselves.

Most expert readers and language users use morphemes to make sense out of and remember new words. The Incidental Morpheme method (Manzo & Manzo, 1990a), teaches students to apply existing knowledge of morphemes to new words encountered in content reading. It also offers a way to teach new morphemes by raising sensitivity to word parts and explicitly providing instruction in a set of morphemes with a high frequency of occurrence in "school" words.

Generally speaking, the students with a weak orientation toward words, and therefore the greatest need, are the ones least likely to warm to direct instruction in morphemic study. Hence, it is best to make these lessons brief, frequent, and spaced. A bulletin board display with space for adding examples can help to keep the project ongoing and the students able to readily participate as they come across new words containing meaningful word parts.

Steps in Incidental Morpheme Method
Preparation: Watch for words in reading assignments that probably are unfamiliar to students but contain familiar word parts, or morphemes. Use the following steps to *preteach* these terms.

Step 1   Write the term on the chalkboard or overhead, and underline meaningful word parts, or morphemic elements, that might help students understand the word's concept base.

    Example: <u>seis</u>   <u>mo</u>   <u>graph</u>

Step 2   Ask students if they can use the underlined parts to grasp the word meaning, and why. If the word meaning is predicted correctly, write the meaning under the word and proceed with steps 3 and 4 as reinforcement.

Step 3   Tell students you will give them additional clues for pre-
             dicting (or remembering) the word meaning. Beneath the
             underlined word parts, write level-1 clues, which are other,
             easier words using those morphemes. If students have not
             yet correctly predicted the word meaning, continue to ask
             for predictions.

Example:	*seis*	*mo*	*graph*
Level 1 clues:	*seizure*		*telegraph*
			graphic

Step 4   Beneath the level-1 clues, write level-2 clues, which are word
             part meanings, and continue to ask for predictions until the
             correct definition is reached and written below the clues.

Example:	*seis*	*mo*	*graph*
Level 1 clues:	*seizure*		*telegraph*
			graphic
Level 2 clues:	*to shake*		*written*

*Meaning: An instrument that records the direction,
time, and intensity of earthquakes*

See Figure 12.3 for a sample listing of common Latin roots. Many dictionaries will provide lists of Latin and Greek prefixes, suffixes, and roots.

Cooperative Glossaries: To Assist With Unfamiliar Word Meanings

A glossary is a handy minidictionary of terms used in a given book or
field. Definitions are context specific, and therefore more concrete. Even
proficient readers appreciate these when wading into a new field. Pupils
spend each day wading through new fields. If there is not a glossary in
the class text, or the particular book or novel being read, there is a relatively
easy and instructive way to create one cooperatively.

Steps in Constructing a Cooperative Glossary

Step 1   The teacher constructs a simple glossary to a few pages of
             a longer selection or book.

Step 2   Students are urged to use the cooperative glossary as they
             read.

Step 3   Students are urged to read a few pages beyond those covered
             by the guide.

Figure 12.3

Common Latin roots and derivative words.

Root	Meaning	Derivatives
-aud-, -audit-	hear	auditorium, audio,
-avi-	bird	aviation, aviary
-caput-	head	capital
-ced-, -cess-	move, yield	recede
-clar-	clear	clarify
-clin-	lean	incline
-clud-, -claud-, -clus-	shut	seclude
-cord-	heart	cordial
-corp-	body	corporal, marine corp
-cred-	to believe	credible
-curr-, -curs-	run	current
-dic-, -dict-	say	predict
-domin-	master	dominate
-duc-, -duct-	lead	conduct
-fac-, -fic-, -fact-, -fect-	to make, do	factory
-fer-	bear, carry	transfer
-fin-	end	finish
-fort-	strong	fortitude
-jun-, -junct-	join	junction
-laud-, -laudat-	praise	applause
-let-, -lect-	gather, read	lecture, collect
-legis-, -lex-	law	legislate
-lux-, -luc-	light	elucidate
-magn-	great	magnificent, magnify
-mal-	bad	malevolent
-man-	hand	manual
-mit-, -miss-	send	missile
-mov-, -mot-	set in motion	motor
-nov-, -novus-	new	renovation
-pac-	peace	pacific, pacify
-pel-, -puls-	urge, drive	propel
-pend-, -pens-	hang, weigh	pensive
-plic-, -plex-	bend, fold	plexiglass
-pon-, -pos-	place, put	postpone
-sci-	know	science
-scrib-, -script-	write	describe
-solv-, -solut-	loosen	solution, solve
-sepec-, -spect-	look	spectator
-sta-	stand firm	stable
-stru-, -struct-	build	construct
-tend-, -tens-	stretch	tendency
-tort-	to twist	distort
-ven-, -vent-	come	convention
-ver-	true	veritable
-vert-, -vers-	turn	reverse
-viv-, -vit-	live, life	vitality
-vid-, -vis-	see	evident
-voc-	call	vocation

Figure 12.4
Cooperative glossary for *A Tale of Two Cities.*

Page	Chapter	Word	Definition	Pronunciation
67	3	inscrutable	cannot be under-stood	in-screw-ta-ble
68		lamentation	cry out	la-men-ta-shun
70		opiate	a drug to help a person sleep	o-pee-ut
71		perpetuation	continuing	per-pet-chu-a-shun
72		specter	ghost	speck-tur
81	4	consignment	delivery	cun-sine-ment
83		disconcerted	confused	dis-cun-sir-ted
84		oblivion	complete forget-fulness	o-bli-vee-un
85		sonorous	loud praise	sah-nore-us
87		supplicatory	begging	suh-pli-cu-tory

Step 4   Discussion develops about how the guide helped and which additional words and/or phrases might need definition.

Step 5   Each student is assigned to prepare a glossary for a few pages of the remainder of the text. Students should be told to note the page number for each word they select and to record *only* the dictionary definition that applies to the way the word is used in the selection.

Step 6   Glossaries are compiled and reproduced for the entire class.

Step 7   (Optional) The teacher adds a pronunciation guide. This step is optional because it is difficult to do; however, most students like—and need—one.

Figure 12.4 presents an example of a cooperative glossary.

OTHER INCLUSION METHODS

Federal Public Law 94-142 mandates that youngsters with learning disabilities and handicaps attend school in a least-restrictive environment. This has been taken to mean that wherever possible such students will be accommodated in regular classes.

Most of the methodology of the content area literacy movement is suitable for meeting this requirement. Maring and Furman (1985) have made an especially strong case for seven methods for helping at-risk readers by teaching fundamental language and literacy strategies in the context of whole-class content instruction.

1. Use the Oral Reading Method (described in Chapter 6) at least once a week to increase familiarity and comfortableness with the language of the text.

2. Use the whole-class graphic organizer called *pyramiding* (Clewell & Haidemos, 1983). This activity offers group assistance to students with learning disabilities in identifying, classifying, and properly subordinating terms and ideas found in text.

   a. Each student reads silently to identify and write down key facts and ideas.

   b. The teacher leads a discussion, using the chalkboard to pyramid, or group, facts and phrases into logical categories.

   c. The class decides on a sentence that answers the question, "What is the author saying about these ideas?" This sentence forms the base of the triangle (see Figure 12.5).

3. Enhance and review the informal textbook inventory described in Chapter 3 and add some easier questions to help make the course textbook more instructive and user friendly, for example:

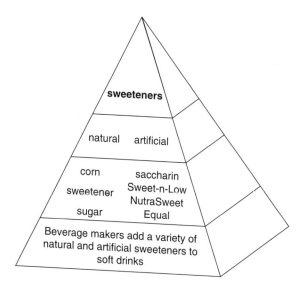

Figure 12.5
Pyramiding: a graphic organizer method for special-needs students.
Source: From G. Maring and G. Furman (1985), "Seven 'Whole Class' Strategies to Help Mainstreamed Young People Read and Listen Better in Content Area Classes," *Journal of Reading* 28, pp. 694–700. Reprinted with permission of G. Maring and the International Reading Association. All rights reserved.

a. How many pages are in the glossary?

b. Where could you find more information about a term defined in the glossary? (Answer: the index.)

c. What are the first and last page numbers of the index?

4. Use the contextual redefinition method described in Chapter 8 to improve vocabulary while reading (Moore, Readence, & Rickelman, 1982).

5. Use Words on the Wall (Cunningham, Cunningham, & Arthur, 1981) as an uncomplicated means of providing students with learning disabilities and other students with an easily available set of key words from the text to which they can refer for meaning, significance, spelling, and increased familiarity. Simply write key words with a felt-tip marker on half-sheets of paper, and tape them on the walls during a given unit of study.

6. Conduct the Guided Reading Procedure (see Chapter 6 for details) with the following specifications:

a. Use the procedure every two weeks, and administer a delayed retention test in the intervening week.

b. Try to get mainstreamed readers to contribute free recalls early in the lesson before the more-able students contribute all of the easiest information.

c. Reread the information on the board as students try to decide which items are main ideas, which are related details, and how to sequence the information.

7. Build further crutches, or scaffolding, into reading guides:

a. Mark with asterisks those questions you feel are most necessary and appropriate for mainstreamed youngsters to answer. Tell them to answer these questions first.

b. Put page, column, and paragraph numbers after certain questions to better guide those students who might have difficulty finding these (Wilkins & Miller, 1983); for example, "92, 2, 2" means page 92, second column, second paragraph.

LIMITED ENGLISH PROFICIENCY, CULTURAL DIFFERENCES, AND PROMOTING DIVERSITY

Methods for Second-Language Students

The increasing numbers of youngsters pouring into our schools from foreign and diverse cultural backgrounds are once again hastening the need for all educators to be conversant with the precepts of teaching those with limited English proficiency. Recent efforts to accommodate non-English-speaking American youngsters consistently result in a richer, more diverse, and stronger nation.

Many of the methods devised and developed for content area literacy have proved especially appropriate for use with linguistically and culturally different students. In many instances, these methods need not even be modified but merely used as described. This certainly applies to methods that create a rich instructional conversation such as ReQuest, reported to be profoundly effective in English-as-a-second-language classes (McKenzie, Ericson, & Hunter, 1988), as well as other interactive methods such as Question-Only, the Cultural-Academic Trivia game, the Subjective Approach to Vocabulary, vocabulary development through cooperative learning, most variations on the cloze procedure, and the various discussion methods presented in Chapters 8 through 10 on promoting higher-order literacy.

The most appealing feature of the methods presented next is that, in addressing second-language and limited-English needs, they simultaneously account for certain universal needs shared by all students. Among the most prominent of these are the need for a multicultural outlook; the need to reconnect ourselves to certain traditional human values and wisdom; the need to think abstractly as a requisite to thinking adaptively; and the need to actively participate in class, that is, conduct ourselves in harmony with others while pursuing individual goals. The final method presented in this chapter can help teachers achieve these and other valued educational goals. This method is appropriate for the unmotivated and occasionally disruptive student as well.

Note Cue: For Improving Oral Language, Comprehension, and Class Participation

Typically, students are not taught how to participate in class discussion, that is, how to ask, answer, and make relevant and appropriate comments. Students with LEP, students learning English as a second language, and culturally different and other at-risk students typically have found these social-academic strategies especially difficult to acquire. These students often are unfamiliar with the more subtle aspects of the English language, for example, tempo, volume, and social protocols such as waiting one's turn to speak, and speaking cogently.

Note Cue (Manzo & Manzo, 1987), as discussed in Chapter 6, is a form of highly scaffolded practice designed to have students experience what it feels like to participate in a well-orchestrated literacy lesson. In some ways it resembles *spotting*, a technique used in physical education to guide initial attempts at tumbling (see Figure 12.6). It is a form of sensorimotor involvement in which the mind and the body learn complex language, thinking, and social routines. Here are some guidelines for using Note Cue to structure a *prereading* interaction as well as a postreading discussion.

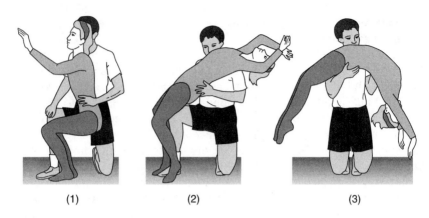

(1)   (2)   (3)

Figure 12.6
Note Cue is like acrobatic spotting.

Steps in Preparing For and Conducting a Pre and Postreading Note Cue Lesson

Teacher Preparation

✦ Prepare two sets of cards, one for *prereading* and one for *postreading*. On the *prereading* cards, write *prereading* questions (one per card), answers (one per card), and comments (one per card). Write the label "Question," "Answer," or "Comment" at the top of each card. Leave a few blank cards, initially just one, then about one more blank each time you use the method until only 20% of the cards contain statements. The prereading questions, answers, and comments should focus on predicting main topics and recalling related information and experiences. Write in pencil, and remember to reread and edit your cards. Prepare the *postreading* cards the same way, but shift the focus from prediction to verification—what the passage actually states—and related evaluative questions and comments.

✦ In preparing both sets of cards, be sure the answer card is phrased clearly enough to be easily matched to the question card (e.g., Q: Who followed Abraham Lincoln into the presidency? A: Andrew Johnson followed Abraham Lincoln into the presidency [not simply A: Andrew Johnson]).

Prereading Activity

Step 1   Instruct students to survey the reading material to try to predict what it will be about. Inform them that a brief written test will follow reading and discussion of the selection.

Step 2	While students are surveying, place one or more random or selected prereading cards on each student's desk.
Step 3	Instruct students to read their card(s) silently and think about when they should read it (them) and about whether they wish to add anything else.
Step 4	Instruct students with blank cards to think of a question, answer, or comment and, if time permits, write it on their cards.
Step 5	Begin the prereading, or prediction, stage of the discussion by asking who has a question or comment that seems to provide a good idea of what the selection will be about. If a question is read, ask who has an answer that seems to fit it. This process continues until students have a sense of what the passage will be about. This should take no more than ten minutes; a brisk pace and aura of evolving a purpose for reading will convey to students that not all cards need to be read to establish a reasonable purpose for reading.
Step 6	Instruct students to read the selection silently to test their predictions. Remind them to read their postreading cards, which will be placed on their desks while they are reading. Announce that you will come to the desk of any student who raises a hand for assistance.
Step 7	Postreading discussion.
Step 8	Ask, "Who has a good question to check comprehension of this selection?" then, "Who has a good answer to that question?" then, "Who has a comment that seems right to state?" and finally, "Who has reaction(s) or personal comment(s)?" The last question is intended to encourage extemporaneous statements as well as statements read from cards.
Step 9	Follow-up.
Step 10	Within the same class period, or later if preferred, give a test of five to ten questions that require brief written responses. Most questions should be taken directly from the cards to build an appreciation of the cooperative value in reading a cue card for all to hear and profit from.

Notes on Note Cue
If initial participation is slow to develop, try these options:

✦ Get things going by reading a question or comment card yourself.

✦ Simply call on students by name to read their card.

✦ Stimulate interest by inverting the process slightly: request that an answer card be read, then ask, "What is the question?"

✦ Call on at least two students with question cards to read their cards aloud. Then, rather than immediately requesting an answer, ask, "Which question do you think should come first?"

✦ Have students write their names in pencil on the back of each card. Middle school teacher Betty Bennett says this heightens students' sense of ownership and accountability for the cards' contents and offers a good way to check afterward which students did not volunteer to read their cards.

To foster greater independence and transfer of learning, try these options:

✦ Reinforce high-quality extemporaneous responses by handing the student a blank card and saying, "That was very good. Would you please write it on this card for further use?"

✦ Divide the class into groups, and have them prepare the Note Cue cards for the next selections to be read.

✦ Once students are familiar with the activity, prepare some cards with prompts ("Try to ask a question to show that one should doubt what is being said") or an incomplete statement to be completed by students ("Make a comment by completing this statement: 'I enjoyed reading this story because . . .' or 'The reaction would have been different in my family or culture. We would have . . .'"). Other types of prompter cards can be personalized ("Come on, Fred, don't you have something you can say about this selection?").

To foster higher-level thinking, develop evocative comment cards, preferably ones related to students' experiences. One vivid example of this kind of bridging comes to mind from a lesson observed in an English class. The selection read had been excerpted from a popular book. It described how a fifteen-year-old boy set out on a solitary voyage across the Pacific in a small craft. The questions and answers the teacher had put on the cue cards were primarily from the teacher's manual for the text. One of the comments that she added, however, raised the class's interest and even indignation: "How in the world did this young man raise the money and supplies to do this, and why did his parents permit him to risk his life in such a silly venture?" A student might not have worded the comment quite like that, but such real reactions tend to invite equally real responses and lively discussion.

Finally, Note Cue, unlike many conventional lesson designs, is cumulative. The cards a teacher composes for today's lesson can be stored for future use. Through cooperative work and sharing, teachers can develop starter sets of Note Cues for most key selections of a text. More important, with each use, previously written cards can be modified following use, and new cards generated by students can be added. In this way, lessons can be kept fresh and current.

✦ *Back Words* ✦

This chapter strongly endorsed the need for remedial reading programs and offered supportive methods to improve reading, language, thinking, and personal-social adjustment among special-needs students in content classrooms. Methods included means of motivating the unmotivated, mainstreaming strategies, biblio-support and dialogue journals, Glass Analysis to manage decoding problems, and Note Cue to heighten classroom participation and language experience. Most of these methods are applicable to broader student groups. The next chapter sets out ways to bring students, faculty, and community together in programs and activities that are beneficial to all. It is for those who would like to be able to identify, and potentially be, literacy leaders.

CHAPTER 13

Literacy Leadership and Content Area Programming

We know what we will have if we operate as we have in the past—and the prospects are not promising.

—Carl D. Glickman

✦ Fore Words ✦

This chapter is structured to answer several organizing questions that a principal, classroom teacher, or literacy specialist would need to understand to be an effective participant in a school's content area literacy program at almost any level of schooling.

1. What is meant by *literacy leadership*, and how does it align with current views of leadership?
2. What do schoolwide content area literacy programs typically look like?
3. What are some newer directions for content area literacy programming and curriculum?
4. How do charter school and other educational reform movements reconcile with content area literacy methods and programming ideas?

Also in the chapter are invitations to join some of the more pioneering efforts in school programming, especially as these are finding expression on the World Wide Web.

LITERACY LEADERSHIP: PREPARE NOW TO LEAD LATER

Sara Van Horn spent the better part of her early adult life raising children and keeping her teaching career and credentials current. She did not anticipate that one day while still relatively young and with children still in school, and with little formal training, she would find herself appointed as interim principal, and then principal, of a 600-plus-pupil middle school. Ironically, it turned out that her best preparation, and in fact her stepping stone to this new level of responsibility, was the precious, guarded time that she spent on the school's literacy committee, where she distinguished herself with her knowledge of this most basic aspect of curriculum and instructional planning.

The baby-boomer generation that is rapidly moving toward retirement is much larger than the one behind it. This is creating a considerable leadership vacuum at every level of American life, and no less so in the nation's schools. For this reason it is useful to be informed about the latest thinking on"leadership." It is in your personal interest, and in the interests of the nation as a whole, to prepare to meet this great need. The primary source for this update is Linda Lampert's (1998) summative work.

Building School Literacy Leadership Capacity

Leadership does not begin or end with an appointment as designated leader. It starts with a sense of responsibility for a school's mission, and a willingness to share one's limited energy and time toward some greater end. Older models of leadership were based more on charisma, core-culture features, connections and status, and, in more recent years, on being part of a previously underrepresented group enjoying some catchup opportunity. With the gap now closing on underrepresentation of women and certain minorities, this issue is no longer a major consideration in determining who shall be selected to provide leadership. Organizations of all types, schools included, now are being assessed in terms of bottom-line effectiveness. For schools this means higher test scores, lower dropout rate, improved school attendance, increased parent satisfaction surveys, and the like. Professional knowledge and skill are gaining new currency. Lampert (1998) offers a keen summary of what *leadership* is evolving to in the new millennium.

✦ Leadership is about learning together. It is about continuing conversations that enquire and generate ideas collaboratively, though not because this is sociable and nice, but because it is effective.

✦ Leaders build leaders. They are not controlling; sometimes they are even inspiring. They know when to follow someone else's lead. They build adult relationships that are not based on a "codependency" arrangement, where the leader is a benevolent authoritarian figure, and all others are the *led*, and therefore more likely to be *misled*.

✦ Leaders pose and constructively respond to questions that lead to reexamination of assumptions and beliefs.

✦ Leaders raise a range of possibilities in order to avoid simplistic answers.

✦ Leaders turn concerns into questions.

✦ Leaders recognize that they sometimes will be wrong and do so with candor, grace, and humility.

✦ Leaders also recognize that getting in front of a populist movement may win short-term support, but it is not the same as offering workable solutions; further, with the growing trend toward independent evaluators of progress, such political posturing will result in discredit to those who practice it.

There are five other notions, or awakenings, that are coming to be understood as influencing organizational change and school leadership. In summary, as noted by Glickman (1985), these are as follows:

1. What we have in education is *predicaments*, or recurring issues and needs, more so than onetime problems with final solutions (originally from Jerome Bruner).

2. Organizational effectiveness depends in great measure on the group buying into a *cause beyond oneself.*

3. Leadership styles can be roughly characterized as nondirective, collaborative, and/or direct. Importantly, directiveness need not be adversarial or capricious, but an honest regard for the different roles that may need to be played by school leaders and appointed supervisors.

4. The probability of achieving durable change can be predicted from situational factors, especially those that characterize the *maturity of the group as well as the designated leader.* According to the Hersey-Blanchard Situational-Leadership model (1977), group maturity can be characterized as "high," "medium," or "low" on three critical factors: (1) the *achievement* level or self-motivation of the group; (2) the sense of *responsibility* of group members to assume the various leadership roles necessary to keep an organizational goal on target despite competing and distracting events; and (3) the background or *education* and experience of the group to accomplish the subtasks comprising the larger goal.

5. To be effective change agents, leaders may need to adopt a leadership style that at least initially matches the culture or characteristic ways of functioning of the group . . . even great leadership can be dissonance producing and inviting of resistance (see Figure 13.1).

Healthy change, or "developmental directionality" (Glickman, 1985), is an evolutionary more than a revolutionary process. Old ways die hard. Nor does time and change pass even handedly across places and circumstances. At the moment, it is safe to say that there are few institutions run by enlightened executive thinkers working in "frictionless synchronicity" with fully competent and dedicated professionals. Institutions tend to be quirky; hence the need to actively develop *thought leaders*, or *informed advocates*, who can help a school to identify, formulate, and hold to a set of mission-based guidelines.

Needed: Informed Advocates

Where content area literacy is concerned leadership is urgently needed. Most postelementary teachers are trained to give optimal focus to subject learning or product over process learning. Similarly, most elementary teachers have little training or orientation in fusing reading, writing, and thinking to subject mastery. Both as a cause and a reflection of this situation, most school districts and state departments of education are muted

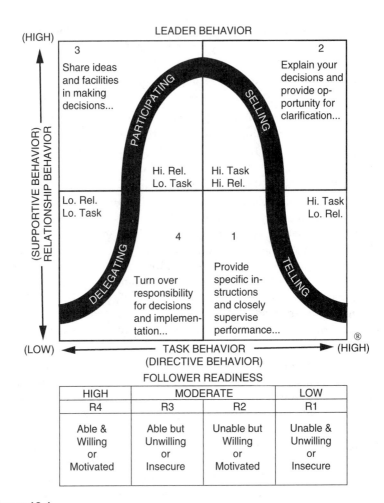

Figure 13.1
Matching on the Hersey-Blanchard Situational Leadership model.
Source: From *supervision of instruction: A developmental approach* (p. 173), by C. D. Glickman. © 1985 by Leadership Studios, Inc. Reprinted with permission.

on content area literacy objectives at elementary levels and silent at the postelementary levels. Hence, content area literacy often finds itself without *informed advocates.* This is quite different from the *uninformed advocates* who sometimes springup and can lead literacy programming into energized but ill-advised quagmires. While education greatly needs leadership, this should not be confused with the *ungrounded leadership* of the quirky types that often creates something of a megamess. There are three common routes to developing *informed advocacy* or shoring up the literacy content knowledge of appointed school and state department administrators:

1. Have on-site or internal specialist(s) providing daily information and guidance—be careful, however, of appointing Czars.

2. Develop a leadership committee.

3. Arrange for external consultants and reviews.

All of the above are necessary to initiate and sustain an effective school-based literacy programs. The roles of principal and literacy specialist are discussed below in the section on essential components of content area literacy programs. The roles of committees and consultants are addressed next.

The Literacy Leadership Committee

Everything about newer concepts of leadership suggests the importance of building a bottom-up consensus for the content area literacy program. Leadership today is based on consensus building. The chapters on how to build consensus and get it pointed in the best direction are still being written. The idea of a *literacy leadership committee*, however, is looking like one fairly sound way to proceed. The confounding nature of group dynamics notwithstanding, a literacy leadership committee has merit for several reasons.

- ✦ It creates an advocacy group for an area of programming that otherwise tends to be underrepresented within the organizational structure of most schools.
- ✦ It allows leadership to emerge from within the organization.
- ✦ It provides a means of building consensus and systemic support over time.
- ✦ It creates responsible parties, but is not vested in one individual and hence is not likely to rise and fall with that person's social influence.
- ✦ It tells faculty, students, community, and central administration that literacy is a valued goal . . . *a cause beyond oneself.*
- ✦ It almost always leads to seeking higher levels of expertise as issues are refined and important implementation decisions are pending.

For ongoing informational and personal support in organizing and guiding a content area literacy leadership committee, see ⟨www.LiteracyLeaders.com⟩. Now consider the always-daunting issue of identifying appropriate consultants.

Consultants: Look for Certified Experts

External literacy consultants are a logical progression for most schools. It is unrealistic to expect school administrators and leaders, and even on-site literacy specialists and advocates, to know all they need to about this area of school programming. But, this need for external assistance always raises the specter of who is an expert and "don't experts often disagree?"

A recent, broadly sampled research report says that over 50% of teachers do not know about proven content area literacy methods, and of those who have been taught these in undergraduate and graduate school, few are using them (Spor & Schneider, 1999). There are a lot of predicaments inherent in this scenario, and they are not of leadership but of competent stewardship, attention to details, and lack of professional knowledge.

While schools of education are not blameless for such lapses in effective teacher education and training, they are most likely the best hope for fixing such problems in the near term. *Certified*, that is, college- and university-educated *experts*, tend to disagree much less than one would think and on fewer matters. Most of the seeming dilemmas of conflicting experts come from failure to establish who is certified and who is somehow self-proclaimed. While it is true that there are certified experts who might give less than the best advice, it is more common to receive misinformation and misdirection from self-made and populous types. In fact, as we mentally review some of the more high-profile fads and misdirections in literacy education of the last thirty years, not one of them was under the *leadership* of a university-certified reading/literacy specialist; however, a few were involved in higher education although working outside their areas of certified educational training, without naming names (why further their notoriety?), here is a sample list of the "theses" and misguided intervention strategies that have been proposed by these self-made "literacy leaders" along with their true backgrounds.

✦ A heavily literature-based literacy program with little or no direct instruction or attention to science and mathematics or subject mastery. Leaders: a psycholinguist and, with slight variations on this theme, a professor of English literature with minimal training in any branch of education.

✦ An "individualized reading" program based on reading "self-selected" books and having little or no direct instruction. Leader: an elementary education specialist in language arts, and with no formal training in the teaching of reading.

✦ A highly prescriptive program of creeping and crawling to ostensibly correct underdeveloped brain connections and presumably almost all reading problems. Leaders: a school counselor and a generalist educator.

✦ A program to remedy dyslexia (severe reading failure) by correcting for undescended testicles in boys (with the help of a tuning fork . . . don't ask). Leaders: osteopathic doctors in a Scandinavian country.

✦ A program of visual-perceptual training, and several variations that followed for vision (eye) training. Leaders: a child psychologist, several physicians, and many small-town optometrists.

✦ A program that prescribes customized colored lenses that are said to improve reading and comprehension. Leader: a college remedial education program director with no formal training in any branch of education.

Many other "programs" and "experts" could be added to this list, as could the names of a flock of celebrities, corporations, and well-known foundations who have enthusiastically supported such ungrounded programs. (For a more complete listing with names, see Manzo & Manzo, 1993). Much of this misdirection could have been avoided or at least properly proportioned, if more people had asked for the credentials of these charismatic but somewhat misguided "literacy leaders." For this reason, it is proper and necessary to check the credentials of school consultants and to challenge the credentials of internal administrators who may fancy themselves "universal leaders" in everything and everywhere strong leadership is recognized as a need. We hate to bring it up, but you will need to be especially watchful of reading programs that seek a halo effect by tying themselves to socially desirable goals and religious groups.

For a list of a certified consultants, with brief biographies, and by geographic area and specialties see www.LiteracyConsultants.com (web site under construction).

Use of Consultants

In general, a certified specialist in one realm can serve as commentator or helpful guide in framing the key questions and issues of a related area. This is due to the fact there are underlying principles of effective instruction, and certified professionals are more likely to be sensitive to what they do not know, and cautious about claiming that they know how to deal with issues outside their realm of training. However, as a matter of course, expertise in one realm cannot pass for expertise in another. Even subtle differences in the aim and purpose of seemingly related fields can be deceiving for all concerned. One frequent problem is acceptance of qualifications in learning disabilities or English education as preparation for guiding literacy programming. The literacy specialist may be trained to provide consultation to the LD and Language Arts program, but the inverse is not likely to be as true.

Evaluation of commercial programs is one area that certified consultants are expected to be of most value. However, this often is problematic even for certified experts for several reasons.

✦ There simply are too many commercial programs for the specialist to follow.

✦ Schools typically are not willing to retain someone to do a careful analysis of a commercial program.

✦ Schools often are not clear about what they intend to do with the program (e.g., use it as a supplement or a primary program, and if the first, with precisely what other methods?).

✦ Schools will sometimes buy programs without training and technical support.

✦ Schools are shy about discussing the political-social tie-ins of a particular set of practices or commercial program with a particular interest group.

✦ Literacy programming is "rocket science." It does not appear to be, because almost anyone can launch this rocket; however, with each distance it travels in space and time, it can move further off its mark. Launching a quality program not only requires proper preprogramming and stability, something commercial materials tend to do well, but also periodic course corrections as well.

Issues such as these can limit effective use of a consultant, but they also make it necessary, as can be seen by the last point above. In general, a consultant's value on arrival is determined by the preparation time that goes into that visit. If a particular decision is of great or long-lasting importance, it may be necessary to confer with more than one consultant. Finally, on this topic, do not confuse "workshops" with "consultations." Workshops are organized presentations, or information sharing on a topic. A consultation is a focused analysis of a fairly specific problem, even if the problem sounds general, such as "What might we be doing wrong in the area of [say, vocabulary] to be getting these marginal or weak scores?"

Finally, there is a way to roughly judge a consultant's wisdom as well as knowledge. The wise consultant will offer solutions that are more elegant than simplistic. The wise consultant will not have a long list of don'ts, such as "Never lecture," "Never ask questions following reading, only before," "Don't use [unnatural] books with a controlled vocabulary." The wise consultant will support enlightened methods and approaches without damning more traditional methods: a new item on one end of the shelf need not shove a more traditional one off the other end, unless this has been fully justified. For the most part, logic suggests that unless there is definitive information on the countereffectiveness of a traditional practice, it is best to assume that the innovation offered is the "new kid" needing proof and clinical (classroom) testing. In other words, *traditional* should not be considered a bad word, although it may not be the last or best word. It should not be necessary to upset most working systems to install better ones.

In general, unless there is evidence of an imminent instructional crisis, changes sought in a professional or knowledge-based arena should, again, be more evolutionary—as in requiring tweaking, elaborating, and/or focusing—than revolutionary—as in radically altering direction or abandoning traditional practices.

ESSENTIAL COMPONENTS OF CONTENT AREA LITERACY PROGRAMS

The term *program* here means any plan targeted at a stated goal or objective. Programs are necessary, because day-to-day events can become random and even fragmented when unfolding in quasi-isolated classrooms. For this reason alone, it can be satisfying to get and have a place to refer back to the big picture. Another reason to try to gain a top-down perspective is its value in giving the professional educator an opportunity to exercise a more assertive role in defining, refining, and aligning classroom practices with larger school goals and objectives.

Successful content area literacy programs, typically, are built around nine key elements that together equal the big picture:

1. Leadership
2. A grounded ideology or philosophy
3. Objectives and goals
4. Clear roles and responsibilities
5. Special services for various segments of the student body
6. Ongoing needs assessment and program evaluation
7. A curriculum plan
8. A staff development program that provides consultation, in-service training, and sharing opportunities
9. Activities that are results oriented and promote collaboration and cooperation

The following sections show how some of these elements might be or are being implemented in actual school programs. The examples and discussions include some optional as well as essential elements.

Ideology, or Guiding Ideas

The term *ideology* is used here not in its more recent connotation of *blinding beliefs*, but rather in its stricter sense of a set of professionally accepted *ideas* and proven practices, or guiding philosophy. It usually is expressed in the form of a unifying theme or focus that serves as the conceptual basis or organizing principle(s) for programming.

Several philosophies have held sway in recent years. Most notable among these has been the mastery-learning perspective that emphasizes heavy doses of direct instruction, a strong dose of testing for transmission of knowledge, and a skills-based orientation. In counterpoint is the whole-language orientation, which emphasizes indirect teaching; transactional, or constructionist, subjectivity in reading; virtually no testing; and the integration of content mastery, reading, writing, and speaking largely through literature-based learning.

The most popular philosophy, however, is an eclectic one. *Eclecticism* is a philosophy that permits one to pragmatically pick and choose parts, principles, and practices from all others. Our own choice is a form of eclecticism that has been labeled the *new, or informed, eclecticism* (Manzo & Manzo, 1997b). This philosophy differs from conventional eclecticism, or "balanced" programming (Duffy & Hoffman, 1999), which often means a"little of this and that." There are three distinguishing characteristics of *informed eclecticism*:

1. Every effort must be made to reconcile (seemingly) competing ideas and political crosscurrents, since there is a good chance that these will enhance rather than displace each other.

2. Instructional decisions should be guided not merely by subjective judgments and equal proportions, but rather by assessment of student needs and reference to research findings that support or fail to support given practices and their degrees of value.

3. There must be an emphasis on critical-constructive or inquiry-based learning, since this is the fundamental purpose of schooling. (See the section on quest fusion literacy curriculum below for a current attempt to formulate such a focus.)

The chief value of these simple guidelines is that they encourage attention to innovation but help schools to resist fads and hollow buzzwords, even when the new buzzwords are *balance* and *eclectic*.

Objectives and Goals

Attempts to state specific goals and objectives represent the first fleshing out of an ideology or philosophical bent. School districts are very good at cranking out hair-splittingly specific objectives, and/or goals that may be socially significant, and appropriate to be represented but not necessarily central to school learning. It is important to take this exercise seriously. The words chosen are an institution's public declarations and logically the basis for the development of strategic planning and allocations of resources. Since resources are almost always limited, this is where priorities and compromises should be negotiated. Everything cannot be a top priority.

Here are some examples of sentences and phrases that align with the themes in this text and that can be combined into descriptive statements to guide content area literacy programs and curricula:

✦ Promoting progress toward reading-language-thinking-content-social/emotional maturity as opposed to mere reading competence

✦ Promoting higher-order literacy, or working to assess and remedy shortfalls in critical-constructive thinking, among the academically proficient as well as those reading below age-grade expectations

✦ The improvement of reading, writing, speaking, listening, and thinking

✦ Promoting multiple literacies, including knowledge of diverse cultures and backgrounds

✦ Fusing literacy, content teaching, telecomputing, and diverse cultures

✦ Creating an inquiry or quest-based multiple-literacy and learning curriculum

✦ Fusing content, literacy, and thinking to the demands of the "new economy"

See the final chapter and the text web site for more on this new-millennium theme.

"Best" Literacy Practices Can Be a Tough Sell

Realistically speaking, the above words and themes may not always play well in a particular school or community, even though they should be an integral part of the school's philosophical or ideological goals. For example, it might be fairly easy to get a faculty committee to say that the school literacy program should include attention to the higher literacy needs of the three near-dysfunctional subtypes of "proficient" readers identified in Chapter 8. In practice, however, there likely would be several objections. Objections would range from "limited resources" to "lack of knowledge" about what to do. In such situations, it is more practical to first express the focus for the school program in more traditional terms, such as the following:

✦ Advance comprehension and vocabulary

✦ Efficient reading and study habits

✦ Reading and writing to learn

✦ Preparation for standardized tests

Ironically, the most concrete-looking item, "preparation for standardized tests," may best open the door for attention to higher literacy since questions on such tests can tend to be of a more abstract nature than those on conventional classroom tests. As such, the standardized test will show which students have been receiving much higher grades in class than is perhaps justified by the quality of their abstract thinking. In most cases, the ideology of the school program will be expressed in a combination of the preceding terms with some locally recognized need. Examples of specific local needs might include functional literacy for job flexibility, college preparation, or effective reading and use of technology. See the section on curriculum implementation below for further thoughts and strategies for advancing important objectives like higher literacy.

ORGANIZATION, ROLES, AND RESPONSIBILITIES

The chief element in translating program ideals into practice is the assignment of role responsibilities. Following are the most commonly acknowledged responsibilities of the school administrator, reading specialist, and classroom teacher.

The School Principal

The school principal has the primary responsibility for initiating and supporting the development and implementation of the goals, objectives, curriculum, and design of the literacy program. In this capacity, the principal is the one who needs to know enough to initiate schoolwide survey testing, program evaluation, and ongoing literacy-related faculty development programs. It also is the principal's responsibility to cultivate a positive school climate. It is important to note, however, that "a poor climate can inhibit learning, but a positive climate does not guarantee success" (Hoffman, 1991, p. 926). In other words, the highly vaunted objective of "team building," while truly important to faculty morale, should not become a primary goal since it is not easily translated into improved student performance. As one leading educator confided in a private conversation regarding the evaluation of principals, "We've got them by the data now." Overall, leadership/supervision should not be viewed as quite so glamorous, because it is not. Administrative leadership is like glue on a chair; largely unrecognized or appreciated when working, but evident and faulted when it is not (Glickman, 1985).

In school design something has to be secondary, and even tertiary, and this "team building" stuff may be it. This does not mean that it is valueless, but it may not be as primary as our social instincts would suggest. Gilbert and Sullivan created some of the most durable and lyrical musicals of the early twentieth century, yet they so intensely disliked one another that they did virtually all of their collaboration by mail. They were competent and even creatively productive, that is, they produced great synergies, but they were never a social team; they simply recognized a goal greater than themselves. Working as a team, or *synergizing*, does not require holding hands and loving your leader and even one another; it requires competency and even the suspension of personal goals in favor of larger, professional goals. This is not to say that good feelings are not important to one's sense of personal worth and the overwhelming human need for affiliation, but it is not why professionals are hired. Unless, of course, they are professional psychologists and counselors brought in to help prevent or correct social dysfunctionality that is spilling over into the deterioration of duties.

We will do much of our collaborating in this new century through various forms of telecomputing that result in fewer conventional teams and fewer leaders to guide us. However, we will have more information and better critiques than ever before, and fewer leaders controlling our access to it. It is true that mythmakers have greater access to promoting ill-advised programs, but so too will they have to weather the scrutiny of *myth-breaking* information, web sites, and perspectives. Chat groups and interactive web sites are helping everyone not merely to access more information, but to get help in processing and digesting it. Much of this open access should keep professionals at every level current but grounded. More than ever, *authority* will be determined by good sense and ability to stand up under cross-examination. This should not diminish the importance of college and postgraduate education, as many fear, but further validate it as people and institutions seek more analytical help, as well as access to basic information.

The Literacy Specialist

Literacy specialists essentially are people who have not only information, or data points, but *knowledge*, which is the grasp of potentially unifying concepts that make it possible to connect those dots in different arrangements as required by given predicaments or sets of circumstances.

As a rule of thumb, an intermediate and secondary school should have one full-time reading/literacy specialist for every 250 students. Reading specialists are expected to serve as resource persons in the development of the goals, objectives, curriculum, and design of the literacy program. They typically are responsible for coordinating and interpreting schoolwide survey testing to assist in the ongoing evaluation of the literacy program and for administering additional diagnostic tests as needed based on survey test results and/or referrals. Reading specialists provide ongoing assistance to teachers in a variety of forms: determining their felt needs, helping them to better understand the nature and implications of those needs, planning in-service activities, evaluating and/or preparing instructional materials, and demonstrating new methods. In addition, they should be responsible for eliciting and coordinating the contributions of other support services such as librarians, counselors, outside consultants, and parents.

The Content Area Teacher

The ultimate power and responsibility for the overall literacy program rests with classroom teachers. A vital content area literacy program enlists teachers' participation in the identification and development of the goals, objectives, curriculum, design, and evaluation procedures for the school-wide literacy program. This participation helps to ensure whole-hearted implementation of the program.

There is a growing belief that teachers may be the chief agents for change in literacy programming. For a solid source book on supporting this movement, see Lawrence G. Erickson's *Supervision of Literacy Programs—Teachers as Grass-Roots Change Agents* (1995; Boston, Allyn and Bacon). Importantly, durable results are not possible without scheduled time for classroom teachers to make their contribution (Glickman, 1985).

Special Services Component

In the context of schoolwide programming, *special services* means assistance available for students with special needs that cannot easily be met in a regular class situation. This typically involves pull-out programs, elective or minicourses, resource rooms, and drop-in help. It now also can include e-mail and phone hotline help. At this time, the authors among others are attempting to develop on-line special services in the form of digital tutoring and mentoring programs. These should assist teachers in providing a virtual form of up-close-and-personal support to students in reading, writing, and thinking to higher levels. The chief benefit of such programs is that they would increase the amount of engaged time students spend in reading and writing with feedback and encouragement. The program that the authors are embracing uses the REAP annotation exchange system described in Chapter 8 as its primary delivery vehicle. This type of programming resembles conventional pull-out services, except it is asynchronous—not occurring in real time, but rather as tutor and tutee are able and willing to engage tasks.

Pull-Out Services

In *pull-out programs*, a reading/literacy specialist offers diagnostic and/or remedial/corrective tutoring for youngsters who cannot be adequately provided for in regular classes. This component is intended to ensure the following:

✦ No remedial-level reader falls between the cracks and leaves school quasi-literate after thirteen years in our charge.

✦ Foreign-born and other language-handicapped students receive special attention where this appears necessary.

✦ Assessment and treatment are provided for other difficult, different, or sometimes overlooked problems (e.g., higher-order literacy needs, cultural differences, study-skills deficiencies, and reading-related writing, grammar, and spelling).

✦ Ideally, consultation is provided for all teachers in selecting and using appropriate methods and materials.

In general, pull-out programs create a safety net where a member of the faculty becomes responsible for the subject that no one seems to think that they teach. It also tasks someone with providing attention to literacy needs that may require out-of-class conferences with parents and the marshalling of available resources, in the school and in the community, for those youngsters at risk of becoming school dropouts or social graduates.

Elective Courses

Content area literacy specialists in upper elementary, middle, and high schools frequently offer exploratory minicourses or full elective courses on topics such as study strategies, reading rate, critical reading, and vocabulary enrichment. This type of short-term, focused instruction reinforces and builds on the ongoing content reading instruction provided daily in content classrooms. It also extends the services of the literacy specialist and committee to a fuller complement of the student body.

Learning Centers

The learning center usually is the hub out of which a reading or literacy department may operate. Bernice Bragstad (1985), an International Reading Association award-winning content area literacy specialist, says that her former high school's learning center provided these three services:

1. Individualized or small-group tutoring in any subject or skill, provided by a select cadre of proficient student-tutors or the reading specialist
2. Individualized help with writing, provided by several English teachers who served their duty periods in this way
3. A preventative biweekly summer tutoring program conducted by high school students for middle and junior high students

In addition to these services, learning centers can offer walk-in assistance with almost any pressing homework or academic problem. Many school districts have extended this concept to a homework hotline. The hotline is available after school hours and staffed by volunteer teachers.

Needs Assessment and Evaluation

Information about students' academic status and about the effects of the school program on this basic school obligation is essential to determining what needs to be done and how to best do it. This type of information should be collected regularly by school leaders and cross-verified by an independent audit from an outside team of consultants about every three to five years. Surveys guided by outside consultants help identify problems that have a way of cropping up in virtually every operation in which day-to-day pressures erode educators' sensitivity to basic flaws in policy and procedure. Most effective businesses routinely budget for such periodic surveys and reviews. It is a fundamental form of quality control. One often-overlooked aspect of evaluation is to look at student progress in terms of key "process variables" that tend to support prevention or program failure. One key variable that should be monitored is in-school "engaged time on-task." There needs to be clear evidence that sufficient time (we estimate, no less than 30–40% of the total school day) be spent on basics such as these:

+ Organized presentation of information
+ Frontloading, or preparation for guided silent reading
+ Discussion and supervised study
+ Frequent, brief periods of additional help to students with special needs

Almost everything else, including popular issues such as diversity, use of cooperative structures, gender concerns, character education, and meeting learning-style differences, will be more attainable with full commitment to monitoring and nurturing these fundamental programming requirements.

Another important part of needs assessment is determination of areas of suboptimal, though not necessarily failing, levels of literacy development. This would include informal assessments of factors such as study habits, writing, listening, and higher literacy.

Implementing Sustainable Programs

The literacy leadership committee can facilitate program implementation in a variety of ways. However, it typically has no authority but advisory. Therefore, a full implementation cycle may need to be measured in years, not weeks or semesters. The committee will win respect for its purposes largely by the quality of its information and recommendations, and by patient construction and introduction of its programming ideas. Achieving these goals requires a great deal of prioritizing and decision making. Methods such as the Regression Equation Technique (see Chapter 8), or similar decision-making structures (cf., Erickson, 1995) can be of considerable assistance in converting a literacy leadership *deliberative* committee into a literacy leadership *action* committee. The basic strategy of an *action committee* should be to TNT, or to specify the *tasks, names,* and *times* of people responsible for getting strategically important things done in a timely manner (Erickson, 1995).

Launching a sustainable new program also tends to require a special level of monitoring for"allergic reactions." These generally can be traced to almost anything that upsets existing routines or social structures. These can be quite subtle and difficult to detect. For example, an effort to increase reflective reading and writing of literature (i.e., stories) will easily win the support of the English department. However, efforts to identify those who read too much story literature and who do not connect their reading to real-life situations will almost surely induce an allergic reaction from that same English department, because this is something that literature majors generally do not do well. When reading beyond the lines is connected to real-life problem solving, or action planning, it amounts to a culture clash, or introduction of a foreign substance into the literature major's environment; literature majors routinely have low scores on psychological measures of *pragmatism*, the essence of applied thinking. Review the profiles of four proficient reader subgroups in Chapter 8 for further verification of this point.

One manageable way to anticipate and establish readiness for such allergic sensitivity is to provide "allergy shots," which amount to small quantities of exposure to the offending element, and then monitoring for reactions. One way to do this is to increasingly nest information and stratagem into a periodic newsletter, electronic billboard, and web site with hyperlinks to appropriate sites. In general, the most tangible and discussion provoking of these is the one-page newsletter. By the way, literature majors have other effective characteristics that make them inclined to be persuaded to do what is best for their students, namely high empathy, compassion, and capacity to be influenced by personal stories.

To begin to construct a newsletter that is professional and authoritative, the committee need only decompose a text such as this one into a series of one-page summaries of *content area literacy methods*. The burden of selecting and editing can be shared with other schools in the district, or outside the district for that matter, having similar goals and objectives. Also, consult free web sites, such as http://members.aol.com/ReadShop/LiteracyExpress.html, for other suggestions and implementation strategies.

Curriculum Implementation Plan

Apart from the obvious effort to infuse each content subject with the necessary reading-related teaching methods and student strategies, each discipline can be designated, by common agreement, to give special attention to specific features of the content area literacy curriculum. Distribution and assignment of reading and literacy-related objectives to each subject area proceeds best when school units volunteer to play designated roles.

This horizontal distribution also can be detailed vertically by age/grade level (see Figure 13.2).

Staff Development

A well-planned staff development program is an important means of ensuring that programs endure and evolve over time in an institutional setting that undergoes frequent changes in administration and staff. An effective plan for staff development should include four basic components:

1. Teacher involvement in program development and an ongoing sense of program ownership
2. Regular program review and revitalization
3. Flexible leadership, with emphasis on fine-tuning the program and accommodating individual teachers' needs
4. Attention to innovation and resistance to fads and hollow words

Discussed next are several means for addressing of these components.

Determining Training Needs

The first question that a staff development program should ask, according to Marzano (1997), is "What part of the learning process needs to be improved?" This question then is converted into consideration of the various possible resources—from books, to web sites, to workshops—that could be brought to fill those needs for the school, subgroups within it, or for individuals. See www.mcrel.org, a federal teaching-learning laboratory, for Marzano's excellent "Framework for Planning Staff Development."

Beware of Bad Currency

One important precaution should be exercised in using the Internet for in-service education. It is the currency of its data banks. Things that are"-current" by definition are not time-tested. They may become gold-plated standards, but they also may prove to be unsupportable. In any case, most on-line journals and touted programs do not reach back prior to 1990, yet the knowledge bases for most fields extend much further back. In the case of content area literacy, its "golden age" of development was between 1969 and 1990. Much of value has occurred since, but much was created prior to the dawning of telecomputing. So, consult textbooks and look for sites that reference these classic works.

Action Research

Classroom experimentation is a proven way to change instructional routines. It has been pointed out that by involving teachers in planning, con-

Figure 13.2
Vertical content area literacy implementation curriculum plan.

Distribution of Literacy Skills and Objectives by Major Disciplines

English

1. Story comprehension
2. Poetry comprehension
3. Language patterns
4. Creative writing
5. Summary writing
6. Systematic vocabulary
7. Literary reference books

Social Studies

1. Analytical discussion
2. Critical reading
3. Metaphorical thinking
4. Critique and reaction writing
5. Note taking
6. Social studies vocabulary
7. Almanac, encyclopedia, and related reference skills
8. Reading maps, charts, graphs, and cartoons

Science

1. Inquiry training
2. Thesis and detail writing from expository material and observation
3. Cooperative reading-learning
4. Accurate recall
5. Science vocabulary
6. Hypothesis formulation and testing
7. Abstract thinking

Mathematics

1. Recitation
2. Translation
3. Test taking
4. Mathematics vocabulary
5. Expository writing: What did this problem ask, and why did I solve it as I did?
6. Cooperative problem solving

ducting, and reporting classroom research, teachers greatly increased their sense of ownership of ideas while providing hands-on evidence of the value of several basic content area literacy methods (Santa, Isaacson, & Manning, 1987).

The process of involving teachers in action research projects is more manageable today than ever before. Assistance with research design and statistics usually can be had for a small fee or even free from a school district's own office of research, from advanced degree-seeking teachers, and/or from nearby university campuses. *Action research* need not be limited to doing, but can involve searching, as in web and textbook questing for certain types of information. For example, teachers might go on a *great paradigm quest* to find and identify some very basic structures for teaching in specific CAL areas. In this text that would include the Directed Reading–Thinking Activity for text comprehension and the Frayer model for teaching vocabulary and concepts. There are several others; see if you can find a paradigm for inquiry-based learning, and one for teaching writing, and . . . you get the idea. Activities such as these tend to increase feelings of ownership, and to stimulate a good deal of creative problem solving.

The idea of teacher-scholars has a rich history in education (Chall, 1986). No doubt you have noticed that several of the methods and ideas presented in this text were suggested by classroom teachers and other school practitioners.

In-Service Education

In-service education, or staff informing and transforming, is a key feature of successful school programming. This can take several forms. The action research model just discussed is one means of broadening horizons. The most practical methods, however, involve direct in-service training.

There are no clear formulas for conducting in-service teacher training. Nonetheless, there has been a good deal of research on the efficacy of various generic approaches. A meta-analysis (broad-summary analysis) of many studies (Wade, 1984–85) and our own more recent research (Manzo & Manzo, 1995) support the following conclusions.

✦ Regardless of who conducts in-service sessions (trainers come under many different job classifications), teachers are more likely to benefit when they use methods that permit learning by doing.

✦ Move beyond *doing* to discovery learning workshops that are built around *heuristic* tasks, actions, and activities that result in penetrating insights (see Figure 13.3).

✦ There is no magical combination of methods for successful in-service education. Nevertheless, in-service programs that use observation, microteaching, auditory and visual feedback, and practice, either

Figure 13.3
Suggested in-service heuristic/discovery workshop activities.

1. Make informal textbook diagnostic tests.
2. Create a reading-study-thinking guide.
3. Identify key questions that underlie a course's content.
4. Search for instructional paradigms that virtually define the most complete way to teach something that is fundamental. Three such paradigms include the Directed Reading–Thinking Activity (a design for teaching a complete content literacy lesson), the Frayer model (for teaching vocabulary and concepts), and the "writing process" (for teaching all phases of effective writing).
5. To further ensure that teachers are becoming investors in a school program, invite them to participate in identifying and solving instructional problems. (See Chapter 8 on critical-constructive teaching and learning for relevant ideas.)
6. Recommend the Listen-Read-Discuss method from Chapter 1 as an initial offering. This *time-release* method was designed to stimulate professional discussion and to invite increasingly more sophisticated discussion among the professional staff.
7. Administer instruments that tend to uncover areas of suboptimal literacy development, for example, *The Informal Reading–Thinking Inventory* (Manzo, Manzo & McKenna, 1995), for middle grades.

individually or in some combination, are more effective than programs that do not use these methods.

✦ Contrary to recent populist trends, in-service education is most successful when led by an expert but organized to encourage participant involvement and contributions.

Increasingly, into the future, the Internet will play an important role in in-service and preservice education. It provides a platform for dialogue, information, and demonstration lessons.

Evaluation

Quality control must be a fundamental part of every intervention effort. It begins with a careful perusal of the literature in a field and extends into field tests. Chapter 9 on assessment provides a solid array of options for preassessing need and evaluating outcomes. Your effort to learn the contents of this and other such textbooks is the best preparation for learning the literature and guiding concepts of the field.

Content Area Literacy and Educational Reform

There are several larger reform movements in education that are proving to be meaningful and durable. Unfortunately, each of these tends to function in relative isolation of all others. It seems reasonable to begin to fuse these collateral movements to content area literacy's highly refined principles and procedures. This would be a fortunate merger since content area literacy is well grounded in teaching practices. As such, it would "put legs under" many of reform programs that are steeped in an enlightened philosophy, but light on specific practices. Conversely, these reform programs tend to be recognizable to most school administrators and boards but frankly not to most teachers and literacy specialists. Technology transfer and sharing across related fields are a logical next step to the great increase in availability of information. To date, issues in policy studies, school decision making, reform, and just what constitutes "best practices" are matters that have proceeded on relatively parallel and therefore noninteracting paths.

School reform in general is not without problems. Reform movements vary widely in purpose, method, and degree of development. They can be quite political in purpose, or just quirky as when they reflect a particularly well-leveraged person's or group's special interests. In fact, there is a reaction growing to the large and overleveraged abilities of some reforms and reformers. The twenty-nine superintendents of Orange County, California voted unanimously to call for a moratorium on state legislative reforms. They say the barrage of laws passed in almost every session are willy-nilly and picayunish—they have mandated something as specific as teaching about the Irish potato famine. In general, these interferences are causing chaos and financial strain, and the legislatures almost never appropriate new funds to implement their quirky laws and regulations (based on a news story in the *Los Angles Times*, 5/29/99). For a quick summary of school reforms and reformers visit our web site.

As noble and influential as these reform efforts have been, none is likely to have the impact of the *charter school movement*. It will affect every educator's work and career even if they never teach in one.

Charter Schools

What are charter schools, once you get past anecdotal headlines like "Gritty Harding High Charter: A Place Where Kids SUCCEED"? Essentially, charter schools are public schools that are licensed to operate with many of the same freedoms as private schools, with no additional charges to parents allowed. Generally, this means that teachers need not meet the same credential requirements, and hundreds of lesser rules and regulations either do not apply or are more liberally interpreted. Most charter schools are allowed to have up to 20% of teachers that have no teaching credential whatsoever. To get a feel for what this means, think what you have learned about content area literacy this semester, and realize that one-fifth of the teachers in these schools may not have a clue that these options even exist.

Almost anyone can apply to the state to operate a charter school. This includes parents, teachers, organizations, and even religious groups as long as they do not operate as a sectarian institution. If approved, they receive state funding on the same per-pupil bases as other public schools (about $7,100 per year on average, although varying widely from Maine to Mississippi). Charter schools also may qualify for additional support from county and local municipal governments. Importantly, they are not exempt from most state criterion-based tests, but may be from nationally normed, standardized tests.

These common factors aside, charter schools are very different from one another. Some are built around themes, such as art or foreign language, others around an idea, such as operating twelve-month schools or meeting kids' learning styles. The nation's first charter school, City Academy, was founded by teachers in St. Paul, Minnesota, to attract and provide for kids who felt alienated by conventional education. Other charters, such as in Oakland, California, have responded to parents who expressed frustration with lack of attention to their children's special needs (in this case Latino students).

Teacher groups are split on charter schools. Some feel that these have diminished the status of teachers and teaching; others see them as a way to curb excessive bureaucracy and top-heavy administration. Clearly, both of these are reasonable objections. However, each time a district or new administrative grouping tries to eliminate workers they tend to reduce the number of curriculum coordinators, and master teachers with release time to work with others; a move that seems to have little negative effect immediately, but that eventually stalls progress. To counter this impact, schools then try to import whole plans "that work!" from elsewhere. These franchise operations seldom are able to sustain themselves, even when done by the same people who were successful in a different location. There also is a history of eventual collapse of "alternative schools." The reasons vary, but certain intrinsic factors tend to sabotage the best efforts.

Alternative Schools and Their Sometimes Naïve Experiments

Alternative schools often are based upon some unsupportable premise or principle. For example, the initially successful KIPP program in New York City has a school day that begins at 7 A.M. and lasts until 5 P.M., and a school calendar that goes through the summer. This apparent solution flies in the face of recent findings by William Demont, of the Sleep Disorders Center of Stanford University, that say that most teenagers can't fall asleep before 11 P.M. and require nine full hours of sleep. It is no wonder, then, that the program's initial grade increases now are slipping. Other researchers, such as Mary Carskadon of Brown University, are finding that about half of youngsters attending school on this schedule are so chronically tired and unfocused that their brains lapse into deep, REM sleeplike states within three or four minutes in tests done at different periods during the day.

For quirky reasons such as these, experimental schools seldom are able to maintain a diversified student population. Most alternative schools must first play up and then live down the mark of being different. At first they have a low ratio of administrators, but in time recruitment necessitates administrative overgrowth and advertising and public relations necessitate cost overruns. Experimental schools begin life *without* a local tradition and alumni, which is an initial advantage but a recruiting and public relations problem thereafter. Experimental schools are founded to implement a new idea about curriculum or instruction that is, by definition, outside the mainstream and often unproven and undeveloped. As a result, they must constantly be engaged in a heavy level of research and development and extraordinary efforts to explain and justify themselves, something they are seldom equipped to do.

Parenthically, something like charter schools happened on a mass scale in the mid-1970s. It was called Experienced-Based Career Education (EBCE). By 1978 it covered over 250 secondary schools in almost every state. It came about through an unlikely marriage of the counterculture movement and massive federal spending. It was commonly held that the spending was insincere and largely prompted by an effort to use the schools to quell revolutionary thinking by institutionalizing it. EBCE fizzled essentially for the reasons noted above and for one other that does not fit the charter school movement; EBCE programs tended to become the place that administrators sent their lowest-performing and most difficult students (Meyer, 1988). Charter schools should do much better in this regard.

TOWARD A QUEST FUSION CURRICULUM

No effort to bring about syntheses of loosely associated parts, such as of content mastery and reading, writing, and thinking processes, is likely to gain strength without some overarching concepts and metaphors to guide thinking into a unifying action plan. With this in mind, the authors have begun to set out some concerns, principles, and practices that we are calling the *quest fusion literacy curriculum*. In concert with its inquiry-based theme, we invite the reader to consider the forming tenets of this curriculum and to join the effort to further refine and specify it as it evolves on our web site into guidelines and practices (although several of the latter have been detailed in previous chapters). One goal is to help teachers to more fully value and use the content area literacy methods that Spor and Schneider (1999) found to be so underutilized. This open-ended approach to learning and creating together is the essence of the "community of learners" approach to education that has been given such great currency and meaning by telecomputing.

Quest Fusion Literacy Curriculum (QFLC): Basic Idea

The QFLC is a cluster of largely content area literacy methods selected to advance curiosity, inquiry, and creative thinking. The curriculum has a strong constructivist orientation, but also seeks to find value in traditional educational goals and practices and to build on these rather than to reject all that came before modern constructivism. To be more precise, it is based on constructive thinking, more so than on the philosophy of constructivism. The goal of collectively constructing a more dynamic curriculum aimed at creative reading, writing, and thinking serves as the quest, or cause beyond oneself, that is so important to supporting durable and sensible changes in current educational practices. This quest literacy curriculum also attempts to address a number of problems and issues in contemporary education. (See Figures 13.4 and Figure 13.5.)

Figure 13.4
Summary of problems, predicaments, and needs addressed by the quest fusion curriculum.

1. Curriculum impediment to creativity: neither art nor science seems to invite innovation in training minds to think creatively. Art tends to treat it as springing from mysticism or the muses; and science as commonly practiced sees it as nearly contradictory: ". . . it is impossible to devise rules [of logic and science] that would enable one to infer new hypotheses from observations" (Longino, 1990, p. 24).

2. School progress can be slowed more than advanced by the demands of a"never-ending stream of new curricular initiatives"(Labbo & Ash, 1998, p. 181) that tend to be played out as competing with traditional theories and practices.

3. There is a need for a cohesive, coherent, and stable body of knowledge and objectives that remain open to new perspectives, but are not easily or overly swayed by every new or revisited challenge and educational fad.

Figure 13.4, *continued*

4. Many sensible school solutions do not achieve a significant level of sustained value because they cannot break through one form or another of political barriers that bias discourse of their efficacy (e.g., the sometimes/someplace excesses of radical multiculturalism, bilingualism, feminism, LD-ism, pop-psychology overemphasis on self-esteem and/or religiosity).

5. Few politically inspired reform themes have addressed the fundamental need to change how teachers teach and how students learn in the classroom. Nonetheless, a revolution has taken place in pedagogy, one that few outside of education are aware of. Educators have shown that they can increase the performance of remedial-level students by four grade levels in twenty days of instruction, and methods based on these cognitive science approaches have resulted in some sixth-graders understanding Newtonian physics as well as do high school students (Bruer, 1993).

6. Our relative ignorance of pedagogical content knowledge has been called "the missing research program." (Bruer, 1993, p. 282, citing Shulman).

7. Schools need to be restructured to better align with human physiology and consequently psychology. They need to be made more conducive to the sprint-and-rest nature of the human attention span and to the circadian rhythms of adolescent sleep needs being reported at several sleep disorder centers—(high school kids need nine hours of sleep per day and cannot be expected to fall asleep much before 11 P.M.).

8. Means must be engineered to expose more students to the "influential teachers" who are able to tap internal motivation that stimulates intellectual curiosity and the desire to solve problems, deal with predicaments, and use clearly formulated teaching methods (Ruddell, 1999).

9. Educators must figure out how to induce more of transformational learning; alternately known as *peak learning experiences* (Bloom, 1981), FLOW (Csikszentmihalyi, 1991), and *manifest curiosity* (Manzo & Sherk, 1978).

10. Schooling must be redesigned so as to gear minds to overcome what sociobiologist E. O. Wilson in his recent book, *Consilience* (1998) notes as the mind's remarkable inability to see the world as an integrated whole, despite our great need to do so.

Figure 13.5

Examples of the methods that combine to form a quest-based fusion and literacy (QFL) curriculum.

A QFL curriculum would be achieved simply by selecting and routinely using content area literacy methods that already fuse reading, writing, thinking, and content mastery to "questing," or inquiry-based learning. Selecting from the methods covered in previous chapters, these might include the following:

+ Question-Only method
+ ReQuest procedure
+ K-W-L plus
+ Enabling Questions
+ Note Cue technique
+ Problem-solving approach to study skills

What others might you add, and to what purpose? See our web site to join the quest for a practical and effective way to build a more seamless, interdisciplinary, and inquiry-based content area literacy curriculum.

QFLC DECLARES FOR DISCOVERY LEARNING AND SYNTHESIS OF FRAGMENTED THEORIES OF TEACHING/LEARNING

In brief, the feeling is that teaching toward attributes such as wonder, curiosity, and constructive thinking-responding are more likely to be sustainable parts of school practices when they are *declared* purposes of education. Achieving this is difficult, perhaps because of the absence of a metaphor or synthesizing construct to guide education out of the room-for-only-one-theme-or-conflict-at-a-time kind of thinking. Strictly speaking, this should not be so difficult. It is not like trying to create a unified theory of macro and quantum (or atomic) physics. It is more like a manageable engineering feat, like Hoover Dam, that simply needs our collective attention and resources. Much of what we need to know to do this is known. It simply is unintegrated, intermittent, and diluted by passing interests, fads, and special-interest groups. The only way to avoid another thirty years of the "reading wars" (between "whole language" and "skills" advocates) is to set integration of theories and parts of educational process as a goal for every graduate of every school of education and every conference on education, everywhere.

To aid in this process, see Appendix B, which summarizes several of the major reform movements in education. More on this in the next chapter, and read more immediately below on the possible value of *questing* and *fusion* as a helpful metaphor for this daunting engineering feat.

The Quest and Fusion Metaphors

To help individual minds and institutions to become more able to address this complex task, two working metaphors are offered. It is the multilevel value in the terms *quest*—which conjures the *wonder* and *invent* part of learning—and *fusion*—a term that speaks to the melding of dissimilar parts into new entities that complement rather than compete. Where this has occurred in the past there often has been a release of energy and spirit that is greater than would be suggested by the simple sum of the parts. Beyond the obvious example of the power released in nuclear fusion is "fusion cooking," or the unique blending of ethnic and American cuisines into dishes that not only fuse styles of cooking, but the art and science of food preparation into dishes that further fuse "haute cuisine" with home cooking. Two concrete examples that most any amateur chef could duplicate, and be inspired by, will help you to see the metaphor. Take old-fashioned (packaged) beef barley soup and add "five-star oriental spices" (available in most grocery stores), and you have a spectacular new flavor that is capturing supporters everywhere it is tried. Another, which is slightly more difficult, starts with a plate of pasta with fresh tomatoes. To this is added a ladle of rich chicken broth and ideally, a link of chicken sausage with apple (your local butcher will not only make it up for you, but you can expect to see him offering it and variations on it in short order), and voila, you have a Sacramento Hilton Hotel treat.

Seeing and knowing about innovations such as these inspires and teaches in ways that transcend our best efforts to teach in conventional ways. As noted in Chapter 8, we tend to disbelieve our capacities to be inventive, and hence do not ask for it in school; but, as you will note in the final chapter, it is increasingly becoming part of life beyond the classroom, where being creative now is ranked as the number-one survival skill in this increasingly entrepreneurial world. See our website for more details and to participate in the further development of the *quest fusion literacy curriculum*, now spanning pre- to high school.

✦   *After Words*   ✦

The final chapter attempts to peer into the future by addressing two contemporary themes that appear to be taking on the force of megatrends. They are interdisciplinarity and entrepreneurism. Both have strong implications for the way content teaching is likely to be conducted and the way we conduct commerce in ideas as well as dollars in the future. These topics also are good examples of literacies that are fusing themselves into education and our collective future.

CHAPTER 14

Multiple Literacies in the Twenty-first Century: Interdisciplinarity, Entrepreneurism, and Other Mooga-Mooga

Let's talk.

✦ Fore Words ✦

Truth be told, this chapter is on the edge. We are not sure where it is going or where it easily fits. New things are like that. We speak more definitively on the topics ahead than we feel about them, in the spirit of the chapter's opening quote, "Let's talk." The intent is to stir interest in, and discussion of some of the newer ideas, knowledge areas, and ways to think that are weaving their way into the American educational psyche. Since there are many possible candidates for "ways to think," the emphasis here is on those that have become movements that are more than passing trends. There are several such *megatrends* that seem to be affecting definitions of what it means to be "literate." Professional educators will need to follow these to be current and able to influence the paths of these behemoths. This chapter focuses on two of these: *interdisciplinary studies* and *entrepreneurism*, particularly e-commerce. To many classroom-oriented educators this preface is already beginning to sound like a foreign language. If this describes you, steel yourself for some ideas and perspectives that at worst could be disorienting, and at best could provide viable and authentic ways to spur effective reading, writing, and thinking. Look also for more on these evolving educational notions: theme study, experiential "authentic" learning, writing-to-learn, and wraparound programming.

MEGATRENDS SWEEPING EDUCATION, LITERACY, AND MAJOR SOCIAL SYSTEMS

Platform shoes for women are a trend. Pets for unmarried adults are a trend. Live plants were once a trend. Home offices, women's rights, telecomputing, free trade, assistance for working parents, these are megatrends. The term *megatrends* is most often ascribed to John Naisbitt's 1982 book of that name.

Megatrends are glacial; they can press, brew, and gurgle for years with intermittent notice. But they just keep coming, slowly and surely, though not always predictably in any given period of time. Which is to say, they can be counterinfluenced by shorter-term events, fads, and lesser trends.

Content area literacy is being influenced by and is influencing several social, societal, and economic trends. The influence of telecomputing as a megatrend is of such great import that it is addressed throughout the text. Here we shall discuss two trends: interdisciplinary studies and entrepreneurism.

Meld to the Methods

Virtually all of the methods described to this point are relevant to interdisciplinary and entrepreneurial studies. To enhance your own reading of this section, assume that the methods previously discussed are "sticky notes," and try to place at least one or two of these alongside each idea and project described in this chapter. Here is a reminder list of some of those methods and instructional practices:

✦ Directed Reading–Thinking Activity

✦ ReQuest, or Reciprocal Questioning, Procedure

✦ Guided Reading Procedure

✦ Writing for a targeted audience

✦ REAP writing

✦ Listen-Read-Discuss heuristic

✦ K-W-L Plus

✦ Group reading activity

✦ Graphic organizers

✦ Critical reading for suasive techniques

✦ Creative-constructive reading-writing-thinking

There is a great deal of redundancy in this chapter. It is intended to achieve the powerful effects of several easily overlooked methods for aiding effective reading in the content areas. Their names describe their functions: *reading before reading, advance ideational organizers,* and *repeated readings.*

THE REAWAKENING OF INTERDISCIPLINARITY AND THEME STUDY: BACK TO THE FUTURE

It is a strange new coinage, sounding almost like a spoof, but for the moment, *interdisciplinarity* is the label of choice for a long-in-coming movement that spans the grades from kindergarten to graduate school. It represents a reawakening to the problem of overspecialization and the benefits of cross-disciplinary teaching and learning. The movement could be likened to an earnest attempt to resurrect the "renaissance man," now "renaissance person": a supraliterate who knew almost all of what there was to know. Of course, this romantic notion would be impossible today, but the essential elements remain the same: one who has a depth of knowledge in some micro-area; a sound conceptual grasp of the fundamental ideas and challenges facing humankind; a lifelong-learning outlook; and an inclination to be artistically sensitive and poetically inclined. This may seem a tall order at a time when most of us would be satisfied to simply guarantee literacy to all who attend school and stem the coarsening of society. However, *interdisciplinarity*, now a topic itself, is a *process* goal that serves education and society well.

Themes Serve as Catalysts to Mental Traffic

Interdisciplinarity essentially is about reconnecting that which has been artificially disconnected. Interdisciplinary curriculum themes and designs are reported to have wide-ranging effects, including improved student attitudes toward learning and school, heightened interest in extracurricular activities and hobbies, improved teacher collegiality, as well as measurable, sometimes spectacular improvements in quantity and quality of learning outcomes (Gilbert, 1989; Manzo, Manzo, & Riley, 1996). While there is no single format for an *interdisciplinary* curriculum, most versions share a few basic elements. The organizing framework is a series of theme-based or concept-based units that serve as catalysts for this otherwise slow-to-develop integrative reaction. Within each unit, activities are designed to engage students, or bring mental traffic to exploring real-life problems and projects. A curriculum that involves several disciplines but does not use themes and/or problem-centered heuristics or mental traffic builders is strictly referred to as *cross-disciplinary* or *multidisciplinary*. These also are worthwhile, but they do not tend to contain that active ingredient of "authentic" or more correctly "evocative" contexts and connectivity that tend to spark curiosity and deep conceptual learning. Importantly, interdisciplinary begets cross-disciplinary and single-disciplinary study, but the inverse does not tend to true.

Interdisciplinary curriculum planning and teaching become largely a matter of posing questions and challenges that encourage student learning. Hence, the central aim of this interdisciplinary model is to bring together the discipline perspectives and focus them on the investigation of a target theme, issue, or problem (Jacobs, 1989). Typically, these include both text-based and hands-on activities for both individual and group efforts. Such activities create their own force field. They take on the influential properties of what is being called *situated cognition* (Kirshner & Whitson, 1997). They become part of the learners' community, environment, and experience. These are powerful and durable forces because they are vested in concepts and ideas that are not as easily forgotten as are facts or data points: exploration of seemingly simple notions, such as that of *civil* war or a nation at war against itself, results in more meaningful learning, thinking, and conceptualizing than the thorough memorization of the names and outcomes of generals and battles; remembering dates, by the way, can be more worthwhile since these help to anchor concepts of time, place, and circumstances.

Why Theme Study Works, But Also Requires Work and Collaboration

The power of theme study probably rests on the fact that it tends to connect informational dots into more vivid images. Theme study takes on more of the character of real-life experience. It is more toothy and tangible. But, it does require extra effort and collaboration to plan and conduct.

Consider a unit on the American Civil War taught in the conventional way. It would contain a textbook, some lecture material, discussion, note taking and test questions, followed by rapid forgetting as the likes of Gettysburg, Fort Sumpter, and Vicksburg begin to meld into one confusing swirl of words that before year's end become further confused with battles, names, and events surrounding the Revolutionary War. Now consider that same unit organized and engaged as a theme. It would invite collaboration with other subject teachers and resource people. It would take on something of a distinguishable life of its own. The English teacher could cover related fiction like *Red Badge of Courage* while the science teacher deals with several of the technological breakthroughs that had impact on the war, such as iron-clad ships and rapid-fire weapons. A team of students and teachers could brainstorm other complementary activities. These might include:

+ Visits to local historical sites

+ Review of the cable guide for related film and documentaries

+ Contacting related community interest groups, libraries, colleges, and museums for artifacts, visiting experts, and bibliographies

+ Selection of some appropriate films for a mini–film festival, from *Roots* to *Young Abe Lincoln*, with each shown in different classroom theaters with a brief libretto and postviewing discussion questions prepared by teachers and/or students

+ REAP-like annotations and interactions on relevant fiction and non-fiction

+ Speculative discussions and essays on how the war might have ended differently if say the South had been more fully industrialized

+ Some new-fashioned webquests focused on myriad topics that could further color in the life and times of the Civil War, and on stories or situations that would deepen comprehension of the concept of civil wars, such as are unfolding in Africa and Eastern Europe

In short, the topic of the Civil War becomes converted into a theme. The theme, with some imaginative planning, can become the frontload for more empowered reading, viewing, writing, and potentially playacting, possibly with a review of the lyrics and music of that time. To further personalize and individualize the theme, students could be encouraged or required to keep a journal of what they did, saw, and investigated. And, yes, it is okay to give a unit test over the concepts that are central to the different subject area curricula. This typical fun killer could be a rewarding moment itself as students would have a much richer background of knowledge and preparation than they may have experienced ever before for a unit test.

Realistically, a teacher or team should try to plan and conduct not more than two or three *new* interdisciplinary units of this magnitude per year. Even at this rate, within a few years, cooperating teachers can build an impressive portfolio of engaging theme units that may even have students looking forward to a class or topic of study.

Generative Topics and Themes

Finding a generative topic or theme is something of a quest in itself. We do not yet understand the subtle dynamics of this form of learning well enough to easily generalize and define what will be evocative and what will not. However, it is not difficult to note when one has been identified; a tremendous energy of interest and thought is released. Recall the story in Chapter 8 where Mary Salibrici (1999) describes how her students reacted to a unit of reading, writing, and discussion on the Rosenberg trial of the early 1950s. Again, that which started as a topical unit in literature soon became almost indistinguishable from a unit in social studies on the mass psychology of fear.

Supporters of direct instruction also tend to emphasize the importance of concept- and theme-centered curricula. Klausmeier, for example, cites the findings of several researchers to illustrate the "powerful effects of focused concept instruction, preschool through college" (1992). These citations include Nelson's (1976) finding that sixteen minutes of one-on-one instruction on the concept "equilateral triangle" enabled three-year-olds to progress beyond the level of their five-year-old controls. Manzo, Manzo, and Riley (1996) investigated the proposition that at-risk students would benefit from theme-based, interdisciplinary units connecting science, social studies, and language arts to their daily lives. These students significantly outscored their peers in a control group receiving a traditional curriculum.

Ula Manzo's trial-and-error experience with her undergraduate students in teacher education supports the generative value of concepts as the centering strand for interdisciplinary units. Preservice teachers working in groups to create interdisciplinary theme units typically struggled to even understand the assignment until they worked their way from flat topics to richer concept themes. Once they had made this conversion, as in the examples given below, creative lesson ideas seemed to emerge almost effortlessly.

A concept theme should start with an idea that is of genuine interest to most kids at a particular age-grade level. It is best stated as a question or a few related questions. Theme activities are designed to challenge students to use what they are learning in specific subjects to solve real problems or create products. Beginning with popular *topic themes* ("oceans," "regions," etc.), preservice teachers have transformed these into *concept themes* as follows:

✦ Oceans—is there treasure under the sea?

> *From sunken ships to edible kelp to drinking water for arid regions—the concept theme includes recognizing value in unexpected places.*

✦ Regions—what do kids in other places do for fun?

> *Most kids think they have nothing to do—what do kids in other parts of the country do? How is it related to the climate and regional characteristics? Use pen-pal connections here—travel brochures.*

✦ Community—what can one person do?

> *What real problems exist in our own community? What would it take to solve them? Are there problems that aren't being recognized or addressed? Kids might work in groups to explore different community functions—postal delivery, library services, street maintenance, and so on.*

✦ Space—what do we really need?

> *Starting with the virtual vacuum of outer space, what would it take for a human to survive there? How much air/water/ etc. do we have to have? How could these be produced/stored? What else do we need (recreation/privacy/etc.)? If you were going to spend six months in a space capsule, and could take anything you wanted that would fit in a conventional foot locker and weigh no more than 50 pounds, what would you take?*

Here are some other themes that we have not tried yet, but which seem to hold promise:

✦ *Internet*—how is it affecting learning, wealth, sense of community, and other viewing and entertainment habits?

✦ *Computer imaging*—or the parallels between the way computers work and minds seem to operate, and the way it is affecting language, allusions, and thought (e.g., *fund of knowledge* being referred to as "bandwidth," *temperament* as "machine language,"and *input*, which now is synonymous with "participation").

✦ *The new economy*—or the circumstances that are making it possible for startup companies like eBay and Amazon.com to challenge established giants like Sotheby's auction house (with whom they have now joined) and 110-year-old Barnes and Noble book vendors.

A bulletin board and/or a classroom web site can be used to display the ideas generated in interdisciplinary explorations. The homepage can also be used to welcome outside comments and related stories from interested others.

Interdisciplinarity Reduces Divisiveness and Increases Collaborations

The growing popularity of this more holistic approach to organizing instruction is likely due to the fact that it has support from the indirect, literature-based or whole-language and constructivist communities, as well as from behavioral psychology and cognitive science. The message of behavioral psychology simply is: get people doing something and it becomes part of their repertoire of things they can and will do. The message of cognitive science essentially is to support traditional subjects, although with a form of direct instruction that builds underlying cognitive processes. It relies in great measure on mental modeling, or cognitive apprenticeships. All proponents, however, seem to agree that the key to cognitive enrichment is a certain amount of interdisciplinary planning with an emphasis on authentic contexts for learning and doing. The whole-language/constructivist group tends to see this happening rather exclusively through literature-study. All agree on the need to flexibly introduce information and ideas as the need arises:

> When literacy skills are developed in an integrated fashion, through themed units and literacy activities serving a realistic function, then children see purposes and reasons for becoming literate. Conversely, if we teach literacy skills that do not reflect real-life experiences and that lack interesting content, children perceive no usefulness in the skills. (Strickland & Morrow, 1990, p. 604)

Whole-language enthusiasts, cognitive scientists, and constructivists all view interdisciplinary curriculum designs as a means of providing instruction that is better aligned with the way we typically think and learn, that is, in response to perceived problems and incongruities, more so than to traditional subject-oriented models. Traditional school subjects tend to impose artificial boundaries on thought, and a narrow vertical incline of information and concepts to master. Often the only reason for studying the next topic in a conventional curriculum is its organizational, but not necessarily conceptual, link to a topic or problem. Ironically, things that are categorically alike, such as the reasons for the first and second world wars, are more likely to be confused as time passes, than are facts that are embedded in a sensible context or story. However, schooling, as distinct from education in the abstract, has certain management needs. It must see to the orderly education of 58 million children and $2\frac{1}{2}$ million of their teachers, many of whom are changing schools on a daily basis. In any case, the addition of these school-based realities with cognitive science, and instructional methods such as are detailed in previous chapters, are together creating a new alignment of motivational topics, conceptual themes, management systems, and instructional practices. The results of this better alignment can be remarkable. A well-known constructivist educator, Joseph Bruer, noted that "teaching methods based on this [cognitive science] research . . . are the educational equivalents of polio vaccine and penicillin" (Bruer, 1993, p. 2).

The Effect of the Internet on Interdisciplinarity

Some informed observers are beginning to believe that the Internet is so good at getting people of like minds together that it maybe acting to further narrow discourse and thinking. We respectfully disagree. We believe that the Internet does underscore the human tendency to gravitate toward our perceived best interests and fellow-believers. However, it also puts information in front of our eyes quickly that we otherwise would have to go out of our way to look up, access, and read. What is more, it quickly creates new categories of thought where there previously were few or none. To that extent, it is a mind tool. To test this proposition, cast your nets now and again for interdisciplinary studies/interdisciplinarity, and watch the growth in this rather obscure topic.

Project Alexandria.com

At this writing, Wired_College.com, in conjunction with the authors is assembling teams of scholars from colleges and universities across the nation to distill and publish on a single web site almost everything an educated person might reasonably be expected to know in the major subject categories and in laymen's terms. This effort is a further attempt to distinguish: what is essential knowledge; what the questions or quests are around which vast bodies of knowledge are organized; and, to establish some common frames of reference for real interdisciplinary dialogues. (See the box Site Seeing 1.)

Site Seeing 1

Browse these sites to get an idea of the breadth and depth of the resource now easily accessible via the Internet.

Dragonfly Project
http://www.muohio.edu/dragonfly

Gender Academy's Theme-Related Resources
http://www.stemnet.nf.ca/CITE/themes.html

Kathy Schrock's Guide for Educators
http://www.capecod.net/schrockguide

Integrating the Internet into K-12 Classrooms
http://www.indirect.com/www/dhixson/index.html

The Gateway
http://www.thegateway.org

Blue Web'n Library
http://www.kn.pacbell.com/wired/bluewebn

FURTHER MOOGA-MOOGA: PREFACE TO BUSINESS AND ENTREPRENEURISM

SES—Socioeconomic Status

Much of the research in education, sociology, and psychology, and a great deal of the public policy of the nation, is based on and interpreted in terms of high and low SES of the "subjects." Nonetheless, relatively little that is done in schools is designed to directly influence SES. Of course, in an indirect way, the efforts of educators to raise literacy levels can and do make a difference. Now, however, change is in the air as we redefine *multiple literacies* to mean "knowledge, experience, and orientation" as well as mere conversance, or shallow, passive reading and understanding. There are issues that will make this transformation something of an uphill battle. Content area literacy, by its nature, will play a role.

Maybe It's a Brain Thing

A popular humor columnist recently wrote despairingly of his "English-major brain," to which every other word spoken by businesspeople sounds like so much "Mooga, mooga." (Dave Barry, *Kansas City Star*, December 27, 1998, "How to Get Rich? Mooga Mooga"). It is true that English majors, as a group, score quite low on "pragmatism" scales on psychological tests, (though high on empathy and compassion) and tend toward a life of the mind. And, apparently, they are not alone. In a study by the authors on over a hundred possible characteristics of mature proficient readers, entrepreneurism did not emerge as a trait or strand in *any* of the subgroups identified (Manzo, Manzo, Barnhill, & Thomas, in press). If sixteen-plus years of conventional schooling does not result in some entrepreneurial orientation in some of our highest achievers, it would seem to follow that we probably need to do a better job of addressing this option in the nation's schools. One source of information on this new dimension to education is the Kauffman Center for Entrepreneurial Leadership (www.emkf.org)

Demands of the "New Economy"

Don't nod off now, but the capitalist or free market system under which we live and the global economy operates will require most youngsters now in school to deal with:

✦ Complex concepts about money management

✦ Job dislocation, reinvention, and downsizing

✦ Employment tending to be project based, with continuation determined by the worker's ability to define the next project

✦ Planning and customizing their own retirement package

✦ Lifetime schooling-learning

✦ Being pressed into becoming more entrepreneurial

Entrepreneurial Means . . .

Entrepreneurial generally refers to someone committed to growth more than maintenance, someone who takes risks, someone who is enterprising. In a manner of speaking everyone is entrepreneurial; however, we are referring to those who intentionally assume more risk than their resources strictly allow. Many of us are moving in this direction with great doubt and uncertainty. And, if there is one thing most of us, and ironically the financial markets, cannot tolerate, it is uncertainty.

Pressed Into Business

The fundamental reason that many people will be pressed into this kind of entrepreneurial stance is simple enough: few firms hire for the long term any longer. This makes more and more of us contract workers or minibusinesses unto ourselves, and with reading and learning and paper rituals and related demands equal to most small businesses.

Pressed Into Teaching About Business: Entrepreneurial versus Economics Education

Accordingly, youngsters need better preparation to read, write, and think adroitly about the executive-level decisions they will be making about their personal energies and resources for the rest of their lives. Since the better part of what humans are inclined to learn is dispositional and situational, preparation for such pressured decision-making is largely a matter of orientation and experience. The problem is the lack of such orientation in the schools. The closest most schools tend to get to these real-life conundrums is a unit somewhere on "careers" and "economics education." Not that this is unimportant—in fact, it is being called the "next frontier in the civil rights movement" by the Rev. Joseph E. Washington, chief executive of the Organization for a New Equality. But, programs to teach personal credit, property insurance, and home ownership are *economic literacy*, not *entrepreneurial literacy*. However, this difference may not be evident, since most of us who are or are becoming teachers tend to have a great work ethic, but not much of a business orientation. Hence, we do not use business terms and analogies and we are not particularly empathetic or in-tune with the high-risk mental outlook that significantly changes SES for families and generations.

This Could Be Tough

As teachers, then, we will need to stretch a bit to encourage language and reading, and hence thought, related to finance, investing, and business startup. In order to add a "business orientation" to our agenda and options, it first will require that schools and teachers acknowledge that we have not done a terrific job with this growing life obligation to date. This is changing, but as recently as the 1990 edition of this book we were firmly discouraged by reviewers and editors from including a three-paragraph piece on a great financial opportunity granted teachers by the tax code, or 403b deferred income plan. With no stock options or bonuses, this plan is an important part of a teacher's career, income planning, and peace of mind. In a related vein, there are solid opportunities for career teachers as corporate trainers. Investment in company-based education programs is up sharply in recent years. In fact, trainers of electronic and computer retail store employees earn, on average, more than teachers at the top of most public school pay scales. (For more information, see the web site of the American Society for Trainers and Development.)

Financial Literacy

To get *business think* going for you and your pupils, and possibly in meeting your own life obligations, begin by inviting REAP-like annotative responses to brief business articles, investment guidelines, and ideas for small business startups. Discuss and reference the "capital markets" (stocks, bonds, futures). Reference to and use of such new terms can be worked into most any discipline. Business-vocational-life requires many proficiencies and subject competencies; for example, a claims adjuster needs math and writing; a physical therapist needs science, math, physical education, and proficient writing; and teachers need to know something about almost everything, no matter what their subject specialty or orientation. So let's get mooga-mooga-literate ourselves, and then try to share the enthusiasm for this new quest with the youngsters in our charge.

Open Your Own Mooga Learning Lab

To achieve maximum professional advantage from your efforts to develop a *business orientation*, begin a journal and keep account of your plans, trials, and journey to financial literacy. In this way, you will have constructed a personal laboratory for imparting knowledge and orientation to read, write, and think in a personally new direction to reluctant reader-learners.

Make a plan, beginning right now, for how you will immerse and instruct yourself:

✦ Reorient yourself to perceive as well as to merely see what is happening about you that is financial and entrepreneurial.

✦ Read and write about things financial. (See Figure 14.1 as a sample reading written just for educators.)

✦ Learn the new vocabulary and idioms of business.

✦ Acquire basic *businessspeak* knowledge.

✦ Get yourself to "love and appreciate" financial reading (or are you having second thoughts about the merits of "loving to read"?).

✦ Build *oracy*, or oral language conversance, with finance and business.

✦ Gain experiences for yourself by joining discourse and chat groups that will keep learning fresh, situationally supported, and ongoing.

In attempting to address these objectives, think about the utility of what you have learned thus far in this text about promoting content area literacy. Which methods do you feel would be most useful in a conventional class on business and finance? Compare your choices with your classmates'. Gather your courage and resolve before you begin this venture. It will be a sobering experience, and no one really likes sobering experiences, no matter how good for you they are supposed to be.

Figure 14.1
On a teacher's pay.

As part of the complex tapestry of modern life, teachers need to plan for how to meet their rudimentary financial needs. This is complicated by several factors: the huge financial demand of your continuing education; the decrease in job security due to elimination of tenure; our modest salaries; and the absence of opportunities for bonuses, stock options, and ownership that are common in the private sector. Further, there are these external macrofactors: home purchases no longer can be expected to accrue greatly in value; and the aging of the population is adding greatly to the burden on Social Security and other retirement systems.

However, there is a way to keep pace and perhaps even establish some financial security. It is through supplementary retirement savings plans, technically known as 403b's and 401k's. Basically, these are special-opportunity IRAs—or deferred-income plans that allow teachers and some government workers to save up to about $9,800 of an annual salary in a program managed by designated insurance and mutual fund companies.

Talk to your business or personnel office about this option. It is one that shouldn't be overlooked. Basically, it will permit you to save between $25 and $800 dollars per month in a plan that invests it as "before-tax" income. In other words, each such investment automatically gains from 15 to 40% in value for the period it is invested, depending upon your federal and state tax bracket at the time it is invested. Some companies even will permit you to borrow against this retirement money at a reduced interest rate for further schooling for you or your children, and for a first-home purchase.

Don't overlook this opportunity to build a personally secure future. In so doing, you will be building respect for one of the less well known benefits in being a professional teacher. Now go find out how a Roth IRA works and whether this isn't best for you. But, be smart and don't delay starting payroll deduction for either your 403b or 401k immediately. Given prior rates of return, this is a much wiser investment policy than paying off a conventional mortgage. By the way, if you operate a small business on the side or during vacation periods, whether it be writing, tutoring, or house painting, you're entitled to certain tax advantages and another form of deferred savings called a *money purchase pension plan.*

Minding Your Own Business: The Age of Entrepreneurism

One of the more valuable and exciting ways to build interdisciplinarity is to ride America's, for that matter the globe's, new enthusiasm for the "entrepreneurial spirit." This modern-life theme is a combination of business, economics, civics, English, and nearly every other conceivable subject. The blunt remark of one teacher, "What does *entrepreneurism* have to do with education?" says loudly that some teachers are not yet enthusiastic about it. This may be because they do not yet understand that entrepreneurism is more than a money game, it is a resources game and a play for greater freedom and the opportunity to be influential. But yes, it is about money too, and how to get and help others to get what it can buy. At an anecdotal level, here is a brief account of how "conversions to opportunity" can cascade, especially in some communities where the need is greatest.

Conversions to Opportunity Can Cascade

Back in the early 1970s some of us at the University of Missouri–Kansas City, an urban campus, ran a small, volunteer program to help more individuals on the janitorial staff to become literate. We were told that about 30% could not read and write well enough to keep their jobs. The five individuals who came to our evening sessions regularly were well rewarded. Before long we began to talk about how to step up their careers and fell on the idea that they should learn more about how bids to clean the campus were submitted. It turned out that there were no bids; the janitorial staff were all employees. However, from this elementary query, a quest began. Through a brother-in-law in Terre Haute, the two then-janitors became involved with a bid opportunity on three small locations in that city. The other three janitors, who now were part of the group, agreed to work for less than standard wages in exchange for help with relocating and a small share in the new company. We helped them to assemble and submit that bid, and put them in touch with an empathetic woman in the Small Business Administration—a quasi-federal program to help fund and guide new programs. They easily won a six-month cleaning contract. Our then-secretary, an outspoken African-American woman who knew these men well, was converted to the possibilities. It took nearly three years, but she ultimately set up her own clerical help agency, and with no help from us. Who knows how many lives and aspirants she has reached. Of course, there were several other factors and media images that came into play at that time, such as television's characterization of the feisty George Jefferson who, "moved on up" from an hourly wage earner to become owner-operator of several dry cleaning shops. Disappointingly, the *Los Angeles Times* (May 1999) reports that not one of the twenty-six new shows to debut in fall, 1999, contains a single African-American or any other minority group member in a major role. This is the downside of a "free market" society, which is why we do not see entrepreneurism and an unfettered market as being quite the same thing, and why we must keep alive the more charitable ideas that drive social entrepreneurial thinking.

Social Entrepreneurs and Social Capital

There can be a good deal of *social capital* or personal goodwill and public image that is put at risk in a *social entrepreneurial* effort or cause. There is no single meaning for *social entrepreneurship*. Most often it means using market-based approaches to bring answers to social needs. However, it also can more broadly mean almost any effort where a mission-related impact, rather than money, is the major criterion of success. Social entrepreneurship can mean one-on-one help, but generally it refers to efforts to bring about systemic changes for sustainable improvements. In general, the term *social entrepreneur* is another name for a constructive, adventuresome spirit.

For example, Jay Leno and his wife, Mavis, are risking a great deal of social capital or personal goodwill and possible public reversal in supporting women's rights in foreign lands. They risk the accusation of this being a too-easy and hollow Hollywood cause. Social capital is everything and anything one might give, such as time, energy, public support, expertise, and money, toward some greater good. *Entrepreneur* magazine (April 1999) tells a familiar story of Mark Kushner, who gave up an unsatisfying career as a lawyer and a San Francisco penthouse to open a charter high school for the needy in this otherwise-affluent city. *Reader's Digest* (April 1999) carried several similar stories. One told of a young woman, Heather Metzger, whose father crashed his midlife-crisis motorcycle while drunk. With uncommon courage, Heather began her own battle against alcohol, first speaking to a local high school, and then starting an organization that she operates while still a student at the University of Maryland. The group, "Drug-Free Me," uses volunteers to stuff statistics on drunk driving accidents into the tuxedos of promgoers. Then there is the story of thirty-four-year-old Ann Gusiff, who read about a Chicago-based clothes recycling program in *Working Woman* magazine and founded "Clothes The Deal," an organization that helps needy people to get proper clothing to wear to job interviews. There also are frequent stories on the evening news of superstars, particularly African-American athletes, who negotiate their contracts so as to include funding to a private foundation devoted to a humanitarian cause. The greatest contemporary use of social capital still paying huge dividends toward some greater good probably is John F. Kennedy's use of the presidency as a "bully Pulpit" to create the still-continuing Peace Corps. Somewhat more recently, former President George Bush envisioned an America with a rising interest in volunteerism—"a thousand points of light," is how he characterized it. Well, it is here. Several polls are showing that nearly 40% of the adult population is involved with some form of giving of their personal time and labors. President Bush can rightly claim having set this expansive spirit in motion, but other social dynamics and the institutionalization of charitable works in the nation's schools has helped to propel it. The chief dynamics probably can be traced to the aging of America, and with that, a renewed interest in community, family, and stability. To paraphrase an elderly women friend, "Americans are growing more mature. I can tell by the way they've stopped making fun of my thirty-seven-year-old book club and now are even forming their own," and in record-bending numbers, Margaret (see Figure 14.2).

Figure 14.2
The book club phenomenon: Fighting isolation.

Book discussion clubs are springing up all over America. Once there were several women's associations dedicated to this purpose. The most successful was the Delphi Society, which once had over two million members and hundreds of chapters all over small-town America (*Delphi Society Manual,* 1912). The success of the women's suffrage movement in gaining the vote, and the competing effects of a depression and two world wars seems to have extinguished the compelling need for the Delphi Society. The new movement is different in any case. It still is largely a women's movement, but there is no driving association, or large-scale, communal membership group. It is local, personal, and without a super-sponsor or a mountain of related web sites. It could be called an extraordinary level of social entrepreneurism.

Oprah Winfrey has given book discussion great currency with her afternoon talk show, but the movement predates this media connection. Another recent impetus has been the popular book, *The Mother-Daughter Book Club* (Harper Perennial, 1997), by Shireen Dodson, assistant director of the Center for African American History and Culture at the Smithsonian Institution.

This phenomenon seems to be grounded in some very basic needs of women, and especially women with young and adolescent children. Where the group has younger members, it is serving as a way for youngsters and mothers to talk about complex human emotions and conflicts through the thin veil of story and largely fictional characters. Where it is adults only, it is a way for diverse people, who happen to be neighbors, to connect and reconnect to those who they would not see in the conventional places, like church, school PTAs, and once-interruptive coffee klatsches.

For more information on forming such a club, although few seem to need it, write a letter (now there's a quaint old custom) to: the Association of Book Group Readers and Leaders (ABGRL, P.O. Box 885, Highland Park, IL 60035). They probably will have a web site by the time we go to press.

Enlightened Self-Interest

With charity there is no need that the donor be altruistic. Giving intrinsically gratifies and generally "ups" the social approval of the giver. For that reason, it probably is more correct to think of social entrepreneurial efforts as "enlightened self-interest," as John Locke referred to this healthy state of mind.

At a deep human level, the motivation for social entrepreneurism probably can be found in the fact that we still haven't evolved away from needing one another (Suarez, 1999). It was response to our need to feel connected that earlier agrarian America created civic groups such as the PTA, NAACP,

Rotary, Lions, and Scouts (Diuguid, 1999). The social trauma of moving from the farms to the cities, where at least there were neighborhoods, is only slightly less than the isolation created in suburbs that often are not even connected by sidewalks. People are depressed in record numbers while our individual wealth reaches record levels. The social entrepreneur is one who realizes that the effort to redistribute wealth or even to grow "the pie" is only a part of meeting human needs. The other part is to spread and personally enjoy that feeling of affiliation captured in the sitcom *Cheers*, the place "where everybody knows your name, and you're always glad you came."

"We need to be as creative now as we were then," is the way Robert Putnam, professor at Harvard's Kennedy School of Government, put the charge to social entrepreneurs (as quoted in Diuguid, 1999). Accordingly, many social entrepreneurs are finding value in telecomputing for re-connecting people in ways that are personally rewarding and socially uplifting, despite its criticisms for being a source of social isolation.

A prime example of enlightened self-interest is the *value network* called ThinkQuest (http://www.thinkquest.org/tatt/app99.html). This quasi-commercial operation encourages educators to form teams to develop materials and project ideas for use on the Internet. They then provide assistance and cash awards for the best ideas and projects developed over a fixed period of time. In this way, everyone contributes and everyone wins.

For a more socially uplifting and educationally grounded example of social capital and social entrepreneurism in progress, consider the Opportunity Network (Manzo, Manzo, Lang & Barnhill, 1996) detailed in Figure 14.9. In this web-based, social entrepreneurial proposal, the writers and their associates essentially are using their leverage as educators and writers to encourage others to give of their time and money to a project that advances social, educational, and humanitarian objectives in a personally connective and systemic way. In this case, the project is designed to match needy youngsters with well-off baby-boomers in ways that bring essential financial assistance to those in need, while satisfying a personal need in this age group, most known for generous and humanitarian ideals. (See Figure 14.3 for a summary of *social/educational entrepreneurial projects* that the authors and their associates, such as Matt Thomas and Amy Barnhill, are adventuring on the leveraging capability of the web.)

A Legacy Opportunity

The free land offered west of Oklahoma to homesteaders opened the western half of the U.S. continent to a period of spectacular opportunities and developments that continue to unfold to this day. The opening of the cyberspace around the globe to *homepaging* is a legacy opportunity of far greater proportions. It is not restricted to a fixed parcel of acreage, but crisscrosses international boundaries without equivocation or passport

Figure 14.3
Summary of authors' and associates' social/educational entrepreneurial
adventures on the web.

+ REAP—reader annotation and exchange networks designed to assist
  readers to higher levels of analysis of text and ideas (K–16) (http://
  members.aol.com/ReadShop/REAP1.html)

+ LiteracyExpress—free information on literacy programming and methods
  for teachers and interested others (http;//members.aol.com/readshop/
  LiteracyExpress.html)

+ Volunteers for Higher-Order Literacy—a confederation of "digital tutors"
  designed to assist teachers in reading and reacting to pupils' attempts
  to write

+ Opportunity Network—a social system proposal to voluntarily redistribute
  wealth to those without the hidden support of the middle class (details
  later in the chapter)

+ Fertile Minds Society—a webtrap for creative minds, so that we might
  be able to continue to study and learn from them

+ Pedagogy for Professors—free tips for professors with noneducation
  backgrounds on teaching at the college level (http;//members.aol.com/
  ReadShop/pedagogy.html)

+ Registry for Better Ideas—a system designed to provide voluntary financial incentives and acknowledgment for creative problem solving, especially of social and procedural issues that are not rewarded by royalties
  or conventional product sales (details in Chapter 9; http://members.aol.
  com/csholumkc/RBI.html)

+ Virtual Center for the Study of Educational Entrepreneurism—an information and discussion site for educators and interested others on the various
  projects, stories, thinking, and experiments in social, economic, and
  educational enterprises (tentatively to be called Responsible College &
  University Entrepreneurship, or RES-Cue.org).

---

restrictions. Further, its development and impact already are at web speed;
for those who are wired and aware, the future is not coming; it is now.

"Commercialization" of Colleges

The story of what has happened and is happening to postsecondary institutions may be a forecast of what is coming to the nation's elementary and
secondary schools. We shall advocate here for limited development of
commercial interests, but not for complete commercialization, especially
where this may jeopardize a nonprofit institution's integrity and basic
mission. Nonetheless, progress is likely to be anything but smooth as
events now in progress continue to unfold.

Peter Drucker (1989), an eminent social scientist and business watcher, has observed that colleges and universities are born of entrepreneurs and are themselves inherently entrepreneurial. By this he means that capitalist money has funded the creation and support of higher education, and the business of idea making and influencing thinking is driven by its own kind of publish-or-perish free market. Nonetheless, what we are seeing today is an unparalleled spread of sector commercialization within the collegiate enterprise. Michael Milkin, of "junk bond" infamy, has announced his involvement in the creation of a "virtual graduate school" that will offer postgraduate education to people in business over the Internet, and in collaboration with several of the major institutions in America. This development also speaks to another trend that is having businesses become more like universities. They are not merely contracting for and doing extensive training, but they have research and development, or viable new idea needs that have them in a push-ahead-or-perish situation as well. The *new economy* is based essentially on ideas that take advantage of the added tools that cyberspace brings to problem solving. There is an alternate world of possibilities for the imaginative mind to draw from. The timing for the colleges and universities could not be better.

State colleges that once received about 75% of their costs for operating from government now receive less than 20%. College tuition has risen much faster than inflation and much, much faster than personal income for the last two decades. Established colleges have been in the business of commercialization for centuries. Much of the world's technical progress stems from partnerships of business and research universities. However, the sale of "business seminars," the contracts to operate public schools, and the issuing of credit cards bearing college logos is new and not without its sticky issues and concerned critics. Even the seemingly innocuous move of professional schools into the operation of hospitals, dental and reading clinics, and a variety of mental health and social services can be problematic. Some of the more obvious issues involve the following:

+ The clash of cultures and the repackaging of mission statements
+ The equitable distribution of new revenue
+ The redefining of professorial roles
+ The fact that collegiate-based businesses may unfairly compete with conventional enterprises
+ The reconciling of low-monetary-reward research with higher-profit-potential research and "contract grants"
+ The reduced will to be objective about ideas in which there is a vested interest
+ The mixed value of treating students too much like customers (who therefore are "always right" because they are sources of revenue)

✦ The likely impact on the current dynamics; some will have their social and professional stock rise and others will feel as if theirs has fallen; a recipe for strained relations

✦ The inevitable miscues and errors in judgment that will follow as public institutions sort out distinctions, such as between "offerings" that are a legitimate part of business-related income and institutional sponsorships and endorsements, which may be over the top and even misrepresentations

These issues are not new and not without workable (though not ideal) resolves. Professors in schools of business are encouraged to be in business. Coaches run teams with an eye toward possible profitability, although few are profitable. College bookstores, soon to face stiff competition from Internet textbook vendors, have been charging students list price for books for three generations. Federal grants have been a source of revenue for an equally long time, despite the fact that they rarely have been instrumental in producing innovations. In the book, *The Cathedral Within*, Bill Shore (1999) describes dozens of charitable organizations that are engaging in a wide variety of enterprises designed to raise business-related income. In other words, this ship has left the port; the questions remaining are of more of a "how" and "where" than a "should we" nature.

Colleges Can Lead Economic Literacy and the Resourcing of Education

The next step for profit sharing of advertising and direct marketing dollars on the Internet will go to nonprofit homepage locations and individual Internet users. Colleges, and soon school districts, will have more than two-thirds of the activity on the web. Students and teachers simply have the best and most unchanging reasons for communicating in print. This financial force needs only to be aggregated and represented to advertisers so that school web sites carry these revenue-rich possibilities.

FrameCast Communications (a company with which the writers are affiliated), for example, operates the WiredCollege.Com that is bringing advertisers and marketers to collegiate sites with an unobtrusive frame that can go around one to four sides of a homepage, but most often is a linked, click away. Through it, colleges can instantly add a commercial stream income, at no cost or delay to school leadership and administration. Cybergold offers on-line payments of several dollars per click to people who sign up with the site and make purchases at the dozen-or-so participating merchants. Another group of companies, first founded by Stanford University scientists, is planning to offer e-mail that pays the user. They plan to send you a monthly check for the number of times that you or those you get to sign on permit yourselves to see ads placed on the screen. This innovation of "permission marketing" (Godin, 1999) was prompted by the fact that eyes have value to advertisers. Another innovation strikes down one of the Internet's chief means of generating income, namely (annoying) banner ads. New software, costing about twenty dollars, will eliminate most banner ads from your personal computer. In other words, advertising and marketing is being democratized, and made voluntary. The financial drought in education could be over. Children can help finance their own education simply by allowing them to see ads for which they personally or their schools gain accounting credit. They will see these ads in any case as soon as they click on to the currently commercialized web.

The New Economy Creates Entrepreneurs

The new economy is not only about telecomputing and information. It also is being influenced by certain other global trends.

The current trend to drop trade restrictions (tariffs) not only reduces prices on products and their flow across international borders, it also creates competition for the cheapest places to manufacture those products, and hence for lower labor costs. This means that Chu, Juan, and Mohsen are standing with equal strength alongside their American labor counterparts on every assembly contract that Ford and General Motors offers and on many electronically provided services. Even with the costs of shipping factored in, it still may be cheaper to manufacture and assemble a car in Taiwan or Chile than in one of the currently heavily industrialized nations. Add to this *new global economy* the rapid technological progress that eliminates many menial jobs and makes the exportation of other jobs, such as the credit card industry to Ireland, possible, and the picture gets even more perplexing. Together, these comprise a formula for the future where there is a greater distribution of the world's wealth, but where employers no longer need to offer fringe benefits or job security. In fact, employers could be heavily penalized if they tried to do so; they would loose their competitive edge and soon their clients. Through out the 1990s, according to a *Los Angeles Times* article (May 9, 1999), the inflation-adjusted income even for college graduates, the most technically advanced and computer-literate workers, fell by a stunning 10%. Newly minted biologists, chemists, and physicists saw their starting salaries plummet by about 11% to 14%.

Reluctant Entrepreneurs

These changes have the effect of converting almost all of us into freelance workers. While not for everyone, entrepreneurial *chutzpah* and resilience are the traits that will be increasingly necessary in America and globally. Many are becoming *reluctant entrepreneurs*, in the sense of subcontractors of our labors, skills, contacts, and personal resources from our autos (delivering pizza) to our home computers. There are many new jobs being created, but there are few that can be counted on to be a stable form of employment over a lifetime. Just consider the rapid decline in tooth decay and the toll this is taking on the need for dentists and dental technicians. Once a high-paying job, many states are changing and eliminating the credentialing requirements for dental technicians, and allowing hourly workers to clean teeth with new, safer equipment. The teaching profession is under attack too. Consider the charter school movement where a teaching degree is not a requisite for employment, hence altering the dynamics that have supported credentialed teachers and credentialing agencies, like schools of education. There is a parallel movement to forge school themes and subjects that are more *client-based*, meaning that students and parents are being viewed more as customers with choices. The need to defend the relevance of entrepreneurism in the schools to teachers could soon be matched by the need for teachers to defend the relevance of conventional English literature and social studies in the schools to kids and their parents.

The Family Farm Is Being Replaced by the Family Business

The challenges of the new economy are neither all bad nor as radical as they might first seem. It does, however, require that we reevaluate schooling so as to better prepare ourselves and our children for the changes taking place in the way commerce is being conducted. Curiously, our nostalgia for the way jobs, business, and commerce have been in the recent past, say from 1945 to the present, may be the interruption of the more historical state of things past. It was only a short time ago, historically speaking, that almost everyone worked at home, and with his or her family; it was called the family farm. On a purely economic level, the movement back to home-based schooling, business, and sale of one's craft skills and labors was the basis for a quite efficient system in which persons of every age were involved. Children born and raised in the last two or three decades often have grown up in rather isolated suburban communities that have sheltered them from seeing people work, strive, and even grow old, get sick, and die. In the time prior to suburbanization, maturity for youngsters followed more rapidly, and being dependent on one another was a healthier form of what today is the disturbing trend toward *codependency*. Thousands of young, able-bodied people (more so men than women) are living home *off* their parents, rather than continuing the family enterprise and providing *for* their parents. Large corporations are reevaluating the *way they work* as well. Many, for example, have not merely downsized, but are engaging in *intra*preneurship where smaller companies operate autonomously within larger ones. This is being done with the expectation that each unit should carry its own costs for operation. This approach also reduces bureaucratization and the tendency of some groups within a company for growing unresponsive to customers and rapidly changing market conditions. Even government is being asked to reinvent itself and to be more client centered and self-supporting (Osbourne & Gaebler, 1993).

Municipal, state, and federal government is being told to figure out how to better serve its citizens, and be resourceful in creating commercial streams of income from the yearly bounty of funds they receive from taxpayers. This movement is all a bit foreboding. There is no place to hide from the reach of the new economy. Even such givens as teacher and professorial tenure are under constant review, with an eye toward elimination. However, this level of scrutiny does help to keep labor costs down, making services and products cheaper and more widely available. This in turn helps to control inflation and the bloating of business and government with unproductive people, costs, and bureaucratically self-serving practices such as have cropped up in agencies who felt they had monopolies on certain products and services—for example, the post offices and motor vehicle bureaus who are closed or taking lunch at the very times that the most people are able to use their services. No private-sector business would dream of not being fully staffed when their customers were standing at the door. Competition is every worker's enemy and every consumer's friend.

Diversity Benefits

Surprisingly, free enterprise and business startup also seem to create more bonding, more easily, of diverse peoples, even more so than many campaigns for tolerance and affirmative action (Miniter, 1999). Women, especially African-American women, according to the U.S. Department of Labor Statistics are opening new businesses in record-breaking numbers. Hence, the former concentration of wealth in the hands of a few is being somewhat relieved through a process that is less invasive than that through taxation and experimental social programs that often run amuck of their goals and siphon off resources through several levels of state, municipal, and federal bureaucracies.

For all its downside on a short-term basis, nothing stimulates wealth and improves quality of life like new technology. As a matter of fact, however, it does tend to help the most advantaged and then the next-most advantaged before it reaches the less and finally the least advantaged. But, this is all the more reason to build business savvy into conventional schooling, and to wrap it all in some larger programs that would enlarge the pools of minority applicants who have the capacity and experience both to attain better jobs and to create new ones.

E-Commerce or Net Income

The new, high-participation, fast-moving economy rests on telecomputing for some simple reasons. Internet businesses stand the best chance for success because net advertising and sales make it possible to open a store with *virtually* no rent, salespeople, or expensive inventory. Importantly, if it does not go well, the venturer just changes the product mix and reopens. If eye traffic and sales go well, and they can go very well, it is a relatively simple matter for the *ad-venturer* to add related and even unrelated advertisements for products at no additional cost to the new business. For example, Amazon.com went into the music business with much greater ease than could conventional book vendors.

This is not to say that on-line business is inherently better and more profitable. Cyberbusinesses are quickly discovering that they also must provide customer service. In other words, they are not "on-line business," as much as "business on-line." Further, there are not only fortunes being made on the web, something that will only happen to a few of us, but there also are modest small businesses being founded of the type that would support a family. For a telling graphic display of how money is being made on the web, see Figure 14.4.

Notice the sums being spent on education (Figure 14.4). These more realistic-size businesses can be pioneered with students over a term in a variety of ways. One simple way is to see what is out there and to duplicate it in one's own region or neighborhood, though not based solely on one's

Figure 14.4
Cash course.

Category	Money Spent Yearly
Satellite	$151.4 million[1]
Tutoring	$37.5 billion[2]
Books	$7.4 billion[1]
Administration	$1 billion[2]
Software	$683.1 million[1]
Internet	$63.8 million[1]
Training	$59 billion[3]
Toys	less than $1 billion[2]
Television	not available

[1] Simba Information
[2] Solomon Smith Barney
[3] Montgomery Securities
Figures taken from WIRED, September 1998, pp. 126–127

Source: Figures taken from "Smart Kids, Who Needs 'Em," by M. Baer, *Wired Magazine.* © 1998. Reprinted with permission. Artwork © 1998 by P. Hobbs, www.lpamorama.com. Reprinted with permission.

own labors, but as a business with other human resources—for example, a neighborhood or area lawn service, or baby-sitting referral service: "Call us, or indicate through e-mail when you would like your yard cut, or your child watched, and we will get back to you promptly with someone to do it, and at a price you can afford."

In business such an organization would be called an *aggregator* or a *broker.* Putting any demand together with a matching service provider or product constitutes grounds for forming a successful business. The Internet merely permits anyone to open a virtual store with a minimal investment (see Figure 14.5). However, computers, software, and technical assistance are necessary and expensive. There almost always is a *dollar equity* requirement to business as well as considerable *sweat equity.* The effort to form a business can be very instructive. It can help to close the gap between school literacy and workplace literacy (Erickson, 1995). As in most ventures, it requires conceptualizing, writing, reading, recordkeeping, and other academic proficiencies. It appears that schools must make an effort to help youngsters actually start businesses, and to work in some started by near-age peers. Doing so increases to an incalculable degree the likelihood that pupils will do so themselves. It is an established psychological axiom that few of us will ever do something we have not done or experienced in some way before. It almost defies human nature to do so.

For all the criticism it receives, business tends to teach collaboration, division of labor, and personal responsibility. It is not often that one hears of employers shooting their employees, or their families, or their neighbors

Figure 14.5
E-commerce made easy.

How easy is it to set up a business on the web? This easy:

✦ Get a domain name (URL) from interNIC, about $70

✦ Assemble your own website, about $99

✦ Accept credit cards, about $15 a month

✦ Get a site manager, about $20 a month

✦ Get e-mail; it comes with web site management

✦ Advertise by hiring a company like Submit It! to register you with search engines, $59*

✦ Put your product out there

You are in business!

*Estimates based on NetNations Communications, Inc. (www.netnations.com).

(although, sometimes their business partners). We do hear often of businesspeople contributing to and supporting friends, family, and neighbors. All and all, most business operators seem to be honorable people with a great desire to see others do well. It cannot be easy to have to meet a weekly payroll, or to invest one's assets and labors in a venture that, if it proves successful, will invite a host of imitators by day's end.

Entrepreneurial Literacy:
Teaching It; Learning From It

Teaching social and economic entrepreneurism essentially is governed by the properties of most other types of cognitive and performance-related theories of learning. For example, "social and imitation learning" theory (Bandura, 1969) is still the prevalent approach. You will recall it is based on modeling, interaction, situational opportunity, and real and vicarious experience. It is learned like almost everything else that is both idea and action based. Unlike most other "subjects," however, social and economic entrepreneurism also teaches almost everything else, since it is inherently cross-disciplinary, *results* oriented, and hence interdisciplinary and demanding of routinely high levels of critical, constructive, and applied thinking.

There are some things that teachers and schools can do to promote the entrepreneurial spirit and a certain amount of intradisciplinarity as well. As educators we have only begun this journey; there will need to be some considerable new commitments to this megatrend to meet this challenge and need into the future. See the box Site Seeing 2 on page 411 for some snappy entrepreneurial ideas, magazines, and information sites on the web.

Reorientation Through Stories,
Images, and Experiences

The chief means of reorienting people of any age are essentially the same. It is through stories, images, and experiences with the desired learning objectives. These in turn form the analogs, or *knowns*, for accumulating and personalizing the unknowns, such as facts, concepts, and ideas. Achieving these is best done by culling human experience for what is known. In this case, discussion could begin with, or at least include, films, books, and media events that involve finance and entrepreneurial spirit. The film *Other People's Money* (with Michael Douglas and Danny DeVito) is one that most youngsters would have seen. To develop platform understandings, work with a class to understand the wheelings and dealings depicted in precise terms. This movie alone includes references to the Consumer Price Index, leveraged buyouts, and angle networks. From this starting place, there will come the means that to increase an individual's *apperceptive mass*, as it once was known in psychology, or *bandwidth*, to use a contemporary metaphor, to better connect to and comprehend a brief news story, a conversational allusion, or a new piece of factual financial information—in other words, the "prior knowledge" necessary to read effectively.

Direct Instructional Approach: The *Construct* Side of *Constructive*

Direct instruction can be very helpful, if not totally necessary in building the *construct*, or ideas and factual side of the constructive process of reading. As suggested above, many of the content area literacy methods that have been described throughout the text are relevant. Figure 14.6 provides an example of the direct instructional way to improve entrepreneurial reading using the ReQuest procedure (Manzo, 1969a&b). In this case, however, ReQuest is used on several sentences at a time, and with the teacher going first. These adaptations were selected because of the assumption that the reader-learners who are the object of this lesson are fundamentally competent readers but have limited knowledge and experience reading in the topic and might need some priming to engage this rather esoteric piece. Remember that the basis of this procedure is to establish a *cognitive apprenticeship* between teacher and pupils, and also to serve as a heuristic from which the teacher can reasonably be expected to learn as well. To set this in motion, the teacher and group reciprocally ask each other as many questions as they wish about each sentence, or in this case group of sentences, and to answer as fully as suits the question—no game playing. Remind students to try to ask the kind of questions the teacher might. This gambit is designed to key students into the teacher's more sophisticated questioning strategies, and to provide students with a socially protected way to ask questions for which they do not have an answer. This structured dialog, or "instructional conversation" (Tharp & Galimore, 1989), continues until a logical or congruent purpose has been evolved for reading the remainder of the article. Only after reading the full article can it be firmly determined if the purpose selected was the most defining one.

There are several somewhat less direct ways to keep reading and learning going and growing. Brief writing and research writing are two examples from Chapter 8. For example, see how REAP is applied in Figure 14.7. Keep in mind as you read below of other methods and means of promoting entrepreneurial literacy that at every age and grade level, the most implosive, transforming lessons are learned from seeing and reading about the achievements and behaviors of peers more so than about adults and from teachers: it's that old, "if she can do it, I bet I can" feeling that tends to convert observation and talk into desire and deeds.

Figure 14.6
ReQuest procedure example: "Touched by an Angel."

Hatch marks are used to note where the teacher would stop for each set of questions noted below.

"Touched by an Angel"/
*Meeting the perfect entrepreneurial
match is easier on the Internet.*
By Jennifer Fischl Kruger/

/Good news, if you want to be an angel. The Internet has made winning your wings—along with potentially market-beating returns—a lot easier./

Angels provide seed capital to developing companies that are far too small to get investment bankers to underwrite initial public offerings. These entrepreneurial ventures are typically trying to raise $100,000 to $1 million. An angel usually contributes $100,000 and in exchange gets in on the ground floor of the start-up. It can be a very profitable trade-off./ Remember, even America Online and Microsoft were once in this position. Investors buying Mr. Softee's shares on Nasdaq can count on a nice return, and those who managed to get a piece of its IPO did a little bit better—okay, much better. But imagine the reward reaped by the select group who backed the company in the angel phase. They didn't just beat the market; they creamed it./

Unfortunately, few venture-capital rainbows lead to Microsoft-style pots of gold. Companies seeking angel backing are generally tiny, with no track records to speak of. Most fail. Uncovering the good values is a daunting task, requiring a working knowledge of your prospects' business, market, and competition, as well as the ability to assess management's plans and capacity to implement them. The Internet doesn't eliminate the need for hard research and number crunching, but several sites have made the quest somewhat easier by bringing together in one spot investors and ventures seeking capital. So, angel wannabes no longer have to comb through community contacts or shell out money to consultants to find attractive projects./

These sites proffer two types of investment opportunities: private placements and direct public offerings. In the first, the investor buys shares in a private company and, if the stake is big enough, a seat on the board or a sufficiently active role in the company to assure that it's moving in the right direction. That type of operating control is usually out of the question with public companies. The downside is that investors are generally locked in for three to seven years./

Figure 14.6, *continued*

The questions the teacher would most want to model are those that would allow her or him to scaffold some of the writer's overassumptions regarding readers' prior knowledge. Accordingly, the teacher might ask the following:

✦ "What do you think is meant by the 'teaser' statement, 'Meeting the perfect entrepreneurial match is easier on the Internet'?"

✦ "Realizing that this is an article in a business magazine, what do you make of the title, 'Touched by an Angel'?"

The class might ask the following questions at this point:

✦ "Who wrote this article?"

✦ "What does 'entrepreneurial match' mean?"

The teacher might then add:

✦ "Do you think that it is significant that the writer is a woman?"

Next, after reading the first short paragraph, students might ask:

✦ "What does the author mean by being an 'angel'?"

✦ "What does the author mean by 'winning your wings'?"

The teacher could follow with:

✦ "Can you rephrase the first two sentences in your own words?"

[This is that all-important "translation" question again, the one so seldom asked and yet so important for building bridges from lower to higher-order thinking.]

On the next cluster of sentences, student questions might include:

✦ "Why would angels take such risks in startup companies?"

✦ "How much might they invest?"

Teacher followup:

✦ "Does this 'angel' investor system remind you of anything we've studied about regarding America's foreign aid policies?"

Figure 14.6, *continued*

Student questions:

✦ "What does 'on Nasdaq' mean?"
✦ "What's an IPO?" [*not really mentioned in article*]
✦ "How do you pronounce 'p-r-o-f-f-e-r', and what does it mean?"

[*This is a question students typically come up with once they figure out that they can simultaneously relieve ignorance and learn, and look clever doing it.*]

Teacher followup:

✦ "Do you think this article is going to be about alternatives to IPOs?"

Student questions:

✦ "What's a 'private placement'?"
✦ "How do you do a direct public offering?"

Teacher followup:

✦ "What do you now think that this article is going to be about?"

The class and teacher agree that the article likely will be about the different ways to raise investment capital, with an emphasis on 'angel investors,' and translate these ideas into the following purpose question, written on the board as a reminder:

✦ "What are some ways in which small businesses raise investment capital, and how are 'angel investors' now helping them to do so?"

From this point, it is a matter of keeping the learning momentum up.

Source: Bloomberg Personal Finance, June 1999, pp. 46–51. Full article can be found online at ⟨www.bloomberg.com⟩.

ThemedSchool: Free Enterprise, Invention, Physical World, the Arts

ThemedSchool (Manzo & Manzo, 1990a) is a grade-level, school: or districtwide simulation of a significant aspect of real life, from entrepreneurism to healthy uses of time and leisure. These *action-themes* could be as valuable as the power-packet *concept-themes* detailed above. ThemedSchool fosters a sense of the relevance of school subjects while putting academics in perspective. It is built around simulations. These tend to (1) take place over an extended period of time, as much as a school year; (2) require participation by practically every department, unit, and student in the school; (3) culminate in some tangible product or event; (4) rehearse students for meeting real-life demands; and (5) involve the community as *extant teachers* (Manzo & Manzo, 1990). Quality themes can be repeated on an appropriate cycle, such as every fourth year in a typical three-grade-level middle school.

ThemedSchool simulations are heuristics, or thought-stimulating experiences, put into a broad scale. They do require extraordinary planning and care. There are some possible liability issues that should be checked out, although most can be overcome by having parents sign a consent agreement, and through a well-thought-out orientation session for students, a must in any case. It is a good idea to put the orientation on videotape to be run for absentees and for any parents who may wish to see and hear what this unusual stream of activity will entail. While the demands are

Figure 14.7
REAP financial application.

Directions and Example

✦ Tell students that you will be demonstrating a study strategy that they can use as they read textbook material and learn content information. To demonstrate the REAP strategy, use an example from your content area or the following example.

✦ Identify a passage that you want students to read. Tell them to read the passage independently. After they have read the passage, tell students to identify the main points and restate them in their own words. The following is an example of a textbook passage and an encoded message based on that passage. Write the passage and message on the chalkboard or an overhead transparency, or use a computer with an LCD panel.

INVESTING IN SAVINGS ACCOUNTS

When you invest in savings accounts, the money is essentially risk-free; it has the greatest safety of any investments you might choose. Even though banks might fail, as long as your investment in a bank is insured by either the Federal Deposit Insurance Corporation (FDIC) or the Federal Savings and Loan Insurance Corporation (FSLIC), your savings are risk-free. Even if the bank fails, your money is insured. Bank savings accounts are virtually risk-free investments; however, money invested in banks does not return a high rate of interest.

Source: Adapted from *Business: Stock Market and Investment Practice Set* (1993). Englewood Cliffs, NJ: Prentice-Hall.

Figure 14.7, *continued*

ENCODED MESSAGE

This paragraph is about investing in savings accounts. When you invest in savings accounts your money will not accrue much interest, but it will be safe.

1. Distribute note cards to students. After students have practiced encoding, or restating, the main points of the passage, have them write their restatements on the cards. Tell students that there could be many different ways to write a summary and that one type of message is not superior to any other type.

2. Divide the class into groups of three or four students. Have students share their statements with each other. Then have them think about the different types of messages represented by the group.

3. Tell students that there are four main types of annotations: summary annotations, thesis annotations, critical annotations, and question annotations. Write an example of each type of annotation on the chalkboard or an overhead transparency, or use a computer with an LCD panel. Use examples from your content area or the examples that follow. Have the students identify the type of annotation they have written. Then remind students to use the REAP strategy as they study content information.

REAP ANNOTATIONS

Summary Annotation
Money invested in banks is insured, so it is virtually risk-free.

Thesis Annotation
Investing money in banks has low risks and low returns.

Critical Annotation
Investing money in banks has low risks and low returns. I don't think money that is not needed to pay bills should be invested in banks. The low risks don't compensate for the low returns.

Question Annotation
I thought that there was a ceiling on the amount of money that is insured by the banks. Are all savings entirely insured?

Source: From S. D. Lenski, M. A. Wham, & J. L. L. John, 1999, *Reading and Learning Strategies for Middle and High School Students,* pp. 207–208), Dubuque, IA, Kendall/Hunt Publishing.

extraordinary, so too are the lessons learned. Students gain new respect for one another's talents and abilities while in school and come to appreciate the importance of effective communication, research cooperation, and social skills that will be useful throughout life. They establish working ties with their community and respect for its industry and problems. Learning, in effect, becomes transformational as well as informational. Some sample ThemedSchools include:

✦ *Free Enterprise Zone:* The final product is a trade fair held in the spring at which students would sell various goods and products that they either manufactured or purchased for resale. The fair should follow the rules and regulations of state and local governments. Students would be urged to find and study these, seeking the assistance of teachers, parents, friends, attorneys, and participating business-people. They would form companies and bid for contracts (e.g., construction, maintenance, and security of fairgrounds). Students could keep money earned, or it could go toward some worthwhile charitable or common goal. Have students work collaboratively to draw up an elementary business plan for a social or a commercial entrepreneurial effort. The best of these may be reviewed and prizes awarded by the local chamber of commerce or media. See Figure 14.8 for the particulars of a basic business plan.

✦ *Home Business:* Do a unit in social studies, business class, and/or economics on home businesses. There are stories and details on the web, and in almost every community, to make this a lively way to

Figure 14.8
Business plan.

These can be relatively difficult to do, but very rewarding in the sense that completing one is empowering, since it converts images and dreams into an action plan. Ingredients of a basic business plan (BP) include:

✦ Purpose of the business

✦ Market analysis—target group(s); size of target

✦ The company or foundation—needs you will satisfy; the specific products or services you will provide

✦ Marketing and sales strategy—how will you get people to select your offerings

✦ Product development—how will you ensure quality service, and refine your offering to a changeable market

✦ Organization and personnel—who will operate and manage the company

✦ Financials—do the math! Funds needed for startup; when you will be self-supporting, and when profitable

Local law firms and college or community business incubators may have other BP outlines for different kinds of ventures. Of course, there is the web, where almost everything informational can be found. See Site Seeing 2 for web sites and magazines for entrepreneurs and product inventors.

connect kids who otherwise might never experience this option to potentially savvy home-based entrepreneurs with whom they might serve internships. There are good magazines, most with web sites, that provide lively articles and actual leads on business opportunities.

✦ *Invention Convention:* Throughout the year, students work with one another, friends, parents, teachers, and senior citizens to identify everyday problems. Typical problems might range from catching pesky flies to meeting catastrophic health care needs that may befall a family.

Students, working either in self-formed groups or individually, attempt to solve at least one problem. The proposed solutions are written up and screened by a faculty and student team. The most promising solutions are selected for presentation at an Invention Convention. At the convention, a panel of judges determines further levels of distinction and selects prizewinners.

Other themes might include:

✦ *Personal Expressions*—from cartooning to music and movement.

✦ *Our Physical World*—Where are we geographically? What is physically under, above, around, and even in us? It has been noted, for example, that our blood has the same proportion of salt as that of the sea.

✦ *Fitness and Resiliency*—our mental and physical fitness needs and development of collective and personal programs to meet these.

✦ *LeisureWorld*—exploration of hobbies, games, volunteer work, and other healthy forms of diversion . . . we all need it.

Using BusinessThink to Do Critical Reading-Writing-Thinking

The topics of this chapter lend themselves to teaching critical reading, writing, and thinking. They are controversial, evocative, and authentic. If a teacher were to teach toward these topics, it would be necessary to address some of the alternate perspectives that students would bring to their efforts to construct both meaning and stance on these issues.

The Anticipation-Reaction Guide is nicely suited to helping with these purposes. Read each of the following statements, and mark the "Before Reading" column with *A* for Agree or *D* for Disagree. After you have read the next three segments, re-read the Anticipation-Reaction Guide statements, and mark the "After Reading" column on the right to indicate whether you now agree or disagree. Discuss your initial stance and any changes in your positions with a group of classmates.

Site Seeing 2

Web Sites and Magazines for Entrepreneurs and Product Inventors

✦ BUSINESS 2.0 ⟨www.imaginemedia.com⟩ (look here for a wide variety of franchise opportunities)

✦ HOMEOFFICE ⟨www.homeofficemag.com⟩ (look here for advice on equipment and services)

✦ ENTREPRENUER ⟨www.entrpreneurmag.com⟩ (look here for discussions on topics of general interest to one starting his or her own business)

✦ BUSINESS START•UPS ⟨www.bizstartups.com⟩ (smart ideas for new businesses and reports on affordable franchise opportunities)

✦ INVENTOR'S DIGEST ⟨www.inventorsdigest.com⟩ (look here for opportunities and advice on patents, licensing, marketing, and inventors' personal stories; there also is an *Inventions Wanted* section)

✦ FOUNDATION FOR BETTER IDEAS ⟨http://members.aol.com/csholumkc/fbi.html⟩ (features a unique strategy for gaining remuneration for and collaboration on "better ideas," and even for "better question/problems")

✦ YOUNG AMERICANS BANK & EDUCATION FOUNDATION ⟨www.theyoungamericans.org/youngent.html⟩ (a complete site for young entrepreneurs, including summer camps built around various aspects of business, banking, and simulations on operating an entire town)

Anticipation-Reaction Guide

Before Reading (A/D)			*After Reading (A/D)*
_____	1.	Owning your own business makes more sense than preparing for a lifetime of groveling and job insecurity.	_____
_____	2.	Social entrepreneurism is an unequivocal force for goodness and personal empowerment.	_____
_____	3.	We must teach pupils to raise their expectations and still seek contentment.	_____
_____	4.	Contentment comes only from lowering expectations: to strive is to be consumed.	_____

Not for the Faint of Heart, or Maybe Even the Sane

The chief outcome for a stab at owning one's own business is failure. Ninety-five percent of new businesses fail. On the other hand, few people go into business with proper training and orientation. This takes time, mentoring, and better teaching toward this objective. This begins with learning some basic rules, or conventions and protocols for business success. Keep in mind that one need not be a business advocate to help make students conversant with it. The early twentieth-century motto [Calvin Coolidge, Jan. 17, 1925 (*Bartlett's*)] that "the business of America is business" is more true today than ever before. It is not merely a bit of *cachet* or trendy way to speak, but a fundamental *literacy* that describes our way of thinking, speaking, writing, and conducting ourselves.

Rosabeth Moss Kanter, a Harvard professor and business guru, has been writing and speaking about four C's that any new company needs to possess to prosper on the Internet. She refers to them as:

+ *Concept*—come up with a viable idea, not necessarily a new one.
+ *Competence*—be sure you can do what is necessary to provide the product or service (partnering helps).
+ *Connections*—mine your neighbors, friends, and family for people that might be customers or otherwise help launch your new venture.
+ *Choice* (or respect for competition)—realize that people have choices in where they can do business; decide how you will offer better value.

We would round these out to a half-dozen by adding:

+ *Culture*—link with people and groups that are in business; just as athletes need the companionship of athletes to stay motivated and continue learning, so too will you in your new business venture.
+ *Capital*—you are going to need money, so get ready to beg and borrow, but definitely do not steal.

There is one more thing about starting a business that needs to be said; it is not over when you have achieved profitability; it has just begun. Owning a business, with only a few exceptions, is very taxing, and often not very profitable until it is sold. Finding a good, solid job that you like can be much more satisfying for most people.

Social Entrepreneurism: Not Without Its Problems

The democratization of power and influence is not without its dilemmas. There are hundreds of new pieces of legislation (such as "Megan's Law," requiring that a community be alerted to a pedophile in their midst) being passed each year that bear the names of victims of one crime or another. Many of these "systemic solutions" are unenforceable, or constitutionally invalidated in time.

These laws almost always are the result of ordinary people reaching out to do extraordinary things. Victims' families form foundations from the contributions of the sympathetic and create conundrums for legislators through what has come to be called the "politics of grief."

Connie and Howard Cleary, for example, had their daughter raped, beaten, and strangled in a college dorm. They pressed for legislation that now requires colleges to regularly report all crimes on and near their campuses.

The cost for this is not as enormous by itself as its critics would suggest, but it adds to the bureaucratic requirements that are together strangling business and (ironically) social enterprise, and are of very limited to social value. Burdett Loomi, a University of Kansas expert on "interest groups," calls this the *power of story*, or how anecdotes have become evidence (as quoted in the *Los Angeles Times*, June 3, 1999).

In contrast to these problematic grassroots efforts, there are those social enterprises that have established roles and purposes that are beyond what was being achieved by a designated branch of government. The American Civil Liberties Union, for example, was born in 1920 when civil rights in the United States was at a dismal level. At that time American citizens were being arrested for being antiwar protesters, and there was forced deportation of alien workers and violent oppression of labor unions. For all the criticism that has been leveled against the ACLU for being "too liberal," it has been a significant social influence in precipitating constitutional challenges to several laws that appear to have been born out of crowd-pleasing demagoguery. For an evocative reason to seek, read, and write, have a class do a web search on the ACLU with electronic and classroom-based bulletin boards critiquing findings from web sites and allowing REAP-ANX type interactions. Ask the librarian to recommend relevant books.

The "Pace" Factor in the Ambition Equation

Entrepreneurism in its various forms still is a new topic; as such educators still are culling its possible meanings and values from experience and story as well as from conventional sources such as professional journals. The "pace" (*pa-chae*) factor comes from this more personal source.

If you are roused to add a stream of references and encouragement on the entrepreneurial spirit to your discipline, please be reminded, of the importance of supporting "pace." I (Anthony Manzo) learned it from my grandfather, an entrepreneur who operated a fresh fruit and vegetable store for much of his adult life.

Grandpa, a Sicilian immigrant, was always perplexed about why Americans seemed unable to strive without becoming consumed by ambition. "Where is their 'pace' [sense of peace and contentment]?" he would ask rhetorically. For him contentment was a palpable thing, a concrete noun more than an elusive or nominal feeling. He found contentment, or satisfaction, in making wine, dressing in suit and tie to smoke his one cigarette a day on the front stoop, cultivating a spectacular garden in the middle of Brooklyn, New York, and in eating from the same large plate at the end of the table with his wife, the mother of his sixteen children. He was successful and content, though less than middle-class by contemporary standards.

It is important that we teach children that "pace" is a life goal and a way of life. Few things are more disquieting, if not disruptive, than raised expectations that are dashed by circumstances or personal shortcomings, especially in areas of achievement that are highly valued by one's society, such as wealth is in the United States. Most of us will experience many more "unsuccesses," or marginal accomplishments, than standout successes. For this reason alone, cultivating areas of personal satisfaction does not cost—it pays. Reminders to "enjoy the moment" can be found in St. Augustine's *Confessions*, where he talks about "joying," as well as in James Daly's editorial (October 1999) in *Business 2.0* where he chides entrepreneurs to take a break from e-commerce and to "get a life."

Of course, Americans did and do have diversions. They are called sports, film, books, health clubs, and vacations. We tend to do these more intensely than in other cultures. Think of how we play golf with a vengeance and turn almost every hobby from growing plants to making jam into a competition. Even leisure reading is driven by "book floods" and competition to see who can read the most books. So, it is not simply a matter of finding a hobby, or even an aesthetic that pleases. It is more in learning how to find comfort and solace in some nonsaleable skills and diversions, much as the Japanese do in origami, or the way many Celtic peoples use their pubs and Mediterraneans the "lunch hour." Share your stories and have youngsters share theirs on where they might find simple diversions and contentment. Satirist George Carlin's monologue, "The Paradoxes of Our Times," provides this reminder of our need to make this a conscious part of schooling: "We've learned how to make a living but not a life. We've added years to life, but not life to years."

Wrap around Support

Educational objectives have the best chance of success when they are supported in a variety ways in and beyond school, or in pupils' life-space and personal experiences. ThemedSchools, for example, amounts to one *wraparound* way to build leisure and contentment as well social and economic opportunity options into the architecture of the house every youngster will live in. Here now is another wraparound plan that you may be interested in joining in its current nascent state. It is a good example of the mergers that can take place to foster social, educational, and economic entrepreneurism.

Opportunity Network (ON)

This idea-in-progress (Figure 14.9) is tied to our larger social responsibility as educators. It fits best under the idea of a "curriculum of caring" (Rasin-

Figure 14.9
Very authentic writing: Abstracts of sample submissions to
Opportunity Network.

1. My grandparents are old enough to have lived through times of intense racial discrimination but too old to have enjoyed some of the benefits that the civil rights movement is providing to younger African-Americans. At this time, they are living in a house that needs many exterior repairs and painting. I would like to raise about $2000 to be able to buy the materials for some of these repairs and painting ($400), and to be able to hire the help of a younger cousin (who would receive about $500) and still earn the $3000 I need to return to college this fall. I hope to be able to earn approximately $2000 selling encyclopedias, and ideally would like to raise an additional $1000 for the eight weekends it would take my cousin and myself to complete exterior painting and repairs.

   Jeffery Combs, 20 yrs. old
   Sophomore, Baker University
   (Assisted by Dr. Roger Wells, Assistant Professor of Mathematics and Opportunity Network Facilitator)

2. My sixth grade teacher told us about an interesting study. The study showed that remedial readers in a sixth grade class were able to serve as effective tutors to first and second graders, and along the way to have greatly improved their own reading and writing skills. My friend Charles and I would like to setup such a program. We need a teacher to train and supervise us. Tutors would work with younger kids for 3 hours a week from October to May. We think we can get 5 other students who would be willing to tutor. We would like to pay the teacher $1000, and each tutor $250. So, I guess we would need about $2500. Our school said it would provide materials and a place to work.

   Nancy Dean, 12 yrs. old
   6th grade, Kevin Elementary School
   (Assisted by Nathan Limes, Social Studies teacher and Opportunity Network Facilitator)

Figure 14.9, *continued*

3. Recently, I learned that two office buildings near my house invite yearly bids for cleaning. They provide all the supplies. My dad is a janitor and he knows how to do this, and where to find good and reliable workers. I would like to help him and myself to start our own business by preparing a bid. I think that we could do this with help from a woman in our church who ran a commercial cleaning company before she retired. We also need help from someone with editing and typing. We would greatly appreciate receiving $500 for the assistance we need to enter a bid, and for the $5000 bond that I am told is required. If we are successful, we will use $2500 of the bond money by 1998–99 to help someone else through the network.

    Ellen Rich, 16 yrs. old, 11th grade
    (Assisted by Mrs. Jane Gold, P.E. teacher and Opportunity Network Facilitator)

4. I love music and play the oboe pretty well. I want to continue my oboe lessons, but my father who has been caught in corporate downsizing, says that it is impossible to pay for more lessons with one brother in college and two kids to go. I have one after-school job that helps with my clothing and personal care costs. I don't think I could work another without hurting my grades. If I could raise the $1800 necessary for another year of lessons, I could offer such lessons myself in the future, and perhaps create an income possibility for my college education. If I could get help myself now, I promise to teach music for more affordable rates, and to give partial and full scholarships each year I teach to someone else in need.

    Thom Barlow, high school senior
    (Assisted by Wm Watts, English-Business teacher, Opportunity Network Facilitator)

5. I have been looking for an opportunity in the large commercial cleaning sector, where I have worked part-time and summers since I was a sophomore. I believe that I have found that opportunity in a niche just being discovered, dirty blinds. They can be found in an apartment complex, restaurant, medical and office building. No one has had an easy way of cleaning them, until Ultra-Sonic. Because their equipment is expensive, folks would rather not buy it, but just pay a quarterly, semi-annual or annual fee for routine cleaning. So, there is plenty of repeat business. The cost for a 60 day trial rental of equipment (90% of which is credited toward the purchase price), with long-term financing for purchase, and with training and assistance in advertising is $1800. With my younger brother and Dad, who is retired, to help part-time, I think I can safely repay this loan with $100 per month installments, over 24 months, allowing the lender to earn 25% interest on the money over about a two-year period.

    Nancy Rankin, high school junior
    (Assisted by Terry Francis, English teacher, and Opportunity Network Facilitator)

Figure 14.9, *continued*

6. We think of ourselves as the best black/white tag wrestling team in the state of Kansas, and plan to go to a local business college together next fall. In the meantime, we're looking for experience in starting and running a small business. The business we have chosen is cleaning and restoring wooden decks. We worked in this trade last summer for someone else. We need $2500 worth of equipment to go into business for ourselves. The equipment essentially is a power spray system that uses no harmful chemicals. We expect to charge approximately $400 per job (one hundred dollars less than competitors), our salaries would be $10 per hour each, and other costs would run about $5 per hour. A job takes about 8 hours, so labor costs should be about $160 per job, with other expenses averaging $35 per job. We expect to be able to get about 4 jobs per week. Hence, our weekly profit could be as high as $800. We would share 60% of profits with investors for all jobs done in a two-year period. After that, we would like an option to buy out our investors for three times their original investments. If business justifies buying more equipment and hiring other workers, and/or to extend the business to resealing and painting decks, we would invite our original investors to invest further, and to receive profits for up to 5 years before a buyout.

    Chuck Storm and Terrance Eubanks
    (Assisted by Opportunity Network facilitators and mentors, Francis Robertson, Home Economics teacher; & Charles Franks, Economics teacher)

ski, 1989) or cultivating altruism. This attribute has been characteristic of American society almost from its inception, although no one seems to know just why.

ON is something of an interagency and interdisciplinary programming idea. It is an attempt to enlarge the reach of the *hidden systems* that have been helping middle- and upper-middle-class people to succeed in business for generations. The strategy is to use newsletters to church and civic groups to link students from upper elementary grades to college level with outside sources who might wish to make a donation, a low- or no-interest loan, or an investment in social and/or entrepreneurial proposals from these youngsters. The thought is to provide more students with the experience of trying to take advantage of the "free market" economy. Currently, there is not much "free" about it. It clearly is biased toward those who already have some resources, along with a healthy dose of prior knowledge, exposure, infrastructure support, and access to funds; in other words, concept, competence, connections, choice, culture, and capital.

The ON system would be monitored at a local level largely by teachers and community leaders. They would be trained to operate workshops on how to write and submit individual or small group proposals. Notably, the proposed system provides considerable and authentic motivation to write and think in ways that encourage personal responsibility, humanitarian caring, and upward economic mobility through a merger of charity and entrepreneurship.

Currently, we continue to seek startup funds and a school-based pilot site that would be willing to collaborate on such an effort. There are many details that would work themselves out in trials, for example, determining age-grade appropriate projects. A fifth-grader might be interested in "playing school" with preschool and primary grade children two days a week during summer break, but would she be able to sustain her effort, and how much supervision would be necessary. Importantly there is reason to believe that such "influential children" positively affect successful early reading, even before kids enter school (Manzo & Manzo, 1995). If this is true, then why not build on this strength by helping the young teacher to envision a summer or afterschool project for which she might be granted say $100 spending money and a $500 contribution to her college fund? Micro-loan and cash infusion programs akin to this one are performing miracles in underdeveloped nations such as Bangladesh, where they are giving poor but ambitious people a running chance at business and life betterment. Each such successful social betterment and business startup becomes a map and a landmark to show others the way.

Admittedly, there are inherent risks, even possible liabilities in such ventures. There is always the problem, for example, that a large number will feel mocked by the headline successes of the few. However, it is axiomatic that the professions that are the most respected and best paid are the ones that deal with high-risk situations, such as pilots in whose hands we all fly, or physicians who regularly prescribe dangerous and hence "controlled substances," and entrepreneurs who try to reach out beyond their resources. Simulations and authentic educational, business, and social involvements could be the "controlled substances" that educators need to add to our repertories to win a more respectful place at the table of professionals.

Ye Olde and Virtual Bookshoppe

Braught (1992) suggests that schools and businesses can cooperate to establish student-managed paperback bookstores, usually in some small area of the school building itself. The bookstore need not operate every day, but more like an occasional book fair. Local merchants, including bookstores, often are willing to contribute the $500 or so necessary to buy some inventory. This program does not compete with typical bookstore sales, and may even stimulate such sales.

Bookstores of this type usually operate under the supervision of an adult Board of Directors and a teacher-parent sponsor. (More information on school-based bookstores, including names of book wholesalers, is available from School Bookshops Project, SE710, Indiana State University, Terre Haute, Ind. 47809, phone, 812-237-2836). This project can turn out to be a genuine lesson in entrepreneurism. It is quickly becoming a lesson in free market competition.

If your students are up to building web sites, as many now are, there is a faster, less complicated route to opening a bookstore. Merely look up one of the major retailers on the web, such as Amazon.com or Barnes and Noble, and sign up with them as an "affiliate." In this way, the web site is credited with 5 to 15% of the purchase price of each book or music CD, and they do all the bookkeeping for you. In the case of the latter, students can get experience in marketing by creating campaigns to get as many avid adult readers and young folkmusic lovers as they can to go through their respective web sites to make purchases. This can be a lively source of replacement income to schools whose current bookstores are on the verge of extinction, though few realize it. Ironically, the Internet that is cutting into their former small monopoly could be the source of their great wealth.

"Scooping Up" Experience in Social and Economic Entrepreneurism

I was telling a graduate class one night about some of the less investment-costly ways that people are finding to be economically enterprising. I mentioned window washing and "reping." The latter is where one works as an independent representative for a retailer, such as Amway, or a manufacturer say of paint or cards or some other largely business-to-business product or service. The class, beginning with high school principal Bob Bloch and his group, added these other old and new opportunities for both social and economic entrepreneurism:

✦ Lawn mowing and total care

✦ Lawn poop scooping—a fast-growing, high-paying, if lowly job

✦ Tutoring for free, for school credit, or for cash

✦ "Professional" babysitting/house cleaning where a bill is provided with the provider's name and Social Security number so that the service can be taken as a tax credit allowed under "cafeteria" plans

✦ Offer to work as an "intern" for whatever the professional or company will pay you while you learn a new role

Wherever a need can be found, there is the potential to fill that need, and in so doing to provide a social and potentially viable economic good.

It can be instructive to send a class on a mental journey to find possible needs that would be fulfilled by knowledge and skill in math, English, history, or virtually any subject. In any case, it will not be dull, and it could be fun; and it is sure to involve more authentic reading, writing, and critical-constructive thinking.

Merging of Social and Business Interests and Trends

Several times in the past and now again, groups are coming forward who see educational and economic opportunity in operating schools. The Edison Group, for example, currently is fully operating over fifty schools. This company is a remake of the one that put "free televisions" in schools a few years ago and offered Channel 1 educational programming in exchange for the right to also offer commercial advertising to kids in school. Now, however, they are providing over a million dollars' worth of "free" computers, along with total, microcontrolled administration. It is a safe bet that they eventually will offer ads over the computers, their own published books, and other such means of becoming profitable. They will need to do this soon to justify the twenty-five million dollars that Morgan-Stanley, a New York Stock Exchange–listed banking company, reportedly invested in them. There is nothing fundamentally unsavory about this kind of school and business partnership, unless either or both parties misrepresent what they are doing or their ability to provide results for those in our charge. We have met groups that have slightly to seriously misrepresented what they could and were doing. Nonetheless, this merging of the charter school movement with the entrepreneurial and interdisciplinary spirit is likely to have a fair share of influence on what is taught, how it is taught, and by whom. (Recently, the New York City Public Schools voted to create their own web site with ads. Income from "views" by the district's 1.1 million bids will be used to buy laptop, take-home computers for those in need.)

Virtual Center for the Study of Educational Entrepreneurism

The particulars of the changes we have discussed are in progress as we go to print. Most every college and university worldwide is actively seeking ways to increase revenue rather than merely reducing costs; K–12 education cannot be far behind. The experiments undertaken and policies enacted in the near future will not only need to be monitored, but as educators some of us will need to provide honest *leadership* in conceptualizing, assessing, and giving honest testimony as to what is occurring and with what consequences. These changes are shaping up to be one of those "either you make this a part of your dialogues or it will make you part of it."

To assist you and others in becoming more conversant and influential in this area, we are constructing a web site and newsletter that will attempt to aggregate key information and invite appropriate dialogue on business-related income for nonprofit schools. Look for links from our book and UMKC sites, especially literacyleaders.com.

✦ *After Words* ✦

There is a good chance that much in this chapter was relatively new to you. Do now what you would have your students do with new ideas—take them with you as you encounter media and friends, and let experience and daily living flesh out these new perspectives. It wouldn't hurt, on occasion, to reread this chapter and other parts of this and other books in your professional library. You will bring so much more to it each time.

Appendix A

Model Professional Portfolio Recorder and Planner

A professional portfolio, begun early in your career, can be an invaluable lifelong resource. To construct a model portfolio, you will need the following materials:

+ A three-ring binder (you may want to begin with a one-inch binder and transfer materials to a larger-size binder as your collection grows)
+ Nine three-hole notebook pockets for storing materials in various sections of the portfolio (see below)
+ Attachable index tabs to mark each section (attach these to the pockets, since these extend farther than regular-sized sheets)
+ Section titles (described next), copied onto separate sheets for insertion into the notebook, between pockets

With these simple materials, and a bit of reflection on your past, present, and future, you are ready to assemble a model portfolio that will grow with you through your professional career.

Section I: Guiding Thoughts
In this section, record relevant quotations you run across that strike you as worth remembering and that can serve to keep your thinking and instructional decision making on track.

A. Thoughts and perspectives on careers in general

Examples
+ Successful careers don't just happen; they are the result of vision, planning, and effort.
+ Most successful careers are beset by occasional setbacks. Expect these, and be ready to push on.
+ When truth stands in your way, you are headed in the wrong direction.

B.   Thoughts and perspectives on teachers and teaching

Examples

 ✦ The art of teaching is the art of assisting discovery.

 ✦ The enthusiastic teacher is a lifelong student.

 ✦ The finer the instruction, the more it invites; the poorer it is, the more it compels.

C.   Thoughts and perspectives on schools and schooling

Examples

 ✦ Nowadays, school heads are chosen to run a school rather than lead it.

 ✦ The school's task is to take a lot of live wires and see that they get well grounded.

Section II: Employment Record
In this section, keep a running record of both teaching and nonteaching experiences, and store an updated résumé.

A.   Nonteaching job experiences

B.   Educational job experiences

C.   Other

(Pocket: current résumé)

Section III: Personal History (Birth to High School)
In this section, make relevant notes about your family and early school background, and store related documents.

A.   Family background

B.   Medical/health factors

C.   Social, athletic affiliations

D.   Academic record, K–12

E.   Hobbies and interests

F.   Significant memories

(Pocket: birth certificate, passport, school records, early photos, letters, memorabilia)

Section IV: Personal History (Postsecondary)
In this section, make notes about your college life and education, and store related documents.

A. Academic record (degrees, majors, minors)

B. Activities (extracurricular; organizations, religious, athletic)

C. Social life (personal and family)

D. Intellectual development (books, magazines, ideas)

(Pocket: transcripts, letters of reference, other records)

Section V: Material Accounting
In this section, keep notes about your financial standing and store related documents.

A. Gifts, trusts, support

B. Income history

C. Loan history

D. Assets (stocks, car, furniture, property)

E. Approximate net worth

F. Prospects (likely legacies and/or opportunities)

(Pocket: financial records, photos, memorabilia)

Section VI: Professional History
In this section, make notes about your teaching career, and store related documents.

A. Certificates

B. Evaluations/recommendations

C. Memorable teachers and colleagues

D. Teaching experiences: subjects, grade levels, situations

E. Related nonteaching roles and experiences

F. Memorable in-service sessions, conferences, sabbaticals

G. Memorable articles, books, papers

H. Membership and roles in committees and professional organizations

I. Grants, travel, awards

J. Summer activities and employment

(Pocket: teaching certificates, letters, articles or summaries)

Section VII: Self-Appraisals
In this section, keep notes on an ongoing self-assessment, and store related records.

A.   Attitudes

B.   Interests and abilities

C.   Temperament/personality

D.   Teaching/learning style

E.   Personal assessment of strengths and weaknesses as a person and as a teacher

(Pocket: records)

Section VIII: Occasional Notes

In this section, make additional notes of memorable events and experiences, and store related records.

A.   Notes on memorable personal events (marriage, deaths, births, friendships)

B.   Notes on memorable professional experiences (significant mentor relationships, special students)

(Pocket: records)

Section IX: Blueprints

In this section, keep notes about long-term career plans, and store related documents.

A.   Personal career goals

B.   Objectives that might contribute to your professional education

(Pocket: related articles, notes, and documents)

Section X: Teaching Competence

In this section, keep notes about your experiences in using various teaching approaches and methods, and store related materials.

A.   Teaching methods you have mastered

B.   Teaching methods you intend to try

(Pocket: related articles and notes on each method)

Appendix B

School Reforms and Reformers

Ambition without knowledge is like a boat on dry dock.

—Mark Lee, *The Next Karate Kid*

DO SOME SITE SEEING FOR DURABLE EDUCATIONAL REFORMS AND MODEL REFORMERS

There are several reforms and reformers who have proven especially durable over time. They tend to be characterized by a core theme or purpose, a certain degree of flexibility and accommodation of other trends, and the support of some foundation, sponsoring company, or other source of private funding. Go site seeing on the web and see what more you can learn about these in terms of their impact on literacy and professional education.

CAST YOUR NET: MODEL REFORMERS, DURABLE REFORMS

✦ Neil Postman, a professor of education at New York University, is well known for his insightful books and journalistic pieces, especially those examining issues pertaining to education and technology. One of his earliest works, *Teaching as a Subversive Activity* (1969), is a classic.

✦ John Goodlad has been at the forefront of educational change and renewal for the past fifty years as a teacher, researcher, administrator, writer, and scholar. Throughout his career, he has demonstrated unflagging optimism regarding education. Goodlad is Co-Director of the Center for Educational Renewal, which established the National Network for Educational Renewal (NNER), dedicated to implementing the Center's core agenda: the simultaneous renewal of schooling and the education of educators, with an emphasis on the relationship between education and democracy. The focus on "renewal," rather than "restructuring" or "reform," suggests an ongoing process of self-examination, reflection, and change. The NNER settings represent a broad cross-section of teacher education institutions and school districts in the United States that share a common commitment to fostering collaborative relationships among faculties in education departments, arts and sciences departments, and P–12 schools.

✦ Henry Levin is the founder and former director of the Accelerated Schools Project, which is based on the belief that all children are gifted and that acceleration, not remediation, will narrow the achievement gap between diverse students. The three principles that guide Accelerated Schools are unity of purpose, school-site empowerment coupled with responsibility, and an instructional approach that builds on students' strengths.

✦ Mary Catherine Swanson is executive director of Advancement Via Individual Determination (AVID), a college-preparatory program supported by the College Board, Inc., that targets underachieving minority and low-income students who traditionally have been underrepresented at four-year colleges and universities. Among other activities, AVID students enroll in regular college-preparatory classes at their schools and then receive extensive support through special classes covering such topics as writing, note taking, and study skills.

✦ Theodore Sizer is the founder and chairman of the Coalition of Essential Schools, a network of more than a thousand schools that share a commitment to ten Common Principles. These include emphasis on helping students learn to use their minds well; curriculum structured around the philosophy of "less is more"; personalized teaching and learning; guiding metaphors of student as worker, teacher as coach; and exhibition of mastery. The Coalition does not promote a single model; instead, it encourages schools to use the Principles as a foundation for rethinking teaching and learning to address their particular needs.

✦ Kati Haycock is director of Community Compacts for Student Success, a program that brings together all parts of the local community and the K–16 educational system to improve the education of all students, particularly those from minority and poor backgrounds. Collaboration between K–12 and postsecondary education is a major focus of the Compacts initiative. At each site, the CEOs of leading education, business, and public/private nonprofit organizations serve as the Compacts' chief decision-making body. The Compacts are administered by the Education Trust on behalf of the Pew Charitable Trusts.

✦ Paul Heckman was director of the Educational and Community Change Project, which advocated the "reinvention" of every aspect of schooling so that all children can benefit from public education. The Project assumed that the knowledge necessary for effective change exists within, not outside of, the individual school, and it provides facilitation and other support services for regular, frequent dialogue among teachers and administrators to reveal that knowledge. The Project encourages creativity in discovering and implementing new ideas and practices, and it supports individual and group reflection and inquiry.

+ Marilyn Watson is director of programs for the Developmental Studies Center (DSC), a nonprofit organization that conducts research and develops programs and materials to integrate children's intellectual, ethical, and social development. Its mission is to help children become kind, helpful, responsible, and respectful of others, and to develop their analytical and critical-thinking skills. DSC's Child Development Project involves long-term collaboration with elementary schools nationwide to create caring communities of learners. In addition, it has helped build a national advocacy alliance to increase awareness of the important role that schools have in children's ethical and social development.

+ Vinetta Jones is executive director of the College Board's Equity 2000 program, a K–12 reform effort that seeks to close the achievement gap between minority and nonminority students and advantages and disadvantaged students, specifically by eliminating "tracking" at all grade levels and in all subjects. The program's major components include a districtwide requirement that all students complete Algebra I and Geometry by the end of tenth grade; academic enrichment "safety nets," such as Saturday academies and special summer classes; and school, community, and higher education partnerships.

+ Linda Johannesen is president of the Galef Institute, which collaborates with educators in public schools, schools of education, and other agencies to create and implement programs that will help children develop positive attitudes toward learning, school, and themselves. Galef's three-part approach to reform, called Different Ways of Knowing (DWoK), encompasses an educational philosophy, a professional development program, and an arts-infused, interdisciplinary curriculum.

+ Howard Gardner is director of Harvard Project Zero, an educational research group that has spent more than thirty years investigating the learning process in children and adults. Its mission is to understand and enhance learning, thinking, and creativity in the arts and other disciplines for individuals and institutions. Much of its work takes place in public schools, particularly those that serve students in disadvantaged situations. Project Zero is best known for its advocacy of the theory of multiple intelligences, developed by Gardner.

✦ Richard Kunkel, dean of education at Auburn University, and Mary Hatwood Futrell, Dean of Education at the George Washington University, coordinate the Holmes Partnership, formerly known as the Holmes Group. This partnership joins research universities and public school districts in the effort to improve schooling and teacher education program simultaneously. Much of the work of the Holmes Partnership, including scholarly inquiry attention to equity and diversity, faculty development, and policy initiation, takes place in professional development schools—public elementary and secondary schools where novice teachers learn to teach and where university and school faculty jointly investigate questions of teaching and learning that arise in the school.

✦ Carl Glickman is founder and director of the League of Professional Schools, which promotes the school as a democratic learning community that is student oriented and focused on improving teaching and learning for all. Depending on local needs and preferences, each League school creates its own programs and guidance structures, but all schools follow a three-part school renewal framework: (1) a democratically derived covenant of teaching and learning that captures a school's beliefs about the characteristics and expected results of exemplary teaching and learning; (2) a democratic school-governance process; and (3) an action-research process that provides the school with information about its progress and the effects of its efforts.

✦ Michael Fullan is founder of the Learning Consortium, a school/university partnership formed in 1988 between four large school districts in the Toronto metropolitan area and the Ontario Institute for Studies in Education of the University of Toronto. The Consortium plans and initiates programs in teacher development and school improvement, generates knowledge about these initiatives through research and documentation, and disseminates new learning in these areas. Collaboration allows Consortium partners to share expertise and resources and to gain access to professional development that might otherwise be too costly or difficult for them to undertake individually.

✦ Linda Darling-Hammond is executive director of the National Commission on Teaching & America's Future (NCTAF). Launched in 1994, the Commission was a bipartisan, blue-ribbon group of public officials, business and community leaders, and educators. Following a two-year, nationwide study of teacher education and teaching, the Commission published a report, *What Matters Most: Teaching for America's Future*, that called for putting teaching quality at the center of education reform and set for the nation the goal that, by 2006, the United States should provide competent, caring, and qualified teachers in every classroom in the country. The members of the state and district network created by NCTAF after the release of the report are now working, with the support and participation of their governors or mayors, legislative leaders, and business and education leaders, to develop strategies for improving the quality of teaching.

✦ Sophie Sa is executive director of Panasonic Foundation. Established in 1984, the Foundation works with public school systems that have high percentages of disadvantaged youth to improve learning for all students. It focuses on systemic, school-based, whole-school reform through the Panasonic Partnership Program, and uses a nationwide network of consultants to provide technical assistance to partner districts. Such assistance includes, for example, on-site consultations to help schools and districts develop and implement plans for improvement; community forums to increase support for reform; and workshops, seminars, and conferences on such topics as student assessment and coalition building.

✦ George D. Nelson is Director of Project 2061, launched by the American Association for the Advancement of Science in 1985—the year Halley's comet was last visible from Earth. Project 2061 seeks to reform K–12 education in science, math, and technology, and to make all Americans science literate by the time the comet reappears in 2061. The nationwide project has involved educators, scientists, mathematicians, and technologists in establishing standards for student achievement and in developing teachers' skills and knowledge. Ongoing efforts are geared toward developing tools to help educators change how they think about and use curriculum materials, instructional strategies, and assessments.

✦ Mary Sudzina is executive director of the Project 30 Alliance, which links university faculty in the arts and sciences with faculty in education for the purpose of improving teacher education. The Alliance focuses on five major themes: Subject Matter Understanding; General and Liberal Education; Pedagogical Content Knowledge; International, Cultural, and Other Human Perspectives; and Recruitment of Underrepresented Groups into Teaching. The themes provide a focus for discussion and joint work by faculties from the arts and sciences and education, with the goal of effective and durable redesign of the teacher education curriculum.

✦ Richard Wisniewski is director of Recreating Colleges of Teacher Education Programs, two parallel efforts aimed at the same goal: fundamental redesign of teacher preparation programs. In 1996, in line with its commitment to public education in the South, the Bell-South Foundation announced its Recreating Colleges of Teacher Education Grants Program. Then, in 1997, the J.A. and Kathryn T. Albertson Foundation announced its Recreating Idaho Colleges and Schools of Education Grant initiative. The two initiatives hold certain fundamental assertions in common, including an emphasis on close collaboration with K–12 schools; cooperation with other college or university departments not traditionally involved in teacher education; and the application of technology to enhance teaching, learning, and assessment.

✦ James Comer is director of the Child Study Center of the School Development Program. This program, founded by child psychologist Comer of Yale University, is committed to the total development of all children by creating learning environments that support their physical, cognitive, psychological, language, social, and ethical development. SDP schools use three mechanisms for development (School Planning and Management Team, Student and Staff Support Team, and Parent Team), three operations (comprehensive school plan, staff development plan, and monitoring and assessment), and three guiding principles (no-fault problem solving, consensus decision making, and collaboration among all stakeholders). Together, these nine components are intended to improve educators' understanding of child development and to foster healthier relations between school and home.

✦ Kenneth Howey is Director of the Urban Network to Improve Teacher Education (UNITE). This consortium of nine universities is committed to transforming their teacher preparation programs and practices, in partnership with K–12 schools, with the ultimate goal of preparing high-quality teachers for urban schools. The consortium serves as a catalyst for change, working primarily through teams made up of four individuals (the dean and three other faculty members) at each participating university. The consortium enables coordinated programs of research and development regarding how best to prepare teachers for urban settings.

Source: In Praise of Education: A National Conference Celebrating Educational Renewal, hosted by John I. Goodlad's Institute for Educational Inquiry, June 18–21, 1999, Seattle, Washington, Conference Program. Amanda Froh, Program Coordinator, Institute for Educational Inquiry; 124 East Edgar Street; Seattle, WA 98102.

Appendix C

Core Functioning Inventory

Directions: There are no right or wrong answers to the following questions. Indicate your responses by marking Y (yes), N (no), or? (not sure) in the space before each question. A few questions require an "a" or "b" answer. Do not spend time pondering questions. You should mark an item? (not sure) only when it is *impossible* to say yes or no. Be sure to answer every question.

____ 1. Are you given to quick retorts and snap judgments?

____ 2. When you meet someone new, do you usually start the conversation?

____ 3. Are you inclined to express your thoughts without much hesitation?

____ 4. Are you apt to say things you may regret later rather than keep still?

____ 5. Do you think much and speak little?

____ 6. Do you get very excited by new ideas and new people?

____ 7. Would you say that you have (a) many friends or (b) just a few friends?

____ 8. Do you often find yourself making comments to a friend while listening to a lecture or watching a movie?

____ 9. In discussion, do you think better when you are challenged to defend your position?

____ 10. Would you rather take (a) an oral test or (b) a written test?

____ 11. Does it irritate you to listen to someone who speaks slowly?

____ 12. Do you recover your emotions rapidly after a sudden upset?

____ 13. Are you inclined to be quick and a little careless in your actions?

____ 14. Would you rather talk than listen in a social situation?

____ 15. Can you turn out a large amount of work in a short time if you are under pressure?

____ 16. Do you usually start to work on a new academic subject with a great amount of enthusiasm?

____ 17. Do you hesitate to volunteer remarks in class?

___ 18. Do you quickly form larger concepts from a few disconnected ideas?

___ 19. Do you find that your recall of past conversations is more accurate than that of most of your friends?

___ 20. Do you usually find that you understand a complex situation with a minimum of explanation?

___ 21. Do you tend to be submissive and apologetic (a) often or (b) seldom?

___ 22. Are you likely to complain about your suffering and hardships?

___ 23. Do you sometimes have a feeling of fear as though you had done something wrong?

___ 24. Do you often have trouble falling asleep at night?

___ 25. Do people tell you that you worry too much?

___ 26. Do you become discouraged when things go wrong?

___ 27. Are you usually tired when you get up in the morning?

___ 28. Do you have nightmares (a) seldom or (b) often?

___ 29. Do you usually have a feeling of being able to handle minor crises?

___ 30. Do you sometimes feel that life would be happier if people only treated you better?

___ 31. Do you sometimes perspire or feel tense without any reason?

___ 32. Do you think of yourself sometimes as neglected and unloved?

___ 33. Would you say that one is wise to be very careful about whom one trusts?

___ 34. Are your ideas generally well organized and systematic?

___ 35. Are you frequently troubled by pangs of conscience?

___ 36. Are you often concerned that you may not have done right in social situations?

___ 37. Do you feel sometimes that people disapprove of you?

___ 38. Is the control of your emotions (a) easy or (b) difficult?

___ 39. Are you easily discouraged when people make fun of you?

___ 40. Are there times when you can't help feeling sorry for yourself?

Impulsivity–Stability Scoring and Interpretation Guide

The Core Functioning Inventory (CFI) is a variation or the Learning Styles Inventory (D. E. P. Smith, 1967) which was created from the Impulsivity–Stability Scales of the Minnesota Multiphasic Personality Inventory. The balance between one's *impulsivity* and *stability* is a fundamental affective characteristic that influences motivation, cognitive style, career interests and daily functioning.

Key: There are no *right* answers, but put a check beside the item numbers where your answer (or the paper you are scoring) is the same as that on the Key. A total score between 0 and 8 is considered a *low* score; 9 to 11 is *moderate;* 12 to 20 is *high.*

1. Yes	11. Yes	21. b	31. No
2. Yes	12. Yes	22. No	32. No
3. Yes	13. Yes	23. No	33. No
4. Yes	14. Yes	24. No	34. Yes
5. No	15. Yes	25. No	35. No
6. Yes	16. Yes	26. No	36. No
7. a	17. No	27. No	37. No
8. Yes	18. Yes	28. a	38. a
9. Yes	19. No	29. Yes	39. No
10. a	20. Yes	30. No	40. No

Total, Items 1–20 _____   Total, Items 21–40 _____
(Impulsivity Score)   (Stability Score)

Quadrant Scores

Use this chart to convert your Impulsivity and Stability scores into a *Quadrant Score (I, II, III, or IV)*, and see the accompanying CFI profile description below.

II High Stability Low Impulsivity	I High Stability High Impulsivity
IV Low Stability Low Impulsivity	III Low Stability High Impulsivity

[Note: In general, scores between 9 and 12 constitute an indefinite range. In all probability, the factor such a scale measures simply is not critical in your life. But that's the way it is with most dispositional factors: They are important when they are definitive, and otherwise inconsequential as life determinants.]

CFI Profile Descriptions of Quadrant Scores

With no other factors taken into account, here is what placement in each quadrant tends to mean:

✦ *Quadrant I:* High stability/high impulsivity. Quick and creative minds; self confident; gregarious; intrinsically motivated; executive type; tend to like social studies, generally not as inclined to arithmetic calculations and precise work.

✦ *Quadrant II:* High stability/low impulsivity. Secure; reserved and methodical; gravitate toward accounting: tend to like math, grammar, and lengthy books.

✦ *Quadrant III:* Low stability/high impulsivity. Tend to be worriers; given to exaggeration; driven, but seldom feel able to satisfy needs; gravitate toward sales; preference for subject is strongly influenced by who is teaching it.

✦ *Quadrant IV:* Low stability/low impulsivity. Tend to be worriers; aversively motivated (motivated by what one *doesn't* want to happen); may appear either apathetic or standoffish; gravitate toward library science or computer-oriented careers; tend to like literature, art history, crafts, and repetitive tasks.

References

Aaronson, E., Blaney, N., Sikes, J., Stevan, C., & Snapp, N. (1975, February). The jigsaw route to learning and liking. *Psychology Today*, 43–50.

Aaronson, E., Stephan, C., Sikes, J., Blaney, N., & Snapp, M. (1978). *The jigsaw classroom.* Beverly Hills, CA: Sage.

Adams, E. K. (1982). What research says to the disciplinarian. In G. H. McNinch (Ed.), *Readings in the disciplines, Second yearbook of the American Reading Forum* (pp. 109–111). Athens, GA: American Reading Forum.

Adams, M. J. (1990). *Beginning to read: Thinking and learning about print.* Cambridge, MA: MIT Press.

Adler, M. J. (1982). *The paideia proposal.* New York: Macmillan.

Alley, G., & Deshler, D. (1980). *Teaching the learning disabled adolescent: Strategies and methods.* Denver, CO: Love.

Alvermann, D. E., & Boothby, P. R. (1983). A preliminary investigation of the differences in children's retention of "inconsiderate" text. *Reading Psychology*, *4*, 237–246.

Alvermann, D. E., Dillon, D. R., & O'Brien, D. G. (1987). Using discussion to promote reading comprehension. Newark, DE: International Reading Association.

Alvermann, D. E. & Hagood, M. C. (2000). Fandom and critical media literacy.

Alvermann, D. E., Moon, J. S., & Hagood, M. C. (1999) *Popular Culture in the Classroom: Teaching And Researching Critical Media Literacy*, Newark, DE: International Reading Association.

Anders, P. L., Bos, C. S., & Filip, D. (1984). The effect of semantic feature analysis on the reading comprehension of learning-disabled students. In J. A. Niles & L. A. Harris (Eds.), *Changing perspectives on research in reading/language processing and instruction. Thirty-third yearbook of the National Reading Conference* (pp. 162–166). Rochester, New York: National Reading Conference.

Anderson, R. C., & Nagy, W. E. (1989). *Word meanings.* (Tech. Rep. No. 485). Cambridge, MA: Bolt, Beranek and Newman.

Ankney, P., & McClurg, E. (1981). Testing Manzo's Guided Reading Procedure. *The Reading Teacher*, *34*, 681–685.

Applebee, A. N. (1981). *Writing in the secondary school.* Urbana, IL: National Council of Teachers of English.

Applebee, A., Langer, J., Mullis, I., Lathan, A., & Gentile, C. (1994). *NAEP 1992 writing Report Card.* Washington, DC: U. S. Department of Education, Office of Educational Research and Improvement.

Artley, A. S. (1944). A study of certain relationships existing between general reading comprehension and reading comprehension in a specific subject-matter area. *Journal of Educational Research*, *37*, 464–473.

Aschner, M. J., Gallagher, J. J., Perry, J. M., Afsar, S. S., Jenne, W., & Farr, H. (1962). *A system for classifying thought processes in the context of classroom verbal interaction.* Champaign: University of Illinois, Institute for Research on Exceptional Children.

Athanases, S. (1988). Developing a classroom community of interpreters. *English Journal*, *77*, 45–48.

Ausubel, D. P. (1960). The use of advance organizers in the learning and retention of meaningful verbal material. *Journal of Educational Psychology*, *51*, 267–272.

Bacon, E. (1963). *Notes on the piano.* Syracuse, New York: Syracuse University Press.

Baer, M. (1998). Smart kids? Who needs 'em. *Wired Magazine. 6:9,* 123–127.

Baines, L. (1998). The future of the written word. In J. S. Simmons & L. Baines (Eds.) *Language study in middle school, high school and beyond: Views on enhancing the study of language.* Newark, DE: International Reading Association.

Baker, L., & Brown, A. L. (1984). Metacognitive skills and reading. In P. D. Pearson (Ed.), *Handbook of reading research* (pp. 333–394). New York: Longman.

Baker, R. L., & Schutz, R. E. (Eds). (1972). *Instructional product research.* New York: Van Nostrand.

Baldwin, R. S., & Kaufman, R. K. (1979). A concurrent validity study of the Raygor readability estimate. *Journal of Reading, 23,* 148–153.

Baloche, L., Mauger, M. L., Willis, T. M., Filinuk, J. R., & Michalsky, B. V. (1993). Fishbowls, creative controversy, talking chips: Exploring literature cooperatively. *English Journal, 82,* 43–48.

Bandura, A., & Walters, R. (1963). *Social learning and personality development.* New York: Holt, Rinehart & Winston.

Barrett, T. C. (1967). *The evaluation of children's reading achievement.* Newark, DE: International Reading Association.

Barry, D. (1998). How to get rich? Mooga mooga. *KC Star Magazine,* December 27, Kansas City, MO: The Kansas City Star.

Barton, J. (1995). Conducting effective classroom discussions. *Journal of Reading. 38,* 346–350.

Barton, W. A. (1930). *Outlining as a study procedure.* New York: Columbia University, Teacher's College.

Baumann, J. F., & Kameenui, E. J. (1991). Research on vocabulary instruction. In J. Flood, J. M. Jensen, D. Lapp, & J. Squire (Eds.), *Handbook of research on teaching the English language arts* (pp. 604–631). Upper Saddle River, NJ: Prentice Hall.

Bean T. W., Bean, S. K., & Bean, K. F., (1999). Intergenerational conversations and two adolescents' multiple literacies: Implications for redefining content area literacy. *Journal of Adolescent and Adult Literacy, 42,* 438–448.

Bean, T. W., & Pardi, R. (1979). A field test of a guided reading strategy. *Journal of Reading, 23,* 144–147.

Behle, P. (Ed). (1982). *The double helix: Teaching the writing process.* Florissant, MO: Ferguson-Florissant Writers Project.

Bereiter, C. & Scardamalia, M. (1985). Cognitive coping strategies and the problem of inert knowledge. In S. S. Chipman, J. W. Segal, & R. Glazer, (Eds.) *Thinking and learning skills, Vol. 2: Current research and open questions* (pp. 65–80). Hillsdale, NJ: Erlbaum.

Bintz, W. (1997). Exploring reading nightmares of middle and secondary school teachers. *Journal of Adolescent & Adult Literacy, 41,* 12–24.

Blanc, R. A. (1977). Cloze-plus as an alternative to "guides" for understanding and appreciating poetry. *Journal of Reading, 21,* 215–218.

Bloom, B. S. (Ed.). (1956). *Taxonomy of educational objectives: The classification of educational goals. Handbook 1. Cognitive domain.* New York: Longman, Green.

Bloom, B. S. (1976). *Human characteristics and school learning.* New York: McGraw-Hill.

Bloom, B. S. (1981). *All our children learning.* New York: McGraw-Hill.

Bormuth, J. R. (1965). Validities of grammatical and semantic classifications of cloze test scores. In J. A. Figurel (Ed.), *Reading and inquiry. International Reading Association Conference Proceedings* (Vol. 10, pp. 283–286). Newark, DE: International Reading Association.

Bradley, A. (1999). Science group finds middle school textbooks inadequate. *Education Week, 19:6,* 5.

Bragstad, B. (1985, March). *Mapping: Using both sides of the brain.* Lecture handout, International Reading Association State Council Meeting. Orlando, FL.

Braught, L. R. (1992). Student operated bookshops: A program to encourage middle-grade literacy. *The Reading Teacher, 45,* 438–444.

Bromley, K. D. (1985). Précis writing and outlining enhance content learning. *The Reading Teacher, 38,* 406–411.

Brown, A. L. (1980). Metacognition development and reading. In R. J. Spiro, B. C. Bruce, & W. F. Brewer (Eds.), *Theoretical issues in reading comprehension* (pp. 453–481). Hillsdale, NJ: Erlbaum Associates.

Brozo, W. G., & Simpson, M. L. (1999). *Readers, teachers, learners: Expanding literacy across the content areas* (3rd ed.) Columbus, OH: Merrill, an imprint of Prentice Hall.

Bruer, J. T. (1993). *Schools for thought: A science of learning in the classroom.* Cambridge, MA: A Bradford Book of MIT Press.

Bruner, J. C. (1971). *Toward a theory of instruction.* New York: W.W. Norton.

Burke, K. (1950/1969). *A rhetoric of motives.* Berkeley, CA: University of California Press.

Calfee, R. C., Dunlap, K. L., & Wat, A. Y. (1994). Authentic discussion of texts in middle school. *Journal of Reading, 37*(7), 546–556.

Campbell, J., Donahue, P., Reese, C., & Phillips, G. *NAEP 1994 reading report card for the nation and the states.* Washington, DC: U.S. Department of Education, OERI, 1996.

Camperell, K. (1982). Vygotsky's theory of intellectual development: The effect of subject-matter instruction on self-regulated cognitive processes. In G. H. McNich (Ed.), *Reading in the disciplines. Second yearbook of the American Reading Forum* (pp. 33–35). Athens: University of Georgia.

Carr, E. M., & Ogle, D. M. (1987). K-W-L Plus: A strategy for comprehension and summarization. *Journal of Reading, 30,* 626–631.

Carver, R. P. (1985). Is the Degrees of Reading Power test valid or invalid? *Journal of Reading, 29,* 34–41.

Casale, U. P. (1985). Motor imaging: A reading-vocabulary strategy. *Journal of Reading, 28,* 619–621.

Casale, U. P., & Kelly, B. W. (1980). Problem-solving approach to study skills (PASS) for students in professional schools. *Journal of Reading, 24,* 232–238.

Casale, U. P., & Manzo, A. V. (1983). Differential effects of cognitive, affective, and proprioceptive approaches on vocabulary acquisition. In G. H. McNinch (Ed.), *Reading research to reading practice. Third yearbook of the American Reading Forum* (pp. 71–73). Athens, GA: American Reading Forum.

Caverly, D. C., Burrell, K., & McFarland, J. (1992, November). *Evaluation results of a whole language TASP reading program.* Paper presented at the annual conference of the Conference on Academic Support Programs, Fort Worth, TX.

Caverly, D. C., Mandeville, T. F., & Nicholson, S. A. (1995). PLAN: A study-reading strategy for informational text. *Journal of Adolescent and Adult Literacy, 39,* 190–199.

Chall, J. S. (1986). The teacher as scholar. *The Reading Teacher, 39,* 792–797.

Chapin, S., Illingworth, M., Landau, S., Masingila, O., & McCracken, L. (1995). *Middle Grades Mathematics: An Interactive Approach.* Upper Saddle River, NJ: Prentice Hall.

Chase, R. H. (1926). *The ungeared mind.* Philadelphia: F.A. Davis Company, Publishers.

Ciardiello, A. V. (1998). Did you ask a good question today? Alternative cognitive and metacognitive strategies. *Journal of Adolescent and Adult Literacy. 42,* 210–219.

Ciardiello, A. V., & Cicchelli, T. (1994). The effects of instructional training models and content knowledge on student questioning in social studies. *The Journal of Social Studies Research, 19,* 30–37.

Clewell, S. E., & Haidemos, J. (1983). Organizational strategies to increase comprehension. *Reading World, 22,* 314–321.

Cloer, T., Jr., & Denton, G. R. (1995). The effects of read-along tapes on the comprehension of middle school students. In K. Camparell, B. L. Hayes, & R. Telfer (Eds.), Linking literacy: past, present, and future. *American Reading Forum Yearbook* (Vol. 15, pp. 85–92). Logan, Utah: American Reading Forum Yearbook.

Collins, C. (1987). Content mastery strategies aid classroom discussion. *The Reading Teacher, 40,* 816–818.

Collins, C. (1991). Reading instruction that increases thinking abilities. *Journal of Reading, 34,* 510–516.

Commeyras, M. (1993). Promoting critical thinking through dialogical-thinking reading lessons. *The Reading Teacher, 6,* 486–493.

Condus, M. M., Marshall, K. J., & Miller, S. R. (1986). Effect of the key-word mnemonic strategy on vocabulary acquisition and maintenance by learning disabled children. *Journal of Learning Disabilities, 19,* 609–613.

Cooter, R. B., & Flynt, E. S. (1986). *Reading comprehension: Out of the ivory tower and into the classroom.* Unpublished paper, Northwestern State University, Natchitoches, LA.

Crafton, L. K. (1983). Learning from reading: What happens when students generate their own background information? *Journal of Reading, 26,* 586–592.

Criscoe, B. L., & Gee, T. C. (1984). *Content reading: A diagnostic/prescriptive approach.* Upper Saddle River, NJ: Prentice Hall.

Cronholm, L. (1999). Why Baruch ended remedial classes. *The Chronicle of Higher Education.* September 24.

Csikszentmihalyi, M. (1991) *Flow: The psychology of optimal experience.* New York: Harper Perennial.

Culver, V. I., Godfrey, H. C., & Manzo, A. V. (1972). A partial reanalysis of the validity of the cloze procedure as an appropriate measure of reading comprehension [Research report summary]. *Journal of Reading, 16,* 256–257.

Cunningham, D., & Shablak, S. L. (1975). Selective Reading Guide-O-Rama: The content teacher's best friend. *Journal of Reading, 18,* 380–382.

Cunningham, J. W., Cunningham, P. M., & Arthur, S. V. (1981). *Middle and secondary school reading.* New York: Longman.

Cunningham, P. M., & Cunningham, J. W. (1976). SSSW, better content-writing. *The Clearing House, 49,* 237–238.

Cunningham, P. M., Moore, S. A., Cunningham, J. W., & Moore, D. W. (1983). *Reading in elementary classrooms: Strategies and observations.* New York: Longman.

Dahmus, M. E. (1970). How to teach verbal problems. *School Science and Mathematics, 70,* 121–138.

Daly, J. (1999, October). *Business 2.0.*

Davey, B. (1983). Think aloud—Modeling the cognitive processes of reading comprehension. *Journal of Reading, 27,* 44–47.

Davidson, J. W., & Stoff, M. B. (1995). *The American Nation.* Upper Saddle River, NJ: Prentice Hall.

Derby, T. (1987). Reading instruction and course related materials for vocational high school students. *Journal of Reading, 30,* 308–316.

Diehl, W. A., & Mikulecky, L. (1980). The nature of reading as work. *Journal of Reading, 24,* 221–227.

Diggs, V. M. (1973). The relative effectiveness of the SQ3R method, a mechanized approach, and a combination method for training remedial reading to college freshmen (Doctoral dissertation, West Virginia University, Morgantown, 1972). *Dissertation Abstracts International, 33,* 5964A. (University Microfilms No. 74-4, 786)

Diuguid, L. W. (1999). Weak Social awareness separates us. *Kansas City Star.* August 24, 1999.

Doctorow, M., Wittrock, M. C., & Marks, C. (1978). Generative processes in reading comprehension. *Journal of Educational Psychology, 70,* 109–118.

Dodson, S. (1997). *The mother daughter book club.* New York: Harper Perennial.

Donald, M., Sr. (1967). The SQ3R method in grade seven. *Journal of Reading, 11,* 33–35, 43.

Dortch, S. (1995). Talking with fewer words. *American Demographics.* (April) http://www.demographics.com/publications/.

Drucker, P. (1989). *The new realities: in government and politics, in economy and business, in society, and in world view.* Oxford: Heinemann Professional Publishing.

Duckworth, S., & Taylor, R. (1995). Creating and assessing literacy in at-risk students through hypermedia portfolios. *Reading Improvement, 32*(1), 26–31.

Duffelmeyer, F. (1994). Effective anticipation guide statements for learning from expository prose. *Journal of Reading, 37,* 452–457.

Duffelmeyer, F., Baum, D., & Merkley, D. (1987). Maximizing reader-text confrontation with an extended anticipation guide. *Journal of Reading, 31,* 146–151.

Duffy, G. G., & Hoffman, J. V. (1999). In pursuit of an illusion: The flawed search for a perfect method. *The Reading Teacher, 53*:1, 10–16.

Duke, C. R. (1987). Integrating reading, writing, and thinking skills into the music class. *Journal of Reading, 31,* 152–157.

Durkin, D. (1978–1979). What classroom observations reveal about comprehension instruction. *Reading Research Quarterly, 14,* 481–533.

Eanet, M. G., & Manzo, A. V. (1976). REAP—A strategy for improving reading/writing/study skills. *Journal of Reading, 19,* 647–652.

Ediger, M. (1992). The middle school student and interest in reading. *Journal of Affective Reading Education, 10*(2), 9–13.

Edwards, P. A., & Simpson, L. (1986). Bibliotherapy: A strategy for communication between parents and their children. *Journal of Reading, 30,* 110–118.

Embracing the persecuted: Park College kept Japanese-Americans out of detention camps (1999). *The Kansas City Star*, August 16.

Ennis, R. H. (1962). The concept of critical thinking. *Harvard Educational Review, 32*, 81–111.

Erickson, L. G. (1995). *Supervision of Literacy Programs: Teachers as Grass-Roots Change Agents.* Boston: Allyn and Bacon.

Ericson, B., Hubler, M., Bean, T. W., Smith, C. C., & McKenzie, J. V. (1987). Increasing critical reading in junior high classrooms. *Journal of Reading, 30*, 430–439.

Estes, T. H. (1991). Ten best. In E. Fry (Ed.), *Ten best ideas for reading teachers* (p. 59). New York: Addison Wesley.

Farr, R. (1992). Putting it all together: Solving the reading assessment puzzle. *The Reading Teacher, 46*(1), 26–37.

Feathers, K. M., & Smith, F. R. (1987). Meeting the reading demands of the real world: Literacy based content instruction. *Journal of Reading, 30*, 506–511.

Flower, L., & Hayes, J. R. (1981). A cognitive process theory of writing. *College Composition and Communication, 32*, 365–387.

Fogarty, R. (1992). Beyond test scores: Tracking significant outcomes. *Cogitare, 6*:3, 2.

Fogarty, R. & McTighe, J. (1993, Summer). Educating teachers for higher-order thinking: The three-story intellect. *Theory into Practice, 32*:3, 161–169.

Frager, A. M., & Thompson, L. C. (1985). Conflict: The key to critical reading instruction. *Journal of Reading, 28*, 676–683.

Freire, P. (1985). *The politics of education: Culture, power, and liberation.* South Hadley, MA: Bergin & Garvey.

Freire, P. (1987). Literacy: Reading the word and the world. South Hadley, MA: Bergin & Garvey.

Friedel, G. (1976, September). *Instant study skills.* Workshop handout, University of Missouri-Kansas City.

Fry, E. (1968). A readability formula that saves time. *Journal of Reading, 11*, 513–516, 575–578.

Fry, E. (1977). Fry's readability graph: Clarification, validity, and extension to level 17. *Journal of Reading, 21*, 242–252.

Furchtgott-Roth, D. F., & Stolba, C. (2000). *Women's figures: The economic progress of women in America.* Arlington, VA: Independent Women's Forum.

Garber, K. S. (1995). *The effects of transmissional, transactional, and transformational reader-response strategies on middle school students' thinking complexity and social development.* (Unpublished doctoral dissertation, Kansas City, MO: University of Missouri-Kansas City.)

Gardner, H. (1983). *Frames of mind: The theory of multiple intelligences.* New York: Harper and Row.

Gardner, H. (1985). *The mind's new science.* New York: Basic Books.

Gauthier, L. R. (1996). Using guided conversation to increase students' content area comprehension. *Journal of Adolescent & Adult Literacy, 39*, 310–312.

Gee, T. C., & Rakow, S. J. (1987). Content reading specialists evaluate teaching practices. *Journal of Reading, 31*, 234–237.

Gentile, L. M. (1980). *Using sports and physical education to strengthen content area reading skills.* Newark, DE: International Reading Association.

Gerber, S., & Finn, J. D. (1998). Learning document skills at school and at work. *Journal of Adolescent and Adult Literacy. 42*, 32–44.

Geyer, J. J. (1972). Comprehensive and partial models related to the reading process. *Reading Research Quarterly, 7*, 541–587.

Gipe, J. P. (1978–1979). Investigating techniques for teaching word meanings. *Reading Research Quarterly, 14*, 624–644.

Gilbert, J. C. (1989). A two week K-6 interdisciplinary unit. In H. H. Jacobs (Ed.) *Interdisciplinary curriculum: design and improvement* (pp. 46–51). Alexandria, VA: Association for Supervision and Curriculum Development.

Glickman, C. D. (1985). *Supervision of instruction: A developmental approach.* Newton, MA: Allyn & Bacon.

Glass, G. G. (1973). *Teaching decoding as separate from reading.* Garden City, New York: Adelphi University Press.

Godin, S. (1999). *Permission Marketing: Turning strangers into friends, and friends into customers.* New York: Simon & Schuster.

Gomez, M. L., Graue, M. E., & Bloch, M. N. (1991). Reassessing portfolio assessment: Rhetoric and reality. *Language Arts, 68*:8, 620–628.

Goodman, K. S., Bird, L. B., & Goodman, Y. M. (1991). *The whole language catalog.* Santa Rosa, CA: American School Publishers.

Gough, E. B., & Cosky, M. J. (1977). One second of reading again. In N. J. Castellan, Jr., D. Pisoni, & G. Potts (Eds.), *Cognitive theory* (Vol. 2, pp. 271–288). Hillsdale, NJ: Erlbaum.

Gray, D. (1988, Summer). *Socratic seminars: Basic education and reformation. Basic Education: Issues, Answers, and Facts, 3, 14.* Washington, DC: Council for Basic Education.

Gray, W. S. (1946). *On their own in reading.* Chicago: Scott, Foresman.

Greenewald, M. J., & Wolf, A. E. (1980). Professional journals in secondary education: Which ones do teachers recommend most? *The Clearing House, 53,* 349–350.

Greenhoe, M. L. (1972). Parameters of creativity in music education: An exploratory study (Doctoral dissertation, The University of Tennessee, Knoxville). *Dissertation Abstracts International, 33,* 1766A.

Guinier, L., Fine, M., & Balin, J. (1997). *Becoming gentlemen: Women, law school, and institutional change.* Boston: Beacon Press

Gurian, M. (1998). *A fine young man: What parents, mentors and educators can do to shape adolescent boys into exceptional men.* New York: Jeremy P. Tarcher/Putnam.

Gurrola, S. (1975). Determination of the relative effectiveness and efficiency of selected combinations of SQ3R study method components (Doctoral dissertation, New Mexico State University, 1974). *Dissertation Abstracts International, 35,* 6938A. (University Microfilms No. 75-10, 822)

Guthrie, J. T. (1984). Lexical learning. *The Reading Teacher, 37,* 660–662.

Haggard, M. [Ruddell]. (1976). *Creative Thinking-Reading Activities (CT-RA) as a means for improving comprehension.* Unpublished doctoral dissertation, University of Missouri-Kansas City, Kansas City, MO.

Haggard, M. R. (1978). The effect of creative thinking-reading activities (CT-RA) on reading comprehension. In P. D. Pearson & J. Hansen (Eds.), *Reading: Disciplined inquiry in process and practice. Twenty-seventh yearbook of the National Reading Conference* (pp. 233–236). Clemson, SC: National Reading Conference.

Haggard, M. R. (1982). The vocabulary self-collection strategy: An active approach to word learning. *Journal of Reading, 27,* 203–207.

Haggard, M. R. (1986). The vocabulary self-collection strategy: Using student interest and world knowledge to enhance vocabulary growth. *Journal of Reading, 29,* 634–642

Harker, W. J. (1972–1973). An evaluative summary of models of reading comprehension. *Journal of Reading Behavior, 5,* 26–34.

Harker, W. J. (Ed.). (1977). *Classroom strategies for secondary reading.* Newark, DE: International Reading Association.

Harste, J. (1978). Instructional implications of Rumelhart's model. In W. A. Diehi (Ed.), *Secondary reading: Theory and application. The 1978 Lilly conference on secondary reading* (Monographs in Teaching and Learning No. 1, pp. 21–23). Bloomington: Indiana University, School of Education.

Harste, J. C. (1994). Whole-language assessment. In A. Purves (Ed.), *Encyclopedia of English studies and language arts* (Vol. 2, pp. 1262–1263). New York: Scholastic.

Haven, K. (1999). "Good to the last drop": Making the most of stories to enhance language arts learning. *The California Reader, 32*:2, 5–9.

Heaton, M. M., & Lewis, H. B. (1955). *Reading ladders for human relations* (3rd ed.). Washington, DC: American Council on Education.

Henry, G. H. (1974). *Teaching reading as concept development: Emphasis on affective thinking.* Newark, DE: International Reading Association.

Herber, H. L. (1978). *Teaching reading in content areas* (2nd ed.). Englewood Cliffs, NJ: Prentice Hall.

Hirsch, E. D. (1987). *Cultural literacy: What every American needs to know.* Boston: Houghton Mifflin.

Hittleman, C. (1984, Spring/Summer). Peer response groups: The writing process in action. *Language Connections: Hofstra University Newsletter, 4.*

Hittleman, D. K. (1978). Readability, readability formulas, and cloze: Selecting instructional materials. *Journal of Reading, 22,* 117–122.

Hoffman, J. V. (1977). Intra-Act: A languaging in the content areas teaching procedure (Doctoral dissertation, University of Missouri-Kansas City). *Dissertation Abstracts International, 38,* 3248A.

Hoffman, J. V. (1991). Teacher and school effects in learning to read. In R. Barr, M. Kamil, P. Mosenthal, & D. P. Pearson (Eds.), *Handbook of reading research* (Vol. 11, pp. 911–950). White Plains, NY: Longman.

Hori, A. K. O. (1977). *An investigation of the efficacy of a questioning training procedure on increasing the reading comprehension performance of junior high school learning disabled students.* (Unpublished master's thesis, University of Kansas, Lawrence.)

Jackson-Albee, J. A. (2000). *The effect of Read-Encode-Annotate-Ponder annotation exchange (REAP AnX) on the complex thinking of undergraduate students in children's literature courses.* (Unpublished doctoral dissertation, Kansas City, MO: University of Missouri-Kansas City.)

Jacobs, H. H. (1989). *Interdisciplinary curriculum: Design and implementation.* Alexandria, VA: Association for Supervision and Curriculum Development.

Johnson, A. P. (1995). Science in reading: A harmonic convergence. *Iowa Reading Journal, 8*(1), 12–13.

Johnson, D. D., & Pearson, P. D. (1984). *Teaching reading vocabulary* (2nd ed.). New York: Holt, Rinehart & Winston.

Johnson, D. D., Toms-Bronowski, S., & Pittelman, S. D. (1982). *An investigation of the effectiveness of semantic mapping and semantic feature analysis with intermediate grade students* (Program Report 83–3). Madison: University of Wisconsin, Wisconsin Center for Education Research.

Johnston, P. H., & Allington, R. (1991). Remediation. In R. Barr, M. L. Kamil, P. B. Mosenthal, & P. D. Pearson (Eds.), *Handbook of reading research* (Vol. 2, pp. 984–1012). New York: Longman.

Jonassen, D. H. (1985a). Generative learning vs. mathemagenic control of text processing. In D. H. Jonassen (Ed.), *The technology of text: Principles for structuring, designing, and displaying text* (Vol. 2, pp. 9–45). Englewood Cliffs, NJ: Educational Technology Publications.

Jonassen, D. H. (Ed.). (1982). *The technology of text: Principles for structuring, designing, and displaying text* (Vol. 1). Englewood Cliffs, NJ: Educational Technology Publications.

Jonassen, D. H. (Ed.). (1985b). *The technology of text: Principles for structuring, designing, and displaying text* (Vol. 2). Englewood Cliffs, NJ: Educational Technology Publications.

Kagan, S. (1994). *Cooperative Learning.* San Clemente, CA: Kagan Cooperative Learning.

Kay, L., Young, J. L., & Mottley, R. R. (1986). Using Manzo's ReQuest model with delinquent adolescents. *Journal of Reading, 29,* 506–510.

Kelly, B. W., & Holmes, J. (1979). The Guided Lecture Procedure. *Journal of Reading, 22,* 602–604.

Kibby, M. W. (1995). The organization and teaching of things and the words that signify them. *Journal of Adolescent and Adult Literacy, 39,* 208–223.

King, C. M., & Parent Johnson, L. M. (1999). Constructing meaning via reciprocal teaching. *Reading Research and Instruction, 38*:3, 169–186.

King, A., & Rosenshine, B. (1993). Effects of guided cooperative questioning on children's knowledge construction. *Journal of Experimental Education, 61*:2, 127–148.

Kirby, D., & Liner, T. (1981). *Inside out: Developmental strategies for teaching.* Montclair, NJ: Boynton/Cook.

Kirshner, D., & Whitson, J. A., Eds. (1997). *Situated cognition: Social, semiotic, and psychological perspectives.* Mahwah, NJ: Lawrence Erlbaum Associates, Publishers.

Klausmeier, H. J. (1992). Concept Learning and Concept Teaching. *Educational Psychologist, 27*(3), 267–286

Konopak, B. C., & Williams, N. L. (1988). Using the key word method to help young readers learn content material. *The Reading Teacher, 41,* 682–687.

Konopak, B. C., Martin. S. H., & Martin, M. A. (1987). Reading and writing: Aids to learning in the content areas. In E. K. Dishner, T. W. Bean, J. E. Readence, & D. W. Moore (Eds.), *Reading in the content areas: Improving classroom instruction* (3rd ed.) Dubuque, IA: Kendall/Hunt.

Koskinen, P. S., Wilson, R. M., Gambrell, L. B., & Jensema, C. J. (1987). *Using the technology of closed-captioned television to teach reading to handicapped students.* (Performance Report, U. S. Department of Education Grant No. G-00-84-30067). Falls Church, VA: National Captioning Institute.

Krathwohl, D. R., Bloom, B. S., & Masia, B. B. (Eds.). (1956). *Taxonomy of educational objectives: The classification of educational goals. Handbook 2. Affective domain.* New York: Longman, Green.

Kruger, J. (1999). Touched by an Angel. *Bloomberg Personal Finance,* June, 46–51.

Labbo, L. D., & Ash, G. E. (1998). What is the role of computer-related technology in early literacy? In S. B. Neuman & K. A. Roskos (Eds.) *Children achieving: Best practices in early literacy.* Newark, DE: International Reading Association.

Lampert, M. (1998). *Teaching, multimedia, and mathematics: Investigations of real practice.* New York: Teachers College Press.

Lance, J. (1981). Practicing for touchdowns. *Journal of Physical Education, Recreation, and Dance, 5,* 38.

Laws, K. (1984). The physics of dance. New York: Macmillan, Inc.

Legenza, A. (1978). Inquiry training for reading and learning improvement. *Reading Improvement, 15,* 309–316.

Lenski, S. D., Wham, M. A., & Johns, J. L. (1999). *Reading and learning strategies for middle and high school students.* Dubuque, IA: Kendall/Hunt Publishing Company.

Levin, J. R., Morrison, C. R., McGivern, J. E., Mastropieri, M. A., & Scruggs, T. E. (1986). Mnemonic facilitation of text-embedded science facts. *American Educational Research Journal, 23,* 489–506.

Lindamood, C. H., & Lindamood, P. C. (1975). *The A.D.D. program, auditory discrimination in depth* (Books 1 & 2). Hingham, MA: Teaching Resources.

Lipson, M. Y., & Wixson, K. K. (1997). *Assessment and instruction of reading and writing disability: an interactive approach.* 2nd edition, New York: Longman.

Longino, H. E. (1990). *Science as social knowledge.* Princeton, NJ: Princeton University Press.

Lovett, M. B. (1981). Reading skill and its development: Theoretical and empirical considerations. In G. MacKinnon & T. Waller (Eds.), *Reading research: Advances in theory and practice* (Vol. 3, pp. 1–37). New York: Academic Press.

Luke, A., & Elkins, J. (1998). Reinventing literacy in "new times." *Journal of Adolescent and Adult Literacy, 42,* 4–7.

Maier, N. R. E. (1963). *Problem solving discussions and conferences: Leadership methods and skills.* New York: McGraw-Hill.

MacNeal, E. (1994). *Mathsemantics: Making numbers talk sense.* New York: Viking.

Manthon, A., Hopkins, J., Johnson, S., Lahart, D., McLaughlin, C., Quon Warner, M., & Wright, J. (1994). *Human Biology and Health.* Upper Saddle River, NJ: Prentice Hall.

Manzo, A. V. (1969a). Improving reading comprehension through reciprocal questioning (Doctoral dissertation, Syracuse University, Syracuse, NY, 1968). *Dissertation Abstracts International, 30,* 5344A.

Manzo, A. V. (1969b). The ReQuest procedure. *Journal of Reading, 13,* 123–126.

Manzo, A. V. (1970a). Reading and questioning: The ReQuest procedure. *Reading Improvement, 7,* 80–83.

Manzo, A. V. (1970b). CAT—A game for extending vocabulary and knowledge of allusions. *Journal of Reading, 13,* 367–369.

Manzo, A. V. (1973). CONPASS English: A demonstration project. *Journal of Reading, 16,* 539–545.

Manzo, A. V. (1974). The group reading activity. *Forum for Reading, 3,* 26–33.

Manzo, A. V. (1975). Guided reading procedure. *Journal of Reading, 18,* 287–291.

Manzo, A. V. (1977). *Recent developments in content area reading.* Keynote address, Missouri Council of Teachers of English, Springfield, MO.

Manzo, A. V. (1980). Three "universal" strategies in content area reading and languaging. *Journal of Reading, 24,* 146–149.

Manzo, A. V. (1983). "Subjective approach to vocabulary" acquisition (Or ". . . I think my brother is arboreal!"). *Reading Psychology, 3,* 155–160.

Manzo, A. V. (1985). Expansion modules for the ReQuest, CAT, GRP, and REAP reading/study procedures. *Journal of Reading, 28,* 498–502.

Manzo, A. V. (1998). Teaching for creative outcomes: Why we don't, how we all can. *The Clearinghouse, 71:*5, 287–290.

Manzo, A. V., & Casale, U. P. (1980). The five C's: A problem-solving approach to study skills. *Reading Horizons, 20,* 281–284.

Manzo, A. V., & Casale, U. P. (1985). Listen-read-discuss: A content reading heuristic. *Journal of Reading, 28,* 732–734.

Manzo, A. V., & Garber, K. (1995). Study guides. In A. Purves (Ed.), *Encyclopedia of English studies and language arts* (pp. 1124–1125). New York: Scholastic.

Manzo, A. V., & Legenza, A. (1975). Inquiry training for kindergarten children. *Journal of Educational Leadership, 32,* 479–483.

Manzo, A. V., & Manzo, U. C. (1987). *Asking, answering, commenting: A participation training strategy.* Paper presented at the annual meeting of the International Reading Association, Anaheim, CA.

Manzo, A. V., & Manzo U. C. (1990a). *Content area reading: A heuristic approach.* Upper Saddle River, NJ: Merrill/Prentice Hall.

Manzo, A. V., & Manzo, U. C. (1990b). Note Cue: A comprehension and participation training strategy. *Journal of Reading, 33,* 608–611.

Manzo, A. V., & Manzo, U. C. (1993). *Literacy disorders: Holistic diagnosis and remediation.* Fort Worth, TX: Harcourt Brace Jovanovich.

Manzo, A. V., & Manzo, U. C. (1995). *Teaching children to be literate: A reflective approach.* Fort Worth, TX: Harcourt Brace College Publishers.

Manzo, A. V., & Manzo, U. C. (1997a). *Content area literacy: Interactive teaching for active learning,* 2nd edition. Upper Saddle River, NJ: Merrill.

Manzo, A. V., & Manzo, U. C. (1997b). A new eclecticism for literacy education. *Journal of Reading Research and Instruction, 37:*2, 94–100.

Manzo, A. V., Manzo, U. C., Barnhill, A., & Thomas, M. (in press). Of different minds: Possible reader subtypes—implications for literacy theory and practice. *Reading Psychology.*

Manzo, A. V., Manzo, U. C., Lang, A., & Barnhill, A. (1996). World wide web: Six enterprises connecting schools to authentic commerce in literature, ideas, humanitarianism, and the free market. Paper presented at the American Reading Forum, Sanibel Island, FL.

Manzo, A. V., Manzo, U. C., & McKenna, M. (1995). *The Informal Reading-Thinking Inventory.* Fort Worth, TX: Harcourt Brace College Publishers.

Manzo, A. V. & Martin, D. C. (1974). Writing communal poetry. *Journal of Reading, 17,* 638–643.

Manzo, A. V., & Sherk, J. K. (1971–1972). Some generalizations and strategies for guiding vocabulary acquisition. *Journal of Reading Behavior, 4,* 78–89.

Manzo, A. V., & Sherk, J. K. (1978). Reading and "languaging in the content areas": A third generation approach. *The New England Reading Association Journal, 13:*1, 28–32.

Manzo, A. V., Garber, K., & Warm, J. (1992). *Dialectical thinking: A generative approach to critical/creative reading.* Paper presented at the National Reading Conference, San Antonio, TX, 1992.

Manzo, A. V., Garber, K., Manzo, U. C., & Kahn, R. (1994). *Transmission, transaction, and transformation: Response to text perspectives.* Paper presented at the National Developmental Educators Conference, Kansas City, MO.

Manzo, U. C., Manzo. A. V., & Riley, B. A. (1996). Concepts, content, and cohesion: Impact of concept-based interdisciplinary instruction on the literacy and learning of at-risk fourth graders. Paper. Society for the Scientific Study of Reading, San Francisco, CA.

Maor, E. (1979). A unification of two famous theorems from classical geometry. *Mathematics Teacher, 72,* 363–367.

Maria, K., & MacGinitie, W. (1987). Learning form texts that refute the reader's prior knowledge. *Reading Research and Instruction, 26,* 222–238.

Maring, G. H., & Furman, G. (1985). Seven "whole class" strategies to help mainstreamed young people read and listen better in content area classes. *Journal of Reading, 28,* 694–700.

Maring, G. H. & Ritson, R. (1980). Reading improvement in the gymnasium. *Journal of Reading, 24,* 27–31.

Martin, D. C., Lorton, M., Blanc, R. A., & Evans, C. (1977). *The learning center: A comprehensive model for colleges and universities.* Grand Rapids, MI: Central Trade Plant.

Marzano, R. J. (1997). *Designing standards-based districts, schools, and classrooms.* Alexandria, VA: ASCD.

Marzano, R. J., & Marzano, J. S. (1988). *A cluster approach to elementary vocabulary instruction.* Newark, DE: International Reading Association.

McFadden, C., & Yaeger, R. E. (1993). *Science plus.* Austin, TX: Holt, Rinehart & Winston.

McKeon, R. (Ed.). (1947). *Introduction to Aristotle.* New York: The Modern Library.

McKeough, A., Lupart, J., & Marini, A., Eds. (1995). *Teaching for transfer: Fostering generalization in learning.* Mahway, NJ: Lawrence Erlbaum Associates, Publishers.

McKenzie, J. V., Ericson, B., & Hunter, L. (1988). *Questions may be an answer.* (Unpublished manuscript, California State University at Northridge.)

McNamara, L. P. (1977). A study of the cloze procedure as an alternate group instructional strategy in secondary school American government classes. (Doctoral dissertation, Northern Illinois University, DeKalb). *Dissertation Abstracts International, 39,* 216A.

McNamara, T., Miller, D., & Bransford, J. (1991). Mental models and reading comprehension. In R. Barr, M. Kamil, P. Mosenthal, & P. D. Pearson (Eds.), *Handbook of Reading Research* (Vol. 2). White Plains, NY: Longman.

Meichenbaum, D., & Asarnow, J. (1979). Cognitive-behavioral modifications and metacognitive development. In P. C. Kendall & S. D. Hollan (Eds.), *Cognitive-behavioral interventions: Theory, research and procedures* (pp. 11–35). New York: Academic Press.

Metzger, M. (1998). Teaching reading: Beyond the plot. *Phi Delta Kappan, 80*(3), 240.

Meyer, B. J. E. (1975). *The organization of prose and its effect on memory.* Amsterdam: North-Holland.

Meyer, L. (1988). Research on implementation: What seems to work (pp. 40–57). In S. J. Samuels & P. David Pearson (Eds.), *Changing School Reading Programs: Principles and Case Studies.* Newark, DE: International Reading Association.

Mikulecky, L. (1982). Job literacy: The relationship between school preparation and workplace actuality. *Reading Research Quarterly, 17,* 400–419.

Miller, W. E., & Dollard, J. (1941). *Social learning and imitation.* New Haven, CT: Yale University Press.

Miniter, R. (1999, March). Keepers of The Dream, *Reader's Digest,* 105–109.

Minton, S. C. (1984). Modern dance: Body and mind. Englewood, CO: Morton.

Minton, S., & Beckworth, B. (1986). Dance and sport—the elusive connection. *Journal of Physical Education, Recreation, and Dance, 57*:5, 26, 54.

Missouri Department of Elementary and Secondary Education. (1986). *Core competencies and key skills for Missouri schools: For grades 2 through 10.* Jefferson City, MO: Author.

Mitchell, D. C. (1982). *The process of reading: A cognitive analysis of fluent reading and learning to read.* Somerset, NJ: Wiley.

Moffett, J. (1989). *Storm in the mountains: A case study of censorship, conflict, and consciousness.* Carbondale, IL: Southern Illinois University Press.

Moje, E. B. (1996). "I teach students, not subjects": Teacher-student relationships as contexts for secondary literacy. *Reading Research Quarterly, 31*:2, 172–195.

Moje, E. B., Young, J. P., Readence, J. E., & Moore, D. W. (2000). Reinventing adolescent literacy for new times: Perennial and millennial issues. *Journal of Adolescent and Adult Literacy, 43,* 400–410.

Moller, G., & Bohning, G. (1992, Spring). Setting reading program priorities. *Journal of Reading Education, 17*:3, 22–28.

Moore, D. W., Readence, J. E., & Rickelman, R. J. (1982). *Prereading activities for content area reading and learning.* Newark, DE: International Reading Association.

Mulliken, C. N., & Henk, W. A. (1985). Using music as a background for reading: An exploratory study. *Journal of Reading, 28,* 353–358.

Nagy, W. E. (1988). *Teaching vocabulary to improve reading comprehension.* Newark, DE: International Reading Association.

Naisbitt, J. (1982). *Re-inventing the corporation: Transforming your job and your company for the new information society.* New York: Warner Books.

National Assessment of Educational Progress. *Report in brief: NAEP 1996 trends in academic progress.* Washington, DC: NAEP, 1997.

Newby, T., Stepich, D., Lehman, J., & Russel, J. (1996). *Instructional technology for teaching and learning.* Englewood Cliffs, NJ: Prentice-Hall.

Niles, O. (1965). Organization perceived. In H. L. Herber (Ed.), *Developing study skills in secondary schools* (pp. 57–76). Newark, DE: International Reading Association.

Ogle, D. (1989). Study techniques that ensure content area reading success. In D. Lapp, J. Flood, & N. Farnam (Eds.), *Content area reading and learning* (2nd ed.). Boston: Allyn & Bacon.

Ogle, D. M. (1996). Study techniques that ensure content area reading success. In D. Lapp, J. Flood, & N. Farnan (Eds.), *Content area reading and learning* (2nd ed.). Boston: Allyn & Bacon.

Ollmann, H. E. (1996). Creating higher level thinking with reading response. *Journal of Adolescent and Adult Literacy, 39,* 576–581.

Osbourne, D. & Gaebler, T. (1993). *Reinventing government: How the entrepreneurial spirit is transforming the public sector.* New York: Plume Books.

Otto, W., & Hayes, B. (1982). Glossing for improved comprehension: Progress and prospect. In G. H. McNinch (Ed.), *Reading in the disciplines. Second yearbook of the American Reading Forum* (pp. 16–18). Athens, GA: American Reading Forum.

Padak, N. D. (1986). Teachers' verbal behaviors: A window to the teaching process. In J. A. Niles & R. V. Lalik (Eds.), *Solving problems in literacy: Learners, teachers, and researchers. Thirty-fifth yearbook of the National Reading Conference* (pp. 185–191). Rochester, NY: National Reading Conference.

Paley, V. G. (1986, May). On listening to what the children say. *Harvard Educational Review, 56:2*, 122–131.

Palincsar, A. S., & Brown, A. L. (1984). Reciprocal teaching of comprehension monitoring activities. *Cognition and Instruction, 1*, 117–175.

Palmatier, R. A. (1971). Comparison of four note-taking procedures. *Journal of Reading, 14*, 235–258.

Palmatier, R. A. (1973). A notetaking system for learning. *Journal of Reading, 17*, 36–39.

Palmatier, R. A., & Bennett, J. M. (1974). Notetaking habits of college students. *Journal of Reading, 18*, 215–218.

Pauk, W. (1989). *How to study in college* (4th ed.). Boston: Houghton Mifflin.

Paul, R. W. (1993). *Critical thinking: How to prepare students for a rapidly changing world.* Santa Rosa, CA: Foundation for Critical Thinking.

Pearce, D. L. (1983). Guidelines for the use and evaluation of writing in content classrooms. *Journal of Reading, 27*, 215.

Perry, M. (1971). *Man's unfinished journey.* Boston: Houghton Mifflin.

Peters, C. W. (1982). The content processing model: A new approach to conceptualizing content reading. In J. P. Palberg (Ed.), *Reading in the content areas: Application of a concept* (pp. 100–109). Toledo, OH: University of Toledo, College of Education.

Phelps, S., & Smith, L. (1989). Microcomputer applications for content area vocabulary. *Reading Horizons, 29*, 103–109.

Piercy, D. (1976). *Reading activities in content areas.* Boston: Allyn & Bacon.

Pollution of the Caesars (1998). *Discover, 19:3.*

Postman, N. (1969). *Teaching as a subversive activity.* New York: Dell Publishing Company, Inc.

Pressley, M., Johnson, C. J., & Symons, S. (1987). Elaborating to learn and learning to elaborate. *Journal of Learning Disabilities, 20*, 76–91.

Pressley, M., Levin, J. R., & MacDaniel, M. A. (1987). Remembering versus inferring what a word means: Mnemonic and contextual approaches. In M. C. McKeown & M. E. Curtis (Eds.), *The nature of vocabulary acquisition* (pp. 107–129). Hillsdale, NJ: Erlbaum.

Pressley, M., Levin, J. R., & Miller, G. E. (1981). How does the keyword method affect vocabulary comprehension and usage? *Reading Research Quarterly, 16*, 213–225.

Putnam, L., Bader, L., Bean, R. (1988). Clinic directors share insights into effective strategies. *Journal of Clinical Reading, 3*, 16–20.

Rakes, S. K., & Smith, L. J. (1987). Strengthening comprehension and recall through the principle of recitation. *Journal of Reading, 31*, 260–263.

Rasinski, T. V. (1989). Fluency for everyone: Incorporating fluency instruction in the classroom. *The Reading Teacher, 42*, 690–693.

Ratekin, N., Simpson, M. L., Alvermann, D. E., & Dishner, E. K. (1985). Why teachers resist content area reading instruction. *Journal of Reading, 28*, 432–437.

Raths, L. E., Harmon, M., & Simon, S. B. (1978). *Values and teaching* (2nd ed.). Columbus, OH: Merrill.

Raygor, A. L. (1977). The Raygor readability estimate: A quick and easy way to determine difficulty. In P. D. Pearson (Ed.), *Reading: Theory, research, and practice.* Clemson, SC: National Reading Conference.

Reeve, R. A., Palincsar, A. S., & Brown A. L. (1985). *Everyday and academic thinking: Implications for learning and problem solving* (Journal of Curriculum Studies Technical Report No. 349). Champaign: University of Illinois, Center for the Study of Reading.

Robinson, F. (1946). *Effective study.* New York: Harper Brothers.

Robinson, E. A. (1897). In M. D. Zabel (Ed.) *Selected Poems of Edwin Arlington Robinson.* (1965) London: Macmillan.

Roby, T. (1983, April). *The other side of the question: Controversial turns, the devil's advocate, and reflective responses*. Paper presented at the annual meeting of the American Educational Research Association, Montreal.

Rogoff, B. (1990). *Apprenticeship in thinking: Cognitive development in social context*. New York: Oxford University Press.

Rosenblatt, L. (1938). *Literature as exploration*. New York: Appleton-Century.

Rosenshine, B. V. (1984). Content, time, and direct instruction. In P. L. Peterson & H. J. Walberg (Eds.), *Research on teaching: Concepts, findings, and implications* (pp. 102–106). Berkeley, CA: McCutchan.

Rowe, M. B. (1974). Wait time and rewards as instructional variables, their influences on language, logic, and fate control: Part One—Wait time. *Journal of Research in Science Teaching, 11*, 81–94.

Rowe, M. B. (1986). Wait time: Slowing down may be a way of speeding up! *Journal of Teacher Education, 37*, 43–50.

Rud, A. G. (1997). The use and abuse of Socrates in present day teaching. *Education Policy Analysis Archives, 5:*20. (http://olam.ed.asu.edu/epaa).

Ruddell, M. R. (1993). *Teaching content reading and writing*. Boston: Allyn & Bacon.

Ruddell, M. R. (1997). *Teaching content reading and writing*, (2nd ed). Boston: Allyn & Bacon.

Ruddell, R. B., & Ruddell, M. H. (1995). *Theoretical processes and models of reading* (3rd ed.). Newark, DE: International Reading Association.

Ruddell, R. B. (1999). *Teaching children to read and write: Becoming an influential teacher* (2nd ed.). Boston: Allyn & Bacon.

Rush, T., Moe, A., & Storlie, R. (1986). *Occupational literacy education*. Newark, DE: International Reading Association.

Russell, D. (1961). *Children learn to read* (2nd ed.). New York: Ginn.

Sage, G. H. (1977). *Introduction to motor behavior: A neurophychological approach* (2nd ed.). Reading, MA: Addison-Wesley.

Salibrici, M. (1999). Dissonance and rhetorical inquiry: A Burkean model for critical reading and writing. *Journal of Adolescent and Adult Literacy, 42*, 628–637.

Samuels, S. J. (1977). Introduction to theoretical models of reading. In W. Otto, N. A. Peters, & C. W. Peters (Eds.), *Reading problems: A multidisciplinary perspective* (pp. 7–41). Reading, MA: Addison-Wesley.

Sanders, P. L. (1969). Teaching map reading skills in grade 9. *Journal of Reading, 12*, 283–286, 337.

Santa, C. M., Dailey, S. C., & Nelson, M. (1985). Free-response and opinion proof: A reading and writing strategy for middle grade and secondary teachers. *Journal of Reading, 28*, 346–352.

Santa, C. M., Isaacson, L., & Manning, G. (1987). Changing content instruction through action research. *The Reading Teacher, 40*, 434–438.

Schell, L. M. (1988). Dilemmas in assessing reading comprehension. *The Reading Teacher, 42*, 12–16.

Schumm, J. S., & Mangrum, C. T., II (1991). FLIP: A framework for content area reading. *Journal of Reading, 35*, 120–123.

Shepherd, D. (1978). *Comprehensive high school reading methods* (3rd ed.). Upper Saddle River, NJ: Merrill/Prentice Hall.

Shor, I., & Freire, P. (1987). *A pedagogy for liberation: Dialogues on transforming education*. South Hadley, MA: Bergin & Garvey.

Shore, B. (1999). *The cathedral within: Transforming your life by giving something back*. New York: Random House.

Shulman, L. S. (1987). Knowledge and teaching: Foundations of the new reform. *Harvard Educational Review, 57*, 1–22.

Simpson, M. (1986). PORPE: A writing strategy for studying and learning in the content areas. *Journal of Reading, 29*, 407–414.

Simpson, M. L., Hayes, C. G., Stahl, N. A., Connor R. T., & Weaver, D. (1988). An initial validation of a study strategy system. *Journal of Reading Behavior, 20*, 149–180.

Singer, H. (1976). Theoretical models of reading. In H. Singer & R. B. Ruddell (Eds.), *Theoretical models and processes of reading* (2nd ed., pp. 634–654). Newark, DE: International Reading Association.

Singer, H., & Dolan, D. (1980). *Reading and learning from text*. Boston: Little, Brown.

Singer, H., & Ruddell, R. B. (1976). *Theoretical models and processes of reading* (2nd ed.). Newark, DE: International Reading Association.

Sizer, T. R. (1984). *Horace's compromise: The dilemma of the American high school*. Boston: Houghton Mifflin.

Smith, R. J., & Dauer, V. L. (1984). A comprehension-monitoring strategy for reading content area materials. *Journal of Reading, 28,* 144–147.

Spache, G. D. (1976). *Diagnosing and correcting reading disabilities.* Boston: Allyn & Bacon.

Spiegel, D. L. (1980). Adaptations of Manzo's guided reading procedure. *Reading Horizons, 20,* 188–192.

Spor, M. W. & Schneider, B. K. (1999). Content reading strategies: What teachers know, use, and want to learn. *Reading Research and Instruction, 38:*3, 221–231.

Stahl, N. A., & Henk, W. A. (1986). Tracing the roots of textbook study systems: An extended historical perspective. In J. A. Niles & R. V. Lalik (Eds.), *Solving problems in literacy: Learners, teachers, and researchers. Thirty-fifth yearbook of the National Reading Conference* (pp. 366–374). Rochester, NY: National Reading Conference.

Stahl, S. A., & Fairbanks, M. M. (1986). The effects of vocabulary instruction: A model-based meta-analysis. *Review of Educational Research, 56,* 72–110.

Staton, J. (1980). Writing and counseling: Using a dialogue journal. *Language Arts, 57,* 514–518.

Stauffer, R. (1969). *Directing reading maturity as a cognitive process.* New York: Harper & Row.

Stenger, C. (1999). *A characterization of undergraduate mathematical thinking.* Paper presented at the Fourth Annual Conference on Undergraduate Mathematics Education. Chicago, IL.

Stevens, K. C. (1982). Can we improve reading by teaching background information? *Journal of Reading, 25,* 326–329.

Stieglitz, E. L., & Stieglitz, V. S. (1981). SAVOR the word to reinforce vocabulary in the content areas. *Journal of Reading, 25,* 48.

Strickland, D., & Morrow, L. (1990). Integrating the emergent literacy curriculum with themes. *The Reading Teacher, 43,* 604–605.

Suarez, R. (1999). *The old neighborhood: what we lost in the great suburban migration, 1966–1999.* New York: Free Press.

Taylor, G. C. (1980). Music in language arts instruction. *Language Arts, 58,* 363–367.

Tchudi, S. (1988). Invisible thinking and the hypertext. *English Journal, 77:*1, 22–30.

Tharp, R. G., & Gallimore, R. (1989). *Rousing minds to life: Teaching, learning, and schooling in social context.* New York: Cambridge University Press.

Tharp, R. G., & Gallimore, R. (1990). *Rousing minds to life: Teaching, learning, and schooling social context.* New York: Cambridge University Press.

Thorndike, E. L. (1917). Reading as reasoning: A study of mistakes in paragraph reading. *Journal of Educational Psychology, 8,* 323–332.

Tierney, R. J., Readence, J. E., & Dishner, E. K. (1990). *Reading strategies and practices* (3rd ed.). Needham Heights, MA: Allyn & Bacon.

Tierney, R. J., Soter, A., O'Flahavan, J. F., & McGinley, W. (1989). The effects of reading and writing upon thinking critically. *Reading Research Quarterly, 24,* 134–137.

Time (March 22, 1993). 54.

Unrau, N. J. (1997). *Thoughtful teachers, thoughtful learners: A guide to helping adolescents think critically.* Scarborough, Ont: Pippin Publishing.

Vacca. R. T. (1998). Forward. In D. E. Alvermann, K. A. Hinchman, D. W. Moore, S. F. Phelps, & D. R. Waff (Eds.). *Reconceptualizing the literacies in adolescents' lives* (pp. xv–xvi). Hillsdale, NJ: Erlbaum.

Vacca, R. T., & Alvermann, D. E. (1998). The crisis in adolescent literacy: Is it real or imagined? *NASSP Bulletin, 82:*600, 4–9.

Vacca, R. T., & Vacca, J. L. (1998). *Content area reading* (2nd ed.). Boston: Little, Brown.

Vaulting Vampires (1998). *Discover Magazine, 19:*3.

Vygotsky, L. S. (1978). *Mind in society: The development of higher psychological process.* Cambridge, MA: Harvard University Press.

Waern, Y. (1977a). Comprehension and belief structure. *Scandinavian Journal of Psychology, 18,* 266–274.

Waern, Y. (1977b). On the relationship between knowledge of the world and comprehension of texts. *Scandinavian Journal of Psychology, 18,* 130–139.

Walker, A., & Parkman, M. (1924). *The study readers: Fifth year.* New York: Merrill.

Walker, B. J. (1985). Right brain strategies for teaching comprehension. *Academic Therapy, 21*, 133–141.

Watkins, J., McKenna, M., Manzo, A., & Manzo, U. (1995). *The effects of the listen-read-discuss procedure on the content learning of high school students.* (Unpublished manuscript.)

Weaver, W. W., & Kingston, A. J. (1963). A factor analysis of cloze procedure and other measures of reading and language ability. *Journal of Communication, 13*, 252–261.

Welker, W. A. (1987). Going from typical to technical meaning. *Journal of Reading, 31*, 275–276.

Wilkins, G., & Miller S. (1983). *Strategies for success: An effective guide for teachers of secondary-level slow learners.* New York: Teachers College Press.

Williams, J. P. (1973). Learning to read: A review of theories and models. *Reading Research Quarterly, 8*, 121–146.

Willmore, D. J. (1967). A comparison of four methods of studying a college textbook. (Doctoral dissertation, University of Minnesota, 1966). *Dissertation Abstracts, 27*, 2413A.

Wilson, E. O. (1998). *Consilience: The unity of knowledge.* New York: Knopf.

Wooster, G. E. (1958). Teaching the SQ3R method of study: An investigation of the instructional approach (Doctoral dissertation, The Ohio State University, 1953). *Dissertation Abstracts International, 18*, 2067–2068.

Worthy, J. (1998). On every page someone gets killed! Book conversations you don't hear in school. *Journal of Adolescent and Adult Literacy, 41*, 508–517.

Index